P A U L

& M O N E Y

PAUL

& MONEY

A BIBLICAL AND THEOLOGICAL ANALYSIS *of the* APOSTLE'S TEACHINGS AND PRACTICES

VERLYN D. VERBRUGGE AND KEITH R. KRELL

ZONDERVAN®

ZONDERVAN

Paul and Money
Copyright © 2015 by Verlyn D. Verbrugge and Keith R. Krell

This title is also available as a Zondervan ebook. Visit www.zondervan.com/ebooks.

Requests for information should be addressed to:

Zondervan, 3900 *Sparks Dr. SE, Grand Rapids, Michigan 49546*

Library of Congress Cataloging-in-Publication Data

Verbrugge, Verlyn D.
    Paul and money : a biblical and theological analysis of the apostle's teachings and practices
/ Verlyn D. Verbrugge and Keith R. Krell.
        pages   cm
    Includes bibliographical references.
    ISBN 978-0-310-51833-4 (softcover)
    1. Money – Biblical teaching. 2. Money – Religious aspects – Christianity. 3. Bible. Epistles
of Paul – Criticism, interpretation, etc. I. Title.
    BS680.M57V47   2015
    262'.00681 – dc23   2015006775

Cover design: Studio Gearbox
Cover images: Zev Radovan/Bibleland Pictures; Thinkstock
Interior design: Matthew Van Zomeren and Kait Lamphere

Printed in the United States of America

15 16 17 18 19 20 21 22 23 24 25 /DCI/ 20 19 18 17 16 15 14 13 12 11 10 9 8 7 6 5 4 3 2 1

To Lori and Lori

TABLE OF CONTENTS

PART 1

PAUL'S WORK AND HIS FINANCIAL POLICIES

CHAPTER 1
EARNING A LIVING FROM THE GOSPEL

CHAPTER 2
PAUL'S RELUCTANCE TO ACCEPT SUPPORT

CHAPTER 3

PAUL AND THE ISSUE OF PATRONAGE IN THE GRECO-ROMAN WORLD

PART 2

RAISING MONEY FOR THE MOTHER CHURCH IN JERUSALEM

CHAPTER 4

PAUL'S CONCERN FOR THE POOR, INCLUDING HIS FIRST FUND-RAISING FOR THE JERUSALEM CHURCH

CHAPTER 5

PAUL'S COLLECTION FOR THE JERUSALEM CHURCH

CHAPTER 6

COMPLICATIONS TO THE COLLECTION IN CORINTH

CHAPTER 7

PAUL'S FUND-RAISING FOR THE COLLECTION IN 2 CORINTHIANS 8 – 9

CHAPTER 8

THE AFTERMATH AND DELIVERY OF PAUL'S COLLECTION

PART 3

OTHER ISSUES CONCERNING FINANCES IN PAUL

CHAPTER 9

THE THESSALONIAN FREELOADERS

CHAPTER 10

THE RICH AND THE POOR IN CORINTH

CHAPTER 11

A MESSAGE TO THE RICH IN THE WORLD

CHAPTER 12

ON TAXES, DEBT, AND TITHING

CHAPTER 13

A THEOLOGICAL AND PRACTICAL CONCLUSION

ABBREVIATIONS

This list of abbreviations generally follows the system as set out by *The SBL Handbook of Style* (2nd ed.; Atlanta: SBL Press, 2014).

SECONDARY SOURCES

AB   Anchor Bible

ABD   *Anchor Bible Dictionary.* Ed. David Noel Freedman. 6 vols. New York: Doubleday, 1992

ANTC   Abingdon New Testament Commentaries

AYBC   Anchor Yale Bible Commentary

BDAG   Danker, Frederick W., Walter Bauer, William F. Arndt, and F. Wilbur Gingrich. *Greek-English Lexicon of the New Testament and Other Early Christian Literature.* 3rd ed. Chicago: University of Chicago Press, 2000 (Danker-Bauer-Arndt-Gingrich)

BECNT   Baker Exegetical Commentary on the New Testament

Bib   *Biblica*

BibInt   *Biblical Interpretation*

BNTC   Black's New Testament Commetnaries

BSac   *Bibliotheca Sacra*

BT   *The Bible Translator*

BTB   *Biblical Theology Bulletin*

BTFL   Biblical Theology for Life

BZNW   Beihefte zur Zeitschrift für die neutestamentliche Wissenschaft

CBC   Cambridge Biblical Commentary

ConBNT   Coniectanea Biblica: New Testament Series

CPNIVC   College Press New International Version Commentary

CTR   *Criswell Theological Review*

CurBR   *Currents in Biblical Research*

DBSJ   *Detroit Baptist Theological Journal*

EC   Epworth Commentaries

EDNT   *Exegetical Dictionary of the New Testament.* Edited by Horst Balz and Gerhard Schneider. ET. 3 vols. Grand Rapids: Eerdmans, 1990–93

HNTC Harper's New Testament Commentaries

IBC Interpretation: A Bible Commentary for Teaching and Preaching

ICC International Critical Commentary

Int *Interpretation*

IVPNTC IVP New Testament Commentary Series

JBL *Journal of Biblical Literature*

JETS *Journal of the Evangelical Theological Society*

JGRChJ *Journal of Greco-Roman Christianity and Judaism*

JOTGES *Journal of the Grace Evangelical Society*

JRS *Journal of Roman Studies*

JSNT *Journal for the Study of the New Testament*

JSNTSup Journal for the Study of the New Testament: Supplement Series

JSOT *Journal for the Study of the Old Testament*

JTS *Journal of Theological Studies*

KEK Kritisch-exegetischer Kommentar über das Neue Testament (Meyer-Kommentar)

L&N Louw, J. P., and Eugene Albert Nida, eds. *Greek-English Lexicon of the New Testament: Based on Semantic Domains.* 2nd ed. 2 vols. New York: United Bible Societies, 1989

LNTS The Library of New Testament Studies

MHT Moulton, James H., Wilbert F. Howard, Nigel Turner. *A Grammar of New Testament Greek.* 3rd ed. 4 vols. Edinburgh: T&T Clark, 1963–2006

MM Moulton, James H., and George Milligan. *The Vocabulary of the Greek Testament Illustrated from the Papyri and Other Non-literary Sources.* Grand Rapids: Eerdmans, 1985

NAC New American Commentary

NCB New Century Bible Commentary

NcBC New Covenant Bible Commentary

NIBCNT New International Biblical Commentary on the New Testament

NICNT New International Commentary on the New Testament

NIDNTTE New International Dictionary of New Testament Theology and Exegesis. Edited by Moises Silva. 2nd ed. 5 vols. Grand Rapids: Zondervan, 2014

NIGTC New International Greek Testament Commentary
NIVAC New International Version Application Commentary
NovTSup Supplements to Novum Nestamentum
NTC New Testament Commentaries
NTL New Testament Library
NSBT New Studies in Biblical Theology
NTS *New Testament Studies*
NTT New Testament Theology
Pillar Pillar New Testament Commentary
PTB Preaching Through the Bible
RGG *Religion in Geschichte und Gegenwart.* Ed. Hans Dieter Betz. 4th ed. Tübingen: Mohr Siebeck, 1998–2007
RTR *Reformed Theological Review*
SBL Society of Biblical Literature
SBLDS Society of Biblical Literature Dissertation Series
SGBC The Story of God Bible Commentary
SNTSMS Society for New Testament Studies Monograph Series
SP Sacra pagina
TDNT *Theological Dictionary of the New Testament.* Edited by Gerhard Kittel and Gerhard Friedrich. Translated by Geoffrey W. Bromiley. 10 vols. Grand Rapids: Eerdmans, 1964–76
TJ *Trinity Journal*
TNTC Tyndale New Testament Commentaries
TynBul *Tyndale Bulletin*
WBC Word Biblical Commentary
WUNT Wissenschaftliche Untersuchungen zum Neuen Testament
WW *Word and World*
ZECNT Zondervan Exegetical Commentary of the New Testament
ZIBBC Zondervan Illustrated Bible Backgrounds Commentary

BIBLE TRANSLATIONS

ESV English Standard Version
HCSB Holman Christian Standard Bible
KJV King James Version
LXX Septuagint

NASB　New American Standard Bible
NET　New English Translation
NETS　*New English Translation of the Septuagint*
NIV　New International Version
NKJV　New King James Version
NLT　New Living Translation
NRSV　New Revised Standard Version
RSV　Revised Standard Version

PREFACES AND ACKNOWLEDGMENTS

In 2014 I had the privilege as academic editor at Zondervan to edit Craig Blomberg's contribution to the Biblical Theology for Life series, *Christians in an Age of Wealth.* He made reference to my published dissertation, *Paul's Style of Church Leadership Illustrated by His Instructions to the Corinthians on the Collection*; authors love to see their works quoted, and I thank him for that! In an offhand comment, Craig said I really should get that dissertation more visibility by getting it out of Mellen Press and into something like Wipf & Stock. For a number of reasons, I did not feel it was appropriate to do that: the dissertation was over twenty-five years old, a lot of research had been done on the subject of the collection since 1988 (when I wrote it), and frankly it looked like a dissertation, not a book. But I sincerely appreciated Craig's comment that there was a lot of value in that material that needed to have more visibility. That comment was the seedbed for this book.

I have continued my study of Paul's collection for the poor among the saints in Jerusalem, and I wanted to update much of the material. Moreover, in doing research on the Internet, I discovered that there was no comprehensive book on the issue of Paul and money—that is, how the apostle interacted with the Jewish and Greco-Roman world of finance. So I decided it made more sense, for a lasting contribution to biblical scholarship, to submit a more comprehensive proposal—and have it typeset as a book, not a manuscript. My first choice of publisher was Zondervan, where I have worked for a fulfilling twenty-eight years now. I suggested it to Katya Covrett, our key academic acquisitions editor, and I am deeply grateful for all she has done to get the book through each stage of the acquisitions process. And I am equally thankful to Nancy Erickson, my colleague at Zondervan, for applying her editorial skills to the manuscript once the manuscript was accepted.

But I knew I would never be able do all the research necessary in those areas of Paul's interaction with the Greco-Roman world of money and finance that I knew were in Paul's letters but which I had never studied. So I asked a good friend of mine, Keith R. Krell, to assist me as coauthor. I became acquainted with Keith when he contacted me while writing his dissertation at the University of Bristol, and I knew he had fantastic writing skills and the energy and ability to cover those remaining areas. I want to thank Keith for all the time and effort he put into the book, and while he may say to you that he was just riding on my coattails, he is wrong. He is a critical part of this book, and it would not have seen the light of day if he had not offered to be a coauthor. Just for the record, I did most of parts 1 and 2, and Keith did most of part 3. But we have read and commented on each other's material.

A number of scholars have assisted us in various ways. In particular, I am thankful for the interactions I had with Lynn Cohick of Wheaton College for her help particularly in keeping me straight on the topic of Paul's Jewish upbringing and education as well as the complicated issue of patronage in the Greco-Roman world.

I want to thank too the rest of the Zondervan CARR team (Church, Academic, Reference, and Reflective books) for the incredible work they do with all of our titles. Their innovative promotional and marketing skills are the best in the business.

I also want to thank my wife, Lori, for her incredibly supportive role and her suggestions whenever I talked over certain parts of the book with her. She patiently spent many hours by herself in the living room while I buried myself in the office, researching and writing the book. She has promised to read this book (but to skip anything in a Greek font!).

I am so grateful for the grace given to me to finish this book. Shortly after completing the finishing touches on this book and sending in the final corrections, I was diagnosed with Stage Four pancreatic cancer. But the book was already in the Lord's hands.

Most of all, I must thank the Lord for the incredible opportunity he opened up for me when he found a place for me at Zondervan. Never in all my years of education did I think that the majority of my career would be working as an editor and a writer, using the skills the Lord gave me in biblical languages and historical research to help shape the lives of scholars and pastors around the world. The phrase from the Protestant Reformation is wringing in my ears:

Soli deo gloria

Verlyn D. Verbrugge
January, 2015

GROWING UP IN A CHRISTIAN HOME, I HAVE ALWAYS ENJOYED READING Zondervan books. During my Bible college and seminary years, I even dreamed of one day writing a book for Zondervan. But, honestly, I never imagined it would happen. It was a dream, nothing more. However, in 2007, I began corresponding with Verlyn in an attempt to learn from his expertise in 1 Corinthians. He then became my stateside doctoral supervisor. More importantly, he became a remarkable mentor and friend. For the last eight years, Verlyn has believed in me. He has given me opportunities I don't deserve. One such opportunity is cowriting this book. I like to say that I have been riding on his coattails for years.

I will always be thankful for the privilege to write on the topic of Paul and money. Much of my career has been spent in the study of Paul's letters while much of my life and ministry in an attempt to follow Paul's financial instructions. I am eternally grateful to my parents, Richard and Pat Krell, who instilled in me a love and commitment to give. It was their influence that cultivated godly stewardship in my life. I am indebted to Dr. Luis and Kerri Vela, my dear friends and patrons, who generously helped finance my doctoral studies. I must also express thanks to my friend Randy Alcorn, who has taught me a great deal about sacrificial giving through his life, ministry, and writing.

I would like to thank Moody Bible Institute-Spokane and Fourth Memorial Church for supporting me in this project. It is a privilege to serve the Lord with you. Along with Verlyn, I, too, would like to express my gratitude to Katya Covrett at Zondervan for her support of this project, along with her deep knowledge of the biblical text and outstanding editing skills.

I also want to thank my wife, Lori, for being my biggest fan and most helpful critic. Without her loving and unwavering support, I would never have lasted in pastoral ministry or academia. I remain grateful that she is a better writer and editor than I am because she has taken me further than I could have ever gone on my own.

Most of all, I thank the Lord Jesus Christ for the privilege of contributing anything in writing, much less in book form. I must also glory in his unending patience and grace. Paul expressed my heart perfectly when he penned these words: "If we are faithless, he remains faithful, for he cannot deny himself" (2 Tim 2:13).

Keith R. Krell
January, 2015

INTRODUCTION

IN 2010, BEN WITHERINGTON III PUBLISHED A BOOK WITH BAKER (Brazos Press) entitled *Jesus and Money*. It was a book that was written in the context of the global recession of 2008–2010 and was more far-reaching than what one would think from the title of the book. That is, it was not limited to what Jesus says in the Gospels about money and our use of it; it was a book about the Bible and money—about what the Bible does and does not say about money.[1] Witherington begins with a theology of creation and moves to some of Israel's legal precepts about wealth and poverty. His second chapter deals with OT wisdom literature and what it says on the subject. From there he moves to several chapters on the NT world—two on the Gospels, one on James, one on Paul, one on John and Revelation, and finally "a New Testament theology of money, stewardship, and giving."

Our goal in the present book is more limited than that of Witherington. We intend to limit ourselves to the life, writings, and legacy of the apostle Paul. We want to probe everything that he says and does in the NT concerning the issue of money. And there is a lot on this topic in Paul, much of which goes unrecognized. Consider the words of N. T. Wright, in response to a thesis proposed by David Downs that we can determine the genuine letters of Paul by the fact that they have something to say about "financial transactions on behalf of the Pauline mission"[2] but the spurious ones do not:

> Galatians mentioned neither the Collection nor Paul's own payment (or lack thereof); 6:6–10 scarcely counts as a counter-example. Philemon does not mention money, except the possibility that Onesimus might have stolen some. Many of the really important themes in [Paul's] letters occur only in one (obvious example: the eucharist in 1 Cor.).[3]

---

1. Ben Witherington III, *Jesus and Money: A Guide for Times of Financial Crisis* (Grand Rapids: Baker, 2010).

2. David Downs, "Paul's Collection and the Book of Acts Revised" (NTS 52 [2006]: 50), as quoted by N. T. Wright, *Paul and the Faithfulness of God* (Minneapolis: Fortress, 2013), 58, n 129.

3. Wright, *Paul*, 58, n 129.

Wright is correct in that we cannot use such arbitrary themes to determine which letters of Paul are genuine. But he is wrong to suggest that a book like Philemon says little about money or financial transactions. That small letter of twenty-five verses has much to say about money issues, though they lie beneath the surface. Let us say at the outset that when we use the word *money* in this book, we are not limiting it to passing coins from one person to another in the purchase of some product or service. Rather, we are using the term broadly. Anything that has to do with how the world of finance intersects with our lives (e.g., jobs, financial transactions, poverty, patronage, theft, taxes) will be summarized under the term *money*.

As we will see, for example, when we discuss Philemon in several places in this book, that letter contains Paul's offer to somehow pay Philemon for what Onesimus has (potentially) stolen (Phlm 19). There is also the value of the ministry that Onesimus has performed for Paul while in prison (vv. 11, 13). And there is Paul's request that Philemon prepare a guest room for Paul, since he hopes to come there soon and enjoy his hospitality (v. 22). There is even the issue of whether Paul is a patron of Philemon, or even Philemon a patron of Paul. All of these are money issues — ones that we will explore in due time.

SOURCES

Because we want to probe what is behind everything Paul says about money, we need to say a word about sources. We are going to assume, without a lot of scholarly argumentation, that the thirteen letters in the NT that are ascribed to Paul can all be used as legitimate sources for the thoughts of the apostle. Scholars, including evangelical scholars (among whom we count ourselves), have argued the pros and cons especially of the genuineness of the Pauline authorship of the Prison Epistles and of the Pastoral Epistles; some are convinced they are genuine Pauline letters; others are not.[4] We are convinced by those who argue for their authenticity.

Furthermore, we will also accept as evidence the history of the early church as described in the book of Acts. It is true that Luke reports less

---

4. Any commentary on Ephesians, Colossians, 1 and 2 Timothy, and Titus has a section where the evidence is weighed for their genuineness of Pauline authorship.

internal conflict in the churches in his second volume than what we read about in some of the Pauline letters (especially in the letters of Corinth). Luke chooses to stress certain conflicts in the history of the church, particularly those between the apostles and the traditional leadership of the Jewish religion in Jerusalem, and he downplays conflict within the early Christian community.[5] It is true that there are perceived differences between what Paul writes in his letters and what Luke writes, and those differences have tended to cast doubt on Luke's accuracy in what he does report. However, none of the verses of Acts are contradictory to the thirteen letters of Paul. Luke, by his own self-assessment, is a careful historian (Luke 1:1–4); he is not a tendentious writer who ignores the facts and writes the history of the church as he wished it might have happened. As a travel companion of the apostle Paul, he spent much time with him. He has recorded what he received from his sources with meticulous accuracy.

This assessment was verified by Sir William Ramsay at the beginning of the twentieth century. Ramsay was educated among the most skeptical of German NT critics at the University of Tübingen and was convinced that the book of Acts "was written during the second half of the second century by an author who wished to influence the minds of people in his own time by a highly wrought and imaginative description of the early Church."[6] But after thirty years of traveling in what the NT calls the Roman province of Asia, Ramsay came to the opposite conclusion: "You may press the words of Luke in a degree beyond any other historian's, and they stand the keenest scrutiny and the hardest treatment."[7] Luke is a trustworthy historian.

---

5. Admittedly, Luke does discuss the issue of the care of Jewish-Gentile widows in Acts 6 and the conflict over circumcision between Jewish Christians and Paul's Gentile mission in Acts 15.

6. William M. Ramsay, *The Bearing of Recent Discovery on the Trustworthiness of the New Testament* (2nd ed.; London: Hodder and Stoughton, 1915), 37, as quoted by W. Ward Gasque, *Sir William M. Ramsay: Archaeologist and New Testament Scholar: A Survey of His Contribution to the Study of the New Testament* (Grand Rapids: Baker, 1966), 25; available at http://www.biblicalstudies.org.uk/pdf/ramsay/ramsay_gasque.pdf.

7. Ibid., (p. 89 in Ramsay, *The Bearing of Recent Discovery*; p. 27 in Gasque, *Sir William Ramsay*).

SCOPE OF INQUIRY

Our goal is not simply to exegete certain statements in Paul's writings about how Christians (particularly wealthy Christians) should use their money. There are many more issues that surface as one examines how financial matters intersect in Paul's letters. We can gain insights, for example, from "the collection" into how Paul viewed himself as the leader of his churches and what his style of leadership was. There is a whole theology of work ethic that he discusses with the church in Thessalonica as he encounters believers who had quit their daily work, perhaps in order to await the imminent return of Jesus. His statements on this issue will lead us to discuss Paul's comments on church discipline practices.

The apostle's instructions about the care of widows in 1 Tim 5 speak not only to the responsibility of the church to widows, but also to the responsibilities of widows to themselves and to the church. The issues of the relationship of believers to the secular government of the Roman Empire and the relationship of the kingdom of Christ to the kingdom of Caesar rise to the surface in Rom 13, where Paul reflects on the matter of paying taxes. And we may even be able to look through a window into the inner soul of Paul as he struggles with his insistence that he would not accept money from believers where he was ministering but rather insisted on working for his own keep as a leatherworker (even though he readily acknowledges that he had the right to be paid for his ministry). Finally, we cannot understand certain passages of Paul without knowing something about Roman reactions to widespread poverty and about the Greco-Roman system of patronage.

OUTLINE OF THE BOOK

With themes such as these in mind, let us outline what we hope to accomplish. The book is divided into three major parts. Part 1 deals with the whole issue of what Paul had to say about support for himself as a missionary and whether (and in what context) it was appropriate to ask for assistance for daily living expenses. Chapter 1 discusses Paul's background as a Pharisee and how those who were teaching rabbis supported themselves. Did they expect fees from their students? Did they require of themselves and others some type of manual labor to earn what they needed for their daily bread? How, if at all, does this intersect with Paul's statement in 1 Cor 9 that people who preach the gospel certainly have a right to earn their living from the gospel? How did the protégés of Paul, such as Timothy and Titus, receive their support (and do we even know)?

Chapter 2 deals with Paul's own reluctance to accept money from those to whom he preached the gospel. Was this merely a matter of pride on his part, or was more at stake? And how did he deal with his opponents in Corinth, who suggested that Paul's reluctance to accept money for his ministry work shows that he felt he wasn't worth as much as the other preachers? Is there a significant difference between Paul's unwillingness to accept money from Christian communities where he was working and his willingness to accept support from Christian communities after he had moved elsewhere? What about the church at Philippi? Why did he accept Lydia's invitation to stay at her house? Is his thank-you note at the end of the letter to the Philippians a reluctant and somewhat embarrassing thank-you, or does he express genuine, heartfelt gratitude?

Chapter 3 takes a look at the whole issue of patronage in the ancient world and how it helps us to understand Paul. What obligations did the patronage system put on those who were recipients of the patron's benefits? Is there any clear evidence that certain people (e.g., Lydia? Phoebe?) served as patrons to support Paul? What expenses might Paul have had (e.g., ship rides, travel expenses, writing letters, support in prison, etc.) that might have required significant outlays of ready cash, and where would Paul have gotten the money from? How can we understand Paul's asking for money to send him and others on their way when he seemed so adamant about being self-sufficient financially? And how might Paul have been able to promise Philemon that he would pay the debts of Onesimus since he seems to have been in prison for up to four years?

Part 2 deals with what is undoubtedly the most prominent topic that immediately comes to mind when we think about Paul and money, namely, the collection that he took during his third missionary journey in the Gentile churches for "the poor among the saints in Jerusalem" (Rom 15:26). Chapter 4 examines the first time we know that Paul assisted in raising money for the church in Jerusalem and was personally involved with delivering the gift there with Barnabas (Acts 11:27–30). Part of the background, of course, has to be the whole alms-giving requirements of the OT and how that might come into play here. Along with that would be the pattern in the early Jerusalem church of sharing possessions. We will also need to delve somewhat into how much poverty there was in the Roman world and in the Christian church. What about Gal 2:10? Is that simply an aphorism that Paul accepts — "remember the poor"? Is it a reference to the Acts 11 event? Does it have anything to do with the collection?

Chapter 5 explores what "the collection" that Paul took on his third missionary journey meant to Paul personally. Why did Paul undertake this venture in the first place? Of the various theories as to what the collection may have meant to Paul, which one(s) might stand out as the most important, and what is the key to his passion for this venture? How does Rom 15:26 – 32 fit into the mix here?

Chapter 6 deals with the process Paul used to get his churches to participate in the collection, and with the complications that developed along the way. It is obvious, for example, that the collection did not go well in Corinth. Why did the apostle have to change his tactics for fund-raising there? How did Paul deal with the opposition that developed in Corinth, and how did the various issues that surfaced at the time he was trying to raise funds for the collection affect his effectiveness as a fund-raiser?

Chapter 7 probes the specific arguments that Paul uses especially in 2 Cor 8 and 9 as he goes about trying to motivate the believers in Corinth to give for the impoverished believers in Jerusalem, regardless of how much opposition there might have been in Corinth. How did he go about raising money, especially when he knew he could no longer command them to participate? What arguments does he use, and what can we learn from them?

Chapter 8 deals with the collection subsequent to Paul's solicitation for money in 2 Cor 8 and 9. In Rom 15 Paul talks about the success of the collection in Macedonia and Achaia. But what about Galatia (1 Cor 16:1)? And what about Asia (Ephesus), from where he wrote 1 Corinthians and from where he sent Titus to Corinth? Did he solicit money in Asia for the collection? What does the strange journey of Paul described in Acts 20:1 – 5 mean? What was "the plot of the Jews" (20:3)? What are the scholarly options? And what about Paul's insistence that he would go to Jerusalem in spite of warnings of trouble there? Was this connected with his deep passion for delivering the collection in person because he was the apostle to the Gentiles? And why does Luke practically ignore the collection? There may be an allusion in Acts 24:17 to "alms for the poor"; is this indeed an allusion to the collection?

Part 3 undertakes a variety of remaining topics in relation to money issues that surface in Paul's letters. Chapter 9 examines the Thessalonian situation, where it seems apparent that there were a number of believers who were freeloading off of others in the church, perhaps because of a false view of the return of Christ. It seems clear in the 1 and 2 Thessalonians letters that Paul valued work and the ability to earn one's own income. Does his own insistence on earning his own keep color his message in 1 and 2 Thessalonians?

Chapter 10 deals with a second issue that developed in the Corinthian church, where there seem to have been differences of opinion and even conflict between the rich and the poor. The rich were looking down on the poor; this comes to light especially in the way in which the Lord's Supper with its accompanying Love Feast was being conducted in that church. How does Paul address these dynamics?

Chapter 11 examines Paul's instructions to those who are wealthy in the world. In 1 Tim 6:10 Paul writes: "the love of money is a root of all kinds of evil" (NIV), where he acknowledges the dangers to the faith of those who are eager for money. In 6:17–19, Paul commands those who are rich in the world to be generous. Moreover, in Eph 4:28 he has instructions for those who steal to stop stealing and to get honest work, so that "they may have something to share with those in need." We will need to say something about all these passages. And also in the Pastoral Epistles, in 1 Tim 5 Paul offers lengthy instructions about younger widows and elderly widows and how the church in Ephesus must approach this issue.

Finally, ch. 12 deals briefly with a few remaining issues. For example, Paul explicitly says in Rom 13:6–7 that believers are responsible to pay taxes to whom taxes are due. How can Paul expect believers to send taxes to a government in Rome that was clearly corrupt? What does this say about his theology? And a few verses later, in Rom 13:8, he writes: "Let no debt remain outstanding, except the continuing debt to love one another." Is the first reference to debt in this text a metaphor, or does Paul actually mean it is wrong for a Christian to go into debt? Another issue that is obviously important to Paul is that of financial integrity, particularly on the part of the leadership in the church, and we need to say a few words on that issue. Finally, we need to discuss briefly something that Paul does *not* say about the Christian's relation to money. Nowhere does Paul (nor does the NT as a whole) instruct believers in Jesus as the Messiah to tithe. Why is this?

The reader may notice that all of these issues deal directly with the concrete world of money and its broader context. That is by design. It is true that Paul uses the world of economics as a metaphor for some of his richest theological exploration of the work of Christ. The word "redemption," for example, comes directly from the buying and selling of slaves, and the way in which many Christians have described the Pauline concept of imputation comes from the world of accounting. We will not analyze such metaphorical uses of Paul's adaptation of the world of finance.[8] Such discussions would have undoubtedly doubled the size of this book; moreover, the past two decades have seen many books published on the theology of Paul the apostle and on his doctrine of the atonement and salvation, and we have no intent to compete with the scholars who have published these erudite tomes.[9]

At the end of the book, we hope to draw up a few conclusions about Paul's message to the church today, for Paul's instructions are not just for his generation. As part of the Word of God, his words apply to us as well.

---

8. The only exception might be our discussion in ch. 12 of Rom 13:8, "Owe nothing to anyone except to love one another." We will include a brief discussion of this verse because while some interpreters see the "debt" owed here as purely metaphorical (a debt of love), others interpret the first couple words in this verse, understood in its context, as containing instructions on how Christians should handle actual monetary debts.

9. See, for example, N. T. Wright, *Justification: God's Plan and Paul's Vision* (Downers Grove, IL: InterVarsity Press, 2009); Brian Vickers, *Jesus' Blood and Righteousness: Paul's Theology of Imputation* (Wheaton, IL: Crossway, 2006); Jeremy R. Treat, *The Crucified King: Atonement and Kingdom in Biblical and Systematic Theology* (Grand Rapids: Zondervan, 2014).

PART 1

PAUL'S WORK AND HIS FINANCIAL POLICIES

CHAPTER 1

EARNING A LIVING FROM THE GOSPEL

THIS IS A BOOK ABOUT PAUL AND MONEY. OUR ATTITUDES ABOUT MONEY are often shaped from childhood, which includes our cultural background. The patterns we grow up with stay with us in one form or another for much of our lives. It is therefore appropriate that we try, as best we can, to see what cultural patterns shaped the Jewish boy Saul/Paul,[1] growing up in the Greco-Roman city of Tarsus in Cilicia.

We read in the book of Acts that at some point in his life, Paul must have learned the skill of working with leather;[2] that was his trade (cf. Acts 18:3). But we also read that relatively early on he moved to Jerusalem to be trained as a rabbi/Pharisee under Gamaliel I (22:3). Moreover, we know that when he went out on his missionary journeys in the Greco-Roman world, he used the skills of leatherworking in order to support himself, rather than expecting that the churches he was serving would provide him with basic life necessities (food, clothing, lodging, etc.). At the same time, he argues in 1 Cor 9:4–6 that other apostle-missionaries did accept financial support for their work—and Paul considered that perfectly acceptable.

This raises a host of questions that revolve around financial issues,

---

1. For the most part we will use the name "Paul" throughout this book, even though the NT does not call him by this name until he was with Barnabas on the island of Cyprus (Acts 13:9).

2. See Ronald Hock, *The Social Context of Paul's Ministry: Tentmaking and Apostleship* (Philadelphia: Fortress, 1980), 20–21. We will discuss the issue of Paul's training as a leatherworker in more detail in the next chapter.

which we will seek to answer in these first two chapters. Why did Paul take the attitude he did toward insisting that he pay his own way for basic living expenses as a missionary? What factors in his background may have shaped his thinking here? How might his thinking have developed over the years—both regarding himself and others? In order to begin to answer these questions, it seems that the best place to start is Paul's training to become a Pharisee under Gamaliel I.

PAUL'S TRAINING AS A PHARISEE

Judging from the NT, we can determine that Paul's training as a Pharisee was one of the most powerful influences on his life as a young man. As he himself admits about his "way of life in Judaism," he advanced quickly in his knowledge of the holy Scriptures and of the traditions of Judaism, surpassing many others his own age (Gal 1:13–14). In fact, he became a fanatic (ζηλωτής) for the traditions of his Jewish ancestors.[3] Whether this zeal for the life of the Pharisees started before or after the martyrdom of Stephen we cannot tell, but it was certainly evident at that time, for Paul was the guardian of the robes of those stoning Stephen (Acts 7:58), and even more so immediately after when he began to do his utmost to destroy (ἐλυμαίνετο) the church (8:3).[4]

TRAINING FOR JEWISH YOUTH

Our intent is not to discuss Paul the persecutor, however. What we want to probe are questions that pertain to financial matters. At what age would a young man likely seek to follow a rabbi and be trained by him? Were

---

3. Note that Paul ascribes the word ζηλωτής to himself in Acts 22:3. We would like to know, of course, if he was always zealous in his knowledge of the Scriptures or if he became radicalized when he entered training as a Pharisee and began a formal study of the Torah, as sometimes happens even today when young people begin studying the writings of their religion, be it the Torah, the Bible, or the Quran. But there is no way to answer that question. We do know, of course, that he had enough of a feeling for his Jewish heritage that he left his home in Tarsus to move to Jerusalem for intense study of the sacred texts of Judaism (see below). Later in Phil 3:5–6, Paul further describes himself as "a Hebrew of Hebrews, as to the law a Pharisee, as for zeal [ζῆλος], persecuting the church, as to righteousness under the law blameless" (cf. Acts 23:6; 26:5); this passage also brings out his "zeal."

4. The verb λυμαίνω is a *hapax legomenon* in the NT. The NIV takes the imperfect tense here as an inceptive imperfect ("began to destroy"); the NRSV simply sees it as a progressive imperfect ("was ravaging"). Either is possible.

any fees involved, and if so, how would a young man get the necessary resources to pay those fees? Were those who were being trained in the way of the Pharisees expected to work at some job in order to earn income to support their education and perhaps also support the one who was training them in the ways of the Torah? Did this have any possible effect on his pattern of working for his own living when he became an apostle of the Lord Jesus Christ?

To find first-century documentation about the process of education for Jewish boys and young men is all but impossible. Josephus does acknowledge that from ages sixteen to nineteen he took some training in the ways of the Pharisees, as well as in the ways of the Sadducees and Essenes, but he tells us nothing about how he went about doing that.[5]

However, certain aspects of the education of Jewish children have remained remarkably stable over the centuries (though, admittedly, some changes have taken place), and it will serve us well to examine them. The education of Jewish children began in the home through their parents' consistent teaching of God's law and how God had dealt with his people in the past (Deut 6:6–9; Prov 1:8). One of the key methods through which teaching took place was attendance at the annual feasts of the Israelites (especially the Passover, but also the Feasts of Weeks and Booths, each of which was connected with significant historical events in Israel's past), which were set up as teaching events.[6] Note Exod 12:26–27: "And when your children ask you, 'What does this ceremony mean to you?' then tell them, 'It is the Passover sacrifice to the LORD, who passed over the houses of the Israelites in Egypt and spared our homes when he struck down the Egyptians'" (NIV). Moreover, undoubtedly whenever children observed sacrifices in the temple, they would ask similar questions about the purposes of those sacrifices, and the parents would teach them about the laws of Yahweh their God.

During the exilic period, when there was no longer a temple in

---

5. Josephus, *Life*, ch. 2 (sec.10–12). Josephus covers this period of his life in just a few lines. Of the three sects that he investigated, he must have liked the Pharisees best, for "[I] began to conduct myself according to the rules of the sect of the Pharisees." Josephus also had a priestly background.

6. Randall C. Bailey, *Exodus* (CPNIVC; Joplin: College Press, 2007), 150. Sadly, history shows that the Passover was not often kept (John H. Sailhamer, *The Pentateuch as Narrative* [Grand Rapids: Zondervan, 1995], 263).

Jerusalem, sacrifices ceased, and God's people lived far away from their homeland, the teaching of the written Scriptures, especially the Torah, became central to Jewish religious life. While the origin of the synagogue is shrouded in mystery and scholars debate its specific details, most agree that synagogues probably started in some fashion during the exile.[7] With the temple destroyed, "the synagogue enabled the Jews to organize their communal life and worship anywhere."[8] What made this institution truly unique from any other religious institution in the ancient world, including the Jewish temple (when it was standing), was "the communal reading and study of the Bible," along with the synagogue's "role as a community center" for almost all aspects of Jewish life.[9] As a consequence, a shift in educational pattern started to take place as the formal teaching of the Torah began to transfer from the home to the synagogue.

The classic description that seeks to probe the history of the education of Jewish youth and adults in the exilic and especially postexilic era is "Education and the Study of the Torah," by S. Safrai.[10] Most of the data used in this article, however, comes from the Mishnah and the Talmuds (the writings of the Pharisees and their successors), and such information is not useful for trying to understand typical Jewish life prior to the destruction of the temple, when the Sadducees were the de facto rulers of the Jewish nation. The rabbinic writings may be useful for describing some of the pre-AD 70 patterns in Judea and perhaps Galilee,[11] but we must remember that Paul grew up in Tarsus in Cilicia.

TRAINING AS A PHARISEE

However, an important passage in Acts indicates Paul's involvement with the movement of the Pharisees did not begin with him; he was υἱὸς

---

7. It would take us too far afield to discuss the origin of synagogue. For one of the best resources of recent scholarship on this issue, see Lee I. Levine, *The Ancient Synagogue: The First Thousand Years* (2nd. ed.; New Haven, CT: Yale University Press, 2005).

8. Ibid., 2.

9. Ibid.

10. S. Safrai, "Education and the Study of the Torah," in *The Jewish People in the First Century* (ed. S. Safrai and M. Stern; 2 vols.; Leiden: Brill, 1988), 2:945–70. We are grateful to Lois Tverberg for her help in pointing us to this essay.

11. See Maristella Botticini and Zvi Eckstein, "Jewish Occupational Selection: Education, Restriction, or Minorities," 12–13; http://www.bu.edu/econ/files/2011/01/2004_22_Botticini.pdf. We are thankful to Lynn Cohick for pointing us to this article.

Φαρισαίων ("a son of Pharisees," Acts 23:6). This does not mean that his father was a Pharisee, but it does suggest that there were Pharisees among his ancestors. Undoubtedly young Paul learned the basics of the Scriptures as a young boy (whether he learned to read the Scriptures in Hebrew in his home province of Cilicia as most of the Pharisees are presumed to have done in Judea and Galilee, we simply do not know, though perhaps so). But somewhere early in his life a desire to study "the traditions of the fathers" grew within the heart of Paul. At some point he moved to Jerusalem in order to be trained by the Pharisees, so much so that he was able to say in Acts 22:3, ἀνατεθραμμένος δὲ ἐν τῇ πόλει ταύτῃ ("[I was] brought up in this city").[12] In general, the verb ἀνατρέφω denotes a significant period of time. From the time that Paul first went to Jerusalem to the time he became a believer in Jesus could easily have been about the same amount of time as he had lived at home in Tarsus. Hengel suggests that this move to Jerusalem took place when he was an adolescent, perhaps about age fifteen.[13]

One of the first things Paul may have experienced in his education was to become involved with "a *bet midrash* [house of instruction] to sit at the teachers of the Law with other adults who studied Torah in their spare time."[14] That such "houses of instruction" existed already in the Second Temple period seems confirmed by Sir 51:23 (titled "A Prayer of Jesus ben Sirach"): "Draw near to me, you who are uneducated, and lodge in a house of instruction" (NETS).[15] While such houses are not known in the Diaspora, there does seem to be evidence that they existed in Palestine.

---

12. Eckhard Schnabel (*Acts* [ZECNT; Grand Rapids: Zondervan, 2012], 900) places this move to Jerusalem relatively early in Paul's life, since Paul had a married sister who lived in Jerusalem (see Acts 23:16), and he could have stayed there and perhaps even attended a *bet midrash* in the Holy City. Schnabel suggests too this may be an implication of Paul's calling himself "a Hebrew of Hebrews" in Phil 3:5. During these years, his Jewish roots seemed more important to him than his birth in Tarsus of Cilicia.

13. See Martin Hengel, *The Pre-Christian Paul* (trans. John Bowden; London: SCM, 1991), 38–40. Earlier in the book Hengel endorses the argument of Gunther Bornkamm that Paul must have received his education as a Pharisee in Jerusalem, "because the sources at our disposal point to Pharisaism as a Palestinian movement and Jerusalem as its centre; we know virtually nothing of a Diaspora Pharisaism" (from Bornkamm's "Paulus," in *RGG*[3], 5 [1961], col. 168).

14. Safras, "Education and the Study of Torah," 953.

15. Note that the NRSV labels Sir 51:13–30 as "Autobiographical Poem on Wisdom." Most scholars date Sirach to about the second century BC.

At some point in his training, promising young Paul was able to "sign on," as it were, with Rabbi Gamaliel I, one of the most prominent leaders of the Pharisees at the time, to be one of his devoted learners (see Acts 22:3). What seems abundantly clear throughout Paul's letters is that he was thoroughly familiar with the sorts of arguments from Scripture that we find in later rabbinic writings.

What about payment to the teachers and the sages? The evidence is somewhat mixed. First, "tannaitic literature [which is well past the NT era] repeatedly affirms the principle that teaching the Law like other public services ought to be performed without financial reward."[16] If the teacher was a member of the priestly class (at least during the time prior to the destruction of the temple), not receiving remuneration for teaching would not present a problem, since priests were already recipients of the tithes of the people.[17] For nonpriestly teachers, however, such as Rabbi Gamaliel, we simply do not know. If we read the later rabbinic literature, there is evidence of ways to get around the principle of no payment for the study of the Torah. Teachers of Torah might receive pay equal to what they were losing by not doing their regular work (i.e., they received compensation for lost wages), "or they would receive a salary for teaching punctuation and accents which are not an integral part of the Torah, or for looking after the children."[18] Or in some cases there might be tuition fees paid directly by the parents. For the most part, it seems, a teacher in a *bet midrash* did receive some compensation, which was considered only fair.

This raises the question of whether Paul may have grown up in a home that could afford a "tuition" fee. Did he grow up in what we might call a "middle class" home, or in a home where people lived basically at subsistence level?[19] Many scholars today argue that most likely Paul's family of origin lived at a somewhat comfortable level.[20] The very fact that Paul's letters appear to demonstrate a familiarity with Greco-Roman rhetoric has

---

16. Safrai, "Education and the Study of the Torah," 956.

17. Ibid., 964.

18. Ibid., 956–57.

19. Much more will be said about the different economic levels in the Greco-Roman world in ch. 4. Suffice it to say here that the majority of people in the Greco-Roman world lived at a subsistence level or even lower, where they had to beg for their daily needs.

20. C. H. Dodd ("The Mind of Paul: I," in *New Testament Studies* [Manchester: University of Manchester Press, 1953], 72) places Paul's childhood home as among "the well-to-do *bourgeois*."

suggested to many he may have had some formal training in that subject,[21] which would likely not have occurred for someone living on a subsistence level.[22] Moreover, when Paul talks about his work as a leatherworker,[23] he talks about the strain and difficulty that his toil and labor brought to him. Note Longenecker's comment: "It is notable that Paul's attitude towards manual labor betrays a man who imagines manual labor to be beneath his normal station in life."[24] If these assumptions are accurate, Paul's father would perhaps have been able to pay fees for his son to train under one of the top rabbis in Jerusalem, especially if he could live at his sister's house in Jerusalem (cf. Acts 23:16).

As Paul advanced in Judaism and in "the traditions of the fathers"

---

21. Cf. Hengel, *The Pre-Christian Paul*, 18–39. Note, however, the recent book of Ryan S. Schellenberg, *Rethinking Paul's Rhetorical Education: Comparative Rhetoric and 2 Corinthians 10–13* (Early Christianity and Its Literature; Atlanta: Society of Biblical Literature, 2013). Schellenberg demonstrates in a variety of ways that Paul's rhetoric does not follow ancient rhetorical handbooks; what rhetorical flourish he does manifest could easily have been acquired through listening to orators. Note his summary: "much of the alleged correspondence between Paul and the theorists and practitioners of formal Greco-Roman rhetoric [have turned] out to be unsubstantiated and illusory" (309). Instead, "what Paul knew of persuasion derived ... from informal social practice" (309–10); for this conclusion he has depended heavily on "George Kennedy's work on comparative rhetoric" (309). Consequently, Schellenberg argues that we cannot use Paul's speech and writing patterns to determine his social position.

22. See Bruce W. Longenecker, *Remember the Poor: Paul, Poverty, and the Greco-Roman World* (Grand Rapids: Eerdmans, 2010), 307. Longenecker defers to Jerome (early fifth century AD in *Lives of Illustrious Men*, 5) who cites a legend that Paul's parents came to Tarsus as slaves after a battle at Gischala in Galilee. But by the time Paul was born, his family was freed from slavery (cf. Acts 22:28, where Paul indicates he was born a Roman citizen). Yet such a birth does not mean his family had become now part of elite society, which one needed in order to qualify for schooling in the famous university in Tarsus. Yet at the same time, for Paul to go to Jerusalem for training as a Pharisee suggests that neither did he live in poverty. Most likely he was what we might today call lower middle class.

23. For more on what Paul's chosen labor involved, see ch. 2.

24. Longenecker, *Remember the Poor*, 305. Longenecker cites in particular 2 Cor 11:7, where "Paul depicts his manual labor as a form of self-humiliation. This is not the language of one who imagined that manual labor was a normal part of his everyday life" (at least, not the life he knew growing up). In other words, when Paul became a Christian, his "economic profile ... drops a level or two" (307; cf. 307–9). But see also Todd Still, ("Did Paul Loathe Manual Labor? Revisiting the World of Ronald F. Hock on the Apostle's Tentmaking and Social Class," *JBL* 125 [2006]: 781–95) who, while acknowledging Paul may have grown up in a home at a comfortable economic level, argues rightly that the assumption that Paul *loathed* his work as a leatherworker is going beyond the evidence in Scripture. For more on the possibility of Paul's possibly downgrading his social-economic status when he became a missionary-evangelist and what may have driven him to do so, see ch. 2.

(Gal 1:13 – 14), it is possible that he became part of a more advanced group, composed of a sage with his disciples. Often such groups had a fund to which everyone contributed and from which they could buy food, especially if they accompanied the sage as he moved from place to place. One is reminded here of the pattern that Jesus and his disciples followed. Note that Jesus was called "Rabbi" on more than one occasion, both by his disciples and by non-disciples (Matt 26:25, 49; Mark 9:5; 10:51; 11:21; John 1:38; 3:2; 6:25; 9:2). This suggests that his manner of traveling about the Judean and Galilean countryside was not unlike what official rabbis did. We know from Mark 15:41 and Luke 8:3b that a group of women traveled with Jesus and "helped"[25] to support him and his disciples "out of their own possessions" (ἐκ τῶν ὑπαρχόντων αὐταῖς). Moreover, we know from John 12:4 – 6 that Judas was the caretaker of the money bag, which means the disciples must have received some voluntary contributions from those who could afford to give, in order to help pay for the ongoing living expenses of Jesus and his disciples.[26]

In other words, while Paul clearly refused to accept support from those among whom he was ministering, it was not because such support for teachers of God's word was forbidden in Jewish society in the first century. That would explain too why the apostles such as Peter had no qualms about receiving support as they went out proclaiming the gospel (see 1 Cor 9:5).

PAUL'S MESSAGE ABOUT FUNDS FOR CHURCH WORKERS: 1 TIMOTHY 5

With this information about the remuneration for teachers of the Torah prior to AD 70 as background, we now turn to a later important issue

---

25. The verb "were helping" is the Greek term διηκόνουν (it occurs in both these verses), from which we get the word "deacon" (cf. Acts 6:1 – 6). Note BDAG, 229, s.v. δαικονέω, 3, which applies to Luke 8:3: "to meet an immediate need, *help*."

26. D. A. Carson, *The Gospel according to John* (Pillar; Grand Rapids: Eerdmans, 1991), 429, expounds: "The *money bag* was doubtless used to meet the disciples' needs, and also to provide alms to the poor. Normally it was replenished by disciples who cherished Jesus' ministry, like the women mentioned in Luke 8:2 – 3. The last clause could almost be taken to mean that Judas used to 'carry' (bastazō) what was put in, but in the right contexts the verb means 'steal' or 'pilfer' — not unlike the verb 'lift' in the United Kingdom. This is the only place in the New Testament where Judas is called a thief — indeed, where any charge other than Judas' ultimate betrayal is leveled against him. Yet the charge is believable: anyone who would betray another person for thirty pieces of silver has an unhealthy avarice for material things."

about Paul and money that surfaces in his letters, namely, his teachings about whether those who worked as teachers and missionaries in the church should receive compensation. We are separating out a discussion of this particular issue from the related issue about whether Paul felt that *he* could or should accept money for his missionary work, and if so, under what conditions. Most of the time scholars discuss these two questions together, partly because these two issues are interwoven in 1 Cor 9. But they are separate issues. It is the difference between a general principle and a specific application — that is, whether Paul personally felt comfortable applying the general principle about payment for workers for the Lord to his own life and ministry. That more specific issue we will explore in the next chapter. In the rest of this chapter we will ask whether, and under what conditions, if any, Paul felt it was appropriate for Christian leaders in the first century to accept some sort of compensation for their work.

JESUS' PATTERN FOR HIS DISCIPLES WHEN SENT OUT

While Paul never refers to the gospel story of Jesus' sending out the twelve disciples on a ministry of teaching and healing, Paul says enough in his speeches in Acts and writes enough in his letters to indicate that he is fully aware of the traditions of the Gospels.[27] It is certainly reasonable to think that Paul knew the story of the sending out of the Twelve (recorded in Matt 10:1, 5–15; Mark 6:6b–13; Luke 9:1–6; cf. Luke 10:1–12 [the sending out of the seventy-two]). One of the key features of these gospel accounts is Jesus' instructions on "financial arrangements" for their support (especially food and lodging). There are, of course, differences among these passages,[28] but there is a general consistency in the instructions.

The disciples were not to take any money along with them when they

---

27. Paul's basic message told about the life, ministry, death, and resurrection of Jesus; see Acts 13:23–39, which follows the preaching of Peter in 2:22–36 as well as the general outline and content of the gospel of Mark. See also 1 Cor 11:23–25; 15:3–7, where Paul indicates he received the apostolic tradition of the salvation-history stories of Jesus. On some occasions in his letters, Paul even shows a familiarity with various dominical sayings of Jesus (e.g., 1 Cor 7:10–11; 1 Thess 4:15). See Craig L. Blomberg, "Quotations, Allusions, and Echoes of Jesus in Paul," in *Studies in the Pauline Epistles: Essays in Honor of Douglas J. Moo* (ed. Matthew S. Harmon and Jay E. Smith; Grand Rapids: Zondervan, 2014), 129–43.

28. Most commentaries on the Synoptic Gospels will point out these differences and, in many cases, attempt to resolve any discrepancies. It is beyond the scope of this book to deal with these in any detail.

left to do their missionary work (Mark 6:8). Nor were they to take any bag along for extra clothing or food. They were to be totally dependent for their daily needs on the people among whom they were ministering, "proclaiming the good news and healing people everywhere" (Luke 9:6). This dependence included lodging; they were to stay with the first person who invited them to stay, and they were to stay there until they left for the next town (note 10:7, "do not move around from house to house").[29] And if no one in a particular village invited them in to stay, they were to depart and "shake the dust off their feet as a testimony against them" (9:5).[30]

In two of the instructions found in the Synoptic Gospels, Jesus included a basic principle about why the disciples should expect daily support: "for the worker is worthy of his food" (ἄξιος γὰρ ὁ ἐργάτης τῆς τροφῆς αὐτοῦ, Matt 10:10); "for the worker is worthy of his wages" (ἄξιος γὰρ ὁ ἐργάτης τοῦ μισθοῦ αὐτοῦ, Luke 10:7).[31] In other words, the Lord Jesus himself did not expect his disciples to set up some shop in a new town in which they would practice a trade or sell goods at a profit; they were workers in the kingdom of God, and such workers should expect that their work was valuable enough to warrant a μισθός.[32]

The basic classical Greek meaning of μισθός is "wages." It was used that way occasionally in the LXX (e.g., Gen 30:26, 28, where Jacob and Laban negotiate Jacob's "wages" [μισθός] as a hired man). It can also be

---

29. Perhaps this was to keep them from "moving up the ladder" to a better, more luxurious house should they be invited.

30. It was to be done as a "testimony against them," a symbolic action that, as the NLT translates, showed that they had "abandoned those people to their fate." That Paul (and Barnabas) were aware of this tradition is suggested by their reaction when they left Pisidian Antioch in Act 13:51: "they shook the dust off their feet as a warning to them" (NIV).

31. One could argue that this sentence comes from Q, the material common to Matthew and Luke. However, Luke's version comes in the sending out of the seventy-two, which is clearly from L. In other words, there is reason to believe that this saying from Jesus is actually found in two strata of the gospel sources. In either case, Luke's record is alluded to in 1 Cor 9:14 and quoted in 1 Tim 5:18 ("wages") and in Did. 13:1 ("food").

32. Darrell L. Bock (Luke: 9:51–24:53 [BECNT; Grand Rapids: Baker Academic, 1996], 999) comments: "Luke's saying states positively what the OT and Jewish tradition state negatively (Lev 19:13; Deut 24:14–15; Mal 3:5; Sir 34:26–27 [NRSV numbering]; Tob 4:14). In the OT the stress is on the crime of withholding a wage from one who has labored. Payment often was made daily in this cultural setting (Preisker, TDNT 4:698). The action contrasts with Cynic philosophers who begged for money (Danker [1988]: 214; cf. the instructions of Luke 10:4). In contrast, the provisionless messengers are to have their needs met in homes of peace."

used that way in the NT, as in Matt 20:8, in the parable of the workers in the vineyard (also Rom 4:4; Jas 5:4).[33] While the word τροφή ("food") in Matt 10:10 does not designate a wage as such, it does refer to that which a disciple-"worker" (ἐργάτης) is worthy of (ἄξιος) by virtue of his activities of preaching the gospel of the kingdom, casting out demons, and healing the sick.

In other words, in the gospel tradition that Paul received, there is clear evidence that anyone who worked as a "kingdom worker" should be able to expect to receive his daily sustenance (esp. food and lodging are mentioned) from the people among whom he was working. In fact, Paul actually quotes the proverb Luke cites in Luke 10:7 in 1 Tim 5:18: ἄξιος ὁ ἐργάτης τοῦ μισθοῦ αὐτοῦ.[34] This verse discusses the work of elders who function well as leaders (οἱ προεστῶτες) of the church (5:17). This term for leadership is derived from the Greek verb προΐστημι, which means to rule or to manage.[35] This verb is used earlier in 1 Tim 3:4, 5, 12 both for elders/overseers and for deacons regarding the management of one's household as a good test to see if someone is able to serve in a leadership capacity in the church.[36]

---

33. See *NIDNTTE*, 3:324–25, s.v. μισθός. See also BDAG, 653, s.v. μισθός, where the first and most prominent meaning is "remuneration for work done, *pay, wages*." Note, however, that the predominant meaning of this term in the NT has to do with eternal reward (e.g., Matt 5:12; 6:1–2, 5, 16; 1 Cor 3:14; Rev 22:12) or eternal punishment, also conceived as reward (2 Pet 2:13, 15).

34. It is perhaps surprising that Paul uses the same text recorded in Luke's gospel in such a different cultural setting. In the sending out of the Twelve, the disciples go into a rural setting in Galilee; the teaching and preaching ministry of the elders in 1 Tim 5 (in Ephesus) is located in a major city of the empire. Yet Paul is able to apply a principle from that rural setting to a significantly different setting. The same can be said for the OT text from Deut 25:4, drawn from an agricultural setting but applied by Paul to the ministry of elders in 1 Tim 5:18 and, as we will soon see, also to Paul's discussion of missionary work in the first century to major cities in the empire. While the setting of the application is different, the principle remains the same.

35. BDAG, 870, s.v. προΐστημι 1.

36. One wonders why Paul did not discuss the importance of the church caring for the needs of elders in ch. 3, where he discusses qualifications for elders. The answer may rest in the fact that when Paul does deal with elders' needs in ch. 5, he is trying to correct church problems—here erring elders (see esp. 5:19–22). Likewise the use of τιμή in 5:17 provides a clear link to the use of the verb τιμάω that Paul used earlier in 5:3, concerning giving "proper recognition" (honor) to widows (see C. Michael Moss, *1, 2 Timothy & Titus* [CPNIVC; Joplin: College Press, 1994], 107).

PAUL'S ARGUMENTS FOR REGULAR SUPPORT
FOR ELDERS IN HIS CHURCHES

In 1 Tim 5:17, Paul says that the elders who served well "were to be worthy" (here the verb ἀξιόω is used) of double honor. There are at least three difficulties in the interpretation regarding this verse. (1) Does it reflect an era in which there were "full-time elders" who received a salary for their work in the church? (2) Are there two types of elders, "those who serve" and "those who serve well"? (3) What is the meaning of "double honor"?[37]

Regarding the first of these, there is no evidence this early in the history of the church that there were certain elders for whom working in the church was considered a full-time job that warranted some sort of salary.[38] It is true that Timothy seems to have been devoting most of his hours in a week in ministry in Ephesus (cf. 1:3), but Paul is not referring to him here (cf. the use of the plural πρεσβύτεροι). Moreover, nowhere does Paul ever refer to Timothy as an "elder."[39]

Regarding the second question, it is important to point out that all elders/overseers were expected to be able to teach in some form (1 Tim 3:2). But as with every position of this nature, some would be more gifted in this area, and it is only natural that those who were the more effective communicators would be called upon to do more of the "preaching and teaching" (5:17) than those who did not have those gifts. This would appear to be the meaning of the word καλῶς ("well") in the phrase "the elders who managed well . . . especially those who labored in the word and teaching."[40]

But what about the third question, regarding τιμή ("honor") — and

---

37. For a thorough discussion of these issues, see William D. Mounce, *Pastoral Epistles* (WBC; Nashville: Nelson, 2000), 306–11.

38. Ibid., 307. Note, of course, Did. 13.1: "But every true prophet who wants to live among you is worthy of his support. So also a true teacher is himself worthy, as the workman, of his support." The Didache, however, is likely a second-century document, well past the time of the writing of the Pastoral Epistles.

39. Whether this is because Timothy was considered a νέος (cf. 4:12), or perhaps had the gift of "shepherd and teacher" (cf. Eph 4:11), or for some other reason cannot be determined. We would love to know how Timothy (and Titus too, for that matter) were able to meet their basic physical needs. Had Paul taught them his leatherworking craft? Did they receive support from the church(es) in Ephesus (Timothy) and Crete (Titus)? Did they have a patron who supported them (see ch. 3)? There is no way we can answer this question, and there is no written source available that we know of through which we can even speculate.

40. See Mounce, *Pastoral Epistles*, 307–8 for discussion.

especially "*double* honor"? A number of scholars have suggested the double honor means that such elders were to be properly honored *and* properly paid.[41] Others argue that they should receive "honor" (not pay) first because they served as elders and second because they served "well."[42] Still others have interpreted "double" to mean double what someone else received, such as perhaps the widows or other elders.[43]

It is true that the term τιμή, along with the corresponding verb τιμάω, does mean "honor, respect" (Rom 13:7; Rev 4:9, 11; cf. the use of the verb in 1 Tim 5:3 regarding respect for widows, and the use in the fifth commandment, "honor your father and mother"). But this word group also has the standard financial meaning of "price, value" (see, for the noun, its use in Acts 4:34; 5:2–3; 19:19; for the verb, Matt 27:9 [along with the noun as cognate accusative]).[44] We think, therefore, that the first option given for "double honor" above seems the best choice. "Double honor" refers to the special respect certain effective elders were to get, *plus* some sort of honorarium (note the double sense in this English *honor* yet today) for those who were notably gifted in communicating God's word to the people, especially in the context of the heresy in Ephesus.[45] This addresses the issue of not ascribing the notion of a regular salary to elders in the first century, but at the same time of keeping consistency in the use of the proverb, "The worker is worthy of his wages" (1 Tim 5:18).[46]

41. Gordon D. Fee, *1 and 2 Timothy, Titus* (NIBCNT; Peabody, MA: Hendrickson, 1988), 129.

42. D. Edmond Hiebert, *Second Timothy* (Chicago: Moody, 1958), 101; William Hendricksen, *Exposition of the Pastoral Epistles* (Grand Rapids: Baker, 1968), 180; Raymond F. Collins (*1 & 2 Timothy and Titus* [NTL; Louisville: Westminster John Knox, 2002], 144) feels that the double honor comes both from the respect intrinsic to the office itself and the joy of a job well done.

43. See W. Lock, *A Critical and Exegetical Commentary on the Pastoral Epistles* (ICC; Edinburgh: T&T Clark, 1924), in loc.

44. See BDAG, 1005, s.v. τιμή, where the first meaning given is "the amount at which someth. is valued; *price, value*." Note too that the corresponding adjective, τίμιος, is often used for that which is precious or costly (such as "costly stones" in 1 Cor 3:12 and precious stones in Rev 17:4; 18:12 [see BDAG, 1005–6, s.v. τίμιος]).

45. See Mounce, *Pastoral Epistles*, 309–10. Note also Titus 1:10–11, where Paul instructs Titus about the rebellious people on the island of Crete. Apparently these people were teaching and were insisting on getting paid for what they said, though Paul writes that their motivation was "for the sake of dishonest gain." In other words, Paul wants to remove financial support for those who refused to teach and preach the true doctrine.

46. The Greek word order places emphasis on the adjective ἄξιος: "worthy are the workers."

The first words of 1 Tim 5:18 seem to suggest that Paul is citing "the worker is worthy of his wages" as "Scripture." The use of ἡ γραφή when it introduces a citation from Scripture is limited in the NT to OT citations; in fact, scholars have pointed out that there are no clear uses of ἡ γραφή for anything other than OT citations well into the second century.[47] Paul, of course, had Luke as a travel companion, and this particular proverb is quoted in Luke 10:7; is Paul therefore trying to ascribe to Luke scriptural authority? Probably not.[48] According to most chronological reckonings, if the Pastorals are indeed written by Paul and the gospel of Luke by Luke, the Gospel was not even written yet when 1 Timothy was written. The best answer to the use of ἡ γραφή in 1 Tim 5:18 is that "the citation 'Scripture' is accounted for by recognizing that 'Scripture' need only apply to Paul's first citation from the OT."[49] That citation, "You shall not muzzle the ox as it is threshing" (βοῦν ἀλοῶντα οὐ φιμώσεις), is from Deut 25:4.

The analogy that Paul is using in this scriptural citation is clear. Oxen were used in the ancient world to do the heavy work of threshing harvested grain. They would pull a heavy sled with sharp objects embedded on the underside to remove the husk from the grain; then the wind would blow the chaff away, so that only the grain, which could be ground into flour, remained. In order to keep a maximum yield of grain for human consumption, farmers were tempted to put muzzles on the mouths of the oxen so they could not eat the grain while they were working. In Deut 25:4 God commanded his people not to do this; after all, the ox was working hard, and he needed food to keep his energy up. This was the ox's "pay."

In conclusion, therefore, it seems appropriate to interpret 1 Tim 5:17–18 to be saying that Paul expected those who did the work of preaching and teaching in the church were to be compensated in some form (whether by money or perhaps by food) for that work. Paul did not expect those engaged in ministry in the church to work for free.

---

47. For evidence, see Mounce, *Pastoral Epistles*, 311; also Fee, *1 and 2 Timothy, Titus*, 93. Note too that the only other place where Paul clearly cites what is in the Gospels (1 Cor 11:24–25; cf. Luke 22:19–21), he follows the Lukan rendering of Jesus' words in the upper room, but he does *not* call it "Scripture"; rather, he cites what "he received" (presumably from the apostles).

48. Phillip H. Towner, *The Letters to Timothy and Titus* (NICNT; Grand Rapids: Eerdmans, 2006), 366–67.

49. Mounce, *Pastoral Epistles*, 311.

PAUL'S MESSAGE ABOUT FUNDS FOR TRAVELING EVANGELISTS: 1 CORINTHIANS 9

What is significant is that Paul used the same quotation from Deut 25:4 in a similar context in 1 Cor 9:9, where he is discussing the issue of whether the apostles and others doing the work of evangelism should receive support from those among whom they were preaching the gospel. As in 1 Tim 5:18, Paul uses a couple of analogies to answer this question in the affirmative, though in contrast to 1 Tim 5:18, he begins in 1 Cor 9:7–11 with a series of analogies rather than with Deut 25:4.

The apostle points out that soldiers are not expected to provide their own food and other provisions while they are fighting in defense of their country; rather, they rightfully could expect to receive all expenses paid (ὀψωνίοις).[50] A farmer who plants a vineyard certainly has the right to use some of the grapes harvested for his own physical needs. And a hired man who takes care of a farmer's sheep can eat, as part of his wages, some of the milk from the ewes.[51] Paul then asks a couple of rhetorical questions: "I don't have to limit myself to human examples, do I? Doesn't the law of Moses say the same thing?" It is at this point that he quotes Deut 25:4: "You shall not muzzle the ox as it is threshing" (1 Cor 9:9).

In contrast to 1 Tim 5:18, Paul is not content to let the quotation from Deut 25:4 simply stand on its own. In 1 Cor 9:9b–11 he expands his explanation in order to justify why this verse from the Mosaic law is relevant to what he is arguing:[52] "It is not about oxen that God is concerned, is it? Doesn't he really say this for our benefit? Yes, this was written for our benefit, because the one who plows does so in hope, and the one who

---

50. Anthony Thiselton (*The First Epistle to the Corinthians* [NIGTC; Grand Rapids: Eerdmans, 2000], 683–84) traces the history of this word. While in classical Greek it could "denote a workman's pay," in Koine Greek it often meant "rations or provisions" given to soldiers as their pay while on duty. Thiselton translates it as "all his own provisions," which includes "both expenses and rations." In the Greek text, the term is in the plural and is preceded by ἰδίοις ("his own"). (Please note that we are not including any of Thiselton's somewhat unusual use of both italics and bold typeface in any quotes from his commentary.)

51. Thiselton (ibid., 684) points to the unusual use of the word "eat" for milk. From this he argues that what is in focus is "the product of the milk," that is, "dairy produce (e.g., including cheeses)."

52. We will discuss aspects of 1 Cor 9 further in the next chapter, where our subject is about why Paul refused to avail himself of his right to receive support from the churches among whom he was ministering.

threshes does so in the hope of partaking in the harvest. If we have sown spiritual things for you, is it too much to expect if we harvest material things from you?"[53]

A number of scholars have taken Paul to task for his interpretation of Deut 25:4.[54] Taken as it stands in the OT, that verse is about the protection of animals as they work hard for human beings. But since Paul uses the verse to endorse the legitimacy of support for those who are doing the work of the Lord, these scholars suggest that Paul is following the allegorical exegetical tendencies of someone like Philo. According to Conzelmann,[55] for Philo God's law is really only interested in human beings, not animals; thus Philo had no choice but to squeeze out a human interpretation in whatever way possible to understand this verse, even if he had to do it by allegory. Fee points out correctly, however, that the particular section of Philo that Conzelmann cites does not use Deut 25:4 as an example; moreover, where Philo does in fact cite Deut 25:4, he uses it "as evidence of the splendid mercy of Israel's God toward even the irrational animals."[56] In other words, it is simply wrong to state that Philo felt that everything in the Torah had to be about people.

It seems to us, therefore, that Paul, even using the principles of interpretation common in the first century, is indeed correctly interpreting Deut 25:4.[57] As Thiselton points out, from the regulations on divorce

---

53. See also William F. Orr and James Arthur Walther, *I Corinthians: A New Translation* (AB; Garden City, NY: Doubleday, 1976), 241.

54. J. Weiss, *Der erste Korintherbrief* (KEK; 9th ed.; Göttingen: Vandenhoeck & Ruprecht, 1910), 236; Archibald Robertson and Alfred Plummer, *A Critical and Exegetical Commentary on the First Epistle of St. Paul to the Corinthians* (2nd ed.; ICC; Edinburgh: T&T Clark, 1914), 183–84; Barrett, *Commentary on the First Epistle to the Corinthians* (HNTC; New York: Harper & Row, 1968), 205; Raymond F. Collins, *First Corinthians* (SP; Collegeville: Liturgical, 1999), 339.

55. Conzelmann quotes Philo's *Spec.* 1.260: "For the law does not prescribe for unreasoning creatures, but for those who have mind and reason"; see Hans Conzelmann, *1 Corinthians* (trans. J. W. Leitch; Herm; Philadelphia: Fortress, 1975), 154.

56. Gordon D. Fee, *The First Epistle to the Corinthians* (NICNT; Grand Rapids: Eerdmans, 1987), 407 n. 57. See also Barrett, *The First Epistle to the Corinthians*, 205. Others have suggested that Paul may be using a rabbinic interpretive principle here, that principle of *qal wahomer* ("the light and the heavy"). This argument would state that "if the law permits animals to eat of crops in fields that they are working, how much more may human laborers do so" (David E. Garland, *1 Corinthians* (BECNT; Grand Rapids: Baker, 2003), 411.

57. See the helpful essays in G. K. Beale, ed., *The Right Doctrine from the Wrong Texts? Essays on the Use of the Old Testament in the New* (Grand Rapids: Baker Academic, 1994).

in Deut 24:1–4 to the regulations on levirate marriage in 25:5–12, everything in the intervening verses deals with human concerns with the exception of 25:4.[58] "The unexpected insertion of one verse about threshing coheres most closely with the encouragement of human sensitivity and humane compassion toward the suffering or defenseless (e.g., the immediately preceding context concerns the plight of widows, orphans, and victims of punishment)."[59] In other words, while Deut 25:4 certainly does suggest that God means what he says that defenseless animals in service of human beings ought to be treated compassionately, the broader context hints that there are appropriate ramifications in this verse for human behavior—in this case, that people who do work for others can expect to reap some benefit from their work and not be forced to work for free.[60]

But there is a second element in 1 Cor 9:10 that has troubled some exegetes, namely, the use of the phrase δι' ἡμᾶς γὰρ ἐγράφη. Is Paul suggesting that Deut 25:4 was not really written for OT Israel, but that God inserted that verse "for our sakes"? Did the verse not mean anything to God's people in OT times? This question could sidetrack us into a lengthy discussion of Paul's use of the OT, which is an enormous topic on which entire books have been written.[61] Most certainly Paul would agree that God had revealed his will to his people in the OT so that by it they might shape their lives in obedience to God, but the apostle's predominant view of the Scriptures is that they have been written for us, "on whom the end of the ages has come" (1 Cor 10:11). Paul had an eschatological view of the Hebrew Scrptures, so that what God was revealing in the past was much more than just a message for the Israelite community; he was preparing

---

58. See the outline of that summary in Anthony C. Thiselton, *The First Epistle to the Corinthians*, 686.

59. Ibid.

60. It is worth noting that the infinitive μετέχειν ("to share") is used five times in 1 Corinthians (1 Cor 9:10, 12; 10:17, 21, 30), and it appears three times in Hebrews (2:14; 5:13; 7:13). It often refers to people consuming portions of food, but it can also refer to participants receiving fair portions of anything.

61. See, for example, Richard N. Longenecker, *Biblical Exegesis in the Apostolic Period* (Grand Rapids: Eerdmans, 1975); Richard B. Hays, *Echoes of Scripture in the Letters of Paul* (New Haven, CT: Yale University Press, 1989); James W. Aageson, *Written for Our Sake: Paul and the Art of Biblical Interpretation* (Louisville: Westminster John Knox, 1993); Stanley E. Porter, ed., *Hearing the Old Testament in the New Testament* (Grand Rapids: Eerdmans, 2006).

the world for the coming of the Lord Jesus Christ and the fulfillment of God's plan of salvation through the ministry of Christ and the establishment of the church. That in essence is what Paul hints at by his δι' ἡμᾶς in 1 Cor 9:10 with respect to Deut 25:4.[62]

In other words, when Paul went to the OT Scriptures, he mined it not simply for what it said to the Israelite community; he wanted to know also what God was saying through those Scriptures to the Christian community. "Paul can accord value to the OT in its proper context, while seeking that which transcends the immediate context. This further ... dimension often embodies a christological content or an eschatological promise."[63] Or, as Fee puts it, Paul generally does not speak to the OT Scriptures as to what they meant to the original hearers (which is often our first step in exegesis);[64] rather, "he is concerned with what it *means*, that is, with its *application* to their present situation. There is a sense in which he clearly keeps the original intent; he simply changes the application."[65]

In conclusion, therefore, Paul is certainly correct hermeneutically to suggest that a clear application of Deut 25:4 for his own day is that those who sow "spiritual things for [people can] ... expect [to] harvest material things" from these same people. In fact, Paul puts it even more pointedly, applying it to himself (and presumably Barnabas) by using "we": "If *we* have sown spiritual things for you, is it too much to expect if *we* harvest material things from you?" It is not just the other apostles and Peter and the Lord's brothers who have a right to food and drink from those among whom they are ministering (1 Cor 9:4–5); rather, Paul and Barnabas have exactly the same right (9:6).

In much of the rest of 1 Cor 9, however, Paul goes on to state forcefully that he and Barnabas forego that right by deciding to work for their own living. Since Barnabas by this time was no longer a travel companion of Paul (1 Corinthians was written on Paul's second missionary journey, after he and Barnabas had separated [Acts 15:36–40]), Paul is probably

---

62. R. E. Oster, *1 Corinthians* (CPNIVC; Joplin: College Press, 1995), 203; Paul Barnett, *1 Corinthians* (Fearn, UK: Christian Focus, 2000), 153.

63. Thiselton, *The First Epistle to the Corinthians*, 687.

64. See the five steps of the exegetical method outline by J. Scott Duvall and J. Daniel Hays in *Grasping God's Word* (3rd ed.; Grand Rapids: Zondervan, 2012). See also the exegetical process outlined for various genres of the Bible in Gordon D. Fee and Douglas Stuart, *How to Read the Bible for All Its Worth* (4th ed.; Grand Rapids: Zondervan, 2014).

65. Fee, *The First Epistle to the Corinthians*, 408 (italics original).

speaking about what he knows Barnabas is doing on his journey with John Mark. It is not impossible, of course, that Barnabas had significant independent income from which he could support himself (cf. Acts 4:36–37).[66] In fact, Barnabas may even have funded Paul's first missionary journey (there is no indication of their working for a living on that trip). But Paul presumably had no independent income. On his second missionary journey, he did engage in his leatherworking business, and in spite of his rights as an apostle-evangelist to receive support, he refused any help from the churches while he was working in their midst. The major question is: Why? Why did Paul refuse support? This is the question for our next chapter.

---

66. David G. Peterson (*The Acts of the Apostles* [Pillar; Grand Rapids: Eerdmans, 2009], 205) remarks: "Several first-century Levites are known to have been outstanding in wealth and education." Ben Witherington III (*The Acts of the Apostles: A Socio-Rhetorical Commentary* [Grand Rapids: Eerdmans / Carlisle: Paternoster, 1998], 205) suggests that "Barnabas is being held up as an example for Theophilus himself as a person of some social status to follow."

CHAPTER 2

PAUL'S RELUCTANCE TO ACCEPT SUPPORT

IN THE PREVIOUS CHAPTER, WE LOOKED AT PAUL'S JEWISH BACKGROUND and his training as a Pharisee. It became clear that there was little in that background that would prohibit Paul from accepting support from the believers to whom he preached the gospel and ministered. In fact, as we saw, he argued in at least two of his letters (1 Cor 9:3–12 and 1 Tim 5:17–18) that those believers who had been appointed to evangelize and preach God's word had every right to receive some sort of support payment for their work. Nevertheless, Paul personally refused to receive any money, at least from churches while he was living in their midst. He insisted on supporting himself by his work as a tentmaker or, perhaps better, leatherworker.[1] Why? What was it that drove Paul to preach the gospel without expecting any compensation? Was it purely theological? Or was something more underlying that decision?

---

1. See Hock (*Social Context of Paul's Ministry*, 20–21) who presents evidence that the Greek word σκηνοποιός (Acts 18:3) denotes a leatherworker. This does not mean that Paul prepared the animal skin; that is, he was not a tanner. Moreover, in the ancient world many tents were made of leather, but so were a lot of other items, such as footware. See also Still ("Did Paul Loathe Manual Labor?" 781–95) who while disagreeing with a number of Hock's contentions, does agree that Paul was most likely a leatherworker. See also the lengthy entry in BDAG, 928–29, s.v. σκηνοποιός, where Danker suggests that a σκηνοποιός was someone involved in theatrical productions; few have adopted this suggestion.

PAUL AS A LEATHERWORKER

In this chapter we need to look at several related issues surrounding this question. We begin by acknowledging that in addition to having been influenced by the Jewish world, Paul was also part of the Greco-Roman world. Paul was born in the city of Tarsus, the major city in the province of Cilicia. This city was associated in antiquity with leather goods.[2]

To learn to become a leatherworker required two to three years of apprenticeship, but it did not require a lot of tools. Here is how Hock describes the ancient craft: "Leatherworking involved two essential tasks: *cutting* the leather, which required round-edge and straight-edge knives; and *sewing* the leather, which required various awls. These tasks would have been done at a workbench, with the leatherworker sitting on a stool and bent over forward to work."[3] This meant that such a craft was easily transported from city to city, for the only things Paul needed to carry along were his knives and awls. Since there were people in every major city who desired goods made from leather, Paul would probably have been able to find work most places he went, even on a temporary basis, without having to carry along large swaths of leather.[4]

The question of when and where Paul learned his craft as a leatherworker is impossible to answer definitively. One of three possible options seems likely: as a young boy from his father (assuming his father was a practitioner of the craft),[5] as a Pharisee-in-training during his time studying under Gamaliel I, or as a young Christian during his "silent years" in

---

2. See the sources cited by Hock, *Social Context of Paul's Ministry*, 21 (with n. 16 on p. 73).

3. Ibid., 24 (italics in original). See also Martin Hengel, *The Pre-Christian Paul*, 17.

4. The most reasonable scenario was not that Paul was an independent businessman who set up his own shop whenever he went to a new city, but that he found work as an experienced leatherworker in the local marketplace. This certainly was the case in Corinth, where he joined the business where Aquila and Priscilla worked and actually ended up staying in their house (Acts 18:2–3).

5. Martin Hengel argues that Paul most likely learned the craft from his father. "In the second century the rabbis required fathers to teach their sons a craft, a practice that ... probably goes back to the early Pharisaic period in the first century BCE; for the Pharisaic scribes in the period before 70 also needed a secure way of earning their bread, and at that time crafts already were 'golden opportunities'" (*The Pre-Christian Paul*, 15–16). However, because there is no clear evidence, Hengel also admits that Paul "*could* have taken [his craft] up in connection with his studies as a scribe or even later as a Christian, in order to be independent as a missionary" (16, italics original). If Paul did learn his craft from his father, and if we are correct (as argued in ch. 1) that Paul grew up at a comfortable economic level, then most likely his father would have been an owner of a business, not simply an artisan.

Tarsus (a period of up to ten years; cf. Acts 9:30; Gal 1:18–24).[6] Of these three, we feel that the least likely is the middle option, that Gamaliel himself was a leatherworker who taught his students both his trade and the Torah (perhaps while they were working together). As prominent a rabbi as Gamaliel I was (being one of the few Pharisees who was part of the Sanhedrin in Jerusalem, Acts 5:34), he would undoubtedly be able to charge his followers a fee to be trained by him.[7]

During those "silent years," Paul was busy "preaching the faith" (εὐαγγελίζεται τὴν πίστιν) in Syria and Cilicia (Gal 1:22–23). One of the perfect places for him to do his preaching would have been in a leatherworking shop (in addition, of course, to speaking in a synagogue). Certainly if Paul had not learned his trade before this time, he did so at that time, and it is entirely possible that he had stints as a preaching artisan in Tarsus and in Damascus (and perhaps other cities in those two provinces). In any case, it seems clear that later, when he was in Thessalonica, Paul combined preaching and working: "while working night and day [νυκτὸς καὶ ἡμέρας ἐργαζόμενοι][8] ... we preached [ἐκηρύξαμεν] to you the gospel of God" (1 Thess 2:9).

Hock also points to the possibility that Paul did this in Athens as well. According to Acts 17:17, Paul discoursed about the gospel both in the synagogue and "in the marketplace every day to those who happened to be there." "These marketplace conversations ... may have taken place in his workshop, which would have been in or near the marketplace."[9] When Paul moved on to Corinth, of course, he met a Jewish couple who were also leatherworkers (18:1–3).[10] He joined them in their business and lived with them, probably earning his keep by working for them.

---

6. See Schnabel, *Acts*, 458. Schnabel points out that during this time, Paul was doing missionary work in Syria and Cilicia.

7. See the discussion of this possibility in ch. 1.

8. Note the present participle in what is essentially a narrative passage — hence, "while."

9. Hock, *Social Context of Paul's Ministry*, 42. We should point out that having just escaped from Berea to Athens and being all alone there, Paul would most likely have needed to find work in one of the local leatherworking shops in Athens (Acts 17:16) to support himself.

10. We do not know whether Aquila and Priscilla were already followers of Jesus as the Messiah when Paul met them or whether they became believers through his preaching. Paul does not include them as people in Corinth whom he baptized (1 Cor 1:14–16), though by the time Paul wrote 1 Corinthians, this couple had left Corinth and moved to Ephesus, and presumably Paul was living with them there as well. According to Schnabel (*Acts*, 756), "Luke's account gives the impression that Aquila and Priscilla were believers when Paul met them in Corinth" (see this section in Schnabel's commentary for more on this issue).

TEACHERS IN THE GRECO-ROMAN WORLD AND THEIR SUPPORT

Paul's brief stint in Athens introduces us to an important reality in the Greco-Roman world, namely, that with the *Pax Romana* and the ease of travel on the Roman roads, the empire was filled with a variety of traveling philosophers and religious promoters who made a living by preaching their brand of truth for a fee. While in Athens, Paul received an opportunity to speak at a meeting of Areopagus, because a group of Epicurean and Stoic philosophers wanted to hear what "this babbler" was teaching, especially since he seemed to be advocating "foreign gods" (Acts 17:18–21). It is obvious, of course, that any traveling teacher needed support of some sort. Since Paul was not unlike them, at least viewed objectively, and since he was thoroughly integrated into the Greco-Roman world, it seems possible that he would draw his financial support pattern from those available to these "wandering philosophers" rather than from the Jewish world.

There were "four options that were open to [such] philosophers: charging fees, entering the households of the rich and powerful, begging, and working."[11] Different groups fit into each category, and each argued that their pattern was the right one. The Sophists — and indeed, some of the philosophical movements that preceded them — charged fees, either by lecture or by course of study.[12] Second, a number of "philosophers, rhetors, even grammar teachers" chose to secure their income by receiving a regular salary after entering into the household of a king or of some other wealthy person. These philosophers lived in the houses of the well-to-do and were often responsible for teaching their sons.[13] One of the most well-known of these was Aristotle, who taught Alexander the Great in the home of his father, King Philip of Macedon. The third means of support, "begging [for] one's daily bread and other necessities," was typical of the Cynic

---

11. Hock, *Social Context of Paul's Ministry*, 52; see also John P. Dickson, *Mission Commitment in Ancient Judaism and in the Pauline Communities* (WUNT 2/159; Tübingen: Mohr Siebeck, 2003), 181; G. W. Peterman, *Paul's Gift from Philippi: Conventions of Gift-Exchange and Christian Giving* (Cambridge: Cambridge University Press, 1997), 209. Hock (*Social Context of Paul's Ministry*, 52–59) especially discusses the pros and cons of each of these options, quoting a variety of sources for each option.

12. Hock, *Social Context of Paul's Ministry*, 52.

13. Ibid., 53. This raises the issue of patronage and the client-patron relationship, which we will discuss in the next chapter.

philosophers; they did this in order to attack greed,[14] which they felt was a characteristic of the first two methods of support.

We need to spend more time on the fourth means, since this is the one that Paul chose: working for one's needs, either in skilled or unskilled labor. This method of support was true of a number of the Sophists, though some of the Cynics also chose to work for a living. According to Hock's analysis of a fragmentary ancient work by Musonius Rufus, a younger contemporary of Paul, entitled "What Means of Support Is Appropriate for a Philosopher?,"[15] this method of working for one's living has two advantages for a philosopher. First, this would mean "the philosopher was not financially dependent on anyone"[16] and left him free to say whatever he wished without jeopardizing his income. Second, depending on the job the philosopher had, he could "work and at the same time engage in philosophical instruction of students."[17] In fact, as Musonius Rufus stresses, working for one's own living actually gives credibility to the philosopher's discussions.[18] Hock also points to the tradition of a certain Cynic philosopher named Simon, who was, like Paul, a shoemaker, and used the place where he worked for philosophical discussions.[19]

---

14. Hock, *Social Context of Paul's Ministry*, 55 – 56. The next few quotes are from this section.

15. See discussion in Hock, ibid., 52, 57 – 58. Musonius Rufus was born AD 20 – 30.

16. Ibid., 57.

17. Ibid.

18. Note the words of Musonius Rufus in *Lecture* 11.16: "Pupils would seem to me rather benefited by not meeting with their teacher in the city nor listening to his formal lectures and discussions, but by seeing him at work in the fields, demonstrating by his own labor the lessons which philosophy inculcates — that one should endure hardships, and suffer the pains of labor with his own body, rather than depend upon another for sustenance" (trans. Cora E Lutz for Yale Classical Studies, vol. 10; see https://sites.google.com/site/thestoiclife/the_teachers/musonius-rufus/lectures/11); note that Rufus is talking here about farming, but what he says can be applied to any number of "peasant occupations" that allow the opportunity for interaction between the philosopher and pupils.

19. See Hock (*Social Context of Paul's Ministry*, 39 – 40) where Simon is analyzed in some detail. It is true that Simon lived several centuries before Paul, but the Cynic tradition underwent a revival in the first century BC to the first century AD. According to Stephen C. Barton ("Paul as Missionary and Pastor," in *The Cambridge Companion to Paul* [ed. James D. G. Dunn; Cambridge: University of Cambridge Press, 2003], 42), "As early as the fifth century BC there is the case of Socrates discoursing on philosophy in the workshop of the Cynic artisan-philosopher Simon the shoemaker." Barton also stresses how working for one's living "protected the integrity of the message that [Paul] preached from any accusation that his words were spoken only in order to please his audience and thereby to gain financially (1 Thess. 2:3 – 6)."

PAUL'S EARNING HIS OWN SUPPORT VERSUS THE WORKING PHILOSOPHER

It is appropriate to ask, therefore, whether that fourth option of the working philosopher is what drove Paul to insist that he and Barnabas should support themselves. While he thoroughly endorsed people like Peter and the other apostles to receive their support from the people among whom they worked (presumably primarily among Jews), Paul, the apostle to the Gentiles, it may at first appear, decided to adopt a more Hellenistic approach, namely, to be a preacher-apostle who earned his own living.

Such a pattern would appear to correspond to some of the passages in the NT where Paul talks about his role as a working apostle and evangelist. To the Thessalonians Paul stresses that he did not want to be a burden to them (see ἐν βάρει in 1 Thess 2:7; πρὸς τὸ μὴ ἐπιβαρῆσαι in 2:9; πρὸς τὸ μὴ ἐπιβαρῆσαι in 2 Thess 3:8).[20] Obviously the issue of not being a burden to others is crucial for Paul, and it fits well with the working philosopher who does not want to sponge off the limited means of other people.[21] Paul would sooner burden himself with the stress of daily work than lay that burden on the people he was trying to reach with the gospel.

---

20. The very fact that Paul uses this word group three separate times when he talks about his work among the Thessalonians demonstrates how important this issue was to him. See Dickson (*Mission Commitment*, 182–83) for a thorough word study of the βάρος word group in the NT. The core meaning of this word is "weight," and it can go in two different directions: "influence, authority" and "burden, especially financial burden." Dickson clearly opts for the latter meaning in all of its NT occurrences. See also BDAG, 167, s.v. βάρος.

21. While many scholars deny the Pauline authorship of 2 Thessalonians, many other scholars argue that this letter was written by Paul not too long after the first letter. If that is so, 2 Thess 3:6–15 likely expands on an issue that may have been in its initial stages in 1 Thess 2:7–12. Paul clearly calls on the Thessalonians to "imitate" (μιμεῖσθαι) him in his pattern of working for his own keep (2 Thess 3:7, 9). It is difficult to define clearly what issue Paul is addressing in 2 Thess. 3:6–15. Gary Shogren, in an excursus in his commentary on the Thessalonian correspondence (*1 and 2 Thessalonians* [ZECNT; Grand Rapids: Zondervan, 2012], 331–35), outlines five positions scholars have taken in trying to identify these meddlesome people. The three that seem the most possible are those who decided to stop working because they felt the return of Christ was imminent (and sought to sponge off others in the church in the meantime), those who simply were lazy and did not want to work, and those who discovered, perhaps from the Greco-Roman pattern of wandering philosophers seeking donations for their teaching or from Paul's own policies about Peter and the other apostles, that they could take Paul's new ideas and make a living off them. (Shogren links this third one with a standard definition of the Greek word περιεργάζομαι, "prying inappropriately into divine matters," 328, 334.) None of these options is without interpretive problems from the data given in 2 Thess 3:6–15.

Furthermore, by working for his own living, Paul was able to feel free, which was an important motif for those working philosophers who chose that option. This comes out particularly in 1 Cor 9 (which we looked at in the previous chapter), where we noted how strongly the apostle wrote that it was appropriate for God's preachers and evangelists to earn their living from their missionary preaching. Paul himself, by contrast, did not make use of this right because he wanted to offer the gospel "free of charge" (ἵνα εὐαγγελιζόμενος ἀδάπανον θήσω τὸ εὐαγγέλιον, "in order that when I evangelize, I may make the gospel free of charge," 1 Cor 9:18). The verb δαπανάω (from which ἀδάπανον is derived), in all of its NT uses, refers to the spending of money (Mark 5:26; Luke 15:14; Acts 21:24; 2 Cor 12:15; Jas 4:3); Paul did not want those who listened to his preaching to have to spend money in order to hear the gospel and become believers. In fact, Paul writes that his making the gospel free of charge is what constitues his "wages" (μισθός, 1 Cor 9:18).[22]

In addition, this pattern of evangelizing also gave Paul himself a sense of personal freedom to say whatever God led him to say. Note that his first word in 1 Cor 9:19 (the next verse to the one quoted above) is Ἐλεύθερος ("free"), and it introduces a paragraph that is put in the first person singular.[23] We should recall that this is precisely what the working philosopher felt when he worked to earn his own wages — freedom! He was not financially dependent on anyone, nor did he have to tailor his message in some way so as not to offend his listeners and thus lose out on his source of income.

However, to relate the concept of freedom that Paul talks about in 1 Cor 9:19 to the freedom championed by the working philosopher is to misunderstand what Paul writes here. First Corinthians 9 comes in the context of 1 Cor 8–10, where the apostle is discussing the freedom some Christians (the "strong" ones) experienced in eating meat sacrificed to idols, in contrast to the weaker Christians, who did not feel free to

---

22. Obviously Paul is not here talking about a monetary reward (μισθός is usually translated "reward" in this verse); rather, the reward is the personal satisfaction he received from knowing that those to whom he preached were receving the gospel message without financial strings attached. That is, people who accepted Paul's message were not doing so in order to get a return on what they had invested in Paul's "lecture."

23. Pointed out by Thiselton, *The First Epistle to the Corinthians*, 700: "Paul signals the conclusion of vv. 1–28 by placing 'free' as the first emphatic word of vv. 19–23. It strikes the keynote for the coda."

eat each such meat. In these three chapters, Paul's main point is that while the strong Christians may personally feel free to each such meat, they should be willing to set aside that freedom out of concern for the weaker brother or sister in Christ. And Paul uses his own example of setting aside his "freedom" to gain income from the gospel (a freedom he readily accepted for all others who preached the gospel) in order to show the strong Christians how they should live in the context of the weaker Christians. In other words, Paul's working for a living as a leatherworker was not a demonstration of his personal financial freedom (as it was with the working philosophers); rather, *it is an example of his giving up his freedom and making himself a slave to the weaker Christians with the goal of leading them to Christ!*[24]

PAUL'S MOTIVATION TO SUPPORT HIMSELF

In the previous chapter we concluded that Paul's Jewish background is likely not what steered him in the direction of deciding to earn his own living. Jewish teachers and rabbis in the first century felt perfectly comfortable in earning income of one sort or another from teaching the Scriptures, from working in the *bet midrash*, or from educating Pharisees-in-training. Likewise, we just have concluded that the pattern of the artisan philosopher did not serve as Paul's primary motivation either. It is true that among the Thessalonians the apostle used his pattern of working night and day so as not to be a burden to the believers in Thessalonica as an example to those who were "busybodies," that they should not sponge off other church members (for whatever reason they may have been doing that). But this cannot be what motivated Paul in the first place to refuse a fee-based ministry; rather, he used his insistence on working as a leatherworker as an ad hoc argument to stress to the Thessalonians how much he loved them and to motivate those not working that they should find a job and start working.

---

24. Note the full context of 1 Cor 9:19: "For although I am free from all people, I have enslaved myself to all people, in order that I may gain the many [for Christ]." Note what Thiselton (*The First Epistle to the Corinthians*) writes: "Paul very subtly but also emphatically presses in what precise sense Christian believers and Christian leaders are free and in what sense voluntary slavery performs a wholesome, even essential, saving purpose in Christ-like obedience and love for the other" (ibid., 701).

The same thing can be said for 1 Cor 9. Paul uses his pattern of freely giving up what he knew was his right (namely, to earn a living from preaching the gospel) as an ad hoc argument to motivate the Corinthians to freely give up their rights to eating food sacrificed to idols because in doing so, they would help strengthen the faith of the weaker Christians—or at least would not destroy the faith of those for whom Christ died (1 Cor 8:9–13). This cannot be the reason why Paul decided, long before he ever ministered in Corinth, to preach the gospel while he supported himself.

In other words, we have not yet located the foundational reason why Paul chose to give up his right to earn his living from the gospel, which apparently began already on his first missionary journey, if not even before that, when he and Barnabas worked for a living (1 Cor 9:6).[25] Neither the situation Paul addresses in Thessalonica nor the one he addresses in Corinth gives the origin of that decision. So where does it come from?

Scholars such as Stephen Chang have suggested that Paul "downgraded" his class status so that he could make the Christian faith more appealing to the lower classes. "There is ample evidence to suggest that he was engaged in manual labour in order to be more accessible to those of lower status, to avoid certain social conventions, and to set an example for his converts."[26] We have already ruled out the third of these reasons. The first reason Chang bases on Paul's testimony in 1 Cor 9:19–23 to be all things to all people. But that would be the case only if Paul had decided at some point early in his ministry that the only people he could hope to reach with the gospel were the lower classes and thus he needed to identify with them. A quick view of the book of Acts will prove this wrong. He evangelized whoever would listen, including the Roman proconsul Sergius Paulus (Acts 13:6–12), the Athenian academics on the Areopagus (17:18–34), and even King Agrippa, his wife Berniece, and Governor Festus (25:23–26:32).

---

25. Note the statement of Thiselton (ibid., 682): "If Acts 13 and 14 provide earlier historical material known among the Pauline communities, the early 'missionary journey' of Paul and Barnabas may have offered a well-known model of missionary-pastors who paid their own way rather than drawing financial support from Antioch or from those to whom they ministered." See also Fee, *The First Epistle to the Corinthians*, 404.

26. Steven S. H. Chang, "Fund-Raising in Corinth: A Socio-Economic Study of the Corinthian Church, the Collection and 2 Corinthians" (PhD diss.; University of Aberdeen, 2000), 151. Chang bases his conclusion mostly on Ronald F. Hock, "Paul's Tentmaking and the Problem of His Social Class," *JBL* 97 (1978): 555–64.

In other words, in order to understand Paul's motivation for insisting on working for his own support, we need to look elsewhere, and we believe there are hints in the Pauline letters of a different motivation. It is to these hints that we now turn.

2 CORINTHIANS 11 – 12 AND 1 CORINTHIANS 4:9 – 13

What most scholars seem not to have observed is that in those places in his letters where Paul points to his pattern of supporting himself, somewhere in the immediate context he refers to the personal cost of suffering that his ministry has cost him. We will begin with the most obvious passage: 2 Cor 11 (plus a few elements from ch. 12). The word that links his working as a leatherworker so as "not to be a burden to anyone" (11:9, κατενάρκησα οὐθενός)[27] together with his listing of his sufferings in 11:23 – 29 is the word "boasting" (the noun καύχησις, 11:10, 17; the verb καυχάοωμαι, which occurs 11x in 2 Cor 11 – 12). Note that Paul's boasting is not about his accomplishments or the numbers of souls he has won for Christ (to use a modern expression); rather, it is about his suffering.[28] And while many of the sufferings he lists were painful experiences instigated by his enemies (such as his beatings) or dangerous experiences that happened while traveling (his shipwrecks), a number of his sufferings can be attributed primarily to his insistence on working for a living and refusing to accept financial help. Note especially 11:27: "in toil [κόπος] and hardship [μόχθος] and often going without sleep; in hunger and thirst, in often going without food, in cold and in nakedness."[29]

All the words listed in 11:27 are situations that would most likely not have taken place if Paul either had had sufficient income to draw on to support himself or if he had been sponsored by a wealthy patron. Most likely there were times when Paul was unable to find a place to work at his leatherworking craft in some city and thus he could not purchase food,

---

27. Cf. the use of this same verb in 12:13, 14, its only three uses in the NT. Later in this same verse (11:9), Paul repeats this theme by saying, "I have kept myself from being a burden to you in anything" (ἐν παντὶ ἀβαρῆ ἐμαυτὸν ὑμῖν ἐτήρησα), which uses the βάρος word group with the alpha privative (see discussion above).

28. Note that 1 Clem. 5:6 mentions Paul's being in chains seven times.

29. Note the A-B-A-B-A pattern of this verse, in which A is a pair of Greek words (cf. "worked hard and long," "hungry and thirsty," and "cold ... without enough clothing") and B is a phrase bookended by the words ἐν ... πολλάκις (cf. "many sleepless nights" and "often ... without food"). All five of these could easily have been the result of his pattern of working for his living.

times when food was expensive during a food shortage and he did not earn enough, times when he needed to work night and day (i.e., go without sleep) to be able to purchase basic necessities, or times when he had to sleep out in the open cold because he had not earned enough to pay for lodging. Note what Raymond Brown writes:

> Paul was an itinerant artisan who would have had to struggle to get money for food.... Paul would not even have been able or willing to spend money for a donkey to carry his baggage.... So we have to picture Paul trudging along the roads ... at a maximum covering twenty miles a day.... He had to sleep somewhere near the road, amidst cold, rain, and snow.[30]

Yet this sort of living condition is precisely what Paul boasts about and delights in (see εὐδοκέω in 12:10) — both that he earned his own keep and that he experienced, in addition to persecution, personal "hardships" (ἐν ἀνάγκαις).[31] As David Garland points out, "as a common artisan hiring his skill out to others, Paul lacked status and authority, power and prestige. His situation was compounded because, 'His labor was a bitter necessity, and perhaps the earnings were not sufficient.' He was not financially secure."[32]

Furthermore, if (as we suggested in ch. 1) Paul grew up in what we might call a middle class home and was used to a certain amount of economic stability, he had deliberately "downgraded himself" to a lower economic class (e.g., in terms of Longenecker's categories that will be discussed in ch. 4, from ES4/ES5 level to an ES5/ES6 level). This was a personal choice he made — certainly not something Paul expected every apostle to imitate. But it was not a downgrading of himself in order to catch the attention of those in the lower classes, but a downgrading so that

---

30. Raymond E. Brown, *An Introduction to the New Testament* (New York: Doubleday, 1997), 447. See also Peterman, *Paul's Gift from Philippi*, 7–8. Note Scott Hafemann (*2 Corinthians* [NIVAC; Grand Rapids: Zondervan, 2000], 440): "Paul labored day and night in order to support himself and preach (cf. Acts 20:9–11, 31), while the uncertainties of his work and travel meant days of hunger and thirst." Cf. also idem, *Suffering in the Spirit: An Exegetical Study of II Cor 2:14–3:3 within the Context of the Corinthian Correspondence* (WUNT 2/19; Tübingen: Mohr, 1986), 219–21.

31. This word can also mean "necessities."

32. David Garland, *2 Corinthians* (NAC; Nashville: Broadman & Holman, 1999), 477 (the quotation is this quote is from POxy 3272); Garland also draws here from T. B. Savage, *Power through Weakness: Paul's Understanding of Christian Ministry in 2 Corinthians* (SNTSMS 86; Cambridge: Cambridge University Press, 1996).

he could enter into the life of the suffering Christ. Note what Paul says in Phil 1:29–30: "Because to you it has been given as a gift [ἐχαρίσθη] on behalf of Christ not only to believe in him but also to suffer on his behalf, so that you now have [ἔχοντες][33] the same sort of struggle that you saw in me and continue to hear about me."[34]

Obviously, Paul's total package of suffering went far beyond the constant strain of his working for a living and the stresses that accompanied such work, but his insistence on earning his own keep certainly added significantly to his suffering. Or, put otherwise, he could have had some relief from his ongoing suffering had he agreed to accept at least food and lodging from people in the cities in which he stayed. But his refusal to do so was part of his boasting: "The truth of Christ is in me that this boasting will not be silenced in me among the regions of Achaia" (2 Cor 11:10).

The apostle had said similar things in 1 Cor 4:9–13, where he addressed some in Corinth who delighted in aligning themselves with the elite. Paul emphasizes in these verses the suffering he routinely goes through (he summarizes this pain as being the περικαθάρματα τοῦ κόσμου, the "dirt, refuse, off-scouring of the world," 4:13).[35] This verse is preceded by a description of how that suffering played itself out in Paul's life: often being hungry and thirsty, dressing in rags, at times being mistreated, and being homeless. Moreover, just to make sure we understand this is linked with Paul's manual labor, he writes: καὶ κοπιῶμεν ἐργαζόμενοι ταῖς ἰδίαις χερσίν ("we become weary by working with our own hands"). As Still

---

33. We understand this adverbial participle to have the nuance of result.

34. David Briones has a lengthy chapter on the κοινωνία between the Philippian believers and Paul, including fellowship in the sufferings of Christ (*Paul's Financial Policy: A Socio-Theological Approach* [LNTS 494; Bloomsbury: T&T Clark, 2013], 58–130; see 95–98 for the discussion of Phil 1:29–30). It is on this basis, so he argues, that Paul was willing to receive gifts from the Philippians, because they understood the message of Paul about suffering as a gift from God. "What emerged was a three-way relational pattern between God, Paul, and the Philippians, being distinguished by a mutuality in *gift* and *suffering*. In other words, the community embraced the gift of the gospel, willingly endured suffering on behalf of it, entered into Paul's ministry of suffering through their gift, and helped mediate the gospel to others" (131). This attitude contrasts with that of many in the church at Corinth, who were enamoured with the honor/patronage culture of the Greco-Roman world (see Briones's analysis of the Corinthians on this matter on 131–218) and were eager to display their wealth; as a result, Paul refused to accept money from the Corinthians. While we could say much more on this analysis, both pro and con, suffice it to say that Briones does establish a clear link between Paul's choice to work for his own support as a common artisan and the suffering that it brought him.

35. See BDAG, 801, s.v. περικάθαρμα. See the entire entry on this *hapax legomenon*.

writes, "Paul was often, if not always (see Phil 4:12), subject to physical exhaustion, social devaluation, and grim working conditions."[36]

That Paul's refusal to accept help especially from the Corinthians hurt his image is understandable when we look at the social-cultural situation in the Greco-Roman world. Paul's rivals did apparently accept money from the Corinthians, and because of cultural expectations, it actually boosted their social status.[37] Historians have noted a pattern of contempt by the leisured class for those who had to work menial jobs or even those who were engaged daily as craftmen and thus could not live the privileged, civilized life.[38] And just as in any culture the lower classes feel honored if the privileged class pays attention to them, it would appear that the Corinthians felt honored to have the people who were criticizing Paul's life pattern pay attention to them, and they were even eager to offer some financial support to them. It made them feel upwardly mobile.[39]

1 CORINTHIANS 9:19 – 23

Just how strongly Paul felt about his own linkage between supporting himself through his leatherworking craft and his boasting in his suffering becomes apparent when we compare 2 Cor 11 with the principles Paul outlined in 1 Cor 9:19–23.[40] There Paul states clearly that he eagerly

---

36. Still, "Did Paul Loathe Manual Labor?" 787. It is important to note also Still's next comment, that this does not "necessarily suggest that he despised manual labor.... That Paul would speak about and even conceive of his labor as an unenviable, if volitional, part of his apostolic remit does not require a reader to perceive him as a former aristocrat who abhorred (his) work."

37. It is important to point out, with Garland (*2 Corinthians*, 475–77), that the issue of Paul's apostleship is not the issue at stake in the conflict with his opponents. Paul's rivals were not trying to claim that Paul could not have viewed himself as an apostle because he insisted on working for a living. "There is no link in this text between the amount of financial support and the legitimacy of apostleship" (475).

38. See R. MacMullen, *Roman Social Relations 50 B.C. to A.D. 284* (New Haven, CT/London: Yale University Press, 1974), esp. 114–15.

39. See Garland (*2 Corinthians*, 477): "Savage concludes that 'an impoverished leader was a contradiction in terms' [*Power through Weakness*, 87]. This issue was particularly important in an affluent city like Corinth, whose citizens took pride in its wealth and aspired to upward mobility."

40. We should note here that in addition to the reason proposed below for why Paul sought suffering, there may be additional elements of value in a life of suffering that he saw for the people he was ministering to. Consider, for example, the perspective of Timothy Savage (*Power through Weakness*, 93), who notes how Paul's refusal to accept compensation for his work would force "his converts to participate in his humility and thus to conform, albeit unwillingly, to the pattern of Christ."

did whatever it took so that people would come to a saving knowledge of Christ. To the Jews he became like a Jew; to those under the law as one under the law; to those not having the law as one free from the law; "to the weak [he] became weak, to win the weak." Then follows the general principle: "I have become all things to all people so that I might by any means save some" (9:22). Now, is it possible for us to imagine Paul saying, however, "To those enamored by the upwardly mobile I became upwardly mobile [i.e., stopped working and accepted support from others] in order to win them for Christ"? Absolutely not! There was a point at which the apostle would say no — that is how strongly he feels about this issue. "The truth of Christ is in me that this [reason for] boasting will not be silenced in me among the regions of Achaia" (2 Cor 11:10).[41] Then, as he goes on to write: "What I am doing, I will also keep on doing, in order to cut off the opportunity of those who are looking for an opportunity" to be people of influence (11:12). There would be no compromise in this area on the part of Paul.[42]

1 CORINTHIANS 9:24 – 27

What we have been trying to demonstrate from Paul's letters is that the apostle linked his insistence on working for a living with his theology of suffering. Since we have just quoted from 1 Cor 9:19 – 23, we will turn briefly to verses in that chapter that we have not yet commented on. In 9:3 – 18, as we noted earlier in this chapter, Paul argues two main points: those who preach the gospel have every right to earn their living from the gospel, but he and Barnabas were freely and voluntarily giving up that right. In a way similar to 2 Cor 11:10 – 12, Paul says that he would rather die than allow anyone to deprive him of his reason for boasting

---

41. We recognize we are coupling 1 Cor 9:19 – 23 with 2 Cor 11:10, but Paul is dealing with the same church and the same theme, namely, why he worked for his own support. Note 2 Cor 11:9: "And when I was with you and needed something, I was not a burden to anyone, for the brothers who came from Macedonia supplied what I needed. I have kept myself from being a burden to you in any way, and will continue to do so" (NIV).

42. We should note here too that if Paul were to say, "To the poor I became poor to win the poor," and then to say, "To the upwardly mobile I became upwardly mobile to win them," his changes of status would eventually clash, for one cannot be both at the same time and in the same place without the question arising, "Who is this guy? Does he identify with our social group, or with a different one? He is a contradiction in self-identity."

(1 Cor 9:15).[43] That is strong language. Then he follows this up with an explanation of how his freedom operates in doing evangelism (9:19–23), as we have just summarized in the preceding section. Finally, before he gets back to the topic of eating meat sacrificed by idols, he writes 9:24–27.

As I (KK) argued in my dissertation, these four verses function as a "literary hinge" between what precedes in 1 Cor 9 and what follows in ch. 10.[44] The linkage to ch. 9 comes in Paul's reference to his rigorous lifestyle as an apostle/evangelist and his closing notation of his suffering, especially stated in 9:27: "I treat my body roughly [ὑπωπιάζω, 'give my body a black eye'] and make it my slave, lest somehow after having preached to others, I myself might be disqualified." Many commentators spend much time here discussing the second half of this verse and its relationship to the doctrine of eternal security, but for our purposes here, we must ask the question *how* Paul treats his body roughly.[45] The only thing that he discusses in the preceding context is the enormous effort he puts forth regularly to earn his own support (which, as 1 Cor 4:11–13 and 2 Cor 11:27 suggest, included a significant amount of pain and suffering). Note Gordon Fee's analysis: Paul's "'bruising of the body' probably refers to the hardships to which he voluntarily subjected himself in preaching to the Corinthians, which included working with his own hands, and which in turn meant suffering the privations expressed in 4:11–13."[46] Once again, therefore, there is a clear linkage between Paul's work ethic and his desire to suffer for the sake of Christ.

---

43. As most commentators recognize (and as even ancient scribes acknowledged by their attempts to make sense of Paul's grammar here), there is an anacoluthon here. See the major commentaries for discussion. While the grammar is not clear, Paul's thought is clear: he will boast about giving up his right to earn a living from the gospel, and do not try to stop him!

44. Keith R. Krell, *Temporal Judgment and the Church: Paul's Remedial Agenda in 1 Corinthians* (Garland, TX: Biblical Studies Press, 2012), 142. That book concentrates on the linkage with 10:1–22; our interest here is its linkage back to ch. 9.

45. See Kent L. Yinger, "Paul and Asceticism in 1 Corinthians 9:27a," *Journal of Religion & Society* 10 (2008): 1–21.

46. Fee, *The First Epistle to the Corinthians*, 439. Fee rightly points us to 4:11–13, for there Paul likewise couples "we toil hard [κοπιάομαι] as we work with our own hands" together with "we go hungry and thirsty, we are poorly clothed … and we are homeless" (along with other sufferings not necessarily connected with his work patterns). Note too the comment of Garland on 9:27 (*1 Corinthians*, 443): "[Paul] knocks out the body's desire for amenities, comfort, ease, abundance, or even small pleasures—anything that would cause him to think twice about going without or making himself a slave of all persons (9:19). He endures physical privations to win over his bodily cravings so that he can then win others over to Christ."

1 THESSALONIANS 2:1 – 9; 2 THESSALONIANS 3:6 – 15

In both 1 and 2 Thessalonians Paul finds it to his advantage to draw the
attention of the Thessalonians to his pattern of supporting himself by
his own hard work. In 1 Thess 2:1 – 12 his mentioning of his daily work
is linked with assurances of his deep love for the Thessalonian believers
(perhaps because detractors in Thessalonica were casting doubt on Paul
since he had left town so hurriedly, thus avoiding persecution). Paul writes
to them in 2:9: "For you remember, brothers and sisters, our toil [κόπος]
and our hardship [μόχθος]; we preached the gospel to you as we kept
working night and day so as not to burden [ἐπιβαρῆσαι] any one of you."
It is important to note that Paul uses the same two words — "toil" and
"hardship" (κόπος and μόχθος) — that he later uses to describe his work
in his catalog of sufferings in 2 Cor 11:27,[47] and he emphasizes here as
well that the labor they did took place "night and day" (no "forty-hour
week" for Paul!).[48]

Not insignificantly, both before and after this section in 1 Thessalonians Paul refers to outright persecution: the outrageous treatment and
physical suffering that Paul (and Silas) had suffered in Philippi along
with the strong opposition they faced in Thessalonica itself (2:2), and the
persecution that the Thessalonians themselves experienced after Paul left
Thessalonica for Berea (2:14 – 15). Once again, when Paul thinks of the
issue of his daily work, he links it closely with the topic of suffering.

In 2 Thess 3:6 – 15, Paul has to deal with the issue of a group of people
in the Thessalonian church who had decided, for whatever reason,[49] to quit
working. In this situation, too, Paul repeats that "with toil [κόπος] and
hardship [μόχθος] we worked night and day with a view to not burdening
[ἐπιβαρῆσαι] any one of you" (3:8). Again, the same three words describe
the strenuous labor Paul exerted in his daily work, just as in 1 Thess 2:9.
Admittedly, in this case there is no reference to Paul's theology of suffering
in the context, but he does go on to say that in this particular situation, he

---

47. Note also the related verb κοπιῶμεν in 1 Cor 4:12.

48. Murray J. Harris (*The Second Epistle to the Corinthians* [NIGTC; Grand Rapids:
Eerdmans, 2005)], 808) notes, "Whereas κόπος occurs eighteen times in the NT (eleven
in Paul), μόχθος is found only three times, always in conjunction with κόπος and always
standing second (11:27; 1 Thess. 2:9; 2 Thess. 3:8)."

49. As noted earlier in this chapter, Shogren (*1 and 2 Thessalonians*, 331 – 35) lists several
possible reasons why this situation developed.

and Silas worked as hard as they did "in order to give you a model so that you could imitate us" (3:9).[50] As we suggested earlier, however, this reason cannot be the *original* reason why, many years earlier, Paul first instituted his insistence on supporting himself. He did not foresee the situation in Thessalonica long before it happened. Rather, he uses his own ministry pattern as an ad hoc reason to encourage a small group of people to stop sponging off others and to get to work, earning their own living.[51]

This is not the place to develop a full-fledged theology of Paul's suffering, but a few words are in order. Kar Yong Lim has made a thorough investigation of Paul's theology of suffering as recorded in 2 Corinthians, particularly from the standpoint of Paul's narrative of Christ. That is to say, Paul's suffering is linked directly to the sufferings of Christ. On 2 Cor 11:23 – 12:10, for example, Lim summarizes his observations as follows:

> For Paul, there is another dimension to his understanding of his weakness that is grounded in the story of Jesus (2 Cor 13:4). From the christological perspective, Paul sees his weaknesses carrying the same sense of the rejection, suffering, and humiliation of Jesus. By identifying his weaknesses with the weakness of Christ (13:4) in dealing with the issues related to the cultural conventions of his day, Paul seeks to prove the unreliability of the criteria used by the Corinthians to evaluate a person's worth by appearance based on personal strengths that stand fundamentally opposed to God's values. For Paul, the only sound criterion to evaluate one's worth is grounded in the Scriptures and the story of Jesus (cf. 1 Cor 1:22 – 23; 2:1 – 5).[52]

---

50. Gene L. Green (*The Letters to the Thessalonians* [Pillar; Grand Rapids: Eerdmans, 2002], 347) notes: "Paul did teach elsewhere that to receive financial support for Christian service was an acceptable practice, although he did not make use of this privilege (3:9; 1 Cor 9:7-14; Gal 6:6; 1 Tim 5:17-18; cf. Matt 10:10). On the other hand, he raised his voice against those who engaged in ministry simply for financial gain (Acts 20:33; 1 Tim 3:3, 8; Titus 1:7)."

51. See also Charles A. Wanamaker, *The Epistles to the Thessalonians* (NIGTC; Grand Rapids: Eerdmans, 1990), 285.

52. Kar Yong Lim, *"The Sufferings of Christ Are Abundant in Us": A Narrative Dynamics Investigation of Paul's Sufferings in 2 Corinthians* (London: T&T Clark, 2009), 174. Note the summary conclusion of Barton ("Paul as Missionary and Pastor," 42): "Paul's sacrificial practice was a way of representing in his own life the self-giving of the crucified and risen Christ whom he was called to proclaim (2 Cor. 4:10 – 11)."

COLOSSIANS 1:24 AND GALATIANS 6:17

The same message stands out in Col 1:24, where Paul affirms, "Now I rejoice in my sufferings for your sake." Paul's sufferings were not something to be avoided; rather, they were something to rejoice about; in fact, through his own suffering in the flesh, Paul "fills up what is lacking of the afflictions of Christ."[53] Douglas Moo points out how Paul switches here from πάθημα ("sufferings") in the first part of the verse to θλῖψις ("afflictions") in the next part as he comments on his sufferings. The latter word is one that Paul never uses for what Christ experienced redemptively on the cross; rather, θλῖψις refers to human afflictions, particularly Paul's own afflictions (cf. 2 Cor 1:4, 8; 4:17; 6:4; 7:4; Phil 4:14; 1 Thess 1:6; 3:3, 7; 2 Thess 1:4). There is something "lacking 'in regard to' the tribulations that pertain to Christ as the Messiah as he is proclaimed in the world."[54] There may even be something eschatological about these sufferings/afflictions, for they "are the tribulations that are inevitable and necessary as God's kingdom faces the opposition of 'the dominion of darkness' (cf. v. 13)."[55] Paul finds affliction as an essential part of the role he plays as the apostle to the Gentiles.

David Pao reminds us that this is not the only place where this theme occurs.

> The coexistence of joy and suffering can be found elsewhere in Paul (cf. 2 Cor 6:10), especially when this suffering is related to his proclamation of the gospel (cf. Phil 1:18–19).... [It] points to Paul's imitation of Christ's suffering (cf. 1 Thess 1:6) and to his authority as an apostle called to this path of suffering (cf. Acts 9:26).[56]

---

53. It would take us too far afield to discuss the variety of interpretations this problematic verse has produced. Suffice it to say that there is a clear link between Paul's willingness to suffer and his desire to thereby participate in what Christ underwent in his earthly life, especially in his sacrifice on the cross.

54. Douglas J. Moo, *The Epistles to Colossians and to Philemon* (Pillar; Grand Rapids: Eerdmans, 2008), 151.

55. Ibid., 152. Note also Jerry Sumney (*Colossians: A Commentary* [NTL; Louisville: Westminster John Knox, 2008], 98) who argues that "Paul makes suffering for the good of his churches a significant part of his apostolic ministry."

56. David W. Pao, *Colossians and Philemon* (ZECNT; Grand Rapids: Zondervan, 2012), 123.

Note too how in Gal 6:17 Paul calls the scars that he bore as a result (presumably) of his beatings "the marks [στίγματα] of Jesus on my body."[57] He wore them as a badge of honor, not (as most people in that society would have seen them) as a symbol of shame (especially insofar as the scars of Christ came from his crucifixion, a most shameful way to die in antiquity).[58]

Through suffering Paul felt closer to Jesus Christ and his sufferings; any spiritual experience that helps us to identify more closely with our Lord is something to rejoice about. This would be reason enough for Paul to decide to experience the hunger, thirst, homelessness, sleepless nights, and even the shame that came from being a common, everyday laborer who eked out just enough income for each day so he could preach the gospel free of charge.[59]

WHAT ABOUT PAUL'S GIFTS FROM HIS CHURCHES?

With this in mind, we must now turn to Phil 4:10–20 and some related passages.[60] At the beginning of this section, there is an element that reminds us of what we explored in the previous section, that Paul voluntarily took on the stress of being a commmon laborer and that it involved suffering. Note Phil 4:12: "I know both what it is to be in need [ταπεινοῦσθαι, "to be humbled"][61] and what it is to abound; in everthing and in all things I have learned the secret both of being well fed and of being hungry, of being both abounding and lacking in necessities." While Paul does not mention here how he has learned this powerful lesson, surely a good share of it must have been because he had chosen to work for his own living rather than to be taken care of through other available means

---

57. As several commentators have noted, there may well be a veiled reference here to the effects of the brutal stoning Paul received outside the city of Lystra during his first preaching mission there (Acts 14:19–20; cf. 2 Cor 11:25).

58. F. F. Bruce (*The Epistle to the Galatians* [NIGTC; Grand Rapids: Eerdmans, 1982], 275) finds a parallel in 2 Cor 4:10, where Paul speaks of carrying around in his body "the dying of Jesus."

59. Perhaps too Paul was fully aware of Christ's suffering as reflected in his saying in Matt 8:20: "Foxes have dens and birds have nests, but the Son of Man has no place to lay his head" (NIV).

60. For helpful insights into the matters discussed below, see Robert C. Swift, "The Theme and Structure of Philippians," *BSac* 141 (July 1984): 234–54.

61. Note the use of the verb ταπεινόω in 2 Cor 11:7, a verse discussed earlier in this chapter.

of support. This verse suggests that at times he had plenty of manual work and at other times he could scarcely scrape by financially (see comments earlier on 2 Cor 11:27).[62]

But this section of Philippians leads into a section in which we discover that there were a few occasions on which the church at Philippi (a city in Macedonia) did send him a contribution toward his ministry so that he did not have to work. Note Phil 4:15–16: "And you yourselves know, Philippians, that when the message of the gospel was beginning among you ... no church shared with me in the matter of giving and receiving except you alone. For even [when I was] in Thessalonica, you sent something to help more than once." Paul says essentially the same thing in 2 Cor 11:9, that "the brothers coming from Macedonia supplied what I lacked."[63] Interestingly, Luke gives a similar report in Acts 18:5; immediately after he reports how Paul joined Aquila and Priscilla in their leatherworking business, he writes: "But when Silas and Timothy came from Macedonia, Paul occupied himself [exclusively] with the word as he witnessed to the Jews that Jesus was the Christ." This can best read as an acknowledgment that Silas and Timothy came with a monetary gift from Macedonia (Philippi alone, or were other churches included?) so that, for a period, Paul did not need to work at his daily job.[64]

PAUL'S THANK-YOU TO THE PHILIPPIANS FOR THEIR GIFT

The question naturally surfaces, then, as to the attitude in which Paul received that gift. After all, as we have seen, he prided himself on earning his own living expenses and not receiving money from others. Would such a gift be a problem for him to accept? First, it is important to note that

---

62. We might note here that earlier in this letter, Paul does have a lot to say about his suffering for the sake of the gospel. He is in prison, and he knew at least for a while that his situation was dire enough that he might lose his life. But that would have been okay for Paul, because "to me to live is Christ and to die is gain" (Phil 1:21; note 1:20–24, 29–30; 2:17; 3:10, where Paul develops the meaning of suffering for him). See also G. Walter Hansen, *The Letter to the Philippians* (Pillar; Grand Rapids: Eerdmans, 2009), 314.

63. While the Macedonian churches were more than just Philippi, it seems likely that 2 Cor 11:9 is referring to Philippi. That is, there is no hint in this verse that more than one church is involved. The "brothers coming from Macedonia" are most likely Christian believers who have come from a single location.

64. "Since [Silas and Timothy] brought financial support for his work from the Macedonian churches, he was able to devote more of his time and energy to preaching and teaching"; Schnabel, *Acts*, 758.

this gift was given to Paul by the church in Philippi (and possibly by other churches in Macedonia) after he had left the area. It came completely voluntarily, and it came with no strings attached. "Paul had no problem accepting money from some of the churches he had previously established, given to help him found new churches (2 Cor 11:8–9). He did not view this as compensation for their having heard the gospel but as 'fruit,' or as 'a fragrant offering, a sacrifice acceptable and pleasing to God' (Phil 4:18)."[65]

Second, and perhaps more important, we actually have in the book of Philippians Paul's "thank-you note" to the believers in Philippi for coming to his aid again in the more recent past. Paul is in prison when he writes this letter,[66] and once again the believers in Philippi have sent him a gift, delivered by Epaphroditus ("I have been filled up since I have received from Epaphroditus the things that came from you," 4:18; he is "your messenger and servant to my need," Phil 2:25; see the entire section, 2:25–30).[67] But as with so many passages of Paul, scholars debate what Paul is really trying to say in this section of Philippians.[68] The way in which he writes his thank-you note sounds ambivalent, as if he is trying to assure the believers in Philippi that he really was doing okay, whether they sent him a gift or not. Is Phil 4:10–20 a genuine thank you or a grudging one, and does Paul perhaps even struggle with accepting this gift?

Lynn Cohick, in her recent commentary on Philippians, probes three questions about this issue, the first two of which are pertinent here.[69] The first question asks why Paul waited until the end of the letter to comment

---

65. Verlyn D. Verbrugge, *Paul's Style of Church Leadership Illustrated by His Instructions to the Corinthians on the Collection* (San Francisco: Mellen Research University Press, 1992), 119. See also P. T. O'Brien (*Commentary on Philippians* [NIGTC; Grand Rapids: Eerdmans, 1991], 539) who writes: "The picture painted by the accounting metaphor is of compound interest that accumulates all the time until the last day. The apostle has employed this commercial language to show that he has set his heart on an ongoing, permanent gain for the Philippians in the spiritual realm. The advantage (*karpos*) that accrues to them as a result of their generous giving is God's blessing in their lives by which they continually grow in the graces of Christ until the parousia."

66. It is a matter of scholarly debate as to which city Paul was imprisoned in: Rome, Caesarea, or perhaps even Ephesus several years earlier. But this issue need not detain us here.

67. It should be noted that people in prison had to locate people to care for their physical needs, because the Roman government did not supply food and clothing, especially not during house arrest as in Acts 28:30.

68. The most thorough analysis of the dynamics involved in 4:10–20 is Peterman's *Paul's Gift from Philippi*.

69. Lynn H. Cohick, *Philippians* (SGBC; Grand Rapids: Zondervan, 2013), 235–44.

about the gift, as if it were an afterthought. This question is only valid, however, if we assume that "Paul's primary intention in writing this letter was a thank-you note."[70] There are other reasons Paul had for writing this letter: to update the Philippians on his situation in prison and on the spread of the gospel, to share with them the example of Christ as a humble servant, certainly to express his concern for Epaphroditus and explain why he was sending him back to them, and to warn the Philippians about a prevalent false teaching that was making the rounds. While we in the Western world tend to forefront the thanksgiving part of a thank-you note even if we intend to include other matters, Greco-Roman rhetoric would sometimes save the best for last.

Note too that Paul wants to set his thank-you letter in the context of his long-standing partnership with the Philippians.[71] He reminds them of their κοινωνία in the gospel and in the Lord Jesus Christ at the beginning of the letter (1:3–6; 2:1; cf. also 3:10), and then he repeats it in the context of the thank-you note (note the verb συγκοινωνέω in 4:14). As Peterman points out, the earlier chapters of Philippians "prepare the reader for the direct response Paul makes to the Philippians' gift in 4.10–20."[72] In fact, Peterman considers the specific use of κοινωνία as a "reference to Paul's suppport," so that the letter actually "opens and closes" with this topic (i.e., an inclusio).[73] Without doubt, therefore, as Cohick summarizes, "the final note left echoing in their minds and hearts will be one of appreciation for their gift."[74]

WAS PAUL'S THANK-YOU NOTE GENUINE?

The second question is more difficult: Why does the actual thank-you portion of the letter seem so anemic? At no time does Paul simply write:

---

70. Ibid., 236.

71. J. Paul Sampley (*Pauline Partnership in Christ: Christian Community and Commitment in Light of Roman Law* [Philadelphia: Fortress, 1980], 52–53) argues that Paul is using the technical terminology of a business partnership contract. He remarks: "The passage is somewhat unusual because of the frequency of commercial technical terms. From many of Paul's letters we know that he used technical terms of law and commerce, but the frequency of them in Philippians 4:10–20 is unparalleled."

72. Peterman, *Paul's Gift from Philippi*, 90.

73. Ibid., 92. For other parallels, see John F. Hart, "Does Philippians 1:6 Guarantee Progressive Sanctification? Part 1," *JOTGES* 9:16 (Spring 1996): 37–58.

74. Cohick, *Philippians*, 237.

εὐχαριστῶ ὑμῖν ("I thank you").[75] Rather, he seems to beat around the bush with comments that sound like this paraphrase: "You do know, of course, I have learned to be content even when I lacked necessities [4:11 – 12]. And you also know that I didn't really ask for this gift, and if I am happy, it is not because you gave me a gift but because what Epaphroditus brought is a fruit [καρπός] of your faith [4:17]. Moreover, in a way, it didn't surprise me that you sent something, because you've done this a couple times before [4:14 – 16]."

We can respond with two comments here. First, we must recognize that there were possible social reasons for Paul not to be overly profuse in his thanks, because that could imply, in the cultural patterns of the Greco-Roman world, that he was acknowledging he was a client of the Philippian congregation rather than, first and foremost, a humble servant of the Lord Jesus Christ, who is the source of all gifts.[76] Paul finds it important to get across that "money is a commodity which one should use to serve others (λειτουργία), an attitude which varies from the Greek and Roman approach that *one displays one's [own] virtue by giving*."[77]

Second, we should expect Paul to turn this gift into an opportunity for instruction, in a section of this letter that is "deliberately crafted to teach the Philippians the proper meaning and significance of their gift."[78] Paul rarely bypasses an opportunity to look beyond the surface of an event to

---

75. Note, however, that Paul rarely thanks people directly in his letters. Rather, he offers thanks to God for what people have done. His first words after the opening letter details (1:1 – 2) is εὐχαριστῶ τῷ θεῷ μου ἐπὶ πάσῃ τῇ μνείᾳ ὑμῶν ("I thank God because of my memory of you," 1:3). Peterman argues successfully that the preposition ἐπί used here is causal, not temporal (*Paul's Gift from Philippi*, 93 – 96). For a thorough analysis of the opening thanksgivings of Paul in his letter and the relationship of these units to Paul's intercessory prayers, see P. T. O'Brien, *Introductory Thanksgivings in the Letters of Paul* (NovTSup 49; Leiden: Brill, 1977).

76. Cohick, *Philippians*, 237 – 42. This brings up the important issue of patronage in the ancient Greco-Roman world. We will be exploring that issue in more detail in the next chapter, when we examine those times when Paul did actually ask for money; at that point, it becomes important to see how the patron-client relationship worked in the ancient world. See here David E. Briones ("Paul's Intentional 'Thankless Thanks" in Philippians 4:10 – 20," *JSNT* 34 [2011]: 47 – 69) who demonstrates from a patron-brokerage-client pattern that sometimes occurred in the Greco-Roman world, that "Paul's seemingly ungrateful silence intentionally discloses a theological conviction which envisages God as the supreme giver of all gifts and the Philippians as mediators of divine resources" (47). David Briones has expanded this theme in his published dissertation, *Paul's Financial Policy*.

77. Peterman, *Paul's Gift from Philippi*, 160 (italics added).

78. Ibid., 121.

probe its theological and spiritual significance. Such "instruction required more than a single line" of thanksgiving.[79]

THE PSYCHOLOGY OF PAUL

So far in this chapter we have stressed how important it was to Paul that he earn his own living expenses as he went out on his missionary trips, even though it would cause him a significant amount of suffering. He did appreciate it when one of his churches spontaneously sent him a gift, but what such a gift meant to him was not the personal relief he may have felt from the daily grind of working in the leatherworking business, but the fact that it was manifesting the fruit of their faith at work in their lives. We want to close this chapter with a few further reflections on whether there is anything in Paul's personality that may further explain why he chose this pathway of suffering beyond his sharing in Christ's sufferings. There is no indication that Paul felt critical of the other apostles for not choosing suffering as he did; in fact, he endorsed their right to earn their living from the gospel. So why did he seem to prefer suffering for himself?

DID PAUL HAVE A GUILT COMPLEX?

In answering this question, what we present in the next few paragraphs is tentative and exploratory, and certainly nothing we can conclusively prove from the exegesis of specific texts. It has to do with what we might call the inner workings of Paul's mind — his psychology, as it were. Biblical scholars are hesitant to go there, first, because it is difficult to interpret the inner workings of any person's mind, let alone Paul's mind from specific passages, but second because we have a tendency to idealize Paul.[80] But Paul was a flawed human being, just as the rest of us are, and there are things in his letters that can make us shake our heads.[81]

---

79. Ibid., 122. Peterman's masterful development of this theme covers thirty-one pages (127–57).

80. Note Longenecker (*Remember the Poor*, 196): "Interpretations based on speculation about the author's psychological state are often suspect." We take this warning under advisement, but at the same time we will try to ground our conclusions in the words of Scripture and not just personal speculation.

81. There are a few people who have looked at Paul from a psychological standpoint. The problem with most of these is that they look at Paul from models of modern psychology and/or personality theory. As James R. Beck writes, "relating Paul's personality to any of the

We begin with a brief quote from Bruce Longnecker and Todd Still: "That Paul was an ardent opponent of believers before his conversion/call is suggested ... [in part] by the ongoing regret (guilt?) he experienced over his persecuting past (1 Cor 15:9; see also 1 Tim 1:12–17)."[82] Guilt? Did Paul experience ongoing guilt from his past as a persecutor of the church, and was he in some way trying to use his choice of suffering to cope with a deep-seated feeling of personal guilt?

Paul specifically records his past life as a persecutor in three of his letters plus two of his speeches in Acts. In Acts 22:3–11 and 26:9–15 as well as in Gal 1:13–14, all three of which give a brief synopsis of his life, Paul refers freely to what he had done prior to his becoming a believer and a preacher of the gospel. He zealously persecuted the church of God. In these reports, he offers this information rather objectively and as an prelude to telling about his conversion experience, when God called him to become the apostle to the Gentiles.

His message in 1 Cor 15:8–10, however, speaks about this event from the standpoint of his personal feelings. When the resurrected Lord Jesus revealed himself to Paul, he recognizes that there is no other explanation for the fact that he became an apostle except for the grace of God. But Paul then goes on to state two other things: (1) that because of his persecuting of the church of God, the process of becoming an apostle was ὡσπερεὶ τῷ ἐκτρώματι; and (2) that he is the ἐλάχιστος ("least") of the apostles and, in fact, not ἱκανός ("worthy, sufficient") to be called an apostle.

Regarding the first of these two notations, there is a significant amount of debate, especially since the word ἔκτρωμα is a *hapax legomenon* in the NT. Fee notes that in Classical Greek, the word "refers to any kind of premature birth (abortion, stillbirth, or miscarriage). Then the word

---

modern theories is risky because his New Testament letters and the book of Acts that we can analyze simply do not give us complete information" (*The Psychology of Paul: A Fresh Look at His Life and Teaching* [Grand Rapids: Kregel, 2002], 81). Gerd Theissen attempted a scholarly analysis of Paul in *Psychological Aspects of Pauline Theology* (trans. John P. Galvin; Minneapolis: Fortress, 1987). But most of his book uses modern theories (learning theory, psychodynamic approach, and cognitive approach) in order to determine "unconscious motives through Pauline theology." Interestingly, guilt is not one of the unconscious motives explored, and none of the passages we have discussed in this chapter are discussed in Theissen's book.

82. Bruce W. Longenecker and Todd D. Still, *Thinking through Paul* (Grand Rapids: Zondervan, 2014), 29.

came to be used figuratively to refer to something horrible or 'freakish.'"[83] Scholars argue whether Paul is perhaps using this term in response to some sort of "slogan" that his enemies in Corinth may have used about him, or whether it is a term of self-deprecation, or whether it is simply a term Paul adopts to highlight God's grace as recorded in v. 10.[84] Because of the deep ambiguity on why Paul chose that word, not much can be deduced from it about Paul's present feelings about his former life as a persecutor.

The second phrase, however, is something that Paul introduces with the present tense of εἰμί twice in this verse, which suggests he is talking about his *present* feelings. While elsewhere Paul does not hesitate to put himself on a par with the other apostles (e.g., Gal 2:1 – 10), when he thinks of his earlier life as a persecutor of the church, he feels himself as "the least of the apostles." Coupled with the next phrase, where Paul suggests that he does not even feel "worthy of being called an apostle," it seems likely that Paul is still chastising himself in some sense for what he had done prior to his conversion/calling by Christ on the road to Damascus. Undoubtedly, Paul knew the story about Peter's denial of Christ, and we know that Peter too felt guilty, for he went out and wept bitterly (Matt 26:75; Mark 14:72; Luke 22:62). But Paul is not trying to rank the apostles in terms of "deserving"; he is only saying about himself that he did not deserve to be an apostle, his reason being that he had been a persecutor.[85] But note again that Paul does not put this phrase in the past tense ("I did not deserve to become an apostle"), but in the present tense; he is still reflecting within himself to some extent on the shameful life-choice he had made nearly twenty years earlier.

---

83. Fee, *The First Epistle to the Corinthians*, 733. Johannes Munck ("Paulus Tanquam Abortivus," in *NT Essays in Memory of T. W. Manson* [ed. A. J. B. Higgins; Manchester: Manchester University Press, 1959], 180) comments that this word "reflects a use found in the LXX to denote dire human wretchedness" (cited in Thiselton, *The First Epistle to the Corinthians*, 1209). The relevant LXX passages are: Num 12:12; Job 3:16; Eccl 6:3.

84. See BDAG, 311, s.v. ἔκτρωμα: "So Paul calls himself, perh. taking up an insult ... hurled at him by his opponents 1 Cor 15:8 (in any case the point relates to some deficiency in the infant ...)."

85. Fee (*The First Epistle to the Corinthians*, 735) argues that Paul was not thinking so much of the grace of salvation as he was of the grace of his apostolic calling to share the good news of salvation.

THE CHIEF OF SINNERS?

This comes out even more strongly in 1 Tim 1:12–17. This section is not in an apologetic section of one of Paul's letters to his churches. Rather, it is in a letter to his friend and coworker, Timothy—who knew Paul better than almost anyone else. Here too Paul describes his former manner of life as a "blasphemer" and "persecutor" and "a violent man." As in 1 Cor 15:7–9, he also celebrates the grace of God that came to him. In fact, he repeats the fact that he "was shown mercy" (1 Tim 1:13, 16). If Paul had stopped there in his reflections on the past, we would think nothing more of it. But Paul goes on *twice* in this section to call himself "the foremost [πρῶτος] of sinners." And note that as in 1 Cor 15:7–9, he uses the present tense εἰμί, but this time he couples it with the word ἐγώ in the position of emphasis, as if to say: "I am the foremost of sinners, yes, I mean it, I." Note that this is now thirty years after he had been a persecutor, and the apostle still seems to feel flooded with guilt over what he had done.[86]

Most commentators in discussing 1 Tim 1:15 concentrate on the precise meaning of πιστὸς ὁ λόγος ("faithful is the saying"), a phrase that occurs later four more times in the Pastoral Epistes (3:1; 4:9; 2 Tim 2:11; Titus 3:8). If commentators have anything to say on the last phrase of 1:15, they usually suggest that this is the way Paul felt about himself after the risen Christ stopped him in his tracks on the way to Damascus with the phrase, "Saul, Saul, why do you persecute me?" (Acts 9:4; 22:7; 26:14). It is true that Paul is alluding to that life-changing event in 1 Tim 1:12–16, but note that the apostle does not use the imperfect ἦν (as in ὧν πρῶτος ἤμην ἐγώ), which we might expect in this mini-narrative of his life. Instead, he uses the present tense, which seems to reflect his present feelings.

Note what Quinn and Wacker write on this verb tense: "The apostle in prayer does not admit, 'I *was* the first of sinners.' He says, 'I am,' as though still poised in that dazzling, overwhelming moment of his conversion-vocation, a moment which gave him an unforgettable and ever present revelation of his own sinfulness in the same instant that it revealed the even greater mercy of God."[87] Then in 1:16 Paul switches back to the past

---

86. Beck does touch on this passage, but only to say that the definition of sin that Paul writes about in 1 Tim 1:15 is not "his former view of sin based in first-century Judaism that had rated him as blameless (Phil. 3:6)," but "the Christian definition of sin" (*Psychology of Paul*, 96).

87. Jerome D. Quinn and William C. Wacker, *The First and Second Letters to Timothy* (Eerdmans Critical Commentary; Grand Rapids: Eerdmans, 2000), 135.

tense, where he repeats the word πρῶτος (in the dative πρώτῳ, modifying ἐμοὶ), but with no accompanying verb this time. That second occurrence clearly points to the Damascus road experience. It is as if Paul is saying in this section, "I was the worst of sinners when I was a persecutor, and I still feel that way."

Guilt can do strange things to people. It seems that even though the apostle glorified deeply the grace of God in his life, he still struggled with guilt over what he had done to God's people who believed in the Lord Jesus as Israel's Messiah.[88] Is it possible that part of his "pride" in working for his own support, along with all the suffering and afflictions that that (theoretically unnecessary) decision involved, roots, in part at least, in a guilt complex? We will never know, of course, but it seems possible.

Moreover, is this perhaps what is behind Paul's exclamation in 1 Cor 9:16b: "Woe [οὐαί][89] to me if I do not preach the gospel." We must recall that this expression comes in the context where he is forcefully asserting that he *must* preach the gospel free of charge, by supporting himself. He feels an inner "compulsion" (ἀνάγκη) to preach the gospel. Where does that sense of compulsion and the feeling of "pain" (an OT nuance of οὐαί) come from? Undoubtedly it comes from within him. "It is agony if Paul tries to escape from the constraints and commission which the love and grace of the 'hound of heaven' presses upon him."[90]

In other words, as 1 Cor 9:16b implies, Paul is going to experience suffering. He will either experience pain by the pattern in which he preaches

---

88. Note the words of Walter Lock, *The Pastoral Epistles*, 16: "'I am,' *not* 'I was.' The sinner remains a sinner even if forgiven; the past is always there as a stimulus to deeper penitence and service ... the longer [Paul] lives, the more he knows the power of Christ and His truth, the severer becomes the self-reproach for having opposed it." Lock goes on to point out that by the time the Pastorals were written, Paul had himself experienced many afflictions, "and so could more keenly enter into the feelings of those whom he had wronged." This could easily have instilled ongoing guilt in Paul's heart.

89. Verlyn D. Verbrugge ("1 Corinthians," *Revised Expositors Bible Commentary* [ed. Tremper Longman III and David E. Garland; Grand Rapids: Zondervan, 2008], 11:338) points out that the word "woe" (οὐαί) occurs frequently in the OT prophets to denote coming disaster and even divine judgment (e.g., Isa 3:11; 5:8–25; Ezek 13:3, 18; Amos 5:18). See also BDAG, 734, s.v. οὐαί: meaning 1: "Interjection denoting pain or displeasure, *woe, alas*"; meaning 2: "A state of intense hardship or distress, *woe*." See also *NIDNTTE*, 3:562, on 1 Cor 9:16: "The compulsion [Paul] felt to proclaim the gospel of Christ was such that he could describe it in terms of both an inward divine constraint and an outward burden pressing upon him (cf. Isa 8:11; Jer 20:9)."

90. Thiselton, *The First Epistle to the Corinthians*, 696.

the gospel—in the way outlined in 1 Cor 9 (i.e., working for his own support)—or he will experience suffering by the personal "woe" he feels if he does not preach the gospel (and presumably, then, he would be able to live a more comfortable life).[91] He sees only these two options.

CONCLUSION

Paul clearly believed he had no other choice than to support himself as he engaged in missionary work. It was difficult; it caused him to suffer, but he would have it no other way. Perhaps there was some residual guilt lurking deeply in his heart that forced on him this way of life—though we must never forget that when all is said and done, he rejoiced in the grace of God that was bestowed on him as a sinner (cf. Luke 18:13–14). In his better moments, he knew that God had forgiven him his past manner of life as a persecutor,[92] but occasionally he opens a window to let us sense that the people whom he had beaten, persecuted, and perhaps even killed weighed heavily on his heart. And it is not unlikely that most of us know people today too who have a shady past and who, from time to time, cope with regret for the past and guilt in the present. But God's grace wins out in the end.

---

91. That is, Paul would feel the weight of severe consequences if he were to choose to forego preaching for another profession.

92. As Thomas D. Lea and H. Payne Griffin Jr. (*1, 2 Timothy, Titus* [NAC; Nashville: Broadman & Holman, 1992], 82) put it, "[Paul] never got beyond a response of wonder and gratitude to God's act of saving him 'warts and all.' We must never move beyond the excitement and joy our conversion generates in us."

CHAPTER 3

PAUL AND THE ISSUE OF PATRONAGE IN THE GRECO-ROMAN WORLD

IN THE PREVIOUS CHAPTER, ONE MAJOR POINT STOOD OUT. PAUL REFUSED to compromise on his policy of earning his own living expenses as a traveling missionary, even though he forcefully argued in 1 Cor 9:3–14 and elsewhere that others who were involved in the spreading of the gospel had every right "to earn their living from the gospel" (9:14). In no way, so it seems, would Paul accept money from people while he was living among them. Instead, he looked for some leatherworking firm in which he could engage in his trade so that he could earn his own keep.

It strikes us as surprising, then — perhaps even shocking — to read Rom 15:23–24: "I have been longing to come to you for many years whenever I travel to Spain. For I hope to see you as I am traveling through and to be sent on my way [προπεμφθῆναι] there by you after I have first enjoyed your company for a while." The verb προπέμπω has a technical meaning here, as pointed out by James D. G. Dunn: "προπέμπω has the specific sense of 'help on one's journey,' that is, in a variety of possible ways: by providing food, money, letters of introduction, arranging transport, accompanying part of the way, etc.... In earliest Christianity it becomes almost a technical term for the provision made by a church missionary support."[1]

---

1. James D. G. Dunn, *Romans 9–16* (WBC 38; Nelson: Nashville, 1988), 872; BDAG, 873, s.v. προπέμπω, meaning 2: "to assist someone in making a journey, *send on one's way* with food, money, by arranging for companions, means of travel, etc." See the use of this verb

In fact, Paul uses this same verb in 1 Cor 16:6 when he talks about *his own* travel plans of going to Macedonia and then coming to visit them in Corinth and perhaps spend the winter there, "in order that you may then send me on my way [προπέμψητε] wherever I go." Thiselton translates προπέμπω here as "send me ... with practical support," and makes the comment that this is "a technical term to denote '*help on one's journey* with food, money, by arranging for companions ... etc.'"[2]

What is going on here? We have spent an entire chapter pointing out how independent Paul wants to be of any financial assistance from those among whom he is living and working, and now we read that he, indirectly at least, is asking the Corinthians, of all people, in this very same letter to support him financially when he leaves from there, perhaps the following spring.[3] And later he writes to the Romans to do the same thing for him as he heads off to Spain. Does Paul feel free to ask for money for his necesssary expenses or not?

To understand what Paul is saying here, as well as to understand other similar passages in the NT, we need to take a small detour and understand something about the patronage system that was part of the social fabric of the Greco-Roman social world. There were essentially two types of patronage: public or political patronage, and personal patronage. We need to say something about both, because we will never understand the complexity of Paul and money matters unless we know a few things about patronage.

---

in 1 Macc 12:4 and 1 Esd 4:47, both of which refer to offering safe conduct on a journey; 3 John 6–8, showing hospitality presumably by offering food and a place of temporary lodging; Titus 3:13, giving help to Zenas and Apollos to see to it that they have everything that they need. See also C. E. B. Cranfield (*Romans* [ICC; 2 vols.; Edinburgh: T&T Clark, 1979], 2:769): "προπέμπειν was used to denote the fulfilment of various services which might be required by a departing traveller, such as the provision of rations, money, means of transport, letters of introduction, and escort for some part of the way"; Longenecker and Still (*Thinking through Paul*, 168–69): "The primary reference in this phrase is economic. Paul is intimating that Christians in Rome might find it in their hearts to back his plans to take the gospel to Spain by offering him the finances necessary to undertake such an enterprise."

2. Thiselton, *The First Epistle to the Corinthians*, 1328.

3. We should point out, of course, that this visit never materialized in the way Paul intended (see 2 Cor 1:15–2:1 and the history reflected there). But that is beside the point as we seek to understand what Paul is asking in 1 Cor 16:6–7.

POLITICAL PATRONAGE IN THE GRECO-ROMAN WORLD

In terms of political patronage, from the time of Augustus, the emperor was the patron of the entire Roman world, and the residents of the empire owed him a debt of gratitude. This particularly took political expression when various governors appointed by him named their cities after Caesar (e.g., references to Caesarea Maritima and Caesarea Philippi in the NT) or constructed temples for the worship of the emperor cult in various cities, beginning with one in Rome itself. Note the observation of Judith A. Diehl: "At the end of the first century, thirty-five cities in Asia Minor held the title of 'temple warden' (*neokoros*) that supported a site of the imperial cult" (note that this is just in one province, Asia Minor).[4]

But such patronage was not only something done for the emperor. Any wealthy person was expected to donate a portion of his or her income as benefaction for the public good—whether it be for a road, for a temple or some other public building, or even for helping to fund a war. Those who did fund such projects received praise from the governing authorities through a monument erected in their honor: "in public places the work of benefactors on inscriptions ... were officially erected by 'the Council and the People.'"[5] The significant thing about inscriptions is that the language was pretty well fixed; it was noted that the wealthy patron had "done the good" (τὸ ἀγαθὸν ποιεῖν; sometimes εὖ ποιεῖν), for which he was receiving "praise" (ἔπαινον).[6]

This language is significant, since it helps us to understand an instruction of Paul in Rom 13:3–4. There Paul uses a second person singular imperative (which, according to Winter, suggests that Paul is addressing an individual, not the church as a whole)[7] to "do the good, and you will receive praise from the benefaction" (τὸ ἀγαθὸν ποίει, καὶ ἕξεις ἔπαινον

---

4. Judith A. Diehl, "Anti-Imperial Rhetoric in the New Testament," in *Jesus Is Lord, Caesar Is Not: Evaluating Empire in New Testament Studies* (ed. Scot McKnight and Joseph B. Modica; Downers Grove, IL: InterVarsity Press, 2013), 72.

5. See Bruce W. Winter, *Seek the Welfare of the City: Christians as Benefactors and Citizens* (Grand Rapids: Eerdmans, 1994), 34. See especially the epigraphic evidence amassed by F. W. Danker, *Benefactor: Epigraphic Study of a Graeco-Roman and New Testament Semantic Field* (St. Louis: Clayton, 1982).

6. See Winter, *Seek the Welfare of the City*, 34–36. In an analogous manner and with similar language, see the examples of the ἐπίδοσις inscriptions in Verbrugge, *Paul's Style of Church Leadership*, 157–76.

7. Winter, *Seek the Welfare of the City*, 37.

ἐξ αὐτῆς).[8] In other words, Paul is instructing believers who have the economic means to participate in this pattern of public benefaction:

> Benefactions included supplying grain in times of necessity by diverting the grain-carrying ships to the city, forcing down the price by selling it in the market below the asking rate, erecting public buildings or adorning old buildings with marble revetments ... refurbishing the theatre, widening roads, helping in the construction of public utilities, going on embassies to gain privileges for the city, and helping the city in times of civil upheaval. There must have been Christians of very considerable means to warrant Paul's injunction in verse 3.[9]

As we will point out further in ch. 4, wealthy believers probably made up only a small segment of the believing community,[10] but Paul does not want such believers to isolate themselves from the broader society in which they lived. Civic responsibilities do not cease when one becomes a believer. And as Paul will soon point out to all the believers, they are to pay taxes to those to whom taxes were due (Rom 13:7; see further comments on this passage in ch. 12).

PERSONAL PATRONAGE IN THE GRECO-ROMAN WORLD

FORMS OF PERSONAL PATRONAGE

The allusions in the NT to personal patronage are far more pervasive than those of political or public patronage. For our purposes, we need to explore briefly three different types of personal patronage. The seminal book that probed the issue of personal patronage is Richard P. Saller's *Personal Patronage under the Early Empire*.[11] Saller directs our attention to two types

---

8. The use of the feminine αὐτῆς here may seem puzzling. The closest feminine noun is ἐξουσία, where it appears to be a synecdoche for a person in authority. But the antecedent could also be an unstated but understood word such as εὐεργεσία, which means "benefaction."

9. Winter, *Seek the Welfare of the City*, 37. Winter also argues in this section that Peter has a similar message in 1 Pet 2:14–15, where both ἔπαινον and the single word ἀγαθοποιέω occur.

10. Note ibid.: "The cost of a benefaction was very considerable and beyond the ability of some, if not most, members of the church."

11. Richard P. Saller, *Personal Patronage under the Early Empire* (Cambridge: University of Cambridge, 1982). It is important also to consult Erlend D. MacGillivray ("Re-evaluating Patronage and Reciprocity in Antiquity and New Testament Studies," *JGRChJ* 6 [2009]: 37–81),

of personal patronage: one based on the patron-client relationship, and the other on the friendship relationship. The patron-client relationship involved "exchange of resources, usually instrumental, economic, and political on the part of the benefactor, while the client responds especially with solidarity and loyalty to the protection, the *fides*, of the patron."[12] The client was expected to greet the patron daily with gratitude and sometimes even to follow him out in public and sing his praises to people whom they may have encountered. On some occasions a number of clients would even pool their meager amount of savings to contract and install a public inscription in honor of their patron. For his part, the patron supported his clients with food and other necessary resources.[13] Both parties would therefore benefit (the term used is *reciprocity*) — the patron by receiving praise and admiration from his clients, and the clients by having their needs met. But as is obvious, it was a relationship based on social inequality.[14]

The other form of patronage was one based on friendship (technically called *amiticia*). Interestingly, "the word *amicus* ['friend'] was sufficiently ambiguous to encompass both social equals and unequals."[15] In fact, in

---

who takes issue with some of the excessive ways in which the patron – client imagery has been used to interpret NT texts by those who champion a social-science hermeneutic. Especially in the Jewish world there is little evidence for patron – client patronage and acknowledged euergetism in the first century. However, MacGillivray does not examine the friendship (*amiticia*) relationship and the reciprocity that might pertain to that relationship. It is this aspect of the Greco-Roman social world that is of significance to us here and is helpful in interpreting the social dynamics of several significant passages of Paul's letters.

12. This summary is offered by Carolyn Osiek, "The Politics of Patronage and the Politics of Kinship," *BTB* 39 (2009): 144.

13. Since there were no government welfare programs throughout the ancient Roman world (except, perhaps, on a city-by-city basis, such as in the city of Rome, where the emperor might function as a patron or benefactor, offering "bread and circuses" to the residents of Rome in return for their loyalty), the patron-client relationship served as a sort of de facto welfare system. At the same time, it is important to point out that the patronage system did not reach the poorest of the poor, those on the lowest rung of the economic scale (see Longenecker, *Remember the Poor*, 73, and our discussion of this issue in ch. 4). The outright poor had no "safety net" for them; they were truly dependent on the occasional coin tossed to them (86), if for no other reason than to stop the beggars from being a nuisance. Yet as we will see in ch. 4, this situation was different in the world of Judaism and, eventually, Christianity. See also MacGillivray, "Re-evaluating Patronage and Reciprocity," 71 – 81.

14. This is clear in letters written by patrons, which were filled with "the language of social subordination [which] may have seemed arrogant when used by the patron, a tactless advertisement of his superiority and the relative weakness of his clients" (Saller, *Personal Patronage*, 10).

15. Ibid., 11.

some cases, a patron might call a person *amicus* rather than *cliens* simply "as a mark of consideration."[16] There was, however, a paradoxical element with the *amiticia* system, namely, that "although friendship was ideally to be based on mutual affection with no thought for profit, a necessary part of friendship was a mutually beneficial exchange of goods and services."[17] In other words, if an *amicus* were to receive a favor, he "was expected to return it at an appropriate time and to show gratitude. Nothing was baser than an *ingratus amicus*, and ingratitude was seen as just cause for the breaking off of *amiticia*."[18] If the *amicus* were of a lower social status, undoubtedly he would not be able to show gratitude by a gift of significant monetary value, but he could do so by responding with "loyalty and *fides*. The latter term carries the 'implication of submission to a superior power as well as confidence in protection.'"[19] Especially in an honor-shame society, clients and patrons as well as friends were "to look out for each other's interests first,"[20] or they would bring shame on themselves.

David Briones has detected a third significant form of patronage (though not nearly as common) that helps us understand certain "transactions" in the NT—a patron-broker-client relationship. This pattern "distinguishes itself by including a three-way bond between a source (patron), a mediator (broker), and a beneficiary (client)." The broker transmits "the patron's material goods and services to the client and, likewise, the client's gratitude and loyalty back to the patron."[21]

---

16. Ibid. Saller goes on to mention that some patrons actually divided their "friends/followers" into three groups: "peers who were received in private," "lesser *amici* [who were] permitted in groups into the atrium for the morning salutation," and "humble *clientes* who were admitted *en masse* and might be humiliated by being kept out of the house."

17. Ibid., 12.

18. Ibid., 14. Hence the paradox: "a man was not supposed to form a friendship or distribute a favor [called the *beneficium*] with a view to the return [called the *officium*], and yet he knew that his *amicus*/recipient was in fact obliged to make a return" (cf. p. 18).

19. Cohick, *Philippians*, 239; her quotation is from Osiek, "The Politics of Patronage," 144.

20. Osiek, "The Politics of Patronage," 144.

21. Briones, *Paul's Financial Policy*, 39. See p. 40 for a couple of examples of this form of patronage. Briones makes an interesting and powerful case for the application of this form of patronage in the book of Philippians (discussed in the previous chapter). The Philippians had sent Paul a gift while he was in prison, but in 1:3–6 the apostle creates "a three-way pattern of exchange, one which envisions God as the source of the gift, the Philippians as the mediator or broker, and Paul as the beneficiary. Similarly, in 4:10–20, Paul's more formal thanksgiving section for their gift, his "joy derives from God's work through the Philippians' contribution, not the supply of material provision *per se* but in what that provision came to represent, their phronetic κοινωνία" (p. 111). Note too how Paul closes this section by noting that "my God

THE LETTER TO PHILEMON AND PERSONAL PATRONAGE

This entire patronage system could get complicated at times, as is clearly illustrated by the NT letter of Philemon. The three main characters in the story in this book are the apostle Paul, Philemon (a man with a large enough house to host a church and with enough resources to own slaves), and Philemon's runaway slave Onesimus.[22] The relationship between Paul and Philemon would be an *amiticia* relationship between equals ("partners," κοινωνοί, Phlm 17).[23] But when Paul introduced Onesimus to Jesus and Onesimus responded in faith, Paul writes that he now considered this slave to be his "son" (v. 10)—and family relationships among adults were considered to be that of "friends." At the same time, however, the formal social relationship between Onesimus and Philemon remained that of master–slave, clearly a relationship of social inequality.

So we have a complicated three-way situation: Paul and Philemon were associated on an *amiticia* basis, as were Paul and Onesimus, but Onesimus and Philemon were on the unequal footing of slave and master (one cannot even call this a patronage relationship). So how should Philemon relate to Onesimus? If Philemon were to insist on receiving Onesimus back *as his slave*, Philemon would be sending a message to Paul that he considered the apostle subordinate to himself, for Paul considered Onesimus his

---

will meet all your needs according to the riches of his glory in Christ Jesus" (NIV). God is the ultimate source [patron] of every gift, and we as humans are only an intermediate supplier [broker]. Or to use the words of Miroslav Volf without the formal patron-client language, Paul "doesn't thank [the Philippians] directly because he believes that he hasn't received gifts *from* them but *through* them. The giver is God. They are his channels" (*Free of Charge: Giving and Forgiving in a Culture Stripped of Grace* [Grand Rapids: Zondervan, 2005], 112–13, italics his).

22. A number of scholars have recently held that Onesimus was not a runaway slave but a slave whom Philemon sent to Paul to help minister to his needs for a limited time. The scenario, then, is that Paul wants to keep Onesimus as a helper, but feels obligated to send him back to Philemon; his hope is that Philemon will return Onesimus to him. However, of the various views of the story underlying what Onesimus had done, the one that makes the most sense to us is that Onesimus is indeed a slave who had fled from his master and somehow linked up with Paul in Rome. See also David E. Garland, *Colossians and Philemon* (NIVAC; Grand Rapids: Zondervan, 1998), 294–300; John G. Nordling, "Onesimus *Fugitivus*: A Defense of the Runaway Slave Hypothesis in Philemon," *JSNT* 41 (1991): 97–119; Moo, *The Epistles to the Colossians and to Philemon*, 365; Ben Witherington III, *The Letters to Philemon, the Colossians, and the Ephesians: A Socio-Rhetorical Commentary on the Captivity Epistles* (Grand Rapids: Eerdmans, 2007), 69–73. But note that our analysis of the complicated patronage issues in the letter to Philemon is not dependent on which of these scenarios is the correct one.

23. If anything, Paul perhaps views himself as superior to Philemon, since he writes that he has the right to order (ἐπιτάσσειν) Philemon what to do (v. 8).

equal. But if he received Onesimus as he would normally receive Paul, undoubtedly there might be neighbors of Philemon who would criticize him severely for demonstrating that a slave could be "rewarded" for running away by being set free. Paul knew of these complicated options, but the whole point of his letter was that Philemon should receive Onesimus back "as you would welcome[24] me" (i.e., as an equal brother, v. 17).[25]

TWO MONEY ISSUES RAISED BY THE LETTER TO PHILEMON

The issues reflected in the book of Philemon raise two other questions that need to be explored, especially in a book on Paul and money. In Phlm 18, Paul makes the promise: "If he [Onesimus] has done you wrong or owes you something, charge this to me." This verse is one of the more problematic verses in this brief letter. We can discount interpretations that have explained the first class condition used here (εἰ plus the indicative) as a subtle way in which Paul knows Onesimus has probably stolen something from Philemon. A first class condition does not necessarily indicate the veracity of the condition's protasis.[26] Moreover, the loss that Paul may be alluding to could be nothing more than the lost work time that the slave Onesimus has cheated his master Philemon.

In any case, the verb translated "charge" (ἐλλόγα) is a *hapax legomenon* in the NT; it appears to be a commercial technical term in the Hellenistic world, meaning to "charge to the account of someone."[27] Paul does not seem to be hinting simply some form of compensation because of the loss of face that Philemon might have experienced as a result of having a slave running away. Rather, he is talking about the possibility of real monetary loss, and Paul assumes personal responsibility for his "son" Onesimus, promising to pay Philemon whatever monetary amount might accrue to

---

24. Paul was thinking of Philemon as a "partner" (κοινωνός) in the gospel enterprise, as a person like Titus or Timothy (cf. 2 Cor 8:23).

25. We have no clear proof of how Philemon chose to respond to this letter, but most commentators agree that the very existence of this letter in the Christian canon suggests that Philemon treasured the letter enough to make sure it did not get destroyed (see, e.g., Pao, *Colossians and Philemon*, 352). That is, he followed through on Paul's advice, regardless of how his unbelieving social equals might have reacted.

26. Daniel B. Wallace, *Greek Grammar Beyond the Basics: An Exegetical Syntax of the New Testament* (Grand Rapids: Zondervan, 1996), 690–91. It is true, of course, that contextual clues on some occasions do allow the word εἰ to be translated "since" (e.g., Col 2:20; 3:1).

27. See BDAG, 319, s.v. ἐλλογέω. See also ch. 12, where we examine this same data from the standpoint of "debt."

this situation. As if this were not enough, Paul writes v. 19 in his own handwriting: "I, Paul, write[28] this with my own hand: I will repay it."[29]

This verse raises, of course, an important issue: "The concrete problem as to how Paul could repay Philemon while he himself is in prison and dependent on others for his daily sustenance is a real one."[30] Some scholars argue that Paul is being ironic here, that he (along with Philemon) knows that he could never follow through on this. Doug Moo, however, rejects this ironic interpretation, but he also rules out further speculation. "Did [Paul] have his own private funds that he could draw upon? Did he have financial backers or 'patrons' willing to help? We simply cannot know."[31] James D. G. Dunn, however, writes that Paul is serious here. "Paul would meet 'the claim in full'. . . . It can only mean that he would be able to call on wealthy backers who presumably knew both Paul and Onesimus, should the IOU be called in."[32]

But we believe that another scenario is equally plausible, and perhaps even more likely to be the case. If, as many scholars argue, Paul wrote Philemon during his Roman imprisonment, he was undoubtedly under house arrest at this time "in his own rented house" (see Acts 28:30) and had freedom to entertain visitors.[33] Thus, it is entirely possible that he may have been able to practice his leatherworking skills by having work brought to him, perhaps even by Onesimus, and thus Paul was able to earn some income. In fact, if (as seems likely from Rom 16:3–4) Aquila and Priscilla were back in Rome, they could have funneled work to him and perhaps even paid his rent. If so, his promise to pay Philemon is a genuine promise and not one that Paul writes either ironically or with the hope that he would never have to fulfill it.

---

28. Almost certainly the use of the aorist ἔγραψα here is an epistolary aorist (see Wallace, *Greek Grammar beyond the Basics*, 563).

29. Note Markus Barth and Helmut Blanke (*The Letter to Philemon: A New Translation with Notes and Commentary* [Eerdmans Critical Commentary; Grand Rapids: Eerdmans, 2000], 483): "With this 'receipt,' Philemon could have required damages of Paul in the court. . . . The fact that Paul . . . chooses a legally binding form may be an indirect but clear indication of the consequences for Paul in case Philemon fails to grant the apostle's 'request' to receive Onesimus as a beloved brother."

30. Pao, *Colossians and Philemon*, 408.

31. Moo, *The Epistles to the Colossians and to Philemon*, 428.

32. James D. J. Dunn, *The Epistles to the Colossians and to Philemon* (NIGTC; Grand Rapids: Eerdmans, 1996), 339.

33. Note that a rented house (μίσθωμα) would have required some access to regular funds.

The second issue raised in this letter about monetary issues is Paul's request in v. 22. He has a strong feeling that he may be released soon from his house arrest, and so he asks Philemon: "And while I am on the topic [of making requests], prepare a guest room for me." This is precisely one of the things we noted in ch. 1 that Jesus instructed his disciples to do on their mission trip, namely, to find a place to stay and then to stay there. But this is also what we saw Paul did not want to do himself, to become financially dependent in any way on those among whom he was working. As we saw in ch. 2, he would sooner sleep out in the cold and rain if he could not afford lodging somewhere by using his own funds, rather than obligate himself to another person.[34] How can we make sense of this? Is Paul changing his mind?

Several things come to mind. It is indeed possible that Paul is changing his mind. After all, he calls himself in this letter a πρεσβύτης, an "old man" (v. 9), and perhaps he is reflecting that he no longer has the stamina he did in his younger years to pay for his own lodging or, if he had no funds, to sleep out in the open. Furthermore, Paul is not going into new territory to preach the gospel to those who had never heard; he is going to a city that had a church that was started under his auspices while he was living in Ephesus.[35] He would be staying with Christian friends, not with strangers.

But most of all, the entire *amicitia* patronage pattern helps explain why Paul feels free to ask for lodging (and, probably, food) from Philemon. As we noted above, Philemon and Paul are socially equals; they are *amici* (note the phrase ἡ κοινωνία τῆς πίστεώς σου ["partnership in the faith"] in v. 6). And friends will do things for each other. In fact, Paul appears to be doing a favor for Philemon in insisting that Onesimus go back to his owner, and if reciprocity means anything, it means that Philemon now "owes one" to Paul. By requesting lodging, Paul is simply giving Philemon an opportunity to return a favor. The request for lodging in Phlm 22 is not that Paul is changing his policy as stated in 1 Cor 9; rather, it is a recognition that Paul lived in the Greco-Roman world with its encouragement of reciprocity for

---

34. It is true, of course, that in Corinth Paul stayed with Aquila and Priscilla. But he did so because he was working for them, and presumably part of his "pay" was room in addition to board.

35. Colossians 2:1 suggests that Paul had not yet personally been in Laodicea or Colossae, and the comparison on names at the end of both Colossians and Philemon strongly suggests that Philemon lives in Colossae. It would appear that Epaphras was the one who started that church (1:7).

favors received, and at times he could work comfortably within that system without compromising his loyalty to the principles of the gospel.

WHAT ABOUT LYDIA?

The account of Lydia in Acts 16 intersects here as well. This incident does present some interesting challenges of trying to understand Paul's mind and policy. We must remember first of all that by this time, Paul (and Barnabas, who had gone with Paul only on his prior missionary journey) had established the policy of not accepting free living expenses from those among whom he was preaching the gospel (1 Cor 9:6). When he and Silas (and Timothy and Luke) arrived in Philippi, it was the first city on his second missionary journey in which he stayed for a period of time. On his first Sabbath there, he discovered that a group of Jewish and God-fearing women met by the riverside for prayer, and Paul joined them. Among them was Lydia. Whatever her prior history may have been,[36] by the time Paul meets her in Philippi, she is a successful businesswoman in the purple cloth trade (her home town was Thyatira in Asia Minor). She appears to be the head of a household (cf. ὁ οἶκος αὐτῆς in Acts 16:15), and as the story progresses, it becomes clear that she has sufficient room to house Paul, Silas, Luke, and Timothy, as well as to invite the church to use her house for a meeting place (16:40).[37] Richard Ascough has concluded that both from her business and from the use of οἶκος, Luke portrays "Lydia as a woman of means who owns her own house."[38]

---

36. See the brief discussion in Schnabel, *Acts*, 680–81.

37. See Richard S. Ascough, *Lydia: Paul's Cosmopolitan Hostess* (Collegeville, MN: Liturgical, 2009), 29. Ascough concludes from a study of Luke–Acts that when we put aside the uses of οἶκος/οἰκία in Acts where it refers to the temple ("house" of God), the majority of the remaining references "refer to an independently owned or rented houses of some size—that is, to a *domus* rather than an *insula* [the latter is more like an apartment]." See, e.g., Luke 7:6, 10; Acts 10:2, 22, 30.

38. Ibid., 32; on p. 34 Ascough discusses, on the basis of archaeological studies, what Lydia's house may have looked like. Cf. the similar conclusion of the type of house by Chaido Koukouli-Chrysantaki, "Colonia Iulia Augusta Philippensis," in *Philippi at the Time of Paul and after His Death* (ed. Charalambos Bakirtzis and Helmut Koester; Harrisburg, PA: Trinity Press International, 1998), 24. On the somewhat meager evidence for the role of women in commerce in the Greco-Roman world, see Bruce W. Winter, *Roman Wives, Roman Widows: The Appearance of New Women and the Pauline Communities* (Grand Rapids: Eerdmans, 2003), 174–76. Note his comment on 174: "Women contributed to commercial and other endeavours using their households as a base."

When Lydia heard Paul bring the message about Jesus Christ, Luke reports that "the Lord opened her heart to give heed to the things spoken by Paul," and she became a believer (Acts 16:14). After being baptized, she "invited" or "encouraged" (παρεκάλεσεν, from παρακαλέω) Paul and his company to stay at her place (presumably up to that point, they had been staying at some temporary lodging place, according to their policy). The verb παρακαλέω has a variety of nuances, such as "to invite, urge, encourage" as well as "to implore, entreat."[39] It seems, however, as if Paul was reluctant to accept her offer, probably for the reasons of policy that we presented in ch. 2. But Lydia was persistent in her invitation, and Luke records her words: "If you have judged me a faithful woman in the Lord, enter my house [οἶκος] and stay here" (v. 15). Luke then concludes the story with these words: καὶ παρεβιάσατο ἡμᾶς ("and she prevailed upon us").[40]

The verb παραβιάζομαι used here contains the root βιάζω, a term that often denotes "force" or even "violence."[41] It would be going too far to say that she forced Paul and company to stay in her house under some sort of threat, but the use of παραβιάζομαι certainly connotes upping the ante from her earlier παρακαλέω.[42] It seems clear that Paul strenuously resisted the invitation to lodge at Lydia's house even though he knew she had the room, but eventually, reluctantly, he gave in. Lydia must have been one persuasive woman![43]

But on what basis could Paul give in to Lydia's invitation to stay at

---

39. See BDAG, 764–65, s.v. παρακαλέω.

40. It may seem strange for a woman rather than a man to invite a group of men to stay at her house. Ascough discusses male-female and marriage customs in the first century in his book *Lydia* and concludes (p. 45): "That [Lydia] was able to offer hospitality to Paul and his colleagues without the approval of anyone suggests that she was not married and was free from legal constraints of a *kyrios*. The most likely scenario that would apply in her case and the one that the ancient reader of Luke's document would have most naturally assumed, is that Lydia was perhaps divorced, but more likely widowed, and had given birth to at least three or four children who survived childbirth." See also Peterson, *Acts*, 460.

41. Cf. BDAG, 175–76, s.v. βιάζω.

42. See BDAG, 759, s.v. παραβιάζομαι ("urge strongly, prevail upon").

43. Most commentators do not comment on the two-stage process Lydia used to get Paul to stay at her place, from "exhortation" to "forceful persuasion." William Larkin Jr. does, however: "Though Paul does not normally accept hospitality and financial support of converts as he is planting a church in their midst (2 Cor. 11:7–9; 1 Thess 2:9), he makes an exception here. He permits Lydia to live out the principle of sharing material good with those who teach the Word of God (1 Cor. 9:11, 14; Gal. 6:6). Apparently his normal hesitation is overcome when she will not take no for an answer (*persuaded*, actually 'prevailed'; compare Phil. 1:5)" (William J. Larkin Jr., *Acts* [IVPNTC; Downers Grove, IL: InterVarsity Press, 1995], 237).

her house and to accept it? Sometime later, both to the Thessalonians and especially to the Corinthians, he wrote so clearly about his policy not to accept free room and board from those to whom he was preaching the gospel. So how could he say yes in this instance (and not admit to the Corinthians in 1 Cor 9 that on at least one occasion he had violated the principle stated there)?

But what we discovered in the Philemon story may apply here as well. First, by the time Lydia was so strenuously urging Paul and the others to stay at her place, she had already become a believer in the Lord and been baptized, along with her household (Acts 16:15). Thus, in no way could Paul argue that he did not want to stay at Lydia's because it was important for him to know that those who did become believers had done so not through any financial incentive (getting their money's worth from paying for Paul's preaching, for example); after all, by this time Lydia and her household had been persuaded of the lordship of Jesus Christ by the power of Paul's message. But second, and perhaps more to the point, since both Lydia and Paul were now believers and hence brother and sister in the Lord, they were now members of God's family, of God's κοινωνία.[44] They were now *amici* of each other. Through the preaching of Paul, Lydia was now no longer just a God-fearer; she was now an heiress of eternal life through Jesus Christ. She had just received an incredible gift from the Lord through Paul's preaching, and her persistence in her invitation was part of the reciprocity of friendship.[45] This story may, in fact, be the first

---

44. Though Luke does not use κοινωνία in Acts 16, it is appropriate to recall Paul's use of κοινωνία language in the letter to the Philippians (see ch. 2). It is not impossible that the one who spearheaded the gifts from the church at Philippi to Paul was Lydia herself—perhaps to the point that Paul was starting to feel uncomfortable and was even beginning to feel the need to reciprocate in some manner. If, as we have noted here, Paul was uncomfortable in being willing to accept the invitation to stay at Lydia's house in the first place, her ongoing support of Paul, even though she could presumably afford it, was met with a certain amount of reluctance. While we did not discuss this as a possibility in ch. 2 when we examined Paul's "thank-you" to the Philippians, this *amicitia* patronage system certainly may have been a part of the complexity of the situation.

45. Ascough (*Lydia*, 47) points out that when Paul and Silas return to Lydia's house after the midnight jail episode in Acts 16, they are returning as "friends to meet and greet those who are part of Lydia's wider social network.... In the case of Paul and Lydia, Paul had already become Lydia's patron by acting as a change agent and brokering for her a connection with a new, powerful deity." Note also p. 53: "Lydia became Paul's client. Her hospitality did not make her Paul's patron but rather was an act of reciprocity for the benefits she had gained through Paul."

time that Paul faced the intersection between Greco-Roman friendship reciprocity and his preaching of the gospel.

As a final footnote, this was not the only time that Paul felt free to live with someone whom he had led to Christ and baptized. At the end of his third missionary journey, Paul spent the winter in Corinth, and he enjoyed the hospitality of Gaius as his "host" (ξένος, Rom 16:23; "a host to me and to the entire church").[46] Why would Paul agree to stay with Gaius as his host? Almost certainly this Gaius is the same Gaius whom Paul had baptized in Corinth (see 1 Cor 1:14). In other words, Paul seems to have had no difficulty accepting the hospitality of those to whom he had preached Christ and who had become believers, either under the basis that they were now family members or, perhaps more so, that it was the reciprocal element in the *amiticia* friendship of someone who had become a believer. This undoubtedly also explains how Paul could say to Philemon, "Prepare a guest room [ξενία] for me, for I hope that through your prayers I may soon accept your graciousness" (Phlm 22). While there is no indication that Paul had baptized Philemon, most certainly he had become a believer as a result of Paul's ministry in Ephesus.

AND NOW PHOEBE

Another story about patronage/benefaction surfaces in Paul's letter to the Romans. In Rom 16:1–2, we read about Phoebe, who is mentioned only in these two verses of the NT. Paul writes what is essentially a letter of recommendation for Phoebe (cf. the verb συνίστημι in 16:1),[47] because she appears there as the one who will be delivering the letter of Romans[48] to the believers in the capital city of the empire.[49] Since Phoebe was most

---

46. The word ξένος is often translated as "stranger" or "foreigner" in many of its NT uses (e.g., Matt 25:35, 38; 27:7; Eph 2:12, 19), but the term also came to denote hospitality (first to strangers, then to anyone). Note the related Greek words: ξενία (guest room), ξενίζω (to stay as a guest), and φιλοξενία (hospitality). See esp. these entries in BDAG, 683–84, 1058.

47. The letter of recommendation is explored as a well-defined genre of letter by Chan-Hie Kim, *The Familiar Letter of Recommendation* [SBLDS 4; Missoula, MT: Scholars, 1972].

48. As is well known, the Romans had an excellent mail delivery system in the first century, using its well-constructed roads. But this system was only available to official government business. Common people had to find their own way to get a letter from point A to point B.

49. We are fully aware of the textual-critical issues connected with Romans 16. While we will not detail the arguments pro and con, we are convinced that the sixteen chapters of Romans belong together and that Romans 16 was the closing chapter of this letter sent to Rome

likely unknown to many of the believers in Rome, Paul certifies through these two verses that she is a trusted member of the body of Christ and can speak for him, should the Roman Christians have any questions about Paul or his theology—or about any of the rumors that may have preceded the arrival of this letter.

Paul calls Phoebe both a διάκονος and a προστάτις in Rom 16:1–2. Most contemporary interpreters have been interested in investigating Phoebe's role as "διάκονος in the church at Cenchreae" (16:1) and what these words might imply about the role of women in the NT church. Our interest here, however, pertains to her role as προστάτις. This word is the feminine form of the masculine noun προστάτης, a word that often denotes a "leader, ruler."[50] But this Greek word was also used to translate the Latin word *patronus*, which means "patron or benefactor," so that προστάτις can also mean "patroness."[51] A third definition for this word is the more general word "helper."[52]

Philip Payne clearly chooses the first of these definitions as the best option, "leader, ruler."[53] But since Paul writes in Rom 16:2 that Phoebe has been a προστάτις "of many others and myself also," it becomes difficult to fathom how the independent Paul would personally submit himself to the leadership of someone else in the churches that he had formed and would allow others (male or female) to hold authority over him. Payne himself does not find this impossible, for he writes: "it should not be thought strange that Paul, who commanded all Christians to 'be subject to one another' (Eph 5:21), should himself be subject to others, at least in certain situations, such as submitting to the local church leadership in the

---

(see also Leon Morris, *The Epistle to the Romans* [Pillar; Grand Rapids: Eerdmans, 1988], 527; Douglas J. Moo, *The Epistle to the Romans* [NICNT; Grand Rapids: Eerdmans, 1996], 927). The listing of people in Rom 16:3–15 was most likely people living in Rome whom Paul, at one time or another, had met in his travels and who could vouch for him among the Roman believers.

50. See BDAG, 885, s.v. προστάτης, which offers this definition: "one who looks out for the interest of others, *defender, guardian, benefactor*" (no NT occurrences are cited); for προστάτις, BDAG offers "a woman in a supportive role, *patron, benefactor*" (only in Rom 16:2).

51. J. A. Fitzmyer, *Romans* (AB; New York: Doubleday, 1993), 731.

52. These three definitions are explored by Esther Yue L. Ng, "Phoebe as *Prostatis*," *TJ* 25 (2004): 3–13. She points the reader to the verb προΐστημι, which is used in the NT to denote "have an interest in, show concern for, care for, give aid" (BDAG, 870, s.v. προΐστημι; e.g., 1 Thess 5:12; perhaps Rom 12:8) as well as to "lead, preside over, rule" (e.g., 1 Tim 3:4–5; 5:17) (Ng, "Phoebe as *Prostatis*," 3–4).

53. See Philip Payne, *Man and Woman: One in Christ* (Grand Rapids: Zondervan, 2009), 62.

churches he visited."[54] Yet without a clear context in which to understand προστάτις in this manner, to use the definition "leader" here seems doubtful. It is also important to note that Paul does not write that Phoebe is a προστάτις of the ἐκκλησία of Cenchreae, but of many (πολλῶν) individuals. He is not referring to her official role in the church but to the way in which she has treated *many individuals* in Cenchreae, including Paul.[55] We should realize as well that Paul turns patronage on its head in 1 Corinthians, for he outlines the most prominent role for the wealthier members of the church at Corinth as service (διακονία, see 1 Cor 16:15), not that of receiving honors.[56]

Ng clearly chooses the definition for προστάτις as applied to Phoebe as a "patroness or benefactor," a term that is increasingly being adopted by standard Bible translations (cf. NRSV and NIV, both of which use "benefactor").[57] "She is envisioned as offering monetary support procuring political advantage, serving as legal representative for individuals, opening her house to receive visitors or provide meeting grounds, etc."[58] In a sense, what Paul is doing is to ask the believers in Rome to give her the same sort of acceptance and aid that she has been giving to others (i.e., a form of reciprocity that perhaps would occur between two believing communities). When Phoebe arrives in Rome, she will need a place to stay as well as food and Christian fellowship; thus, "as she has provided hospitality to

---

54. See ibid., 62. See also R. R. Schulz, "A Case for 'President' Phoebe in Romans 16:2," *LTJ* 24 (1990): 124–27.

55. See Ng, "Phoebe as *Prostatis*," 5; Moo, *The Epistle to the Romans* (NICNT), 916, who writes: "[Perhaps Phoebe supplied] aid to others, especially foreigners, providing housing and financial aid and representing their interests before local authorities." This would pattern Phoebe somewhat after Junia Theodora, a prominent Lycian woman living in Corinth who had a number of inscriptions in her honor for exercising προστασία for Lycians in Corinth; see Winter, *Roman Wives, Roman Widows*, 183–94; see also decree 5, 209–10, where the term is used.

56. See Winter, *Roman Wives, Roman Widows*, 194–96; see also comments in ch. 10 on the Corinthian situation and Paul's attack on the lack of goodwill on the part of the rich toward the poor.

57. Pertinent here is the comment of James Dunn, *Romans 9–16*, 888, who translates this part of 16:2: "for she herself has also been patron of many and of myself." Dunn goes on to elucidate: "The unwillingness of commentators to give προστάτις its most natural and obvious sense of 'patron' is most striking." See his entire discussion on this verse.

58. Ng, "Phoebe as *Prostatis*," 6. Ng goes on to show how this same definition of benefaction (Gk. εὐεργεσία) occurs in inscriptions regarding what several women in the Roman East did; see R. A. Kearsley, "Women in Public Life in the Roman East: Iunia Theodora, Claudia Metrodora and Phoebe, Benefactress of Paul," *TynBul* 50 (1999): 189–211.

many and to Paul in the past, she should be able to receive hospitality in return when she needs it."[59]

Joan Cecelia Campbell compares Paul's request of Phoebe to that of the Jews' request for the Roman centurion in Luke 7:1–10. Some Jews come to Jesus and ask him to heal the severely ill servant of this centurion. "This man deserves to have you do this, because he loves our nation and has built our synagogue" (Luke 7:4b–5 NIV), and Jesus eventually heals this servant.

> In this story, the centurion is a benefactor-patron whose generosity motivates the elders to attempt to broker a favor for him from Jesus.... Both Jesus and the elders exercise brokerage by acting as go-betweens: the elders broker a favor from Jesus for the centurion, and Jesus brokers a favor from God for the centurion. Similar, acting as emissary for the Jesus group in Kenchreai, Phoebe brokers the assistance of [Roman] Jesus groups. To promote her success, Paul acts as her broker by writing a letter of recommendation in which he praises her as a *diakonos* and *prostatis* and exhorts the [Romans] to help her "in whatever matter she may have need of you."[60]

This is the process of benefaction and reciprocity at work,[61] both with the Jews in Capernaum in the Lukan episode and with Christian believers in Rom 16 — the latter one not within a single city (as Capernaum in Luke 7:1), but within an association of Christ followers that has members in more than one location.

Paul freely acknowledges in Rom 16:2 that he himself had been the recipient of Phoebe's kind benefaction. In other words, Paul did indeed accept benefaction from people who were already believers — whether they were male or female. He would not ask for support from strangers when he entered a town for the first time as an evangelist, but as soon as there

---

59. Ng, "Phoebe as *Prostatis*," 10.

60. Joan Cecelia Campbell, *Phoebe: Patron and Emissary* (Collegeville, MN: Liturgical, 2009), 86–87. "Romans" is placed in square brackets because Campbell holds that Rom 16 is a letter sent to Ephesus rather than to Rome; her original has "Ephesians." Note that this book was written before the book by David Briones (*Paul's Financial Policy*), in which he demonstrates, both from Greco-Roman sources and the NT, a form of patronage that has the three-way component of patron-broker-client.

61. Interestingly, while MacGillivray, "Re-evaluating Patronage and Reciprocity," denies that a patronage relationship exists in the somewhat parallel passage of Matt 8:5–13, he acknowledges that this pattern is probably at work "in the most Greco-Roman oriented Gospel, Luke (Lk 7.2–5; 8.41; 22.25)."

was a community of believers, Paul was willing to accept their support. If he could help support himself by doing his leatherworking, he gladly (and perhaps regularly) did so, as he did by working in the leatherworking business of Aquila and Priscilla in Corinth (and perhaps also at their place in Ephesus on his third missionary journey), but for short-term stays among the churches he had started, such as in spending the winter in Corinth, he was not averse to accepting help from other Christian believers.

BACK TO THE VERB προπέμπω

It is undoubtedly in the light of the foregoing discussion that we must understand Paul's use of the verb προπέμπω, with which we began this chapter. While it is true that Paul prided himself in differentiating himself from the wandering philosophers who sought to make a living from going place to place by their rhetorical speaking and by teaching their philosophy for a fee, as we saw in ch. 2, the apostle freely accepted support when he was among believers whom he had evangelized, and on occasion he even asked for it. We have already noted the use of this verb in Rom 15:24, when Paul asks the Romans that when he comes to visit them, he hopes they will be willing to send him on his way to Spain with provisions for the journey and perhaps help pay the fare on a ship. We also noted he was willing to ask for help from the Corinthians when he was planning to head to Jerusalem after he has had a brief visit in Corinth (1 Cor 16:6). Note too that he repeats this plan in 2 Cor 1:16: "[I decided] to pass through your area on my way to Macedonia and again to come to you from Macedonia, and then to be sent on my way [προπεμφθῆναι, from προπέμπω] by you to Judea."

Furthermore, Paul asks the Corinthians for assistance for Timothy if and when he arrives in Corinth, that they may "send him on his way [προπέμψατε αὐτόν] in peace" (1 Cor 16:11). This is asking for money and support—this time for a coworker of his, not for himself.[62] He makes

---

62. The letter of 2 Corinthians, however it may be partitioned, was certainly written later than 1 Corinthians, and it is in 2 Cor 11:5–10 that Paul boasts about the fact that he did not receive any support from the Corinthians. But we must remember that in this section, Paul is talking about his activity on his first missionary trip (he narrates this section in the past tense), not a policy that he would necessarily follow were he to visit them again (cf. again his message in 1 Cor 16:6). He is responding here to "super-apostles" who have just arrived in Corinth and are eager to accept and even expect support from the Corinthians on this first visit. *That* is what Paul would not do.

a similar request on behalf of others in his letter to Titus (3:13), though there, of course, he is writing to a single individual, a personal assistant of his who is ministering on the island of Crete: "Diligently send Zenas the lawyer and Apollos on their way [πρόπεμψον] so that they lack nothing." Unless Paul is expecting Titus to find a way to earn the money to assist Zenas and Apollos, which we seriously doubt, Paul expects Titus to find a source of income from people in the church who will be able to give full assistance to them. Paul is probably suggesting that Titus solicit donations from other church members.[63]

So did Paul accept money from those among whom he ministered? The answer is no and yes. No, he did not accept money when he first arrived in a new city. He preached the gospel free of charge and refused to solicit or even, it seems, accept funds from the people of that city, unlike the wandering philosophers, who made a living of doing precisely that. This, for Paul, was a matter of personal pride — and, as we suggested in the previous chapter, personal yet purposeful suffering. But once the church was well established, he expected his churches to take part in spreading the kingdom of God by offering to him as an apostle/evangelist and to his coworkers the necessary support as they hoped to move on to a new place (or, in the case of 1 Cor 16:6, to pay a visit to the city of Jerusalem). These revisits to the churches he established would, of course, be short occasions, in which there was insufficient time for him to find a place to engage his craft as a leatherworker (though it is entirely possible that when he spent the winter in Corinth, he found a place to work, since he knew the city well). He would not, however, accept such assistance during the initial visit in which he established the church. The only clear exception was Philippi, where Lydia, a woman of some means, kept after Paul until he finally agreed (perhaps grudgingly) to stay with his entourage at her house and accept her *amiticia* patronage.

---

63. While 3 John is not a Pauline letter, John makes a similar request in 3 John 6. He writes to his dear friend Gaius: "you will do well to send [some fellow believers whom have come from John] on their way [προπέμψας] in a manner worthy of God." Here too the verb προπέμπω means to provide the necessary food and transportation so that these fellow believers can return to Ephesus (where John was most likely located).

ONE FINAL EXPENSE

There is one final expense that needs to be examined briefly for which Paul almost certainly needed sponsorship or some form of patronage. That is the cost of writing, producing, and sending a letter. In our age of sending emails and text messages (or a generation ago in typing a letter on paper and mailing it to someone else for less than a dollar), we have little concept of what it may have cost the apostle Paul to write a document the size of the letter to the Romans and to send it off. Even if he were working at his leatherworking craft in Corinth during the winter of AD 57 when he wrote the letter to the Romans, at his relatively low wage it is fair to say he could never have earned the necessary funds to afford to produce such a document. He would have needed significant assistance from someone like Phoebe or perhaps Erastus, "the city's director of the public works [ὁ οἰκονόμος τῆς πόλεως]" (Rom 16:23 NIV; note the translation "city treasurer," NET, NASB, ESV, and others).[64]

Randy Richards has done an excellent job scouring classical sources in an attempt to estimate how much such a letter might cost.[65] We know that Paul made use of an amanuensis when he wrote his letters (cf. Tertius in Rom 16:22; note too those occasions when Paul took the pen from his secretary into his own hand to close with a personal message, Gal 6:11; 2 Thess 3:17; Phlm 19). Unless Paul was able to find a believer who would donate his time, he would have to pay such an individual. Moreover, the presentation of a letter as to its neatness and script was as important rhetorically to the recipient as was the content of a letter. Secretaries who had good literary skills as well as good penmanship were probably scarce and could command a top fee for their handiwork.[66]

Richards estimates that each letter of Paul probably went through a minimum of four drafts. The first one would be a rough draft with copious notes. Then the secretary would put those notes down in a flowing text on papyrus (or on washable pieces of wood), and then this person

---

64. Paul Barnett (*Romans: The Revelation of God's Righteousness* [Fearn, UK: Christian Focus, 2003], 359) writes: "An inscription bearing the name Erastus, 'public works commissioner,' was discovered near the theatre in Corinth. It is not certain if this is the same 'Erastus.'" Regardless, the Erastus mentioned in Rom 16:23 appears to be a man of some means.

65. E. Randolph Richards, *Paul and First-Century Letter-Writing: Secretaries, Composition, and Collection* (Downers Grove, IL: InterVarsity Press, 2004), esp. ch. 10 (156–70).

66. See ibid., 163.

would go over that written text carefully with Paul and make a third copy. After further tweaks or revisions were made, the final draft could be made. But the majority of authors who wrote documents of value would also want to keep a copy of the finished document for themselves (no copy machines or flash drives available!).

That Paul kept copies seems almost certain, for he asks Timothy to come to him and "bring the scrolls, especially the parchments [τὰς μεμβράνας]" (2 Tim 4:13). The term μεμβράνα is an important word (a *hapax legomenon* in the NT and, so it appears, in the first century). We know from Cicero that he kept what are called *codicilli* (small wooden tablets) of his writings. In the first century, these were being replaced by parchment notebooks, called (in Latin) *membranae*. This is the word transliterated into Greek that Paul uses in 2 Tim 4:13, and it suggests that Paul did indeed keep copies of his letters.[67] Thus, at a minimum, a secretary could be involved in writing four drafts of each of Paul's letters.

Richards also tries to estimate how long it would take a skilled secretary to "prepare the papyrus sheets, score the lines on the sheets, mix the ink, etc.," as well as actually write a draft of a letter such as Romans. A reasonable, if conservative, estimate is two to three days for each draft. Richards continues making his estimates, based on actual estimates from Pliny and from an Oxyrhynchus papyrus from the third century that notes how much it cost to have copies of two books made. Based on these estimates and using the minimum amount of time that might be involved, Richards projects that a letter such as Romans cost $2,275.00 in present-day dollars to write.[68] Insofar as a slight variation in figures would not significantly change the total, this is well within the ballpark.

We are not even including in this the cost to transport the letter. In the case of Romans, Phoebe probably carried it to Rome for free, since she was presumably going there on business and agreed to take the letter along. Some of the other letters may have required payment of a hired person who would guarantee the safe delivery of the letter. In our day and age with cheap paper, a high rate of literacy, the ease of transferring

---

67. Colin Roberts and Theodore Skeat (*The Birth of the Codex* [2nd ed.; London: Oxford University Press, 1983], 15–23) discuss the use of the *membranae*. According to them, Paul is the only known writer of the first century to use this word. See also the discussion in Richards, *Paul and First-Century Letter-Writing*, 57.

68. See Richards, *Paul and First-Century Letter-Writing*, 165–69.

our thoughts to paper and making revisions, and no issues as to clearly writing letters since we use keyboards and well-defined fonts, it is almost unfathomable to us that a letter such as Romans could cost that much, but the first century was a vastly different world.

So where would Paul get this amount of money to write such a letter? We suggest it could only have come from a patron of some sort—and that would mean that Paul likely had to ask for money from someone to fund such a project.[69] Would this put him in a client relationship with a patron, so that Paul would have lost some of his freedom, in which he took so much pride? Perhaps there were reciprocal favors that Paul was able to perform for the patron. But perhaps this did not put him in someone else's debt. He may have been able to use someone like Silas or Luke (who may both have had writing skills and rhetorical skills; see 1 Pet 5:12) to assist in the writing (though for Romans, we know Paul did use Tertius).[70] And if Paul did find it necessary to seek funding, he would have stressed that this project was not for him personally, but for the advancement of the kingdom of God. In this way, Paul would have been able both to keep his freedom but also to deliver much-needed messages to his churches.[71]

---

69. Most scholars think that Theophilus (Luke 1:3; Acts 1:1) was a real person and not a pseudonym. He may have been "a specific person of high social standing" (Darrell L. Bock, *Luke* [2 vols.; BECNT; Grand Rapids: Baker, 1984, 1988], 1:63). He may even have been the patron who paid for Luke to write his two-volume work. Note what Robert F. O'Toole ("Theophilus," *ABD*, 6:511) writes: "Among other things, the dedication very probably indicates that Theophilus helps make the two volumes available to potential readers. In the best of circumstances, as an influential patron, he may have also made a considerable contribution to this end." See also Joseph M. Fitzmyer (*Luke* [2 vols.; AB; New York: Doubleday, 1981, 1985], 1:299) for evidence that such a "dedication did at times mean [patronage of a work] in the Greco-Roman world of that time." We should also note that both Luke and Acts are each at least twice as long as the letter to the Romans, which would put its production cost at approximately $7,000 each.

70. We would like to think that Tertius was a believer. It seems unlikely to us that Paul would entrust a letter with such deep theological thoughts to a pagan who had no knowledge of the Jewish writings or of the fulfillment of those Scriptures in Jesus Christ.

71. If there was any patronage talk between Paul and those who may have assisted in the funding of a letter, it would not be that Paul was a personal client of the one funding the letter; rather, the latter was functioning as a client of God and performing a reciprocal favor for God as patron. However, as David Downs has warned in "Is God Paul's Patron? The Economy of Patronage in Pauline Theology" (in *New Testament Scenarios and Early Christian Reception* [ed. Bruce W. Longenecker and Kelly D. Liebengood; Grand Rapids: Eerdmans, 2009], 129–56), Paul avoids all patronage language for a believer's relationship with God. Rather, God is consistently called "Father," and people who assist in any way for the good of the church and kingdom of God are doing so because they live in a family relationship, not a patron relationship.

CONCLUSION

Our conclusion to this chapter and indeed part 1 of this book can be short. While Paul clearly would not accept money for his initial preaching of the gospel in a new community, once a church had been established, Paul expected them to take part in the spread of the gospel. Part of this responsbility meant giving money to Paul and his coworkers, not necessarily for everyday living expenses, but certainly for special projects such as transportation fees, support while on a trip, and writing letters. At times there were people with some discretionary income (such as Lydia and Phoebe) who gladly gave to the cause of the spread of the gospel and even supported Paul while he was living in their midst. Others perhaps became a patron when Paul wrote a letter, though Paul would not have considered himself a client of that individual; rather, he would have emphasized that the sponsor of a letter was responding in gratitude to God, their heavenly Father, who had saved them through the blood of Jesus Christ.

There was, however, one other major financial project that Paul expected his churches to participate in and for which he solicited funds, namely, his collection for the impoverished saints in Jerusalem — a project usually simply called "the collection." The next few chapters, which form part 2 of this book, deal with this important project conceived and carried out by the apostle.

PART 2

RAISING MONEY FOR THE MOTHER CHURCH IN JERUSALEM

PAUL'S CONCERN FOR THE POOR, INCLUDING HIS FIRST FUND-RAISING FOR THE JERUSALEM CHURCH

IT IS CLEAR FROM A NUMBER OF PASSAGES IN THE NT, BOTH IN ACTS AND in some of Paul's letters, that Paul engaged in raising money for impoverished believers of the church in Jerusalem. The most familiar of these is the project called "the collection." Chapters 5 through 8 will delve into various aspects of that effort. But the first fund-raising project took place a number of years earlier (see Acts 11:27–30). We need to look at such questions as to why it was necessary to raise money for the Jerusalem church and why Paul participated in this effort. Equally important is a study of Gal 2:10, which (as we will see) is one of the more disputed texts in Paul's letters, historically speaking. This chapter deals with these issues.

POVERTY IN THE GRECO-ROMAN WORLD

Before we engage these biblical texts, however, we must say a few things about poverty in general in the Greco-Roman world and about Paul's attitude toward the poor. The most recent thorough analysis of this aspect of Paul's life is that of Bruce W. Longenecker, *Remember the Poor: Paul, Poverty, and the Greco-Roman World*. While our intent is not to repeat all of the discussion and conclusions proposed by Longenecker, we need to know a few things because they will be important as we progress in this topic.

In ch. 3, we noted the importance of patronage in the Greco-Roman world, which was one method of addressing economic imbalance. A patron would meet the physical needs of economically depressed clients in return for the praise and honor they would give him or her. This raises the question of how many people might be involved in this system. Asked otherwise, how many poor were there in the ancient world?

It is difficult to obtain accurate statistics about a world where the recording of statistics was not deemed important. As a result, scholars have proposed a variety of theories about poverty in the Greco-Roman world. In 1998 Justin Meggitt claimed that only 1 percent of the Roman population truly escaped poverty.[1] Several years later Steven Friesen, in a seminal article, argued for much more diversity in the urban populations, with as many as seven levels of people, which he placed on a poverty scale (PS). He argued that approximately 3 percent (PS 1–3) could be considered truly wealthy; these were the political and military elite. PS4 (about 7 percent) were the more well-to-do merchants, traders, and military veterans. PS5 comprised about 22 percent of the population; they were economically stable (the rest of the merchants and traders, along with some artisans and farmers). PS6 made up 40 percent of the population; they lived at subsistence level and were made up of unskilled workers, artisans employed by other business owners, common wage earners, and the like. Finally, PS7, the truly poor, made up 28 percent (orphans, widows, day workers, the disabled, and beggars).[2]

Longenecker himself adopts much of Friesen's categories, though he divides the Greco-Roman world with different percentages and uses what he calls an economic scale (ES) rather than a poverty scale (PS).[3] ES1–3 comprised about 3 percent of the Roman world; ES4, about 15 percent; ES5, about 27 percent; ES6, about 30 percent; and ES7, about 25 percent.[4]

---

1. Justin Meggitt, *Paul, Poverty and Survival* (Edinburgh: T&T Clark, 1998). He based his conclusions on elite classical sources, which tended to lump all of the rest of the citizens in one large category. See Longenecker, *Remember the Poor*, 43.

2. See, e.g., Steven J. Friesen, "Poverty and Pauline Studies: Beyond the So-called New Consensus," *JSNT* 26 (2004): 337–47.

3. Longenecker, *Remember the Poor*, 45–53. Longenecker's description of each of the levels is about the same as Friesen's. We will use the ES abbreviation throughout the rest of this chapter.

4. Note that the discussion is ongoing. In 2009 Walter Schneidel and Steven J. Friesen coauthored an article using a different method of analysis: "The Size of the Economy and the Distribution of Income in the Roman Empire," *JRS* 99 (2009): 61–91. See the discussion in

With these figures and statistics, those who may have participated in the patron–client system would almost certainly have been in the ES5 or ES6 category. Not everyone who fit this category was a client of a patron, of course, but at least a number of them were. Those in the ES7 category were virtually shut out of any form of regular public assistance. Deborah Watson shows a particular interest in this last category, which she maintains was virtually ignored in the Roman world.[5] She notes, for example, that the corn dole in Rome, which was a project managed by the emperor, went primarily to benefit people in the ES4 and ES5 levels, and it was (in theory, anyway) restricted to Roman citizens. In other words, grain subsidies were a political move, geared at keeping riots and political instability at bay by those who had a certain amount of economic power.[6] Its motivation was not to alleviate poverty, and those who were the poorest of the poor (ES7 level, and many in ES6) had no access to the dole. Such people were dependent on the compassion of other people for food or for small coins occasionally tossed to them.

It is all but impossible to determine what the percentage make-up of the Christian community was of these different classes, but it seems clear that there was a variety of different economic levels in most Greco-Roman cities,[7] and these different levels appear to be reflected in the names and

---

Longenecker, *Remember the Poor*, 47–53. This article led Longenecker to make some minor revisions to his percentages. But in all of these analyses, what is constant are the same seven categories, with 3 percent in the top three (ES1–3) and 25–28 percent at the bottom (ES7). The middle three levels are much harder to divide, but together comprised the bulk of the populations.

5. See Deborah E. Watson ("Paul's Collection in the Light of Motivations and Mechanisms for Aid to the Poor in the First-Century World" [PhD diss.; Durham University, 2006; available at http://etheses.dur.ac.uk/2601/], 14–55) for her analysis of the extent of poverty in the Roman world. See also Roman Garrison (*Redemptive Almsgiving in Early Christianity* [JSNTSup 77; Sheffield: JSOT Press, 1993], 38–45) who has researched Greco-Roman attitudes to abject poverty and concludes that there are "no specific exhortations to the rich that they should give to the poor" (41); in fact, "the general attitudes to the helpless poor is almost hostile" (43).

6. See Watson, "Paul's Collection," 41–46. Note that Watson does not use a PS or ES scale but her description of those who benefited from the corn dole fit into the ES4 and ES5 levels.

7. See Chang ("Fund-raising in Corinth," 74–124) for an interesting and conclusive description of the economic stratification of just one Roman city, the city of Corinth. He concludes: "The stratified society of Roman Corinth based on 'status' was multidimensional, which made mobility through the acquisition of wealth a greater possibility. The elite of Roman Corinth, furthermore, were mostly *nouveaux riches* and thus, there was a high level of fluidity in the stratification structure of Roman Corinth" (123).

occupations of believers talked about in the NT. Paul himself probably fit into the ES6 or perhaps ES5 category.[8] There may have been an occasional Jesus follower in an ES2 or ES3 category, such as Sergius Paulus, the proconsul of Cyprus (Acts 13:7), Cornelius the centurion (10:1–2), and Erastus, a city official[9] of Corinth (Rom 16:23). Those who were able to host a church in their house, such as Aquila and Priscilla, were probably ES4 or perhaps ES5. The majority of the believers were probably in the ES6 or ES7 levels.[10] With this historical background, we move now to a general discussion of the Christian community's response to poverty and then an analysis of how Paul fits into this aspect of the Greco-Roman world.

THE JERUSALEM CHURCH

The Christian faith, which centered in belief in Jesus as the crucified and risen Messiah, began in Jerusalem. According to Acts 1, when Jesus met with his followers after his resurrection, he told them to wait in Jerusalem for the baptism in the Holy Spirit (1:5). After Jesus was taken up into heaven, his followers continued to meet together for prayer as a community of about 120 persons (1:15). Then, ten days after the ascension, the Holy Spirit came upon them and filled each one of them in an event that we now call Pentecost (2:1–4). Peter and the other apostles proclaimed the message about Jesus as the promised Messiah to a large group of Jews who

---

8. This conclusion concurs with the discussion of Paul's life as a leatherworker as discussed in chs. 1 and 2. For a thorough discussion of Paul's social and economic status, see ibid., 140–51. Chang argues, as have others, that there is a disconnect between Paul's family's economic status (which he argues by birth "probably made him *accessible* to the upper strata groups" 151.) and his social location as a manual laborer.

9. The Greek word used is οἰκονόμος. The NRSV suggests "city treasurer," the NIV, "director of public works." BDAG, 698, s.v. οἰκονόμος, offers "public treasurer." Longenecker discusses a variety of named people in the NT, particularly those named in the letters of Paul, and which ES level they may have belonged to; see *Remember the Poor*, 236–53.

10. As Longenecker (*Remember the Poor*, 262) points out, Celsus, the critic of Christianity, "characterized Christian groups as being attractive only to the poor, the uneducated and the stupid. Even allowing for rhetorical hyperbole, his depiction must have been generally reliable in order to score its rhetorical points." But in n. 10 on p. 262, Longenecker also points to Pliny (*Ep. Tra.* 10.96.9), who wrote that the Christian community was "comprised of 'a great many individuals, of every age, of every class, both men and women.' " So the classical evidence is mixed, but probably enough to say that most believers were in the ES6 and ES7 categories (see ibid., 279–80); such a division reflected society at large. See also ibid., 294–97, where Longenecker postulates a "typical" Jesus community of fifty members.

were in Jerusalem for the Feast of Firstfruits (Weeks). On that day, about three thousand were added to their number and were baptized.

This larger group "devoted themselves to the apostles' teaching and to fellowship, to the breaking of bread and to prayer" (Acts 2:42 NIV). Moreover, they formed a community in which they had everything in common. In order to meet the physical needs of the believing community, "they sold property and possessions to give to anyone who had need" (2:45). This pattern of sharing continued as the numbers of converts grew to at least five thousand (4:4), so that "there were no needy persons among them" (4:34). One of the more notable examples of sharing was a man from Cyprus, Joseph Barnabas, who "sold a field he owned and brought the money and put it at the apostles' feet" (4:37). From the beginning of the Christian church, therefore, there was a concern for the physical needs of people and a sense that the haves would share their possessions with the have-nots. As Garrison points out, this attitude comes from the Jewish worldview rather than the Greco-Roman worldview.[11]

It is not as if no problems developed in this sharing of possessions. Ananias and Sapphira sold some property and decided to keep a part of the proceeds for themselves while pretending to give the entire amount to the apostles. For this deceit they were severely judged (Acts 5:1 – 11). In Acts 6 we read that grumbling arose on the part of the Hellenistic Jews against the Hebraic Jews because their widows were being neglected in daily "service" (διακονία).[12] To solve this problem, the twelve apostles gathered together their large community of followers and commissioned

---

11. Garrison, *Redemptive Almsgiving*, 46–55. See later in this chapter for more on the OT background to concern for the poor. A recent dissertation on this important area is Fiona Jane Robertson Gregson's, *Everything in Common: The Theology of the Sharing of Possessions in Community in the New Testament with Particular Reference to Jesus and His Disciples, the Earliest Christians, and Paul* (PhD diss., Middlesex University, 2014). This resource arrived too late to be incorporated throughout *Paul and Money*. Fiona discusses the early church in Acts 2–6 on pp. 53–88, the Antioch community and its collection for Judea on pp. 89–107, the issues of Corinth and sharing at the Lord's Supper on pp. 108–52, the collection for Jerusalem on pp. 153–202, and the problems in Thessalonica on pp. 203-41.

12. The word διακονία will become important later on when Paul talks about his collection. While it was not a technical word in the Greek language for distribution of food to the needy (the more usual word in the LXX and NT is ἐλεημοσύνη ("almsgiving"; see, e.g., Matt 6:2–4; Acts 3:2–3, 10; 10:2, 4, 31, trans. in NIV as "give to the needy"; see discussion later in this chapter), διακονία is a term that eventually came to be used for that practice. It is the word group from which the English word "deacon" is derived.

them to choose seven men "known to be full of the Spirit and wisdom" and to appoint them "to this need-based ministry" (ἐπὶ τῆς χρείας ταύτης).

A short time later, however, after the preaching and martyrdom of Stephen (who was one of those seven chosen), the Christian community in Jerusalem began to suffer persecution (primarily instigated by Saul/Paul), and many of the believers moved away from the holy city to live elsewhere in Judea and in Samaria (cf. Acts 1:8); they spread the story of Jesus wherever they went (8:1–4). But "Luke does not address the question of what happened to the impoverished believers of the Jerusalem church, especially the widows from a diaspora background."[13] He does, however, note that the apostles remained in Jerusalem, though he does not report any further persecution against them until the death of James the son of Zebedee and the imprisonment of Peter in Acts 12.[14] He records too that some time later, Peter moved to Joppa on the Mediterranean coast (10:5–6).

After Saul/Paul was converted in Acts 9, however, it is clear that believers ("disciples," μαθηταί) were back in Jerusalem, because after Paul left Damascus, he came to Jerusalem and "tried to join the disciples" there. They were (understandably) afraid, but Barnabas (who apparently was also back in Jerusalem) took Paul to the apostles and vouched for the genuineness of his conversion (9:26–27). Paul then began to move about freely in Jerusalem, speaking boldly in the name of the Lord (9:28). He concentrated on preaching to the Hellenistic Jews, but they tried to kill him, so the Christian brothers took him to Caesarea and sent him off to his hometown, Tarsus in Cilicia (9:29–30). This was followed up by a time of peace for the church "throughout all Judea, Galilee, and Samaria," and the Christian movement began to grow even more.

Persecution started up again during the time of Herod Agrippa I, who killed James the son of Zebedee and imprisoned Peter in Jerusalem (Acts 12:1–4), with the intent of killing him. By this time, it appears, James the brother of Jesus was the key leader in the church at Jerusalem (cf. 12:17). It seems that Peter had left Jerusalem permanently for Joppa or elsewhere in Judea, and after his miraculous release from prison, "he traveled to

---

13. Schnabel, *Acts*, 393.

14. John B. Polhill argues that not only did the apostles remain in Jerusalem but also "their fellow Aramaic-speaking Christians," since they "remained faithful to the Jewish institutions" and thus "were likely able to remain in Jerusalem unmolested" (*Acts* [NAC; Nashville: Broadman, 1992], 211).

another place" (ἐπορεύθη εἰς ἕτερον τόπον, 12:17). From hints elsewhere in the NT, Peter probably left to do mission work outside of Judea and Galilee, perhaps limiting his ministry primarily among Jews (Gal 2:8, 11 – 14; 1 Cor 9:5; cf. 1 Pet 1:1).

As a summary of the church of Jerusalem, we can conclude from the record in Acts that it experienced periods of peace alternating with periods of turmoil and persecution. There does seem to have been a significant amount of negative feeling against the church there (as well as, perhaps, in Judea as a whole), especially on the part of the Jewish leadership. While there may not have always been outright persecution, any poor among these believers likely would not have been regular recipients of alms given for the poor in the temple; it was up to the believers in Jesus as the Messiah to care for them. This may have been one factor, at least, that left perpetual need for basic life necessities for the believers in Jerusalem, especially if there was a food shortage (as happened periodically in the ancient world).[15] One wonders, too, as some scholars have speculated, if the selling of property for the initial immediate needs of the new Christian community formed after Pentecost later meant that there was little money left to purchase food when Jesus did not return as quickly as they might have anticipated.

THE FAMINE PREDICTED BY AGABUS AND THE RESPONSE FROM ANTIOCH
THE PROPHECY OF AGABUS

This is a book about Paul and money, and the previous section said little about Paul and even less about Paul and money. We must now explore a historical incident that happened after Paul left for Tarsus and about ten years prior to the collection, namely, the time when Paul and Barnabas took money from the church in Antioch to Jerusalem in response to the prophecy of Agabus that predicted a worldwide famine.

This incident is recorded in Acts 11:27 – 30. It appears as if in the early 40s, Christian disciples from Cyprus and Cyrene traveled to Antioch

---

15. See Peter Garnsey (*Famine and Food Supply in the Greco-Roman World: Response to Risk and Crises* [Cambridge: Cambridge University Press, 1988], 6) who argues that while true famines were rare in the ancient world, "subsistence crises falling short of famine were common."

in Syria (a city located about four hundred miles north of Jerusalem).
Presumably these travelers were diaspora Jews who had become believers
in Jesus as the Messiah and who had either family members or business
interests in Antioch. Antioch was a major city, with an estimated population of about a quarter million, including 25,000 Jews.[16] These believers
proclaimed the good news about Jesus that he is Lord (εὐαγγελιζόμενοι
τὸν κύριον Ἰησοῦν); not only did more Jews in Antioch become believers,
but also a great number of Greeks/Gentiles (Ἑλληνιστάς; 11:20–21). In
other words, "in Antioch we meet the first church that is made up of
Jewish and Gentile believers together."[17]

Word of this new development reached the church leaders in Jerusalem,
and they sent Barnabas to investigate what was going on, probably because
he himself was from Cyprus and undoubtedly knew some of these people.
Barnabas was excited to see how "the grace of God" had worked in
the hearts not only of Jews but also of Gentiles, and he encouraged all
the believers in Antioch to remain firm in their faith (Acts 11:22–23).
Moreover, Barnabas's ministry there led to further conversions (11:24) —
so much so that he knew he needed help to consolidate the ministry and
do further outreach in Antioch. So he traveled to Tarsus, where Saul was
located, and asked him to come to Antioch (11:25–26).

> Paul had proclaimed the gospel in Damascus (9:20–22, 27), in Arabia/
> Nabatea (9:23; Gal 1:17; 2 Cor 11:32–33), in Jerusalem (9:28–29), and in
> the region of Syria and Cilicia (Gal 1:21–24). Thus Barnabas recruited Saul
> for the pastoral ministry and the evangelistic outreach in Antioch because
> he was a trained theologian (a student of Gamaliel) and an experienced
> missionary (for about six years) who could reach out to Jews and Greeks.[18]

A short time later a group of prophets came from Jerusalem to Antioch,
one of whom was Agabus. This man stood up and predicted that a famine would soon occur "over the entire inhabited world" (ἐφ' ὅλην τὴν
οἰκουμένην, Acts 11:28). Luke adds the notation that this famine happened during the time of Emperor Claudius (most likely AD 45–47).[19]

---

16. Schnabel, *Acts*, 520.

17. Peterson, *Acts*, 35.

18. Schnabel, *Acts*, 523.

19. Watson, "Paul's Collection," 35, 42 (cf. Acts 11:28); cf. Schnabel, *Acts*, 525; Hans
Conzelmann, *Acts of the Apostles* (Hermeneia; Philadelphia: Fortress, 1987), 90–91; F. F.

Apparently there was a certain amount of wealth among some of the believers in Antioch (a number were probably at the ES4 and ES5 level), so that while they may have been concerned about food for themselves, they were even more concerned about the availability of food at affordable prices for the Christian brothers and sisters in Jerusalem. Thus, under the presumed leadership of Barnabas and Saul, they encouraged believers in Antioch, "according as each one was prosperous" (καθὼς εὐπορεῖτό τις),[20] to donate money that could be given to the Christian community in Judea to pay for higher food prices (11:29). The chosen delegates to deliver the money to Jerusalem were, not surprisingly, Barnabas and Paul (11:30).

OLD TESTAMENT PERSPECTIVE ON ALMSGIVING

What would motivate the believers in Antioch to take up this collection? Naturally, part of the motivation was the practice of the earliest days of the church, in which Barnabas, a landowner, had played a significant role. Equally important, of course, was the OT, which shaped the theology and practices of the Christian community. Deeply rooted in the OT is God's command for his covenant people to show concern for the poor and needy. God had given instructions to the Israelites in the Torah to protect the poor in a variety of ways.[21] According to Deut 15:4, God said through Moses, "There need be no poor people among you." God provided for the poor by allowing them to glean in the fields of land-owning Israelites (Lev 19:10; Deut 24:19–21), and the rich were not to hinder them. Every seventh year creditors were to cancel debts on any loan made to a fellow Israelite (Exod 21:1–11; Deut 15:1–11), and the fiftieth year was the year of Jubilee, which was a year for resetting the financial clock for all God's

---

Bruce, *The Book of Acts* (NICNT; Grand Rapids: Eerdmans, 1954), 243. See especially Bruce W. Winter ("Acts and Food Shortages," in *The Book of Acts in Its Graeco-Roman Setting* [The Book of Acts in Its First Century Setting 2; ed. David W. J. Gill and Conrad Gempf; Grand Rapids: Eerdmans, 1994], 59–78) who discusses significant literary and inscriptional evidence for food shortages in the 40s and early 50s. Winter also sees evidence for these food shortages in the time of Claudius in the phrase διὰ τὴν ἐνεστῶσαν ἀνάγκην ("on account of the present crisis") in 1 Cor 7:26–28. Severe food shortages were almost invariably times of social unrest.

20. See BDAG, 410, s.v. εὐπορέω: "to prosper financially, *have plenty, be well off.*" Note that this is the same principle that Paul uses to encourage his churches to give for his later collection; see 1 Cor 16:2.

21. For a summary of God's instructions in his Torah as they pertained to the poor and needy, see Watson, "Paul's Collection," 56–68.

people (Lev 25:5 – 55). Moreover, some of Israel's prophets took God's people to task for not only neglecting the poor, but for actually exacerbating the plight of the poor by unscrupulous economic practices (see Neh 5:1 – 13; Isa 3:14 – 15; Jer 2:34; 17:11; Amos 2:6 – 8; 4:1 – 3; Mic 2:1 – 2; 3:1 – 3; Zech 7:8 – 11).[22]

Moreover, God commanded that specific tithes (the so-called third-year tithes) were to be designated for the Levites, resident aliens, widows, and orphans, who had no other means to support themselves (Deut 14:27 – 29; 26:12). In addition, special provisions were included in God's law so that widows and orphans and other poor people could participate in the annual feasts (Deut 16:11, 14).

While none of the laws in the Torah or the words of the prophets is invoked in Acts 11, surely the early Jewish Christian believers in Antioch, including Barnabas and Paul as their leaders, were shaped from the history of Israel as depicted in the Hebrew Scriptures to show concern for the poor. The Lord Jesus himself assailed the rich for their exploitation of the poor (Mark 12:41 – 44; Luke 16:13 – 15) and spent a good share of his ministry with the common people who eked out a living from day to day. When they were hungry and Jesus knew they could faint on the walk home if he dismissed them, he fed them miraculously (Mark 6:35 – 42; 8:1 – 8). Particularly Luke records the words and deeds that demonstrated Jesus' profound care for the poor and what he expected from his followers.[23] Let us remember, too, that Luke was a travel companion of Paul (cf. the "we" sections of Acts [Acts 16:10 – 17; 20:5 – 15; 21:1 – 18; 27:1 – 28:16]; Col 4:14; 2 Tim 4:11; Phlm 24)[24] and undoubtedly was influenced in his views of Jewish and Christian attitudes to the poor by his association with Paul.

---

22. For an explanation of the data in the Prophets and the Writings about concern for the poor as well as Israel's failure to live up to God's expectations, along with comments on the Apocrypha, see ibid., 68 – 87.

23. Watson, "Paul's Collection," 101 – 4. See particularly Watson's introductory comment on Luke: "Luke, with ten references to the poor and their care, refers more to our subject than any of the gospel writers" (101). Note too that almost every introduction to the gospel of Luke will cite the passages unique to Luke that focus on Jesus' concern for the poor (see esp. Darrell L. Bock, *A Theology of Luke's Gospel and Acts* [Grand Rapids: Zondervan, 2011], 352 – 58). See also Longenecker, *Remember the Poor,* 108 – 31.

24. Note that in Acts 11:28, the Western text (D) places Luke in Antioch at this time by the introduction of a "we" text; see Bruce, *Acts,* 243: "Although the Western reading is probably not part of the original text, it does reflect knowledge of the tradition which has been preserved independently in the anti-Marcionate prologue to the third Gospel (c. A.D. 170), that Luke was a native of Syrian Antioch."

ALMSGIVING IN FIRST-CENTURY JUDAISM

We could give additional evidence of Jewish concern for the poor by show-ing evidence from Qumran and Philo and Josephus,[25] but such evidence is only marginally relevant as an influence on Barnabas and Saul/Paul. More relevant, especially for Paul, could be the writings of the rabbis, for Paul himself had been trained as a Pharisee under the famous rabbi Gamaliel the Elder (cf. Acts 22:3) and was thus "thoroughly trained in the law of our ancestors" (NIV). Paul himself admits his rigorous life as a Pharisee when he writes about himself in Gal 1:14 about how much progress he was making "in Judaism beyond many others my own age [ὑπὲρ πολλοὺς συνηλικιώτας] and was extremely zealous [περισσοτέρως ζηλωτής] for the traditions of my fathers" before the Lord stopped him from his violent ways on the road to Damascus. Moreover, in Phil 3:5 the apostle, in writ-ing about his heritage prior to his conversion, calls himself "a Hebrew of Hebrews, according to the law, a Pharisee."

However, it is admittedly difficult to know precisely what the rab-bis believed and practiced during the era in which the NT was written. The thoughts and opinions of the rabbis were not written down until the Mishnah in about AD 200, and in the two Talmuds in AD 500–600. As Watson admits, "The longer a concept was discussed, the greater the pos-sibility that it may become removed from the original meaning in scripture and the more likely to be affected by interaction and/or confrontation with any other culture present on a daily, or at least regular basis."[26] In other words, to cite from the Talmudic tractates Pea'h or Sheqalim and import their rabbinical sayings back into Paul's life as a Pharisee is somewhat risky.[27]

There are, however, evidences from the Gospels themselves, written in the first century, of how the strictest of the Pharisees lived—precisely during the time in which Paul was in his prime as a Pharisee. Consider, for example, the parable of the Pharisee and the tax collector in Luke 18:9–14. While Jesus told this parable to show that the humble tax

---

25. Watson, "Paul's Collection," discusses the evidence from Qumran on pp. 90–95 (they formed an economic association not unlike the earliest Christian community; Watson relies most heavily on the doctoral research of Catherine M. Murphy, published as *Wealth in the Dead Sea Scrolls and in the Qumran Community* [Leiden: Brill, 2001]); Watson discusses Philo and Josephus on pp. 108–13.

26. Watson, "Paul's Collection," 113.

27. See Garrison (*Redemptive Almsgiving*, 56–59) for a scholarly attempt to highlight the sayings and practices of the earliest rabbis on the issue of almsgiving.

collector is the one who went home "justified" (δεδικαιωμένος), what he says about the Pharisee has some relevance here: "I fast twice a week; I give a tenth of all that I get" (18:12). Jesus' judgments on the Pharisees in Matt 23:23 likewise testify to the care with which they kept the OT laws about tithing. Presumably, then, Paul the Pharisee was scrupulous about the laws about tithing, including the third-year tithe designated for the poor.

Jesus similarly criticizes the Pharisees in Luke 11:39–44. In 11:42, he refers to their scrupulous tithing, but then follows that comment up with "you neglect justice and love for God." One cannot fail to hear Jesus pointing out the hypocrisy of the Pharisees because though their goal was to be scrupulously concerned about the poor, they ended up falling under the indictment of the prophets (as noted above) about injustice and even taking advantage of the poor. Note Luke 20:46–47, where Jesus insists that the teachers of the law claim to be especially worthy of respect but they have no problem devouring widows' houses. If Paul as a Pharisee and teacher of the law were in this audience, he would have felt the sting of this indictment. The Pharisees (including Paul) knew what the law taught, though they did not necessarily follow through on its true ramifications — love for God and for one's neighbor as oneself.[28]

It is clear from these examples, of course, that Jesus links the Pharisees with the hypocrites. In his Sermon on the Mount, Jesus has harsh words for "hypocrites," particularly in Matt 6:1–18 (earlier in 5:19–20, he specifically refers to such people as "the Pharisees and the teachers of the law"). In his first example (6:1–4), Jesus tells his disciples that "whenever" they give to the needy (note that the word used is ὅταν ["whenever"], not ἐάν ["if ever"]), they should not do so with great fanfare but "in secret." A clear implication here is that giving alms is something any good Pharisee (including Saul, "in regard to the law, a Pharisee," Phil 3:5) or any teacher of the law would do (only with trumpet blasts).

Finally, in Acts 3 we have the story of the man born crippled who was begging at the temple gate. It would appear that this man's only source of food was to receive "alms from those going into the temple" (ἐλεημοσύνην

---

28. Cf. also the parable of the Good Samaritan, 10:25–37, through which Jesus taught the twofold love command and emphasized the need for showing the importance of concern for the unfortunate and even offering to pay for their care. Admittedly, this parable specifically refers to the priests and Levites, not the Pharisees, but it does show Jesus' commendation of how an occasional non-Jew could and in fact did show mercy to people in desperate need.

παρὰ τῶν εἰσπορευομένων εἰς τὸ ἱερόν). The word ἐλεημοσύνη designated charitable giving for the poor, and any law-abiding Jewish person of some means entering the temple was expected to give "silver or gold" (3:6) to such people. Certainly any Pharisees entering the temple, whether from a heart of compassion or even from an attitude of condescension, would have done that. Giving alms was one of the main responsibilities before God of any God-fearing Jew (note too the commendation that the God-fearing Gentile Cornelius received for his ἐλεημοσύνη, 10:2, 4, 31).[29]

It is appropriate to conclude, therefore, that Paul, who had grown up as a Jew and a Pharisee, was thoroughly ingrained in the responsibility, derived from the Hebrew Scriptures and their subsequent traditions, that Israel's God, who was also the Father of our Lord Jesus Christ, would want his covenant people to show concern for the poor. This thinking did not change when Paul became a believer in Jesus, for this particular message of the Hebrew Scriptures was not abrogated by the coming of Jesus (note the words of James, the brother of Jesus, in Jas 2:14–16). While the motivation for keeping these principles of concern for the poor may have been modified to include obedience to and love for the Lord Jesus Christ (as expressed later in 2 Cor 8:9), this part of the law still stood as part of the moral code for followers of Jesus.

Consequently, when Agabus stood and prophesied that there would be a global famine soon, and since Barnabas and Paul knew fully well what God would want them to do, they organized a collection fund to bring to Jerusalem and to give to the believers there to help them during that time. As noted above, this would fall in line with what Barnabas had done earlier when he sold a piece of property to help take care of the needs of the early Christian community. Moreover, we concur with the assessment of Watson regarding the later fund-raising venture of Paul: "The collection itself is but one example, albeit an unusually large one, of the historically persistent Jewish concern for the poor."[30]

---

29. See the discussion of the history of the word ἐλεημοσύνη in the Jewish world in Garrison, *Redemptive Almsgiving*, 52–55.

30. Watson, "Paul's Collection," 12. Note that concern for the poor, as stressed in the NT, became thoroughly engrained as part of the Christian way of life. In the second and third centuries, even the Roman emperors and other prominent Romans took notice of what Christians were doing in terms of giving aid to the poor, in contrast to the rest of the Greco-Roman world (see Longenecker, *Remember the Poor*, 60–67). Note, for example, this summary from Longenecker: "These ancient evaluations are significant in noting a general lack of concern

Paul's Ongoing Concern for the Poor

The smaller collection in Acts 11 and the larger collection that consumed Paul's energy during his third missionary journey are two indisputable projects that demonstrate Paul's concern for the poor. But is his concern limited only to these two projects? Or is there evidence in Paul's life and letters of an ongoing concern for the poor?

While scholars have pointed out many parallels between the ministry of Jesus and Paul, Jesus' clearly expressed concern for the poor is not one of those parallels usually addressed. As Longenecker points out, "rarely have the economically vulnerable, who took pride of place in Jesus' ministry, been used as a point of comparison between Jesus and Paul."[31] Longenecker then takes up the challenge of exploring evidence in Paul that the apostle expected people in the churches he established to have an ongoing concern for the poor. It is important to summarize Longenecker's arguments in order to show that the two fund-raising projects for the poor in Jerusalem were not anomalies but rather part of a regular pattern of teaching in his churches.[32]

First, among Paul's instructions to the Corinthians in 2 Cor 8 and 9 about the Jerusalem collection, the apostle points out (9:13) that as part of their "obedience to [their] confession in the gospel of Christ" (ἐπὶ τῇ ὑποταγῇ τῆς ὁμολογίας ὑμῶν εἰς τὸ εὐαγγέλιον τοῦ Χριστοῦ), the Corinthians are to manifest their generosity to the Jerusalem group "and to all" (καὶ εἰς πάντας). In other words, Paul did not see the collection for Jerusalem as an "isolated event" but as one example "of a general practice of generosity that was to characterize the on-going corporate life of Jesus-groups 'for all' of the needy."[33]

Moreover, in Gal 6:9–10, Paul exhorts the Galatians to "do good to all

---

for the poor *apart from Judeo-Christian strands in the ancient world*" (63, italics added). For example, as late as the fourth century, Emperor Julian (in Letter 22 in LCL edition; see http://en.wikisource.org/wiki/Letters_of_Julian/Letter_22), sometimes called Julian the Apostate, tried to shame his political appointees into imitating the Jews and Christians into giving aid to the poor; "for it is disgraceful that, when no Jew ever has to beg, and the impious Galilaeans [Christians] support not only their own poor but ours as well, all men see that our people lack aid from us."

31. Longenecker, *Remember the Poor*, 136.

32. See ibid., 141–56, for the complete discussion. There is no doubt that by the time of the Prison Letters (e.g., Eph 4:28) and the Pastoral Letters (e.g., 1 Tim 5:3–16; 6:18) at least some of Paul's communities had established practices of concern for those in need.

33. Ibid., 141.

people" (ἐργαζώμεθα τὸ ἀγαθὸν πρὸς πάντας); note here again the word πάντας. The expression "to do good," Longenecker argues, surely includes "charitable works for the needy and poor."[34]

A third example is 1 Thess 5:14, where Paul includes in his closing instructions to the believers in Thessalonica that they should "help the weak" (ἀντέχεσθε τῶν ἀσθενῶν). The word ἀσθενής can have a variety of nuances. For example, this is the term Paul uses for "the weak in faith" in 1 Cor 8:7, 9–10. But as BDAG points out, there is a standard use of ἀσθενής, evident in the papyri, for the economically weak, the poor.[35] In fact, Paul uses the corresponding verb (ἀσθενέω) as an adjectival participle in his farewell speech in Acts 20:35 to encourage the Ephesian believers to "help those who are weak" (the context of vv. 33–34 is economic—of Paul supplying his own needs and those of his companions).[36]

Finally, we can point to Rom 12:13, where in a list of rapid-fire exhortations of what love is all about, Paul encourages the believers in Jesus in Rome to share what they have "for the needs of the saints" (ταῖς χρείαις τῶν ἁγίων).[37]

34. Ibid., 142. Longenecker is quoting Ben Witherington III, *Grace in Galatians: A Commentary on the Letter to the Galatians* (Edinburgh: T&T Clark, 1998), 434. He goes on to cite similar comments from Winter (*Seek the Welfare of the City*, 11–40) and N. T. Wright (*Paul for Everyone: Galatians and Thessalonians* [London: SPCK, 2002], 79) about the specific meaning of the expression, "to do the good" as including financial contributions. See also N. T. Wright's linking of Gal 6:10 with Jeremiah's statement in Jer 29:7 to "seek the welfare of the city" (cf. again Winter's book) in *Paul*, 380, n. 107. We should note here that this is virtually identical to the language used in patronage inscriptions. Gal 6:10 used the verb ἐργάζομαι whereas patronage inscriptions use the verb ποιέω. Likewise Paul uses ἐργάζομαι as a synonym for ποιέω, which he had just used in 6:9 (he also varies τὸ … καλόν v. 9 with τὸ ἀγαθόν in v. 10). We can go so far as to suggest, therefore, that what Paul commands in 6:9–10 is a Christianized form of patronage as an ongoing pattern of behavior for believers.

35. BDAG, 143, ἀσθενής (meaning 2c). Cf. also Longenecker, *Remember the Poor*, 143, n 23, 151 (on Acts 20:35).

36. Note here BDAG, 142, s.v. ἀσθενέω, meaning 3, "to experience lack of material necessities, *to be in need*."

37. See Longenecker, *Remember the Poor*, 144–45. For more on this verse as well as on verses in the Prison and Pastoral Letters, see chs. 11 and 12. An additional issue beyond the scope of this book is whether Paul would have envisioned the church to help the poor and needy in society at large (e.g., any in society at the ES7 level). While some of the texts discussed above place no limits on Christian charity (cf. the use of "all"), "in general, it is most likely that care for the poor was primarily practiced intra-communally within Jesus-groups. In view of the huge number of destitute and poor within the ancient urban context, and the relatively limited resources of Jesus-groups, it would be foolhardy to imagine much other than an intra-communal practice of extending support in limited supply to a few within a community" (ibid., 291; see the entire section 284–94).

Furthermore, we could delve into Paul's message to the wealthier members of Corinth in the way they conducted the Agape Feast that preceded the Lord's Supper, and how they marginalized the poorer members of the believing community (1 Cor 11:17–34). We will discuss this deplorable situation in greater detail in ch. 10. Suffice it to say here that Paul would tolerate no discrimination against the poor and needy or allow them to go hungry while more prominent members of the Corinthian community were being well fed and even getting drunk.

Finally, it is interesting too that a century after the time of Paul, legends were being developed that show Paul as someone who distributed to the needs of the poor.

> One "rich woman named Queen Tryphaena" (sec. 27) is said to have given up "much clothing and gold so that she could leave many things to Paul for the service of the poor" (sec. 41)…. It is notable … that Paul could be depicted a century or so after his death as one through whom the resources of the rich could reliably be channeled to the poor in an effort to offset their need.[38]

We can reasonably conclude, therefore, that the two collections that Paul helped manage for the poor in Jerusalem are evidence of an ongoing concern on his part for the poor and needy. This is one part of Paul's life as a loyal Jew that he did not abandon when he became a believer. Rather, like Jesus himself, he incorporated concern for the poor into his paradigm for church behavior. We have no evidence, of course, that Paul encouraged each believing community to develop a "benevolent fund"; but he did expect each community to address benevolent needs as they encountered them, especially among the family of believers (Gal 6:10).

GALATIANS 2:10

This brings us, then, to Gal 2:10, one of the most important verses that must be discussed in the issue of Paul and money. This verse comes in the context of a meeting between Paul and the "pillars of the church" — James (the brother of Jesus), Cephas (Peter), and John (son of Zebedee) — in

---

38. Longenecker, *Remember the Poor*, 153. The parts in quotation marks are taken from the apocryphal *Acts of Paul and Thecla*. For this document, see http://scriptural-truth.com/PDF_Apocrypha/The%20Acts%20of%20Paul%20and%20Thecla.pdf.

Jerusalem. The specific issue was whether Gentile believers had to be circumcised, though Paul phrased the central issue this way: "the gospel that I [Paul] preach among the Gentiles" (2:2). Paul wanted to get the blessing of these church leaders that his gospel message for the Gentiles was correct. According to Gal 2, he was successful: James, Peter, and John "added nothing" to Paul's message (2:6). They agreed that Paul could continue his ministry among the Gentiles as he had been doing, while the other three would preach the gospel "to the circumcised" (2:9). But then Paul reports one other phrase that came out of that meeting: μόνον τῶν πτωχῶν ἵνα μνημονεύωμεν, ὃ καὶ ἐσπούδασα αὐτὸ τοῦτο ποιῆσαι, "only that we should remember the poor, which selfsame thing I made effort to do" (2:10). The key issue in this text revolves around the verb ἐσπούδασα.[39]

Ἐσπούδασα IN GALATIANS 2:10

First, we should recognize that beginning in the nineteenth century and throughout the twentieth century, a virtual consensus had developed that this text referred to a mandate given to Paul by the Jerusalem leaders that he should take up a collection for the impoverished believers in Jerusalem. That is, "the term 'the poor' identifies members of the Jesus-movement *in Jerusalem*, either collectively or in part."[40] It is time for scholars, following the exegesis of David Downs and Bruce Longenecker, to end this stranglehold on NT interpretation.[41]

---

39. See also David J. Downs, *The Offering of the Gentiles: Paul's Collection for Jerusalem in Its Chronological, Cultural, and Cultic Contexts* (WUNT 2.248; Tübingen: Mohr Siebeck, 2008), 36, for a slightly different review of aorist tense in ἐσπούδασα from what is offered here.

40. Longenecker, *Remembering the Poor*, 158 (italics in original). Longenecker goes on to demonstrate how unusual this interpretation is in the history of interpretation, because it is without precedent in the early church and did not surface as an option for Gal 2:10 until the late fourth century with Ephrem, Jerome, and Chrysostom (159–82): "'the poor' of Gal 2:10 was ubiquitously interpreted throughout the earliest centuries without geographical specificity" (181, i.e., without assigning the term to Jerusalem). See also Downs (*The Offering of the Gentiles*, 33–34, n. 9) for a long list of scholars "who connect the request in Gal 2:10 with the beginnings of Paul's collection."

41. Downs writes (*The Offering for the Gentiles*, 27) that almost all older studies of the collection work "with the assumption that the project originated in the request of the Jerusalem leadership that Paul and Barnabas, as delegates of the Antioch church, 'remember the poor,' an appeal which is reported by Paul in Gal 2:10." To be honest, the view of Gal 2:10 presented in the rest of this chapter represents a change in thinking from what I (VV) advocated in *Paul's Style of Church Leadership*, 311–14.

Lexically, ἐσπούδασα is an easy verb to parse: first person singular aorist indicative active of σπουδάζω. The verb is intransitive and means either "to *hurry, hasten*" or "to be especially conscientious in discharging an obligation, *be zealous/eager, take pains, make every effort.*"[42] What does Paul imply about himself by this use of the aorist? A review of the uses of the aorist indicative suggests three possibilites.[43] The first is the *constantive* or *punctiliar aorist.* This use of the aorist indicative is the most basic one and records some event in the past, regardless of how long that event may have lasted.[44] Paul, then, would be describing some event in the past in which he demonstrated his eagerness and effort to help out the poor. This could easily refer to the event of Acts 11:27–30, which we have just discussed, when he and Barnabas took the gift for the Christian believers in Jerusalem during the time of the famine predicted by Agabus.

A second option would be the *gnomic aorist.* This use of an aorist describes a generic principle, but without any reference to a specific occasion.[45] If this were Paul's intention with the aorist, it would mean that being concerned for the poor was something that was part of Paul's person and lifestyle without pointing to any specific incident. The phrase in question would be translated something like, "which selfsame thing I have always been eager to do." The apostle would then be describing his life first as a Pharisee, which included regularly giving alms for the poor, but including also his ongoing concern for the poor (cf. the earlier discussion in this chapter on Acts 11:27–30).

The final option would be an *inceptive aorist.* This use of the aorist indicative stresses "the beginning of an action or the entrance into a state."[46] This sort of aorist is particularly common with stative verbs, and σπουδάζω can easily be translated as the state of eagerness that began when the three pillars of the church asked that Paul remember the poor. If this were the nuance to the aorist tense used here, it could be seen as

---

42. BDAG, 939, s.v. σπουδάζω.

43. We are using the categories of the aorist as outlined in Wallace, *Greek Grammar Beyond the Basics,* 554–65. For the punctiliar view, see 557–58.

44. This use would emphasize the verbal aspect of the aorist, which looks at a situation as a whole rather than at a specific moment. See Constantine R. Campbell, *Basics of Verbal Aspect in Biblical Greek* (Grand Rapids: Zondervan, 2008), esp. 19–45.

45. See Wallace (*Greek Grammar Beyond the Basics,* 562) for an explanation of the gnomic aorist.

46. Ibid., 558.

Paul being asked or even mandated to take up a collection for the poor in Jerusalem; as a result, when James, Peter, and John made this request, the idea suddenly energized Paul to the idea of developing a collection among his churches. An inceptive aorist stresses the beginning of the project, but it says nothing about when Paul may have executed this "remembering of the poor" or how long it took to execute this plan.

ANALYSIS AND INTERPRETATION OF GALATIANS 2:10

It is our opinion that the third option is the least likely of the three, though as noted above, this is the most common interpretation of this verse. In the next chapter we will see that one of the standard explanations of the collection is that it was an obligation put on Paul by the mother church in Jerusalem as their right. Keith Nickle goes so far as to call the collection an analogy to the temple tax that Jews all over the world were required to pay annually.[47] First, there is no hint anywhere in Gal 2:10 — and it certainly was not the way in which Paul conducted the collection — that collecting money for the poor in Jerusalem was to be an annual event (Paul's collection certainly took at least three years from the time he began the collection to its delivery in Jerusalem), nor was there a specific amount assessed to each member of the Pauline communities as a tax. In fact, as we will see, Paul emphasizes over and over the voluntary nature of what each person gives.

Moreover, the timing does not work out. There is much scholarly debate on when exactly the book of Galatians was written,[48] though most agree it was one of Paul's earliest letters. Two dates are most frequently adopted. One option is that it was written just after the first missionary journey of Paul but before the Council in Jerusalem reported in Acts 15; Paul's visit to the pillars of the church in Jerusalem recorded in Gal 2:1 – 10 would then likely correspond with the Acts 11 visit. The other option is that Galatians was written some time during the second missionary journey of Paul. If that second option were chosen, then the most likely meeting between

---

47. For the scholarly sources of this view, see the section "A Form of Tax Assessed by the Mother Church in Jerusalem" in ch. 5.

48. We will not argue for any one particular view here of this issue, for the most common views are irrelevant to the point being made here. See the introduction to almost any commentary on Galatians for the arguments on the various views.

Paul and the pillars of the church in Jerusalem would have coincided with the Jerusalem Council in Acts 15.[49]

Let's now suppose, for the sake of argument, the later date, that Galatians was written during Paul's second missionary journey. The inceptive use of the aorist would then suggest that in Gal 2:10, when Paul met with James, Peter, and John, he developed a sudden, great eagerness and enthusiasm to take a collection for the poor in Jerusalem, similar to what he and Barnabas had done earlier (Acts 11:27–30). But that would mean that during his entire second missionary journey he apparently does nothing about acting on that enthusiasm—at least, there is no hint anywhere in Acts or in Paul's letters that after he left Corinth in Acts 18:18, he brought money from his churches to Jerusalem when he "went up [from Caesarea] and greeted the church [in Jerusalem] and then went down to Antioch" (18:22). It would seem odd for a man as dynamic as Paul to wait from three to five years to *begin* to take a collection if he was supposedly fulfilling a mandate or even a suggestion from the pillars of the church in Jerusalem, one that corresponded to his own eagerness.[50] Or if, perchance, he was soliciting funds during his second and third missionary journeys, it took him up to *eight* years before he finally brought that gift to Jerusalem. That, to us, seems an unlikely scenario.[51]

Either of the two other interpretations of the aorist in Gal 2:10 are possibilities. Certainly in Paul's life as a Pharisee, as we outlined above, he would have regularly given alms for the poor, so that the aorist verb ἐσπούδασα could be a gnomic aorist.[52] This would have continued as an

---

49. The chief argument against this view is that according to the record of Acts, the event of Acts 11:27–30 was Paul's second visit to Jerusalem after becoming a Christian (cf. 9:26–30 for his first visit), and Paul implies in Galatians that the visit in Gal 2:1–10 is his second visit. But it seems to us that the key factor in Gal 1–2 is not how often Paul visited *Jerusalem as such*, but how often he visited *Cephas (Peter)* in Jerusalem (in this section he is recording his interactions with Peter). There is no record in Acts 11 that Barnabas and Paul saw Peter on this visit.

50. Note the observations of Ernest Haenchen (*The Acts of the Apostles: A Commentary* [trans. R. McL. Wilson; Philadelphia: Westminster, 1971], 548): on Paul's second missionary journey, Paul did go to Jerusalem (Acts 18:22). "The visit to Jerusalem involved the greatest danger for Paul. He had no great collection to deliver, as is the case in Chapter 21."

51. For further discussion on the inceptive options, see Longenecker, *Remembering the Poor*, 191–93.

52. Admittedly, to take ἐσπούδασα as a gnomic aorist would account most easily for the first person singular here, that throughout Paul's whole life, first as a Pharisee and then as a Christian, he had a passion for remembering the poor. Note Ernest De Witt Burton

important aspect in his ministry as a Christian "church planter," as we have noted earlier in this chapter.[53] Our personal preference, though, is for the first option, the constantive or punctiliar aorist. Paul is recalling a time in which he had already demonstrated an eagerness and a personal effort to take up an offering for the poor, which took place during the Acts 11:27–30 event.[54] Indeed, if the visit in Gal 2:1–10 alludes to the Acts 11:27–30 visit, he had in the not-too-distant past acted on his eagerness to take up a collection for the poor.

Moreover, the grammar of Gal 2:6–10 is rather complex and difficult to sort out. This is all one sentence in Greek (English translations, of course, break it into several smaller sentences). The subject of that sentence is James, Cephas, and John (phrased as οἱ δοκοῦντες [εἶναί τι], "those who seemed to be something," 2:6, and repeated as οἱ δοκοῦντες στῦλοι εἶναι, "those who seemed to be pillars," 2:9a). There are two main actions ascribed to these three men in third person aorist plural verbs: "they added nothing [οὐδὲν προσανέθεντο] to me" (2:6c, a summary of 2:1–5), and "they gave right hands of fellowship [δεξιὰς ἔδωκαν κοινωνίας] to me and Barnabas" (2:9b).[55] These two verbs, joined by the contrasting conjunction ἀλλά, are followed up in 2:9c–10 with two substantival ἵνα clauses,[56] both of which give the content of the conversation that accompanied that handshake: "that we [i.e., Paul and Barnabas] should go to the Gentiles, and they to the circumcised [i.e., the Jews]," and "that we should continue

---

(*A Criticial and Exegetical Commentary on the Epistle to the Galatians* [ICC; Edinburgh: T&T Clark, 1921], 100), "Against the supposition that the reference [Gal 2:10] is to an effort in which Paul and Barnabas had jointly taken (cf. Acts 11:30) is the singular number of ἐσπούδασα."

53. While not citing a specific grammatical category, Longenecker seems to opt for the gnomic aorist (*Remembering the Poor*, 194–99). In his next chapter (207–19), he argues that according to Paul, care for the poor rather than circumcision is the key feature that "would unite Jewish and gentile communities of Jesus-followers" (209) into a single body of Christ.

54. The use of the first person singular in ἐσπούδασα is in keeping with the entire tone of the passage, where Paul is giving his personal testimony (from 1:12–2:14) and only occasionally uses the plural to include Barnabas.

55. See the outlined structure of this sentence in Thomas R. Schreiner, *Galatians* (ZECNT; Grand Rapids: Zondervan, 2010), 116–17.

56. For the substantival ἵνα clause, see Wallace, *Greek Grammar Beyond the Basics*, 474–75. Wallace includes the use of the ἵνα clause in v. 10 as an example of an imperatival ἵνα (p. 477); see also Schreiner, *Galatians*, 131. However, there is no hint anywhere in vv. 6–10 that the three pillars are laying down a command; after all, what they said was done with a handshake of fellowship (δεξιὰς ... κοινωνίας), an agreement among equals.

to remember the poor."[57] In fact, if this second main verb of the sentence (ἔδωκαν) indeed suggests a mild form of indirect discourse,[58] as we have been suggesting, then the aorist indicative in ἐσπούδασα can be pushed back to a time that preceded the handshake: "only that we continue to remember the poor, which selfsame thing I had put forth effort to do."[59]

CONCLUSION ON GALATIANS 2:10

If we are correct in our conclusion that ἐσπούδασα is a constantive or punctiliar aorist, then Gal 2:10 almost certainly refers not to a future event or to a mandated project. The pillars of the church suggested through their handshake that both Paul and Barnabas (note the first person plural in μνημονεύωμεν, which includes Barnabas) continue to remember the poor. Paul could theoretically have followed this up in the second substantival ἵνα clause with a first person plural ἐσπουδάσαμεν, for both he and Barnabas had readily participated in the collection of Acts 11. It seems that while Paul is willing to admit that the suggestion from James, Peter, and John came to both him and Barnabas that they continue to remember the poor, he chooses not to speak for Barnabas but just for himself about his ongoing eagerness to remember the poor.[60]

In any case, Gal 2:10 does not seem to us to speak about the genesis of the collection that consumed Paul during his third missionary

---

57. Note the present tense of μνημονεύωμεν, which suggests that Paul and Barnabas continue an activity that had long been a part of their lives, not that they start a new one.

58. Most translations acknowledge that in some form, this is indirect discourse, but then a verb needs to be supplied to make smooth English. The verb that is inserted to introduce this indirect speech can prejudice interpretation. Most translations supply "asked," which may sound generic but can be read as a mild command (NIV, NRSV, ESV, NASB [the NASB put it in italics, to indicate that is an interpretive addition]). NET has "requested." The RSV has "they only would have us," which is similar to "asked" or "requested," though perhaps less direct. We personally like the NLT: "Their only suggestion was...."

59. On the use of tenses in indirect discourse and their translation into English, see Wallace, *Greek Grammar Beyond the Basics*, 456–58. Downs also suggests that the ἐσπούδασα may relate some past point in time (*The Offering of the Gentiles*, 35). Note the NIV 2011 here: "the very thing I had been eager to do all along."

60. A number of scholars have accounted for the switch from the "we" in μνημονεύωμεν to the "I" in ἐσπούδασα by noting that by the time Paul wrote Galatians, he and Barnabas had separated; see, e.g., Hans Dieter Betz (*Galatians* [Hermeneia; Philadelphia: Fortress, 1979], 102): "In the meantime, between the Jerusalem Conference and the writing of Galatians, Paul and Barnabas have separated, and this may account for Paul's changing from the first person plural to the first person singular."

journey. Especially if the Jerusalem Council came shortly after the letter of Galatians was written, Paul would not have needed to do something to help bridge the growing gap between what we might call Jewish Christianity and Gentile Christianity (see more on this in ch. 5). After all, an agreement had been made, written by James and signed by him and the other leaders in Jerusalem, that the major dividing issue had been resolved. The most we can surmise is that when Paul returned to Jerusalem after his second missionary journey, he discovered that the issue of Gentile Christianity (where circumcision was not required) versus Jewish Christianity (where it was required) had in fact not yet been settled; if anything, things had become more tense on this issue (note his later reservation expressed in Rom 15:30–31). As a result, Paul was bound and determined by the grace of God in him, in part by remembering the poor, that he would develop a monetary project that would at least demonstrate to the mother church in Jerusalem that the Gentile Christians still honored them as the mother church.

We conclude, therefore, that at whatever time the conference reported in Gal 2:1–10 took place, Paul had already been involved in projects for the poor—first as a Pharisee, and then as a leader of the Jesus movement in Antioch and elsewhere. As he established churches in Asia Minor and later in Macedonia and Achaia and he encountered poverty, he was indeed eager to help the poor out (if in no other way, by working for a living and not being a burden to them), and he encouraged his churches to do the same. This is what the Lord Jesus would expect of him, for this is what Jesus himself did when he was on earth. And when he visited Jerusalem after his second missionary journey and (so we can assume) realized the plight of impoverished believers in Jesus there, and when he also realized that the gulf between Jewish Christians and Gentile Christians was growing wider rather than narrower, he determined to develop something that would make a statement on both concerns—the collection. It is to that major monetary project in the life of the apostle Paul that we now turn.[61]

---

61. As we hope to demonstrate in the next chapter, while concern for the poor clearly played an important role in the collection, the chief instigating factor was an attempt by the apostle Paul to heal the growing rift in the church.

CHAPTER 5

PAUL'S COLLECTION FOR THE JERUSALEM CHURCH

AS WE HAVE ALREADY INDICATED, ONE OF THE MOST IMPORTANT EVENTS to discuss in a book on Paul and money is "the collection." This was a fund-raising effort that took place among his churches during his third missionary journey, with the proceeds intended "for the poor among the saints in Jerusalem" (εἰς τοὺς πτωχοὺς τῶν ἁγίων τῶν ἐν Ἰερουσαλήμ, Rom 15:26). While scholars have debated what in Paul's thinking motivated him to undertake this project, about one thing there seems to be little doubt, Paul gathered a significant amount of money from churches in Macedonia, Achaia, and probably Galatia, and perhaps also Asia Minor, which he intended to deliver to Jerusalem for the relief of poverty-stricken believers in Jesus as the Messiah (Rom 15:25–28; 1 Cor 16:1–2; cf. Acts 20:4).[1] In ch. 6 we will examine how Paul managed the fund-raising and how this project intersects with his leadership patterns particularly in

---

1. In 1 Cor 16:1, Paul indicates that he sought to raise money for this project from the churches in Galatia. Both Rom 15:26 and the Corinthian correspondence demonstrate that Paul gathered funds from the churches in Macedonia and Achaia. What about Asia Minor (i.e., Ephesus and environs, where he was located during much of his third missionary journey)? Did Paul also solicit donations from those churches? There is no direct evidence in Romans (where we might expect Asia to be added to Macedonia and Achaia), and Paul's pattern of not soliciting money from churches for his own living expenses where he was currently located (see part 1) may suggest he did not raise money in Asia Minor (though there is no way in which he could have refrained from saying anything about the project; moreover, as we saw in ch. 3, Paul was willing to ask for money from his churches for causes that did not benefit him personally). However, the fact that representatives from Asia accompanied Paul to Jerusalem when he delivered the collection (see Acts 20:3; cf. also 21:27–29) suggests

Corinth; in ch. 7 we will examine the specific arguments he used to motivate believers in Corinth to give (esp. in 2 Cor 8 and 9); and in ch. 8 we will probe the final stages of the collection and its delivery to Jerusalem. The present chapter will examine the collection in a more general way, as we seek to understand what this fund-raising venture meant to Paul and why it appears to be so important to him.

We begin our four chapters on the study of the collection, then, with a survey of the various views scholars have proposed as to why Paul was so intent on collecting money for the impoverished believers in Jerusalem. Why did he do it? What did it mean to him? We could construct this study in two different ways. One is chronological in terms of what scholars have said about the collection. That is, we could analyze, in chronological order, what key scholars have written about the collection, emphasizing particularly how they have viewed Paul's motivation for gathering money for Jerusalem. The second is thematic. That is, we could analyze the various theories that have been proposed about the purpose(s) of the collection and designate which scholars accepted or rejected each proposal. We will take the second approach. But let us say upfront that it is simplistic to limit each scholar to only one purpose, for most of them acknowledge that Paul probably had more than one motivation in mind when he solicited money from his churches for the church in Jerusalem.

Obviously any scholar who writes a commentary on 1 and/or 2 Corinthians will have to say something about the collection; after all, 1 Cor 16:1–4 mention the collection, and two entire chapters in 2 Corinthians (chs. 8 and 9) deal extensively with this topic. Moreover, anyone who writes a history of the apostle Paul will have to mention the collection, for it was beyond doubt an important part of his life and ministry on his third missionary journey. But until relatively recently, there were only two full-length studies that focused on the collection, both written in the 1960s:

---

that the churches there also had a vested interest in the project (for more on this, see ch. 8). David Downs, by contrast, concludes that the Ephesians did not participate, perhaps because persecution in Ephesus did not allow Paul to stay long enough, or because the collection was intended to be primarily from Gentiles and the Ephesian church may have been predominantly Jewish (*The Offering of the Gentiles*, 55–58). We would argue that if Paul did not strongly encourage such giving in Ephesus, it may have been the result of a spill-over of the unhealthy dynamics about money in Corinth making him extra cautious in Asia. Or perhaps his rapid exit from Ephesus under dangerous circumstances (cf. 2 Cor 1:3–11) did not allow for carrying whatever funds had been collected there.

Dieter Georgi's *Die Geschichte der Kollekte des Paulus für Jerusalem* and Keith Nickle's *The Collection: A Study of Paul's Strategy*.[2] Since the later 1980s, however, several other significant studies have been written (many of them dissertations) that focused on the collection.[3] It is these special studies that will be the primary focus of our analysis in this chapter.

THE COLLECTION AS CHARITY

One proposed purpose of the collection is that it roots out of Paul's desire as a Christian leader to assist the poor with food and other physical needs. Virtually everyone who writes on the collection acknowledges that this is a key motivating factor for the apostle. After all, as we discussed in ch. 4, this pattern of activity goes back to the earliest practices of the primitive church in Jerusalem, and even much earlier insofar as concern for the poor and caring for their needs were imbedded in the words of the OT. Moreover, several years later, when Agabus came to Antioch and predicted a famine over the entire inhabited Roman world (Acts 11:28), the believers in Antioch collected money to provide help for their brothers and sisters in Judea (11:29), and they sent that money to Jerusalem by Barnabas and Saul (again, see ch. 4).

Consequently, Paul's "fellowship-gift [κοινωνία] for the poor [εἰς τοὺς πτωχοὺς] among the saints in Jerusalem" (Rom 15:26) almost certainly taps into this history of God's expressed concern for the poor and his people's response to his will. This motivation may not be the whole answer to what drove Paul during his third missionary journey, but it played a significant role. Paul's "use of the noun διακονία and the verb διακονέω

---

2. Dieter Georgi, *Die Geschichte der Kollekte des Paulus für Jerusalem* (Hamburg: Herbert Reich, 1965), published in the 1990s as *Remembering the Poor: A History of Paul's Collection for Jerusalem* (Nashville: Abingdon, 1992); Keith Nickle, *The Collection: A Study of Paul's Strategy* (Naperville, IL: Allenson, 1966).

3. Verbrugge, *Paul's Style of Church Leadership*; Hans Dieter Betz, *2 Corinthians 8 and 9: A Commentary on Two Administrative Letters of the Apostle Paul* (Hermeneia: Philadelphia: Fortress, 1985); Kieran J. O'Mahoney, *Pauline Persuasion: A Sounding in 2 Corinthians 8 and 9* (JSNTSup 199; Sheffield: Sheffield Academic, 2000); Stephen Joubert, *Paul as Benefactor: Reciprocity, Strategy, and Theological Reflection in Paul's Collection* (WUNT 2/124; Tübingen: Mohr Siebeck, 2000); Chang, "Fund-Raising in Corinth"; Gary W. Griffith, "Abounding in Generosity: A Study of *Charis* in 2 Corinthians 8-9" (PhD diss.; University of Durham, 2005); Watson, "Paul's Collection"; Downs, *The Offering of the Gentiles*.

(Rom 15:25, 31) ... suggests the notion of relief for those truly in need."[4] The fact too that this gift came from Gentiles was a significant part of this project. "Taking the proceeds of gentile generosity right to the heart of Jerusalem itself would speak volumes about the transformation of gentile followers of Jesus — precisely since generosity was the very thing that gentiles were generally not known for (or at least not credited with)."[5]

It is also important to point out here the assessment of Downs concerning the nature of the poverty esperienced by the Jerusalem church community, namely, that Paul's gift for the church in Jerusalem was probably not intended to meet a food crisis but rather to give aid for a chronic food shortage:

> We should not overstate the severity of the financial crisis facing the Jerusalem church, for the very fact that Paul seems to have taken a number of years to coordinate the delivery of a relief fund among the churches of his mission suggests that the situation in Jerusalem may not have been ... dire.... Paul's instructions about the delivery of the relief fund lack the urgency that one would expect, if the gift were intended to stave off the imminent threat of starvation among a segment of the Jewish-Christian community in Jerusalem. There is reason to believe, in fact, that the Pauline collection for Jerusalem was a one-time caritative project.[6]

A FORM OF TAX ASSESSED BY THE MOTHER CHURCH IN JERUSALEM

A number of scholars have sought to argue that the collection was an obligation placed on Paul by the church in Jerusalem. The seminal article that lies behind this proposal is an article written by Karl Holl in 1921.[7] Since Paul's collection was intended for Jerusalem, Holl argued from the language Paul used that two words occurring in Rom 15:26 (οἱ πτωχοί and οἱ ἅγιοι) are

---

4. See Verbrugge (*Paul's Style of Church Leadership*, 309) for comments on this word group. See also Nickle, *The Collection*, 106–9. Note the significant discussion of this motivation for the collection in Downs (*The Offering of the Gentiles*, 19–26) under the topic, "The Collection as Material Relief."

5. Longenecker, *Remember the Poor*, 314; see comments in ch. 4.

6. Downs, *The Offering of the Gentiles*, 25.

7. Karl Holl, "Der Kirchenbegreiff des Paulus in seinem Verhältnis zu dem der Urgemeinde," 1921 article reprinted in *Gesammelte Aufsätze zuer Kirchengeschichte* (Tübingen: Mohr [Siebeck], 1928), 2:44–67.

technical designations of the church in Jerusalem, not of people in need. The poverty Paul referred to was not physical poverty but a religious poverty, similar to the "poor in spirit" in Matt 5:3. Because of the importance of Jerusalem as the mother church of all the churches in the Greco-Roman empire, they have a right to expect money as "a certain right of taxation."[8]

Holl himself did not relate this "right of taxation" to the Jewish temple tax that Jews were not only permitted by the Romans to send annually to Jerusalem, but were even obligated to pay; this was a central thesis of Keith Nickle's book on the collection. He concluded, both from the way Paul administered the collection and from the view of church unity apparent in Romans 15, that the idea of the temple tax lies clearly in the background. But this view does not do justice to the language Paul uses. As we will see in ch. 7, one of the key words that Paul uses over and over to describe the collection and to motivate the Corinthians to give is χάρις, which denotes something freely given—from God to us in Christ, and from the Corinthians to the believers in Jerusalem. Moreover, as Downs points out, the temple tax was an annual event to help pay for the sacrifices in Jerusalem, whereas Paul's collection was a one-time event that took place over a number of years, and Paul encouraged the members of his churches to donate voluntarily in keeping with their income (1 Cor 16:1–2; 2 Cor 9:6–7) rather than for each person to give a specific amount.[9]

The only possible hint that there is an "obligation" theme involved in giving "for the poor among the saints in Jerusalem" is the use of ὀφειλέται and ὀφείλουσιν in Rom 15:27. The verb ὀφείλω could be used in the NT for the idea of owing someone something—perhaps money, but especially a moral or religious duty (cf., e.g., Rom 13:8; 15:1; Heb. 5:3).[10] Thus, when Paul uses this word in Rom 15:27 in connection with the collection (it is significant, though, that he never uses this word in his instructions *to the*

---

8. Ibid., esp. 2:58–62. Note that the phrase οἱ πτωχοί also occurs in Gal 2:10, which many scholars have taken as an allusion to the collection (most notably Georgi, *Remembering the Poor*, 34). See ch. 4 for more on this proposal.

9. Downs, *The Offering of the Gentiles*, 10. Note N. T. Wright, *Paul*, 1507, n 84: "The 'Collection' was not a Christian version of the Jewish 'temple tax,' or a levy imposed by the 'mother church.'... It owes much more to the needs of 'the poor' (cf. Gal 2:10). However, Paul cannot have been ignorant of the ironic overtones of the plan he was now implementing."

10. See BDAG, 743, s.v. ὀφείλω: the meaning 1 is "to be indebted to someone in a financial sense, *owe someth. to someone*," and meaning 2 is "to be under obligation to meet certain social or moral expectations, *owe*."

Corinthians on the collection),[11] he is suggesting that in his mind, there is a certain obligation in connection with this project.

But in Rom 15:27 Paul clarifies what that "ought" is. Indirectly, Paul is reminding the believers in Rome that salvation in Christ, which the Gentiles have received, could only have originated through the Jewish Christians in Jerusalem; that is, the Gentiles would not be enjoying redemption in Christ if it had not been for what Messiah Jesus had done and for the message of his cross that went out through the apostles from Jerusalem to the ends of the earth (Acts 1:8). In this way, and in this way only, Gentiles Christians are indebted to the mother church in Jerusalem; "even though Paul sought independence from Jerusalem (see Gal 1:11 – 2:10), he still recognized the central place that that church and its leaders had in the history of salvation."[12] Thus, Paul could acknowledge a debt of the Gentiles in connection with the collection, but it was not intended as a (re-)payment to the Jewish Christians for Gentile salvation. If anything, it was a thank-you gift for a grace freely given (cf. the note earlier in the section about χάρις), not a payment that was to be listed on some ledger somewhere, thus discharging that debt.[13]

ESCHATOLOGICAL PURPOSE

A long-standing and significant interpretation of the collection is the view championed by Johannes Munck in the late 1950s.[14] It is hard to

---

11. See Verbrugge (*Paul's Style of Church Leadership*, ch. 6) where it is strongly argued that if we want to see what the collection really meant to Paul, we need to go to the book of Romans.

12. Ibid., 316.

13. Downs (*The Offering of the Gentiles*, 12 – 14) also discusses and critiques the thesis of Joubert in *Paul as Benefactor*, who sees the collection from the standpoint of Gal 2:1 – 10: the pillars of the church recognized Paul's law-free gospel as a benefaction, and in turn Paul and Barnabas were to remember the poor. Since we have discussed the meaning of Gal 2:10 in the previous chapter, we will not analyze this thesis in depth here. As noted there, Paul may be indicating in that verse that he had always been eager to help the poor; or perhaps it is an allusion to his earlier demonstration of concern for the poor when he and Barnabas together managed the collection for Jerusalem from Antioch (Acts 11:27 – 30). Moreover, as pointed out in ch. 3, the pattern of patron – client relationships is difficult to apply to God's relationship with his people; instead, we need to talk about a father and his children. Note too the warning of MacGillivray "Re-examining Patronage and Reciprocity," that we must be careful not to adopt uncritically the patron – client relationship in the Greco-Roman (and especially Roman) world to the study of the NT.

14. Johannes Munck, *Paul and the Salvation of Mankind* (trans. Frank Clarke; London: SCM, 1959), 299 – 308.

underestimate the profound impact that Munck has had on the last half-century of interpreting the meaning of the collection.[15]

That basic premise for this interpretation starts with Rom 9–11, where Paul expresses his pain and frustration over the fact that many Jews were not coming to a confession of Jesus as the promised Messiah.[16] The apostle was willing to be accursed by God and cut off from his people if only it would result in the salvation of the Jews (Rom 9:3). Paul insisted, however, that God's will for his people cannot be thwarted. The Gentiles are now accepting the gospel of salvation. When the Jews see that the blessings that used to be bestowed on them are now being bestowed on the Gentiles, it will make the Jews envious, and they will want those blessings for themselves (11:11–12, 25). In this way, says Paul, "all Israel will be saved" (11:26).

So how does the collection fit into this? Munck points out that Paul will soon be on the way to Jerusalem, and along with him will be an entourage of Gentiles, who will be carrying the collection (1 Cor 16:3–4; 2 Cor 8:16–23; see also Acts 20:4). Their gift for the believers in Jerusalem will be living proof of what God has been doing among the Gentiles, and that will fulfill the prophecies (particularly in Isaiah) of Gentiles bringing the wealth of the nations to Jerusalem (Isa 56:6–8; 60:1–9; cf. Hag 2:7–8; Zech 14:14). The scholars who adopt this interpretation of the collection also suggest that behind Paul's request for the Romans to pray for him as he goes to Jerusalem in Rom 15:30–31 is a fear that the collection might not accomplish its purpose to provoke the Jews to jealousy.

There are two significant problems with this understanding of the collection. The first is that it requires that the genitive in ἡ προσφορὰ τῶν ἐθνῶν (Rom 15:16) be taken as an objective genitive (that the Gentiles themselves are the offering being made to God). A significant number of scholars, influenced by Munck, have adopted this interpretation. But that is a lot to hang on the slipperiness of an objective genitive versus a subjective genitive (or perhaps a genitive of apposition).[17]

---

15. Munck's view of what Paul intended by the collection can be found in Nickle's *The Collection* and Georgi's *Remembering the Poor*, as well as in many commentaries written and publish since the 1950s. See a sample listing of scholars who have been influenced by this interpretation in Downs (*The Offering of the Gentiles*, 6 n. 18).

16. The analysis and critique of this understanding of the collection follows the line taken in Verbrugge, *Paul's Style of Church Leadership*, 323–27.

17. While some genitives are clearly subjective and some clearly objective, many can be read either way; see Wallace, *Greek Grammar beyond the Basics*, 112–21. We admit, of course, that

The second problem is the total lack of the prophetic pilgrimage texts in Romans and 1 and 2 Corinthians (the only three books in the NT that deal directly with the collection) — most notably in Rom 15:25 – 32.[18] Surely there should be some hint that Paul sees himself as leading an eschatological group of Gentiles to Jerusalem in order to provoke the parousia, and that he therefore asks for prayers that this mission will succeed. Instead, Paul's only prayer request is that he will be rescued from unbelieving Jews in Jerusalem and that the Christian believers in Jerusalem will graciously accept the gift that is being given for the needs of "the poor among the saints" in Jerusalem.

Norman Peterson sought to answer this objection by looking at the rhetorical structure of Rom 15:16 – 32.[19] He sees the key verse as 15:16, where Paul describes his task as "a minister [λειτουργός] of Christ Jesus to the Gentiles ... so that the offering of the Gentiles [ἡ προσφορὰ τῶν ἐθνῶν] might be acceptable to God." "Rhetorically, v 16a is expanded in vv 17 – 24, v 16b in vv 25 – 27. Thus [Peterson] is able to maintain that the προσφορά of the Gentiles is directly related to the collection."[20] That is, Paul's service is to preach to the Gentiles, and the Gentiles service is to bring material gifts to Jerusalem. This interpretation requires that τῶν ἐθνῶν in 15:16 be understood as a subjective genitive ("an offering that the Gentiles make"). As with the previous interpretation, that is a lot to hang on a subjective genitive. It is perhaps for this reason that Dan Wallace has identified and discusses a plenary genitive, i.e., a genitive that is both subjective and objective.[21]

---

in Phil 2:15 – 17 (cf. 1 Thess 2:19 – 20) Paul clearly identifies the Gentiles as his offering to God (i.e., objective genitive or genitive of apposition). But Paul gives no hint in Rom 15 that he will be accompanied by a gathering of Gentiles (cf. Acts 20:1 – 30) when he heads to Jerusalem. As we will soon point out, this is Paul's project, and while the collection is from the Gentiles, the role of Gentiles in helping to bring the collection to Jerusalem plays no role in Rom 15.

18. Cf. Wright, *Paul*, 1203: "It is striking that Paul makes virtually no use of [the pilgrimage of the nations to Zion] tradition, no doubt because he sees the whole Zion tradition itself radically redrawn around the Messiah." Moreover, in n. 569, Wright notes, in agreement with Cranfield and Best: "Paul cannot have been ignorant of the many other lands to the east, north and south which remained unevangelized."

19. Norman Peterson, *Rediscovering Paul: Philemon and the Sociology of Paul's Narrative World* (Phildelphia: Fortress, 1985), 144 – 45.

20. Verbrugge, *Paul's Style of Church Leadership*, 325.

21. Downs bases much of his dissertation on the fact that τῶν ἐθνῶν is a subjective genitive, which indeed it could be — that the collection is an offering that the Gentiles have collected and that Paul will present in Jerusalem to the church there. If we have to choose between the two, the subjective genitive is the better choice, but because of the ambiguity, it may even be better to see it as a plenary genitive and try not to determine Paul's theology from either option.

We should note too that much of Rom 15:23–31 is written in the first person; it would seem unusual to have so much of "I" in this section if Paul's main emphasis in delivering the collection is the role the Gentiles are to play in accompanying him to Jerusalem—that his trip to Jerusalem should be seen as an eschatological journey. About that there is not as much as a hint in Romans. "He essentially places the onus of the delivery [of the collection] squarely on his own shoulders."[22] Moreover, the only fear that Paul expresses overtly in 15:31 relative to the Jews is a fear of persecution from the unbelieving Jews in Jerusalem ("Pray that I may be rescued [ῥυσθῶ] from the disbelievers in Judea"), not a fear that they will fail to appreciate the eschatological significance of the upcoming event. Finally, note too that Paul does not expect the parousia will come through what happens in Jerusalem, for he is busy laying plans for preaching the gospel in Rome and for doing further missionary outreach in Spain (1:13; 15:24, 28).[23]

THE COLLECTION AS AN ACT OF WORSHIP

Of the recent studies of the collection, by far the most thorough and most innovative proposal on the collection is that of David Downs. No further study on Paul's collection can ignore this significant work. We have learned much from Downs's study, *The Offering of the Gentiles*, and it is important to give in summary form how he reads these texts. Let us begin with his conclusion:

> Paul employs a number of cultic metaphors to speak of "the offering of the Gentiles" (Rom 15:16). This clustering of cultic language suggests that Paul's understanding of the collection is governed by a particular structural metaphor, which I have identified as COLLECTION IS WORSHIP. This metaphorical concept structures the way Paul thinks about, experiences, and presents the activity of collecting money for the poor among the saints in Jerusalem. That is, in metaphorically depicting the activity of collecting

---

22. Downs, *The Offering of the Gentiles*, 8 (see ibid., 7–9, for further critique of the eschatological interpretation).

23. Wright too (*Paul*, 1202) reflects on those scholars who have argued that by Paul's "bringing money from gentile churches to help the poor Messiah-community in Jerusalem, this would stir up 'jealousy' among the non-Messiah-believing Jerusalemites." In his estimation, this interpretation seems "somewhat more convoluted than the programme envisaged in [Rom] 11.11–14," though Wright does state that "a connection is not impossible."

money for Jerusalem in terms of cultic practice, Paul frames participation in the relief fund primarily as an act of worship.[24]

As this quote suggests, Downs bases his conclusion on his use of a theory of metaphor, and he carefully explains that theory by using the example of how we talk about the phenomenon of engaging in an argument. Downs shows how many of the phrases we use for arguments have a war theme imbedded in them.[25] With regard to the collection, as noted above, his conclusion is that "COLLECTION IS WORSHIP." Downs reaches this conclusion from the Greek terms that Paul uses to describe the collection, many (though not all) of which can be connected with worship. Here is a list of the concepts and Greek words that he notes:

collection to be given "on the first day of the week"

λογεία, a term used for a collection for a god or a temple

χάρις, collection originates in God's grace

ἐπιτελέω, a term used for the performance of sacred rules

εὐλογία, blessing of God (used in 2 Cor 9:6–10 to mean "generosity")

εὐχαριστία, God as the object of all thanksgiving

ἡ διακονία τῆς λειτουργίας: λειτουργία is used in the LXX for priestly service, and it is also a word that developed as a cultic term in Hellenistic times

ἡ πρόσφορα τῶν ἐθνῶν: πρόσφορα is a term for sacrificial offering[26]

It is particularly this last word that captures Downs's attention, for it shapes the title of his book. As we discussed earlier, most interpreters have viewed τῶν ἐθνῶν in the expression ἡ πρόσφορα τῶν ἐθνῶν as a genitive of apposition or an objective genitive, that the Gentiles themselves are the offering that Paul is offering to God (see the section on "Eschatological Purpose").[27] Downs, however, prefers to see it as a subjective genitive, "the

---

24. Downs, *The Offering of the Gentiles*, 157.

25. Ibid., 121–26. Examples of phrases are "winning an argument" and "demolishing an opponent's arguments." His main source for developing the metaphor theory is George Lakeoff and Mark Johnson, *Metaphors We Live By* (Chicago/London: University of Chicago Press, 1980).

26. See Downs, *The Offering of the Gentiles*, 127–45.

27. See discussion in ibid., 147–49, where Downs cites many scholars who have taken this position.

offering given by the Gentiles." Since this phrase occurs in Rom 15:16, several verses before Paul actually discusses the collection (15:25–32), Downs sees the collection as one facet of this offering.

> There is, therefore, no compelling linguistic reason that with the designation ἡ πρόσφορα τῶν ἐθνῶν Paul cannot be referring to a monetary contribution from his Gentile churches (cf. 15:27), especially if the noun πρόσφορα is taken metaphorically. Moreover, within the same section, the noun ἐθνός occurs in a comparable genitival construction, ὑπακοὴν ἐθνῶν (15:18), and in this latter case the phrase is best understood as a subjective genitive.[28]

As a result, Downs rejects the use of Isa 66:20 as an interpretive framework for Paul's collection and his bringing of the results of that project to Jerusalem. His final conclusion, therefore, is as follows: "In metaphorically depicting the activity of collecting money for Jerusalem in terms of cultic practice, Paul frames participation in the relief fund primarily as an act of worship."[29]

There are many striking observations in Downs's monograph, and he has offered a fresh perspective on the collection. There is little doubt that the cultic metaphor is strongly present. However, it is still appropriate to question whether Paul saw the *purpose* of the collection as a cultic act, or whether he was using the cultic language primarily as a means of *motivating the Corinthians to participate in the collection*. While in 2 Cor 8 and 9 Paul did not command the Corinthians to participate in this project as he had done in 1 Cor 16 (see the next chapter), he is trying to find various means whereby he can gently encourage or motivate them to give. What better way to do this than by suggesting it is an outgrowth of their regular worship of Jesus Christ, their Savior? While the Corinthians are unlikely to give simply because Paul says so, surely they will give because it is a cultic duty to their Lord.

---

28. Ibid., 150.
29. Ibid., 157.

Paul's Personal Attempt to Heal the Growing Rift in the Church

Many scholars have noted that the collection was designed to help foster unity in the church, especially between the two major segments of the church that did not see eye-to-eye on a number of issues — Jewish Christians and Gentile Christians.[30] This understanding of the goal of the collection is primarily derived from Rom 15:26–27:

> For Macedonia and Achaia were pleased to make a contribution for the poor among the saints in Jerusalem. For they were pleased to do so; indeed, they are debtors to them. For insofar as the Gentiles have shared [ἐκοινώνησαν] with them in spiritual blessings, they owe it also to [the believers in Jerusalem] to share [λειτουργῆσαι] in physical blessings.

For a number of reasons, we maintain that this purpose, more than any of the others, stands at the heart of why Paul was so insistent on organizing, promoting, and following through on the collection.[31] Furthermore, there is a good reason why this motivation for the collection surfaces only in the book of Romans.[32]

First, as will be shown in the next chapter, Paul was on a tenuous footing with believers in Corinth during the time between the writing of

---

30. Just to name a few: F. F. Bruce ("Paul and Jerusalem," *TynBul* 19 [1968]: 10) writes that the collection is Paul's "opportunity of strengthening the bonds of fellowship between the Jerusalem church and the Gentile mission." Munck (*Paul and the Salvation of Mankind*, 290) speaks of "an ecumenical aim in the collection among the Gentile Christians for the church in Jerusalem." Bornkamm (*Paul* [trans. D. M. G. Stalker; New York: Harper & Row, 1971], 41), says that "the purpose of the collection was to signal the unity of the church historically founded from Jews and Gentiles, the equal status of its members." Nils Dahl ("Paul and Possessions," in *Studies in Paul* [Minneapolis: Augsburg], 1977) maintains that "the gift of money expresses what is for Paul most important: the unity of Jews and Gentiles in the church of Christ." According to Bengt Holmberg (*Paul and Power: The Structure of Authority in the Primitive Church as Reflected in the Pauline Epistles* [Philadelphia: Fortress, 1978], 38), the collection was a "demonstration of unity between Jews and Gentiles in the church." Finally, Nickle (*The Collection*, 111) asserted that Paul used the collection "to testify to the Jerusalem Christians of the real and full inclusion of Gentile believers into the Body of Christ."

31. Downs (*The Offering of the Gentiles*, 40) writes that "the reasons for this new project are now almost entirely obscured ... and it is wise to exercise caution in speculating on these matters." While speculating always entails dangers, we hope to show that Paul seems clear in Rom 15 as to what the collection meant to him personally and why he organized this significant fund-raising effort.

32. This section draws heavily from ch. 6 of Verbrugge, *Paul's Style of Church Leadership*, 294–307, 318–27.

1 and 2 Corinthians. He had originally planned to leave Ephesus and go to Corinth, then go to Macedonia, and then come back to Corinth (probably to spend the winter); but he changed his mind (2 Cor 1:13–17). This led to a charge against him that he was fickle and undependable. He sought to justify to the Corinthians that this change of plans was not an evidence of fickleness on his part; but the very fact that Paul has to defend himself on such a charge suggests that some in Corinth were indeed charging him with being a yes-and-no man. Paul then goes on to swear with an oath that "I did not come to Corinth as originally planned because I wanted to spare you" (1:23).

There were strong opponents of Paul in Corinth, and they were gaining the confidence of the Corinthians and trying to destroy Paul. The apostle had already had one presumably "painful visit" (ἐν λύπῃ) with the Corinthians (2 Cor 2:1), which seems to have been a brief visit across the Aegean Sea and back again during the time he was in Ephesus, and Paul did not want to have another confrontation like that. He was afraid that he might damage the situation even further by losing control of himself in frustration if he visited Corinth again before he knew whether the Corinthians were once again "in his camp," as it were. In fact, Paul was so agitated about the Corinthian situation that even though God "opened a door" for him to preach the gospel in Troas (2 Cor 2:12–13), he instead ignored the opportunity and left for Macedonia (this is the only time in the NT that we find Paul unable to preach the gospel when there were opportunities God had placed before him).

As we will also note in ch. 6, some of the grief that Paul experienced from his opponents in Corinth actually had to do with the collection. While Paul had the most pure motives for the project he had been devoting himself to, his opponents were charging Paul—and perhaps Titus too—with deceit and trickery (2 Cor 12:16–18). In their way of thinking, Paul, who regularly boasted about refusing to take money from his churches for self-support (see ch. 2), was planning on using the collection as a secret plan to line his pockets with the money for his own personal use (for more on this, see comments in ch. 11).

Furthermore, Paul's pride in not accepting money from this church was viewed by his opponents as a minus, not a plus (cf. 2 Cor 11:7–15, a passage that is dripping with irony). They claimed that Paul's refusal to accept money from the Corinthians portrayed him as an "inferior" servant of Christ to the other apostles, who did apparently accept money for their work (1 Cor 9:3–6). Or perhaps Paul, in contrast to the wandering Sophists, did not think his message was worth much, because these philosophers felt that their message was valuable enough to pass the hat, as it were, whereas Paul had to work for his own living expenses.[33]

Consequently, with all this misunderstanding and even harsh rankling going on in Corinth over money issues, Paul knew he had to tread delicately with the Corinthians on anything connected with money. It is little wonder that he portrayed the collection in 2 Corinthians exclusively as a cultic offering and sought to motivate them to give to the collection as a part of their dedicated worship to the Lord Jesus Christ; in no way did he want to link the collection with his own goals. Moreover, he assured the believers in Corinth that whatever they might give to this cause would not be in his custody but would be with Titus and two other trusted brothers, "chosen by the churches" (2 Cor 8:16–24). In fact, there may even be a hint in 1 Cor 16:3–4 that Paul was already sensing something wrong between him and the Corinthians at that time, because he insisted to the Corinthians that they should be the ones to select people to carry the money to Jerusalem and that he might not even go along.

Now, the believers in Rome, while Paul knew a number of them personally by name (see Rom 16:3–15),[34] did not have a history of monetary issues that was casting an open cloud on the relationship between them and Paul. It is for this reason that we argue that we must restrict ourselves to Rom 15 if we want to understand exactly what the collection meant *to Paul* as well as what he intended to accomplish by it. One of the striking

---

33. David Briones (*Paul's Financial Policy*, esp. 180–218) concludes on the basis of a patronal interpretation "that the Corinthians, with their desire to become patrons over their leaders, exploited the super apostles through their self-interesting and obliging gifts" (189). Paul, however, refused to participate. In his mind, "the Corinthians are being exploited by these perpetrators ... who behave malevolently *over* the church, like a patron over a client" (ibid., italics in original). Briones goes on to state that Paul "did not want dependent clients [whom he could exploit].... He wanted partners in the gospel who recognised God as the supreme giver" (190).

34. We recognize the position of some scholars, based partly on textual issues, that the list of names in Rom 16 is not a part of that letter; rather, it was sent to Ephesus. While we do consider this section to be a part of the autographa on the letter to Romans, if it is not part of Romans, then there is even less connection between Paul and any of the believers in Rome, and he is free to talk about financial issues without hardly anyone knowing about the history of conflict in that particular area.

elements about Rom 15:25–31, as hinted above, is its preponderance of first person singular verbs and pronouns: πορεύομαι in 15:25, ἀπελεύσομαι in 15:28, οἶδα and ἐλεύσομαι in 15:29, παρακαλῶ, μοι, and ὑπὲρ ἐμοῦ in 15:30, ῥυσθῶ and μου in 15:31, and συναναπαύσωμαι in 15:32. In fact, Paul actually calls this fund-raising project "*my* service for Jerusalem" (ἡ διακονία μου ἡ εἰς Ἰερουσαλήμ) in 15:31. It is interesting that when the apostle uses the noun διακονία in 2 Cor 8 and 9, he uses "the service for the saints" (τῆς διακονίας τῆς εἰς τοὺς ἁγίους, 2 Cor 8:4; 9:1), "the service of this ministry" (ἡ διακονία τῆς λειτουργίας ταύτης, 9:12), or simply "this service" (τῆς διακονίας ταύτης, 9:13). He never uses "*my* service"; that is reserved for Romans, where he plays up the fact that the collection is his personal project, and that he has a specific goal in mind.

So, what is that goal? And why does Paul feel so strongly about that goal? The background, as already suggested, appears to be the growing rift between two segments of the church — the same two talked about in Rom 15: the Jewish Christian element and the Gentile Christian element.[35] When controversies erupted, Paul often was one of the central figures in the debate. For example, when key Jewish Christians heard that Paul did not require circumcision for Gentile believers, he and Barnabas were summoned to a council in Jerusalem with the key church leaders there (Acts 15). When Peter reneged his practice of eating with Gentiles because "certain people from James" arrived in Antioch, Paul "stood up against him to his face" (Gal 2:11–14). When Paul got wind of the fact that some Gentile believers in the Galatian churches were seeking circumcision, he wrote: "Christ will not benefit you at all" (5:2), and he became exceptionally harsh in his judgment (esp. 5:12; see similarly Phil 3:2–3).

Moreover, when Paul arrived in Jerusalem after his third missionary journey and reported on his success in bringing many Gentiles to believe in Jesus Christ as Savior and Lord, James and the elders suggested a political move to help placate the many thousands of Jews who had become believers, "all of them zealots of the law" (Acts 21:20) with presumably

---

35. We are not trying to revive the attempt from a couple centuries ago that divided the entire NT into a conflict between Peter and Paul and to read every NT passage through that Hegelian lens. In fact, if we listen carefully to Acts, Paul's letters, and Peter's letters, it seems clear that Peter and Paul respected each other as fellow apostles and got along well together (for the most part). But neither can we deny that there were significant controversies between Jewish Christians and Gentile Christians and their respective viewpoints.

questions about the legitimacy of Paul's gospel. That political move was to undergo a Nazirite vow and pay for the purification rites of four other Jewish believers who had taken a Nazirite vow; doing so would help prove to the Jewish Christians that Paul did not reject the law personally for himself. Rather, the apostle happily complied with that suggestion.[36]

In other words, Paul was deeply concerned about the Jewish-Gentile rift and was willing to do whatever he could in order to heal that wound—except that he would not change his deeply held views that Gentiles did not have to be circumcised and were required to follow all the unique Jewish practices imbedded in the OT law and in the regulations of the Pharisees. At some point in time—and we do not know precisely when—Paul came up with the idea of the collection. Knowing that the Jewish Christian community in the mother church in Jerusalem struggled with perpetual shortages for basic living expenses, Paul reasoned that if he managed to gather a significant amount of cash from among the Gentile believers and brought it to Jerusalem as "an offering from the Gentiles" (ἡ πρόσφορα τῶν ἐθνῶν, Rom 15:16) and as "my service for Jerusalem" (ἡ διακονία μου ἡ εἰς Ἰερουσαλήμ, 15:31), this gift would demonstrate, at least from his end, that the people in his churches considered the Jewish Christians as full brothers and sisters in Christ. How then could the church in Jerusalem not turn their hearts in thanksgiving to God for a sizable gift from fellow church members in the diaspora (2 Cor 9:13–15)? As N. T. Wright so aptly says:

> The "Collection" of money from the gentile churches to take to impoverished Jewish Christians in Jerusalem and Judaea no doubt started as a bright idea, but once it had taken root it deserves to be seen, in worldview terms, at least as an "intention," flowing from the "aim" of Jew/Gentile unity in the Messiah.[37]

---

36. It is for this reason that we reject the view that Longenecker suggests (*Remember the Poor*, 314) for the collection, when he writes that Paul's personal goal in the collection was an almost "in-your-face" proof of "the legitimacy of 'law-free' Jesus-groups." Perhaps some in Jerusalem may have viewed the collection in that way (we will never really know), but as we have argued above, Paul does not bring this gift in a spirit of triumph over against "the circumcision group"; rather, as Rom 15:25–31 demonstrates, his goal is to *heal* the rift, not to make it wider.

37. Wright, *Paul*, 1495. See also 1496: "If the goal of 'reconciliation' thus belongs in Paul's worldview as one of his key *aims*, we may suggest that the Collection, which by the time of 2 Corinthians is a project that Paul and his audience both take for granted, should itself be classified in worldview terms as an *intention*" (italics in original).

But Paul knew that in this life there are no guarantees. He had opponents in the Jewish segment of the church, and he had enemies in the Jerusalem Jewish community. That is why he asks the Romans to pray that when he arrives in Jerusalem, he will be kept safe from unbelievers, and that his gift for the church in Jerusalem will be graciously received by the church leaders and its members (Rom 15:30–31). As we will discuss in ch. 8, we know from Acts 21:37–26:32 what happened to Paul through the instigation of certain diaspora Jews—his unlawful arrest and imprisonment for the next four years. But we do not know much about how the collection was received, and even what hints we do see in Acts are disputed by scholars (for comments on this, see ch. 8).

CONCLUSION

So why did Paul take up the collection for the poor among the saints in Jerusalem? No single answer suffices. Surely the entire OT with its message that God wants his people to be concerned about the poor, as well as Paul's own position that the church should care for the poor, forms the solid basis for his goal to collect money for those in the mother church who were struggling financially. Furthermore, Paul felt so passionate about this project that he sought to motivate the Corinthians to participate by emphasizing that giving money was an essential part of their worship before God. But at the very core of his being, Paul saw the collection as his personal project whereby he was hoping to heal the growing rift in the church between Jewish Christians and Gentile Christians. If through a much-needed monetary gift to the church in Jerusalem the Jewish believers would be convinced that the Gentile believers in Paul's churches saw them as brothers and sisters in Christ, he hoped that the former would reciprocate in their thinking that Gentile Christians are equally and fully within the body of Christ. Paul regularly placed a high priority on church unity (see Eph 4:1–6); this collection was his attempt to foster it in a powerful way.

CHAPTER 6

COMPLICATIONS TO THE COLLECTION IN CORINTH

Since I (VV) wrote my dissertation on Paul's collection, and in particular on how Paul went about the process of fund-raising among the believers in Corinth,[1] the present chapter draws significantly from that dissertation and make the results of it more widely available than has heretofore been the case.

It seems apparent that when Paul decided to take an offering among the Gentile churches he had started "for the poor among the saints in Jerusalem" (Rom 15:26), he felt it would be a rather simple task. He would either tell them directly in person to participate in this fund-raising project, or he would write them a letter with instructions on how to participate.

THE FIRST MESSAGE TO THE CORINTHIANS (1 COR 16:1 – 4)

The first area in which Paul hoped to gather funds for the believers in Jerusalem was Galatia (as reflected in 1 Cor 16:1): ὥσπερ διέταξα ταῖς ἐκκλησίαις τᾶς Γαλατίας ("as I commanded the churches in Galatia"). The verb Paul uses here is διατάσσω, which means "to order."[2] Paul uses this verb five other times in his letters:

---

1. Verbrugge, *Paul's Style of Church Leadership*.
2. BDAG, 237–38, s.v. διατάσσω, meaning 2: "to give (detailed) instructions as to what must be done, *order*."

- 1 Cor 7:17: "Let each person walk in this way, and this is what I command [διατάσσομαι] in all the churches."
- 1 Cor 9:14: "This is also what the Lord commanded [διέταξεν] to those who preach the gospel, to obtain their living by the gospel."
- 1 Cor 11:34: "And about the rest of the matters I will give instructions [διατάξομαι] when I come."
- Gal 3:19: "[The law of God] was commanded [διαταγείς] through angels by the hand of an intermediary."
- Titus 1:5: "This is why I left you in Crete, so that you might put in order the remaining issues and establish elders in each city, as I commanded [διεταξάμην] you."

In two of these occurrences the command comes from the Lord; in the other three the command comes from the apostle Paul—two to believers in his churches, one to the individual Titus. There is a strong authoritarian nuance to this verb:

> According to Moulton and Milligan, words in the family of διατάσσω were used to express a person's instructions in his final will and testament, or as a technical word to introduce an imperial edict or decree. Gerhard Delling relates Paul's use of διατάσσω in 1 Cor 7:17 and 16:1 (along with his seven uses of ἐπιταγή) to his apostolic right to give instructions to his churches.[3]

Paul, therefore, apparently "ordered" or "commanded" the Galatians to participate in this fund-raising effort. Admittedly, we have no actual record of what Paul said to the Galatians or how he communicated it. He could have done so through a letter that is no longer extant, but it seems more likely that Paul gave his instructions to them in person as he passed through Galatia at the start of his third missionary journey (Acts 19:1, following the same route as his second missionary journey, see 15:40–16:6). But whatever he said to them, it was in the nature of διατάσσω. Paul expected them to participate in this project, no questions asked.

Gordon Fee attempts to soften the nature of this command when he

---

3. Verbrugge, *Paul's Style of Church Leadership*, 63; the two sources noted are James H. Moulton and George Milligan, *The Vocabulary of the Greek Testament Illustrated from the Papyri and Other Non-Literary Sources* (Grand Rapids: Eerdmans, 1952), 155; Gerhard Delling, τάσσω, *TDNT*, 8:35–37.

writes concerning διατάσσω: "[this word] can go the range from 'command' to 'arrange.' Here it means 'ordered' in the sense of 'directed' rather than commanded."[4] But it seems to us that the meaning "directed" is just as strong as the meaning "ordered" or "commanded." A director of an event, for example, is the person in charge and expects people to do as he says. Anthony Thiselton is more on target when he writes: "διατάσσω entails unavoidable inferences about apostolic authority."[5]

Having established with the Corinthians that he had ordered the Galatians to participate in this project, Paul now writes to the Corinthians: οὕτως καὶ ὑμεῖς ποιήσατε ("in the same manner you yourselves do"). Paul uses the emphatic pronoun ὑμεῖς, and he offers no motivation for them to participate in this fund-raising project except for (presumably) his authority as an apostle, as the one who established the church in Corinth. And Paul follows this up with a third person imperative (τιθέτω, "set [something] aside"), directed to "each one of you by yourself" (ἕκαστος ὑμῶν παρ᾽ ἑαυτοῦ) to lay aside money.[6]

I need to say a word about a third person imperative. We do not have a third person imperative in English, and beginning Greek students are trained to translate this construction with "let him/her [verb]." This may give the impression that a third person imperative is more optional in the mind of the speaker than a second person imperative — "let him give," "allow her to give," "it might be a good idea to give." We need to adjust our thinking in this regard, for a third person imperative often has the same imperatival thrust as a second person imperative,[7] with the nuance (using the present context in 1 Cor 16:1): "each person should set some money aside," or even, "each person is expected to set some money aside." This τιθέτω is part of Paul's διατάσσω to the Corinthians about the collection.

---

4. Fee, *The First Epistle to the Corinthians*, 812 n. 18.

5. Thiselton, *The First Epistle to the Corinthians*, 1321.

6. It is interesting to ask the question where people were to store this money. Mark Wilson ("Treasures in Clay Jars," http://www.biblicalarchaeology.org/author/markw18/) notes having seen in a museum in Cyprus small clay jars with money spilling out, dating to the Greco-Roman period. (See also the cover of this book for an example.) He relates this to 2 Cor 4:7, how God has put his treasure in earthen vessels.

7. I like to envision the difference between the second and third person imperative in the following manner. While a second person imperative is a command addressed to a person located right in front of you (mentally, if not physically), a third person imperative is a command placed upon a person standing off to the side but who is still within your range of vision.

In my research for my dissertation I came across hundreds of short, pithy letters of instruction that were given by people in authority to those under their charge of what they expected the recipients of the letter to do. The commands, spanning at least six centuries (300 BC to AD 300), almost invariably used second person imperatives. These letters could be from fathers to sons, from husbands to wives, from employers to employees, from political leaders to subjects, and so on.[8] These sorts of letters I identified as "commanding letters,"[9] and I suggested Paul is adopting that style of epistolary writing in 1 Cor 16:1–2. While it is not important to acknowledge that Paul is inserting a well-defined epistolary form or type inside his longer letter of 1 Corinthians,[10] there seems to be little doubt that Paul, in giving two imperatives (along with the word διατάσσω) in 16:1–2, offers no specific reasons or motivations why the Corinthians should participate in the collection, how it might benefit them, or even what it would mean to "the saints." Whether Paul had spoken more on an earlier occasion in person (on his second missionary journey) or expected the person who carried the letter to Corinth to expand on this issue is impossible to say definitively; we have only his direct command to the believers in Corinth to get busy collecting money. What stands behind these two verses is Paul's authority.

That Paul had every reason to consider himself an authority figure among the churches that he started seems clear. This comes out strongest in the book of Galatians, where Paul's authority seems to be under attack. In the first two chapters Paul asserts his divinely appointed position as

---

8. Many of these were papyrus letters, but I also found letters with the same structure in the LXX and in Greek literary writers (see Verbrugge, *Paul's Style of Church Leadership*, 31–53). Just to give one example: P. Lond. 848, a letter from an owner of sheep to a hired caretaker of his flock: Ἰσχυρίων Κούιτι χαίρε[ιν]· δὸς Λάδωνι ὥστε τῇ γύναικι Ἀγαθείνου ἐρίων πόκους πέντε. ἔρρωσαί σε εὔχομαι. "Ischyrion to Kouites, greetings. Give therefore to Ladonis, the wife of Agatheinos, five fleeces of wool. I pray for your health" (pers. trans.).

9. As early as fourth to sixth century AD, Pseudo-Libanius, in a work called *Epistolary Styles*, mentions the ἐπιστολὴ παραγγελματική as a distinct type of letter (see ibid., 27, 53–54, and fn. 10, 60–61; see also Abraham Malherbe, "Ancient Epistolary Theorists," *Ohio Journal of Religious Studies* 5 [1977]: 28–39).

10. Downs (*The Offering of the Gentiles*, 127) writes that "Verbrugge's strategy of isolating 1 Cor 16:1–2 from its present literary context and claiming that these two verses represent the genre of 'commanding letter' is dubious." It is not important to me to insist that these two verses form an epistolary type; what is important is to see that what lies behind these two verses is Paul's authority.

an "apostle" (Gal 1:1),[11] his parity with Peter and the other "pillars" of the church (2:1 – 10), and even his right to stand up to Peter when he was convinced of Peter's "hypocrisy" (2:11 – 14). At the same time, he states forthrightly that the message he has proclaimed is the true gospel and that anyone who deviates from that gospel is under God's curse (1:6 – 9).

Moreover, specifically to the Corinthians, he asserted forthrightly earlier in this letter that he is their father through the gospel, for "he gave birth" (ἐγέννησα) to them (1 Cor 4:14 – 15). This verb illustrates an important metaphor that Paul uses.[12] It is appropriate to read behind Paul's use of γεννάω the Greco-Roman pattern of the *pater familias*. According to Robert N. St. Clair, the father of the Roman family "was the family patriarch (*pater familias*). He owned his family. He could kill them or sell them for he was the sacred priest of the family, the master of their domain."[13] While Paul would never, of course, apply to himself that much power (he was, after all, always under the authority of Christ, 1 Cor 10:21), his consistent use of the "father metaphor" at least suggests that he felt he had the right to tell the churches he had started how they should act and what they should do. This comes to expression in his frequent refrain that those who have come to Christ under his preaching should imitate him (e.g., 1 Cor 4:16; 11:1; cf. Phil 3:17; 4:9; 1 Thess 1:6; 2 Thess 3:7, 9).[14] Children should imitate their father.

In summary, the first direct means we have in Paul's extant writing that he uses in his fund-raising effort for the believers in Jerusalem was simply to order his churches to participate. It seems surprising that in Jouette Bassler's excellent work on asking for money in the NT, in her chapter on "the Great Collection," she completely bypasses the order given

---

11. This "battle" over his authority may be what inspired Paul to choose to strongly assert his apostleship in 1 Cor 9:1 – 2. My personal feeling is that on a number of occasions in his letters, Paul would communicate to Church B some thoughts he had on an issue he was facing in Church A (e.g., Phil 3:2 – 7 may reflect the situation in Galatia rather than a situation in Philippi).

12. Holmberg (*Paul and Power*, 78) argues that Paul uses the metaphor of parenthood (either fatherhood or motherhood) in all his major, uncontested letters except Romans (presumably because the church in Rome was not a church that he had started).

13. Robert N. St. Clair, "Paterfamilias, Rome and Societal Transformations," http://structural-communication.com/Articles/paterfamilias-stclair.html. OT society was also patriarchal, so any Jews in Corinth would likely be in sync with Paul's father metaphor.

14. See Willis P. De Boer, *The Imitation of Paul: An Exegetical Study* (Kampen: Kok, 1962).

in 1 Cor 16:1–2—Paul's first and most direct means of trying to raise money for the collection.[15]

THE SECOND MESSAGE TO THE CORINTHIANS (2 COR 8 – 9)

Apparently Paul's hope of raising money for "the poor among the saints in Jerusalem" as reflected in 1 Cor 16 did not go well, or at least it did not go as Paul had hoped, for the apostle comes back to this issue in 2 Cor 8 and 9. What strikes a person about these two chapters in 2 Corinthians is that whereas there are at best four verses devoted to the collection in 1 Cor 16 (with three clear indications of a command—the διέταξα plus the two imperative verbs), in the thirty-nine verses that deal with the collection in 2 Corinthians, Paul includes *only one imperative* (2 Cor 8:11), and that imperative is set in the context of the phrase οὐ κατ᾽ ἐπιταγὴν λέγω ("I am not speaking in a commanding manner," 8:8). This drastic difference in tone stands out starkly (though few scholars seem to have noticed the contrast). Rather than speaking in a forceful commanding voice as he had done earlier in 1 Cor 16:1–2, Paul constructs in 2 Cor 8–9 a variety of arguments, both theological and moral, in which he attempts to *motivate* the Corinthians to give for this project (see ch. 7 for an exploration of Paul's arguments).

This does not mean that in modern translations of 2 Cor 8 and 9 you will see only one imperative. In fact, translators have often inserted an imperative in 8:7; 8:24; and 9:7. We must discuss these translated imperatives to see if they truly bear an imperative thrust.

2 CORINTHIANS 8:7

Second Corinthians 8:7 reads this way: ἀλλ᾽ ὥσπερ ἐν παντὶ περισσεύετε, πίστει καὶ λόγῳ καὶ γνώσει καὶ πάσῃ σπουδῇ καὶ τῇ ἐξ ἡμῶν ἐν ὑμῖν ἀγάπῃ, ἵνα καὶ ἐν ταύτῃ τῇ χάριτι περισσεύητε ("However, as you abound in everything—in faith and love and knowledge and all zeal, and in love from us to you—in order that you also may abound in this grace"). Obviously as it is translated here, this is a partial sentence; in fact, in the

---

15. See esp. ch. 4 of Jouette M. Bassler, *God and Mammon: Asking for Money in the New Testament* (Nashville: Abingdon, 1991).

Greek, there is no main verb, even though most English translations add one before the ἵνα clause, and often an imperative.[16] What is the nature of the ἵνα clause used here, and what, if anything, should be added to make it a complete sentence?

Many scholars have opted here for a use of the ἵνα clause that functions as an alternate form of the imperative. "Not only do grammars of New Testament Greek discuss the imperatival use of ἵνα, usually referring to this passage as one of the clearest examples, but several articles dealing specifically with this construction in the New Testament have been published."[17] Regarding this grammatical possibility, most scholars agree that the imperatival ἵνα does not occur in Attic Greek and was only starting to be used in the first century in any regular manner; moreover, it was one of the least direct ways for an author to exhort his audience.[18] As to the origin of this grammatical construction, it seems to have begun when a θέλω ("wish") was omitted from a sentence beginning with θέλω ἵνα.[19] In other words, the ἵνα clause as used here expresses more a wish than a command. Margaret Thrall writes, "This would seem consonant with the beginning of the verse, where Paul seems to encourage his readers by expressing his recognition of the spiritual graces he knows them to possess."[20] I suggest the translation for this construction, therefore, "However, as you abound in everything ... our wish is that you may also abound in this gracious work."[21]

---

16. KJV: "see that ye abound"; RSV: "see that you excel"; NIV: "see that you also excel."

17. Verbrugge, *Paul's Style of Church Leadership*," 247; see footnote 10 on pp. 274–75 for a citation of the grammars; footnote 11 (p. 275) cites these articles, both pro and con: "C. J. Cadoux, "The Imperatival Use of ἵνα in the New Testament," *JTS* 42 (1941): 165–73; H. G. Meecham, "The Imperatival Use of ἵνα in the New Testament," *JTS* 43 (1942): 197–80; A. R. George, "The Imperatival Use of ἵνα in the New Testament," *JTS* 45 (1944): 56–60; W. G. Morrice, "The Imperatival ἵνα," *BT* 23 (1972): 326–30. Wallace (*Greek Grammar Beyond the Basics*, 477 [incl. n. 82]) discusses this construction and considers 2 Cor 8:7 as an example.

18. See Verbrugge, *Paul's Style of Church Leadership*, 248–51, for the history of its development.

19. This is acknowledged by Cadoux, "The Imperatival ἵνα," 165; George, "The Imperatival ἵνα," 556–57, and James H. Moulton, *A Grammar of New Testament Greek*, vol. 1, *Prolegomena* (Edinburgh: T&T Clark, 1906), 179.

20. Margaret E. Thrall, *2 Corinthians* (ICC; 2 vols.; Edinburgh: T&T Clark, 2000), 2:529; Thrall adopts my proposal for inserting θέλομεν.

21. Cf. the NRSV here: "Now as you excel in everything—in faith, in speech, in knowledge, in utmost eagerness, and in our love for you—so we want you to excel also in this generous undertaking."

2 CORINTHIANS 8:8, 10

The next two verses for discussion are 2 Cor 8:8 and 10, not because they have a presumed imperative, but because they clearly outline how Paul wants this portion of his letter to be understood. Verse 8 begins: οὐ κατ᾽ ἐπιταγὴν λέγω ("I am not speaking in a commanding manner"). Paul uses ἐπιταγή six other times in his letters. In three of these, it is clearly linked with a genitive (τοῦ) θεοῦ/κυρίου—a "command of God/the Lord" (Rom 16:26; 1 Tim 1:1; Titus 1:3). As to the other three, in Titus 2:15 Paul exhorts Titus to "speak and exhort and rebuke these things with all command"—clearly an emphasis on authoritative speech of Christian doctrine. The last two occurrences are in 1 Cor 7:6 and 25, where Paul contrasts ἐπιταγή with συγγνώμη and γνώμη—precisely the same sort of contrast he is making here (see below). In those two verses Paul is addressing issues for which he does not have a direct command (ἐπιταγή) from the Lord (about abstinence in marriage and about virgins), and so he offers his opinion (γνώμη).[22]

Then, in 2 Cor 8:10, as hinted above, Paul asserts that his message to the Corinthians in this chapter must be seen as γνώμη. This word can mean "purpose, resolve," since it sometimes appears that way in edicts, and it has something of this nuance in the NT in Acts 20:3 and Rev. 17:13, 17. In Paul's writings, however, he uses this word for the notion of advice or opinion (1 Cor 1:10; 7:25, 40; Phlm 14).[23] What Paul is about to say in the next couple of verses of 2 Cor 8, in other words, likely reflects his opinion or advice.

That is, if οὐ κατ᾽ ἐπιταγὴν λέγω tempers the ἵνα clause of 2 Cor 8:7, the γνώμη tempers the rest of v. 10 and v. 11.[24] Paul reminds the Corinthians that about a year earlier they had clearly manifested an eager desire to participate in the collection. It is only natural then, in Paul's

---

22. Note too that ἐπιτάσσω, the verb from the same word group as ἐπιταγή, contains a strong notion of command; it is used most frequently for Jesus' command to evil spirits to come out of a demon-possessed person. The ten occurrences of ἐπιτάσσω are: Mark 1:27; 6:27, 39; 9:25; Luke 4:36; 8:25, 31; 14:22; Acts 23:2; Phlm 8 (where Paul chooses not to give orders to Philemon about Onesimus but appeals on the basis of love instead).

23. See BDAG, 202–3, s.v. γνώμη: "a viewpoint or way of thinking about a matter, *opinion, judgment, way of thinking*." See also R. Bultmann, γινώσκω, *TDNT*, 1:717. The same thing can be said about συγγνώμη as used in 1 Cor 7:6: see BDAG, 950, συγγνώμη, "permission to do something, *concession*...."

24. See Thrall, *2 Corinthians*, 2:535: "The positive γνώμην δίδωμι complements the negative οὐ κατ᾽ ἐπιταγὴν λέγω of v. 8. It is counsel that Paul is giving, not any kind of order."

opinion, that they would want to finish what they had started: νυνὶ δὲ καὶ τὸ ποιῆσαι ἐπιτελέσατε ("and now also complete the doing [of what you have started]"). The verb ἐπιτελέσατε is the only verb in the imperative mood in 2 Cor 8 and 9. In contrast to 1 Cor 16, where Paul had used two imperatives to command the believers in Corinth to do what he had ordered the Galatians to do and to lay aside a certain amount of money regularly, here Paul's imperative is a soft "finish what you have started; I am sure that is what you would want to do; you are not quitters."

2 CORINTHIANS 8:24

The next verse in which scholars have argued for a command in 2 Cor 8 is 8:24. The entire verse reads as follows: τὴν οὖν ἔνδειξιν τῆς ἀγάπης ὑμῶν καὶ ἡμῶν καυχήσεως ὑπὲρ ὑμῶν εἰς αὐτοὺς ἐνδεικνύμενοι εἰς πρόσωπον τῶν ἐκκλησιῶν ("therefore proving the proof of your love and our boasting about you to them in the presence of the churches"). Like 8:7, what stands out again is that there is no finite verb; here there is only a participle and its cognate noun. Some scholars have argued for an imperatival use of the participle here ("Offer the proof of your love ...").[25] The NT does occasionally manifest the imperative use of a group of participles—e.g., in passages such as Rom 12:9–17; Col 3:16–17, 1 Pet 4:8–10—but these sections do not serve as adequate parallels. All of these other passages are general paraenesis, not specific commands for specific situations, such as we find in 2 Cor 8:24. As Daube has pointed out, an imperatival participle seems to be adopted from Aramaic or from later (Tannaitic) Hebrew, where it is limited to general rules and principles.[26] Perhaps the best option available "is to interpret this verse an anacoluthon, with the participle

---

25. Wallace (*Greek Grammar Beyond the Basics*, 650–52) discusses the imperatival participle and admits it is "quite rare." While he lists 2 Cor 8:24, he offers no exegetical discussion about it.

26. David Daube, "Participle and Imperative in I Peter," in *The First Epistle of St. Peter*, by E. J. Selwyn (London: Macmillan, 1947), 467–88. In my dissertation, I argued that this participle might be a remnant participle that modified an ἀσπάσασθε of an original letter ending (*Paul's Style of Church Leadership*, 257–258). This interpretation, of course, is dependent on a particular theory of partition of 2 Corinthians, and it would take us too far afield to introduce that topic here. It is sufficient to mention that as this verse presently stands, the participle bears the marks of an anacoluthon. A participle can take up the nuance of an imperative (cf., e.g., Matt 28:19–20a), but we can only be certain of that nuance if the imperative is directly present in the context.

loosely connected with the ὑμᾶς of v. 22."[27] In any case, if there is any imperative thrust to this verbal form, it is mild and indirect.

2 CORINTHIANS 9:7

One final verse that is often translated with an imperatival thrust is 2 Cor 9:7: ἕκαστος καθὼς προῄρηται τῇ καρδίᾳ, μὴ ἐκ λύπης ἢ ἐξ ἀνάγκης, ἱλαρὸν γὰρ δότην ἀγαπᾷ ὁ θεός ("each one as he has purposed in the heart, not out of sorrow or out of necessity, for God loves a cheerful giver"). Once again, two elements stand out. First, note that most standard translations here insert a sort of third person imperative, or at least offer a sense of personal obligation:

- KJV: "Every man according as he purposeth in his heart, so let him give: not grudgingly, or of necessity, for God loveth a cheerful giver."
- NASB: "Each one *must do* just as he has purposed in his heart, not grudgingly or under compulsion, for God loves a cheerful giver."
- NRSV: "Each of you must give as you have made up your mind, not reluctantly or under compulsion, for God loves a cheerful giver."
- NIV: "Each of you should give what you have decided in your heart to give, not reluctantly or under compulsion, for God loves a cheerful giver."

Second, it is important to point out that there is simply no verb "to give" here in any form; it simply isn't there. Now, of course, verbs in Greek can often be inferred from the context. But since the last imperative verb occurs in 2 Cor 8:11, we can hardly infer an imperative here. If we are going to connect the verse at all to the context (9:6), perhaps we can phrase it this way: "Sowing is what each one does from his own heart, not out of sorrow or out of necessity, for God loves a cheerful giver."[28]

---

27. This is Daube's preference ("Participle and Imperative," 461). He is followed in this by C. K. Barrett (*A Commentary on the Second Epistle of Paul to the Corinthians* [HNTC; New York: Harper and Row, 1973], 231). Note the assessment of A. T. Robertson, *A Grammar of the Greek New Testament in the Light of Historical Research* (New York: Hodder & Stoughton, 1919), 1133: "The participle in itself is never imperative or indicative, though ... because of ellipsis or anacoluthon, the participle carries on the work of either the indicative or the imperative."

28. This follows the suggestion of Betz, *2 Corinthians 8 and 9*, 83. He maintains that Paul is merely stating a common aphorism of antiquity, that true giving is a matter of the heart.

Surely we must reject the suggestion of Plummer, who maintains that "the omission [of an imperative here] makes the sentence more forceful."[29] There is nothing more forceful than a simple imperative, and by this time in our study of 2 Cor 8 and 9 we must conclude that Paul avoids, as much as possible, the direct imperative form of a verb for alternate methods of motivating the Corinthians to give; he tones down any sense of command or obligation for the Corinthians to participate in the collection. What a change from 1 Cor 16:1–2!

THE SITUATION IN CORINTH AND PAUL'S OPPONENTS

So, what happened? Why did Paul switch from such a direct, obligatory form of fund-raising (a note of command issuing from him as an apostle in 1 Cor 16:1–2) to a more hortatory form, in which he attempts to motivate the believers in Corinth to participate in his fund-raising effort? We need to examine some of the clues in 2 Corinthians of what was going on in that community of believers.

As noted above, the very fact that Paul felt free to command the Corinthians in 1 Cor 16:1–2 to participate in the collection suggests that by and large he felt confident that they viewed him as their church leader, as their spiritual father. He had little reason to doubt that they were ready to rally behind his call to participate in the collection, even though in 1 Cor 16 he did not explain to the believers in Corinth what this project was all about.[30] But something drastic happened between 1 and 2 Corinthians that destroyed that confidence; he knew deep within his heart that the Corinthians were beginning to listen to alternate voices, that they were being enamored by other leaders. The biggest clues that we have as to the characteristics of these other leaders are contained in 2 Cor 10–13.

---

29. Alfred Plummer, *A Critical and Exegetical Commentary on the Second Epistle of Paul to the Corinthians* (ICC; New York: Charles Scribner's Sons, 1918), 438.

30. Presumably, of course, the person who delivered 1 Corinthians would have explained to the believers in Corinth the nature of the project. Or perhaps some of the Corinthian visitors to Paul in Ephesus, after returning to Corinth could have done so. John C. Hurd (*The Origin of 1 Corinthians* [New York: Seabury, 1965]) argues from the περὶ δέ in 16:1 that Paul is here responding to questions about the collection mechanics submitted in the Corinthians' letter to him (7:1); that understanding is somewhat doubtful; see Verbrugge, *Paul's Style of Church Leadership*, 58–62.

Below is a list of the characteristics of these opponents and their criticisms of Paul. We can only develop this list by a process of "mirror-reading." Mirror-reading (akin to listening to one side of a telephone conversation) can be risky, especially when the one who describes the actions of one's opponents is in an adversarial relationship with the people he is describing. We will attempt to err on the side of caution, but since we have no original documents from these opponents, it is the only route to go.

- The opponents charged Paul with being bold and brave (θάρρω) when he was absent from the Corinthians and wrote them letters, but humble and timid (ταπεινός) when he was face-to-face with them (2 Cor 10:1, 9–11). In other words, Paul could talk and write big, but he had no ability to follow through on what he wrote about. He was, in their view, something like a spineless wimp who would wave to and fro in the wind, especially when he was face-to-face with people. By contrast (through the process of mirror-reading), the opponents seemed to have some training in rhetorical methods of speaking (see 11:5–6).

- These opponents commended themselves (τῶν ἑαυτοὺς συνιστανόντων, 10:12). The verb συνιστάνω was an important verb in the ancient world. Among the papyri discovered more than a century ago are many letters of recommendation, in which an unknown person would apparently carry a letter of recommendation and offer it to a third party, who personally knew the author of that recommendation.[31] It would be like a man giving a notarized résumé to someone who was a friend of the notary public; such a document would say, "This guy is for real." Paul asserts that these opponents of his living in Corinth, however, had no recommendation outside themselves; they were boasters and braggarts, writing their own recommendations (10:12–17), though they did seem to claim some affiliation with the Jerusalem apostles (see next paragraph). Paul, by contrast, felt that he personally needed no letter of recommendation to show his credentials to the Corinthians,

---

31. The classic reference for letters of recommendations is Chan-Hie Kim, *The Familiar Letter of Recommendation* (SBLDS 4; Missoula, MT: Scholars, 1972). On the verb συνιστάνω (or συνίστημι) see BDAG, 972–73, s.v. συνίστημι: "to bring together as friends or in a trusting relationship by commending/recommending, *present, introduce/recommend someone to someone else.*"

for "you yourselves are our letter, written on our hearts, known and read by everyone" (2 Cor 3:1–3). In other words, he could ask the Corinthians themselves to write a letter of recommendation for him (12:11)!

- Twice Paul uses the term "super-apostles" (see τῶν ὑπερλίαν ἀποστόλων, 2 Cor 11:5; 12:11). The main debate is whether these "super-apostles" is a term Paul uses for his opponents in Corinth or whether the term perhaps refers to the original apostles. Most scholars today seem to agree that this is a negative expression for Paul's opponents in Corinth,[32] whom he clearly labels "false apostles" (11:13). We will not explore the pros and cons of that extensive debate here; suffice it to say that the opponents of Paul in 2 Corinthians undoubtedly claimed some affinity with the original twelve apostles, perhaps claiming that they were their official representatives (but without any special letter to prove that). Most certainly, Paul's statement in 11:22 ("Are they Hebrews? So am I. Are they Israelites? So am I. Are they Abraham's descendants? So am I") would not have been made so emphatically unless these opponents had Jewish ancestry. What is significant, however, is that in Paul's estimation, these men had no legitimacy to speak for James, Peter, and John; they were "false apostles, deceitful workers, masquerading as apostles of Christ" (11:13).

- Another central characteristic of these new opponents in Corinth concerns money issues. They felt strongly that it was their right to ask the believers in the Corinthian church to support them financially. These opponents argued that the very fact that Paul refused to accept money for his work as a missionary from those among whom he was working was a minus, not a plus. In their estimation, Paul did not think his message was worthwhile and substantive enough to charge his listeners.[33] Suffice it to say that "Paul's legitimacy as an apostle was under attack, and one of the central issues was this monetary one. Paul therefore felt forced to

---

32. See the extended discussion in Garland, *2 Corinthians*, 466–69, who concludes that the opponents in Corinth are different from the "super-apostles." See also Thrall, *2 Corinthians*, 2:671–76.

33. This whole issue of Paul's pride in and insistence on his self-support has been discussed in detail in part 1 (esp. ch. 2), so we need not repeat that material here.

defend himself. He insisted that preaching the gospel free of charge was something to boast about (2 Cor 11:7 – 10), not something to be ashamed of."[34]

- A more critical issue concerning money for our purposes in this chapter is that the opponents were apparently charging Paul with double talk on the issue of the collection. He had refused to accept money for his personal support from the Corinthians when he ministered there, but now he was in the business of organizing a rather significant collection of money. To the opponents this was a backhanded way of asking for support. "They apparently thought that Paul would be pocketing a part, if not all, of this collection."[35] We need to explore this charge in a bit more detail.

The verb that Paul's uses to describe this charge against him is πλεονεκτέω, which means "to take advantage of, *exploit, outwit, defraud, cheat.*"[36] Paul asks, in a question that begins with the word μή (thus expecting a negative answer), whether he has, through any of those men he sent to Corinth (he mentions Titus by name), exploited them (2 Cor 12:17).[37] Furthermore, in 12:16 we hear hints of a charge against Paul that he had used "deceit" or "trickery" (δόλος) against the Corinthians, probably in connection with his solicitation of donations for the collection.[38] While he would not accept money from the Corinthians to aid him in his basic needs, the opponents were charging him with double-talk, that he was using the collection to secretly line his own pockets. While it is true that "there is no explicit reference in these verses to a charge of financial fraud … the context renders this interpretation likely."[39]

So who are these opponents of Paul in 2 Corinthians? It is not, of course, that Paul's first letter to the Corinthians reflects a conflict-free

---

34. Verbrugge, *Paul's Style of Church Leadership*, 123.

35. Ibid., 125 – 26.

36. BDAG, 824, s.v. πλεονεκτέω.

37. The verb πλεονεκτέω also occurs earlier in the letter, where Paul states forthrightly, "We have exploited no one" (7:2). Since this section also leads into a section on Titus in ch. 7, these two passages seem linked in some way and refer to the same charge of exploitation.

38. This verse insinuates "that the collection was offered as bait to entrap the Corinthians. Then, when entrusted with the catch, Paul pilfered the money box" (Ralph P. Martin, *2 Corinthians* [WBC; 2nd ed.; Grand Rapids: Zondervan, 2014], 642).

39. Murray J. Harris, "2 Corinthians" (*EBC*; 2nd ed.; ed. Tremper Longman III and David E. Garland; Grand Rapids: Zondervan, 2008), 11:537.

time. As is evident from 1 Corinthians, there was a significant amount of controversy between Paul and the Corinthians while Paul was stationed in Ephesus during the third missionary journey. Apollos had spent some time in Corinth after Paul left the city (Acts 18:24–28), but Apollos was now living in Ephesus (1 Cor 16:12), and either through him or through others, Paul heard about defined factions in the church (1:10–4:20), some of whom had been gravitating to human leaders other than Paul (esp. Apollos and perhaps Peter; see 1:10–17; 4:1–7). Moreover, Paul had received emissaries from Corinth who visited Ephesus, such as people from Chloe's house (1:11), and Stephanas, Fortunatus, and Achaicus (16:17), and they reported further issues of tension. Paul had also received a report at some time about a incestuous man who was being tolerated in the church at Corinth (1 Cor 5:1), and Paul had actually sent a letter to the Corinthians, either dealing with this particular issue or (more likely) with moral issues in general (5:9–10). And finally, the Corinthians themselves had written a letter to Paul, asking for his advice on certain issues (7:1).[40]

Are there any hints in 1 Corinthians of people who match the characteristics of the opponents of Paul as we have outlined them above from data in 2 Corinthians? Most scholars do not think so, because there seems to be little relationship between the various characteristics we have noted about the opponents of Paul in 2 Corinthians and the troubles of the church that are reflected in 1 Corinthians.[41]

So who then are Paul's opponents in 2 Corinthians, who are spoken

---

40. In his classic book on the subject, Hurd (*The Origin of 1 Corinthians*) tries to reconstruct the letter from the Corinthians to Paul. His main argument for this reconstruction of the topics they raised is Paul's use of περὶ δέ in 7:1, 25; 8:1; 12:1; 16:1, 12.

41. Stephen Chang proposes an interesting thesis in his dissertation ("Fund-Raising in Corinth," 226–49). He revives an older theory that the incestuous man of 1 Cor 5 is the same as the one who opposed Paul in 2 Cor 2. The Corinthians obviously had been enamored with this individual and were proud about their relationship with him, which suggests that he was a man of wealth who functioned as a patron of a segment of the Corinthian church. When Paul "delivered this man to Satan" (1 Cor 5:5), this wealthy man was enraged and tried, through his financial power, to wrest control of and influence in the church away from Paul. Eventually this man lost his power in the church and repented. Paul accepted the man's repentance and asked the church to forgive him too, "in order that we might not be outwitted by Satan" (2 Cor 2:11). Some new opponents who had arrived in Corinth (the super-apostles) had also rallied around this incestuous man because he was an opponent of Paul, but they were deeply unhappy when the man repented. As a result, they upped the ante of their own opposition to the apostle by trying to discredit him on financial matters as well as character issues (2 Cor 10-12). Such a scenario supports Chang's view of the unity of 2 Corinthians.

about in such sharp language? C. K. Barrett, primarily on the basis of 2 Cor 11:22, considers them to be Jewish Palestinian Christians.[42] Dieter Georgi has argued that they were itinerant missionaries who came from "the world of Hellenistic Jewish Apologetics."[43] Bultmann and Schmittals narrowed this down further to "Gnostic pneumatics" with a Jewish background.[44]

It doesn't matter for our purposes to identify precisely who these opponents are and which of the above theories best fits the evidence. It is enough to know that they were making it miserable for Paul to retain respect as the founding and main leader of the church at Corinth. He had lost much of his reputation and position as the Corinthians' apostle and father, and Paul could no longer assume that they would automatically listen to his message and fall in line with his instructions/commands about putting aside some of their money for the collection. This new reality required different tactics on Paul's part as to how he had to go about raising money for "the poor among the saints in Jerusalem." He still felt passionate about the collection, and he desperately wanted the Corinthians, as one of his Gentile congregations, to participate. Thus, he had to come up with a variety of theological and moral reasons why they ought to participate, and this is precisely what he does in 2 Cor 8 and 9. It is to these motivational methods that we now turn in ch. 7.

---

42. C. K. Barrett, "Paul's Opponents in 2 Corinthians," *NTS* 17 (1971): 233–54. Barrett is one who argues, like Garland (see above), for a distinction between the "super-apostles" and the "false apostles."

43. Dieter Georgi, *The Opponents of Paul in Second Corinthians* (Philadelphia: Fortress, 1986), passim. He considers the "super-apostles" to be Paul's "ironic statement of the opponents' claim to be apostles" (32). In other words, Georgi identified the "super-apostles" with the "false apostles." For an extended discussion of the history of trying to determine precisely who these opponents were, see Ralph P. Martin, "The Opponents of Paul in 2 Corinthians: An Old Issue Revisited," in Martin, *2 Corinthians*, 105–15; this is reprinted from an article by Martin in *Tradition and Interpretation in the New Testament: Festschrift for E. E. Ellis* (ed. G. R. Hawthorne and O. Betz; Tubingen: Mohr Siebeck, 1987), 279–89.

44. Martin, "The Opponents of Paul."

CHAPTER 7

PAUL'S FUND-RAISING FOR THE COLLECTION IN 2 CORINTHIANS 8 – 9

THE PRESENT CHAPTER EXPLORES THE SPECIFIC ARGUMENTS THAT PAUL uses in 2 Cor 8 and 9 as he goes about trying to motivate the believers in Corinth to give money for the impoverished believers in Jerusalem. What specific tactics does he use to raise money? What expectations does the apostle have for the Corinthian saints? Does Paul hint at all here that new covenant Christians are biblically and morally obligated to give according to the demands of the old covenant laws?

BACKGROUND OF 2 CORINTHIANS 8 – 9

Before we can address questions such as these, we must make a few comments on the various attempts to reconstruct a history of 2 Corinthians.[1] Paul wrote the bulk of this second letter (maybe all of it) to the believers in Corinth from somewhere in Macedonia, perhaps Philippi.[2] It was prompted by Titus's return from Corinth and his report that the

---

1. Almost all commentaries must deal with reconstruction issues. Was 2 Corinthians one continuous letter? A collection of letters edited together? For a thorough discussion of reconstruction issues, see Harris, *The Second Epistle to the Corinthians*, 87 – 100; Martin, *2 Corinthians*, 42 – 49 (excursus 1: "History of the Composition of 2 Corinthians"); Verbrugge, *Paul's Style of Church Leadership*, 95 – 112.

2. Linda L. Belleville, *2 Corinthians* (IVPNTC; Downers Grove, IL: InterVarsity Press, 1996), 19.

Corinthians had responded positively to the exhortations in what has been called "the letter of tears" (cf. 2 Cor 2:3–4).[3] Consequently, when Paul wrote 2 Corinthians, he expressed great joy over their favorable response to the strong words he had used (7:5–16). He was, however, somewhat concerned about their failure to participate enthusiastically in the collection. Sadly, some of the Corinthians were still confused and frustrated about Paul's role in exhorting them to participate in this fund-raising effort, and this had been complicated by those opponents who had gained traction in the church (see ch. 6 for more on the opponents).

The Corinthians had been the first church to respond to Paul's request to raise money for the needy Christians in Jerusalem (8:10), perhaps responding initially to Paul's instructions in 1 Cor 16:1–2 that each of them regularly set aside a sum of money every week, based on their personal income. Paul would have presumably known this from some Corinthians who visited Paul in Ephesus. In fact, it appears that this response had helped motivate the churches of Macedonia also to participate in this project (2 Cor 9:1–2).[4] But now, it seems, Corinthian zeal was lagging, largely due "to intruding missionaries who raised questions about the legitimacy of the collection—perhaps with a view to diverting the funds into their own coffers."[5] When Titus reported this situation to Paul, the apostle penned 2 Cor 8 and 9. After commending them for their positive response in other areas of their Christian lives, he elaborates on what his wish is for their participation in the collection.[6]

There is little agreement about the literary structure of 2 Cor 8–9, in part because some commentators argue that at least one of these chapters once functioned as a separate administrative letter for organizing the

---

3. Paul Barnett, *The Second Epistle to the Corinthians* (NICNT; Grand Rapids: Eerdmans, 1997), 387; Harris, *The Second Epistle to the Corinthians*, 556.

4. The Macedonian churches, Philippi, Berea, and Thessalonica, were founded by Paul on the second missionary journey. See below in this chapter for specific comment on these verses.

5. Belleville, *2 Corinthians*, 207. See comments in the previous chapter on this issue.

6. A. E. Harvey (*Renewal through Suffering: A Study of 2 Corinthians* [Studies of the New Testament and Its World; Edinburgh: T&T Clark, 1996], 81) writes: "Paul certainly had an urgent request to make of the Corinthians, but of the kind which he always preferred to speak of somewhat indirectly. He also evidently needed to express his personal confidence in Titus, who would be assisting in the transaction. What [is] more natural than that he should adopt a more official tone and use some well-tried techniques of persuasion?"

collection.[7] But even if one or both of these chapters were separate letters that a later editor merged into what is now called 2 Corinthians, they now function as a literary unit within the present form of the letter.[8] Although there is disagreement on the literary structure, most commentators recognize the following units within the canonical form of 2 Corinthians: 8:1–6; 8:7–15; 8:16–24; 9:1–5; and 9:6–15.[9]

Those who read quickly through these chapters will immediately be struck by the variety of powerful words Paul uses to describe the collection, though he never specifically mentions money:

διακονία ("ministry," 8:4; 9:1, 12, 13; cf. Rom 15:25)
κοινωνία ("partnership," (8:4; 9:13; cf. Rom 15:27)
ἁδρότης ("generous gift," 8:20)
ἐν τῷ μέρει τούτῳ ("in this matter," 9:3)
ἐν τῇ ὑποστάσει ταύτῃ ("in this undertaking," 9:4)
εὐλογία ("bountiful gift," 9:5; cf. Rom 15:28)
λειτουργία ("service," 9:12; cf. Rom 15:27)

In addition to this vocabulary, Paul makes frequent use of a number of other key words — περισσεύω ("abound," 8:2, 7; 9:8, 12) and περισσεία ("abundance," 8:2, 14; the περισσεύω word group occurs only four other times in the rest of 2 Corinthians),[10] ὑστέρημα ("need," 8:14; 9:12), and ἁπλότης ("generosity," 8:2; 9:11, 13; this word is used only five times in the rest of Paul). In other words, the collection is more than an appeal simply for money; it is an appeal to a Christian lifestyle.

The champion of all the words is χάρις,[11] used ten times in chs. 8 and

---

7. See esp. Betz, *2 Corinthians 8 and 9*, 3–36. Martin (*2 Corinthians*, 460–62) admits that the two chapters may not be from the same letter. Verbrugge (*Paul's Style of Church Leadership*, 95–103) does the same. We should note, however, that the content of the present chapter does not depend on any particular theory of division of 2 Corinthians.

8. Frank J. Matera, *II Corinthians* (NTL; Louisville: Westminster John Knox, 2003), 180. See also Charles H. Talbert (*Reading Corinthians* [New York: Crossroad, 1987] 181–82) who supports the unity of the section based on a perceptive literary and thematic analysis.

9. For a rhetorical study of the structure of these chapters, see Betz, *2 Corinthians 8 and 9*.

10. Matera (*II Corinthians*, 181) says, "it is an invitation to participate in God's abundant grace."

11. Stephen Joubert (*Paul as Benefactor*) views the collection, and 2 Cor 8 and 9 particularly, from the standpoint of Greco-Roman patronage and benefaction. "The collection was the result and the concrete expression of the reciprocal relationship between the Jerusalem leadership and Paul, and also between the Jerusalem church and the rapidly growing early Christian movement under Paul's supervision. *Benefit exchange* provided the basic interpretative framework that informed the collection, from Paul's initial theological

9 (see 8:1, 4, 6, 7, 9, 16, 19; 9:8, 14, 15), but only six times in chs. 1–7 and only twice in chs. 10–13.[12] Most notably, Paul uses this word in 8:1 and 9:14–15 to form an *inclusio*.[13] Garland notes other verbal correspondences of the words listed above that support the unity and *inclusio* of these chapters.[14]

δοκιμή	8:2; 9:13
περισσεύω	8:2; 9:12 (also 8:7 [2x]; 9:8 [2x])
ἁπλότης	8:2; 9:13 (also 9:11)
διακονία	8:4; 9:12–13 (also 9:1)

Let us now take a look at the various units of these two chapters.

PAUL'S USE OF THE MACEDONIANS' EXAMPLE (2 COR 8:1 – 6)

In this first unit Paul attempts to motivate the Corinthians not to a new giving project but to following through on a prior commitment that he knows they have made. This distinction is important. Paul is not soliciting a new pledge; it was the Corinthians who had expressed interest in the collection in the first place (see esp. 2 Cor 9:2).[15]

In a single sentence that spans vv. 1–6,[16] Paul uses the sacrificial giving of the Macedonians in order to help spur the Corinthians to carry out that

---

conceptualisation to the eventual delivery thereof." (215) It seems to us that while benefaction language does in fact appear in these two chapters, with overall framework in Paul's mind is defined by the theology of God's χάρις, not human benefaction. At the same time, however, it is entirely possible that some of Paul's detractors in Corinth did "view the collection as particularly an act of *patronage* rather than a benevolent benefaction" (Chang, "Fund-Raising in Corinth," 216; italics his; see Chang's ensuing discussion for his critique).

12. Craig L. Blomberg (*Neither Poverty Nor Riches: A Biblical Theology of Possessions* [NSBT; Downers Grove, IL: InterVarsity Press, 2000], 191) says that "grace is the central theme of this entire two-chapter section." Nickle (*The Collection*, 109) remarks, "If any one phrase could summarize Paul's theology, it would be 'the grace of God in Christ.'" Note also John D. Harvey, *Listening to the Text: Oral Patterns in Paul's Letters* (Leicester: Apollos / Grand Rapids: Baker, 1998), 202.

13. Harris (*The Second Epistle to the Corinthians*, 560) notes that this is in keeping with how the apostle begins and concludes each of his thirteen letters.

14. Garland, *2 Corinthians*, 400.

15. Belleville, *2 Corinthians*, 209.

16. The Greek text of this unit consists of a single sentence that begins in 8:1 with a disclosure formula ("we want you to know") and concludes in 8:6 with Paul's decision to send Titus to Corinth once more ("so that we appealed to Titus"). Verses 2 and 3 introduce subordinate clauses, each beginning with ὅτι.

previous pledge. In other words, the generous response of the churches in Macedonia serves as an *example*[17] to the believers in Corinth. The remarkable evidence of God's grace (χάρις) is evident in the Macedonians' giving "into the richness of their sincerity" (εἰς τὸ πλοῦτος τῆς ἁπλότητος αὐτῶν)[18] in spite of the most adverse circumstances — "in the midst of severe affliction" (ἐν πολλῇ δοκιμῇ θλίψεως, 8:2). The birth of the churches in Macedonia had originally been accompanied by much opposition, both to the apostolic team and to the new converts.[19] Most likely the churches of Macedonia were still afflicted by some sort of persecution when Paul wrote 2 Corinthians (see 7:5). By using the example of the churches in Macedonia, Paul is exhorting the Corinthians to follow that same pattern of generosity with the grace that they themselves have received.

Second, the Macedonian churches gave out of "their extreme poverty" (8:2). They were experiencing "rock-bottom poverty,"[20] but their hearts welled up with joy in a generosity that "overflowed" (ἐπερίσσευσεν)[21] in response to the needs of other believers while being in a condition of great want themselves.[22] Despite their sacrificial giving, there is no indication that God's grace either lightened their afflictions or removed their deep poverty. God's grace merely opened their hearts and their finances to others.[23]

Third, the Macedonian churches, consisting of Gentile converts, were giving to "the service for the saints" (τῆς διακονίας τῆς εἰς τοὺς ἁγίους, 8:4) in need. While we cannot interpret οἱ ἅγιοι as a technical term limited to the believers in Jerusalem (e.g., Paul uses this word for the Corinthians

---

17. Betz, *2 Corinthians 8–9*, 41–42; Martin (*2 Corinthians*, 255) and others rightly point out that 8:1–6 is a "paradigm" or "example." Raymond F. Collins (*Second Corinthians* [Paideia; Grand Rapids: Baker Academic, 2013], 169–70) remarks: "In Hellenistic rhetoric the giving of examples (*epideigmata exempla*) was considered an important means of persuading people."

18. The word ἁπλότης means "simplicity, sincerity, uprightness, frankness" (BDAG, 104, s.v. ἁπλότης 1). See also meaning 2, which acknowledges that the interpretation "*generosity, liberality*" has frequently been proposed for Rom 12:8; 2 Cor 8:2; 9:11, but concludes that the probable meaning in def. 1 of "sincere concern, simple goodness" is sufficient for all these passages.

19. See the accounts of the mission in Philippi, Thessalonica, and Berea in Acts 16:11–17:15. Paul was still vividly aware of their persecution when he wrote to the churches of Thessalonica and Philippi (Phil 1:27–30; 1 Thess 1:6; 2:1–2, 14–16; 3:1–5; 2 Thess 1:4).

20. Philip Edgcumbe Hughes, *Paul's Second Epistle to the Corinthians* (NICNT; Grand Rapids: Eerdmans, 1962), 288.

21. The verb translated "overflowed" (περισσεύω) also appears in 8:7 (2x, "excel"), 9:8 (2x, "abound"), and in 9:12 ("overflow"); see also 1:5; 3:9; and 4:15.

22. Colin G. Kruse, *2 Corinthians* (TNTC; Downers Grove, IL: InterVarsity Press, 1987), 147.

23. Garland, *2 Corinthians*, 364.

themselves in 1 Cor 1:2), the context of the collection does indicate the referent of τοὺς ἁγίους as the Jerusalem believers.[24] As we have noted in ch. 5, the generosity of these Gentile churches had great potential to help establish unity within the church by bringing Jew and Gentile together.[25] Recall too, especially in light of Rom 15:25–29, that unity in the church was the main motivating factor for Paul in spearheading the collection in his Gentile churches.[26]

Paul's words in 8:3–4 describe further elements of the Macedonians' giving. They gave "according to their means" (κατὰ δύναμιν, "according to [their] power"). This expression is common in the papyri, especially in marriage contracts where a husband promises to provide food and clothing for his wife "according to his means." Hence, Paul testifies that the Macedonians have done all that could be expected of them; they have responded to the appeal "according to their means." But Paul feels obligated to add "and beyond their means." In the papyri, "beyond one's means" (παρὰ δύναμιν, "beyond one's power") is found in the context of a man's complaint against his wife for whom he has provided beyond what his means really allowed. So Paul says of the Macedonians that they have contributed to the collection for the poor in a way that was over and above anything that could be expected, given their situation.[27]

The Macedonians also gave "of their own accord" (αὐθαίρετος, 8:3). The apostle adds this adjective to conclude 8:3 — a word that means "to choose for oneself, of one's accord" (cf. 8:17).[28] Moreover, the Macedonians earnestly "kept begging with much pleading" (μετὰ πολλῆς παρακλήσεως δεόμενοι, 8:4) for the blessing and fellowship of helping the impoverished saints in Jerusalem. Instead of opting out because of their poverty, they kept asking Paul to allow them to give more.

---

24. Martin, *2 Corinthians* 460–62. Paul does not specifically identify the "saints" who are the recipients of the "ministry" (see Rom 15:26). Yet, on the basis of Rom 15:31, where Paul mentions *"my* ministry for Jerusalem," Barnett (*The Second Epistle to the Corinthians*, 397) rightly argues that Paul's various references to "ministry" in these chapters refer to his ministry to Jerusalem to which his churches are contributing.

25. Kelly M. Kapic and Justin L. Borger, *God So Loved, He Gave: Entering the Movement of Divine Generosity* (Grand Rapids: Zondervan, 2010), 206. N. T. Wright (*Paul: In Fresh Perspective* [Minneapolis: Fortress, 2005], 167) describes the collection in this way: "A massive symbol, a great prophetic sign, blazoned across half of the continent, trumpeting the fact that the people of God [were being] redefined around Jesus the Messiah [as] a single family."

26. Verbrugge, *Paul's Style of Church Leadership*, 294–330.

27. Kruse, *2 Corinthians*, 148.

28. BDAG, 150, s.v. αὐθαίρετος.

Paul's primary reason for emphasizing that the Macedonians responded voluntarily and generously is to make clear to the Corinthians that he did not force the Macedonians in any way to bend to his will.[29] Rather, they first gave themselves to the Lord and then to the apostles "by the will of God" (διὰ θελήματος θεοῦ, 8:5).[30] The Macedonians were considering it a privilege to contribute; they were following the Lord's leading in their lives. It seems almost sad in this context of the Macedonian example that Paul has to plead with the more affluent Corinthians to follow through to complete what they had earlier pledged when Titus was in their midst.[31]

In summary, in these first six verses Paul appeals to the Corinthians' emotions in two ways. First, he subtly contrasts the spiritual state of the Corinthians with that of the Macedonians (8:1–2) through the attitude of each toward the collection. The latter were filled with "joy" (χαρά) because of God's "grace" (χάρις) despite much "tribulation" (θλῖψις), and yet they gave in their extreme "poverty" (πτωχεία) with great "richness" (πλοῦτος); the Corinthians, by contrast, were reluctant to part with their money. Second, Paul indirectly praises or honors the Macedonians, who joined the collection in their extreme poverty and offered more than expected, while the Corinthians, who supposedly surpass the Macedonians with every-thing — faith, words, knowledge, earnestness, and love — have stopped collecting money for the poor (8:2, 7).[32]

In an honor-shame culture, such as the Greco-Roman world was, it

---

29. J. Murphy-O'Connor (*The Theology of the Second Letter to the Corinthians* [Cambridge: Cambridge University Press, 1991], 80) writes, "This spontaneous recognition of charity as the essence of Christianity won [the Macedonians] a place in his affections to which no other com-munity could aspire, and which merited them the accolade of 'partners in the gospel' (Phil 1:5, 7). They made the good news something real and vital by demonstrating the power of grace."

30. Garland (*2 Corinthians*, 367) writes, "With the phrase 'by the will of God' Paul makes more specific that the impetus for generosity comes from God and is related to God's grace."

31. Barnett (*The Second Epistle to the Corinthians*, 401, n. 53) believes that Titus actually began the collection. Yet, the collection had clearly already started in Corinth when Paul wrote 1 Cor 16:1–4, and Paul's account of Titus's recent visit to the church suggests that it was his first visit (2 Cor 7:14). During this visit Titus must have made some attempt to revive their interest in the project.

32. J. Murphy-O'Connor ("Paul and Macedonia: The Connection between 2 Corinthians 2.13 and 2.14," *JSNT* 25 [1985]: 102) reflects on the Macedonians' benevolence: "Despite all their own difficulties they did not turn inwards; their concern was for others, the one proof of 'authentic love' (2 Cor. 8:2–8). It was this that released the divine power into the world. What a contrast to the church at Corinth, whose internal divisions risked putting a stumbling-block in the way of the conversion of both Jews and Greeks, and even endangered other Christians (1 Cor 10:32–33)!"

would seem that such high praise for the Macedonians could only result in a feeling of shame in the hearts of the Corinthians in light of their self-expressed pride over their material and spiritual richness (cf. also 9:2–4). Paul hopes "that the Corinthians [will] take [his praise of the Macedonians] to heart and emulate it."[33] One even senses a certain amount of rivalry or competition that Paul is inculcating in the Corinthians, who are proud of their "earnestness" (σπουδή, 8:7, 8; cf. 7:11, 12) and "zealousness" (ζῆλος, 9:2; cf. 7:7, 11). Betz, in fact, asserts that

> Paul must have known of the rivalry, both ethnic and political, between the Macedonians and the Corinthians ... he did not hesitate to make use of such rivalry. By contrasting the Macedonians and the Corinthians in this way, Paul made use of the rhetorical figure of *syncrisis*, a technique used widely in ancient rhetoric and historiography to stimulate competition between rivals by means of comparison.[34]

While it is true that Paul seeks to motivate the Corinthians to resume their participation in the collection by appealing to their emotion of shame and the human reality of competition,[35] David Downs is careful to point out that "the nature of the rivalry in 2 Cor 8:1–6 is quite different from that found in Greco-Roman inscriptions."[36] Paul uses none of the typical language that is associated with such rivalry; rather, "Paul is ultimately interested in the excellence of the Corinthians' love (ἀγάπη)."[37] Moreover, the praise that will ultimately come from the final result of the collection is not praise for the human givers but thanksgiving to God (εὐχαριστίαν τῷ θεῷ, 9:11; cf. 9:12; δοξάζοντες τὸν θεόν, 9:13). Admittedly, while this theological impetus is only implicit in 8:1–6, even such an indirect perspective is foreign to the Greco-Roman honor-shame culture.

---

33. Betz, *2 Corinthians 8 and 9*, 48.

34. Ibid.

35. See also Kota Yamada, "Relationship between 2 Cor. 8 and 9 in Terms of Rhetoric and Ethics," *Queen: A Journal of Rhetoric and Power* (2002): 6. William R. Baker (*2 Corinthians* [CPNIVC; Joplin: College Press, 1999], 297) suggests, "Paul seems to seek to draw upon the very human desire of competitive self-improvement. He seems to list what he knows they are prideful about—even if unwarranted—in order to motivate them to shift their attention to something that would be really valuable for them to excel in, the collection. Maybe he just understands the Corinthians well enough to know the best way to hit a nerve."

36. Downs, *The Offering of the Gentiles*, 133.

37. Ibid.

PAUL'S APPEAL TO GRACE AND FAIRNESS (2 COR 8:7 – 15)

In the second unit (8:7–15), Paul begins by seeking to build on the Corinthians' desire to grow in grace. The apostle lists six virtues in two triads. The first triad includes faith (πίστις), speech (λόγος), and knowledge (γνῶσις). The second triad consists of earnestness (σπουδή), love (ἀγάπη), and grace (χάρις). Even a cursory reading of the Corinthian correspondence reveals the importance of speech and knowledge (cf. 1 Cor 1:5) among the Corinthians. Paul has asserted that they are "not lacking in any spiritual gift" (1:7); now he wants their financial giving to catch up with their spiritual gifts and blessings.

The apostle's backdoor use of simple encouragement instead of "command" (8:8) provides a subtle hint of getting the Corinthians' attention.[38] He also finds it advisable to uphold the Corinthians' freedom. Thus, he encourages purely voluntary participation in the collection (see also 9:5, 7). As Garland rightly notes, "the apostle does not command but instead invites, encourages, and lays out divine principles gleaned from Scripture. He hopes that they will respond out of hearts that have been freed by the gospel and fired by God's grace."[39]

The Corinthians must choose to respond to God's promptings through the apostle for the right reasons and with the right motives. While Paul has confidence in their follow-through because he knows they want to excel in all aspects of Christian living, he moves on to the greatest example possible: Christ himself (8:9).[40] Richard Melick rightly states, "The Macedonians provided the 'near' example (both geographically and temporally near), but Jesus provided the ultimate example for them."[41] As

---

38. As noted in ch. 6, Verbrugge (*Paul's Style of Church Leadership*, 47–51) argues that Paul rejects any notion of command and uses the construction of ἵνα plus the subjunctive in 8:7 as "one of the least direct ways that [he] could use to express the imperatival idea."

39. Garland, *2 Corinthians*, 372.

40. Betz (*2 Corinthians 8-9*, 61), Charles K. Barrett (*The Second Epistle to the Corinthians* [BNTC; Peabody, MA: Hendrickson, 1993], 223) and Thrall (*2 Corinthians*, 2:532) rightly point out that this is a "paradigm" or "example."

41. Richard Melick Jr., "The Collection for the Saints: 2 Corinthians 8–9," *CTR* 4, no. 1 (1989): 101 n. 18. See also David Horrell, "Paul's Collection: Resources for a Materialist Theology," *Epworth Review* 22 (1995): 77. Contra Victor Paul Furnish (*II Corinthians* [AB; New York: Doubleday, 1984], 418), who argues that Paul does not present Christ as an example to follow. He claims that Paul does not mean "Do what Christ did," or even "Do for others what Christ has done for you." It is rather, "Do what is appropriate for your status as those who have been enriched by the grace of Christ."

Paul explains the example of Christ, the "rich" became "poor" in order to "enrich poor" human beings (8:9) — and this is the result of his love (cf. 8:8). This second example is more intensified than the first one, because "the grace of Jesus Christ of our Lord"[42] (τὴν χάριν τοῦ κυρίου ἡμῶν Ἰησοῦ Χριστοῦ) itself (8:9) is the original expression of "the grace of God" (τὴν χάριν τοῦ θεοῦ) given to the Macedonians (8:1).

The apostle is not alluding here to Jesus' poor socioeconomic status, his lowly birth, his carpenter trade, and the lack of a place to lay his head. Instead, he is emphasizing how Christ became "poor" through leaving his heavenly dwelling to come to this earth and through his offering of himself in his sacrificial death on the cross for sin (cf. Phil 2:5–8). William Baker writes:

> It is apparent that Paul does not so much intend for the Corinthians to model Christ's unique kind of poverty. He gave up everything, his very life, even his dignity. Rather, he seeks to motivate by reminding them of the wealth of salvation which they have received from Christ. Sharing material resources in the name of Christ with other needy believers is a drop in the bucket compared to that.[43]

Christ's voluntary and generous sacrifice, then, summarized in the word χάρις, becomes the ultimate motive for giving, rather than trying to imitate or perhaps even to outdo the Macedonians.[44]

Having now provided the ultimate motivational principle for the Corinthians to give to the collection and instead of merely offering them a command (cf. οὐ κατ᾿ ἐπιταγήν in 8:8), Paul now shares with them some practical "advice" or "opinion" (γνώμη) on the matter (8:10).[45] He appeals to their "desire" (τὸ θέλειν) and insists that their deeds of generosity match their desire. We should note the order of these words: the Corinthians' "desire" has preceded their "doing" (τὸ ποιῆσαι). "This comment suggests

---

42. "The grace of our Lord Jesus Christ" is the customary phrase Paul uses to close his letters (Rom 16:20, 24; 1 Cor 16:23; 2 Cor 13:13 [13:14]; Gal 6:18; Phil 4:23; 1 Thess 5:28; 2 Thess 3:18; Phlm 25).

43. Baker, 2 Corinthians, 300.

44. Garland, 2 Corinthians, 375.

45. See ch. 6 for comments on this word. Betz argues that this γνώμη illustrates the rhetorical principle of expediency: "it is more expedient to finish what one has begun than to leave it unfinished ... this commonplace remains at the level of a presupposition. It is not elaborated" (2 Corinthians 8 and 9, 63).

that the orientation of the heart—the self—surpasses in importance the execution of the deed, for it is *zeal* or *desire* that confirms the presence of God's grace within them."[46]

In 8:11 Paul issues the only imperative in 2 Cor 8 and 9. It is simple and pointed, "Finish!" (ἐπιτελέσατε).[47] The apostle yearns for the Corinthians to make good on the promise they have made. It is important to note that Paul never specifies here an amount, nor does he even call for a percentage. Giving is left purely voluntary—the working of God's grace in the heart of the believer. Note the words of Linda Belleville: "For several centuries in the history of the church there was no such thing as a 'tithe' to support Christian workers; instead, freedom in giving was emphasized. In fact, church fathers like Irenaeus argued against the tithe."[48]

Paul does not, however, expect the Corinthians to put themselves into a state of poverty in order to give to this collection. Neither does he encourage them to think that they must somehow outsacrifice the Macedonians.[49] He calls each individual merely to give "out of what you have" (ἐκ τοῦ ἔχειν, 8:11). Paul does not want the Corinthians to give so much to the Jerusalem church that the believers there end up needing to take up a reciprocal offering for the Corinthians (8:13–15).[50] This would be sheer foolishness! The goal is to achieve some degree of equality so that each person does their part at the appropriate time.

Finally, in 8:15 Paul roots this perspective by quoting Exod 16:18. This passage from the Torah originally applied to the time when God sent manna to his people, and it emphasized that every Israelite had sufficient

---

46. Bassler, *God and Mammon*, 105 (italics original).

47. BDAG, 383, s.v ἐπιτελέω 1: "to finish someth. begun, *end, bring to an end, finish*." Baker (*2 Corinthians*, 302) observes that the words "finish" and "completion" (see NIV of 8:11) translate the same Greek word (ἐπιτελέω), used previously in 8:6 and 7:1. Used seven times in Paul's letters (see also Rom 15:28; Gal 3:3; Phil 1:6), it seems to be preferred by Paul to its synonym (τελειόω), which is used only once by Paul (Phil 3:12) but twenty-two other times outside of Paul's writings.

48. Belleville, *2 Corinthians*, 217. For a thorough investigation on the issue of tithing for Christians, see esp. Craig Blomberg, *Christians in an Age of Wealth: A Biblical Theology of Stewardship* (BTFL; Grand Rapids: Zondervan, 2013), 121–33, 141–44. See also further extended comments in ch. 12 on Paul and tithing.

49. Martin, *2 Corinthians*, 265; Barnett, *The Second Epistle to the Corinthians*, 412.

50. Garland, *2 Corinthians*, 382. Note the words of Craig Blomberg: "God did not ask his people to trade places with the poor if they have more resources than the median or average in a given society (v. 13). That would only change who needs financial help from whom" (*Christians in an Age of Wealth*, 133).

food for each day. From this passage, Paul extrapolates what may be called the law of reciprocity, namely, that each person should have sufficient resources for the needs of each day, and that the giver and receiver should be equally involved and equally concerned about each other. When God's people are in need, those who have plenty should help those who have less. True, the future possibility of the Corinthians and the people in Jerusalem interchanging roles is probably more theoretical than real at the time of writing,[51] but it is an excellent principle for the Corinthians to consider. If the Corinthians participate in the collection, they will be following the principles set down by God for his people shortly after the exodus and the pattern practiced by the early church (cf. Acts 2:45; 4:35): sufficient resources for the needs of everyone.

THE FORTHCOMING VISIT OF TITUS AND HIS ASSOCIATES (2 COR 8:16 – 24)

This section serves as a recommendation letter for Titus and two brothers as they complete the collection, and Paul thanks God for these three men. They are being sent to Corinth in order to assure the collection against any suspicion of pilfering and to confirm its integrity (8:20–21).[52] "These arrangements show the pains Paul takes to avoid any hint of unscrupulous behavior and seems to reflect Paul's earlier crisis with this church."[53]

Paul is carefully arranging for the visits of the two additional persons and commending them to accompany Titus in carrying the gifts to Jerusalem. Note 8:21: "For we are taking pains to do what is right, not only in the eyes of the Lord but also in the eyes of man" (NIV). The apostolic messengers are persons of proven worth. Paul appreciates Titus's character as a tested and trusted colleague (8:17, 22–23). The other two unnamed coworkers are persons of similar integrity (8:19, 23).

These three men will function as official "representatives of the churches" (ἀπόστολοι ἐκκλησιῶν),[54] sent to Corinth for the administration

---

51. It is unlikely that the chronic poverty in Jerusalem would ever come to a surplus, even if the Corinthians were to have a deficiency.

52. For more on the importance of integrity, see comments in ch. 12.

53. Bassler, *God and Mammon*, 105.

54. We do not know the number or identity of the churches appointing the brothers in 8:19, 22. It is unlikely that they were from Judea, since the collection was designated for Jerusalem. However, they could have been from Asia Minor, thus reflecting Paul's wider missionary

of the relief fund and the care of the money raised. Therefore, they had to be people of sterling reputation and probity (8:22), and they have the highest endorsement possible (8:23).

While most of 8:16–24 concerns these recommendations that Paul is offering for his personal representatives to Corinth, these verses do indeed contain additional elements intended to motivate the Corinthians to participate in the collection. First, the gathering of this money is "for the glory [δόξα] of the Lord himself" (8:19).[55] Through the giving of a generous gift, the Lord will indeed be honored and praised (see also 8:23; 9:12–15). Second, Paul wants everyone to see the "readiness" or "eagerness" (προθυμία) of his churches to help out the Jerusalem church (8:19; cf. 9:12–13). Paul is hoping to secure better relations between the Gentile churches and the Jewish church in Jerusalem, an issue that was especially important in light of Paul's opponents' claiming their authority from the Jerusalem church. This collection will be a key instrument to aid in securing that sense of unity.

THE NEED FOR GENEROSITY (2 COR 9:1 – 5)

In these verses Paul revisits the issue of the Macedonians. There are some parallels of this section with 8:1–6, though the focus is different. The churches in Macedonia were uppermost in his mind as he wrote 2 Corinthians because he was located there at the time of writing (1:15–16; 2:12–13; 7:5–7; cf. Acts 19:21–22; 20:1–2), and he could not help but contrast the Macedonians' attitude toward giving with the attitude that seemed apparent in Corinth. Paul admits that he has boasted to the Macedonians about the original "eagerness" (προθυμία, cf. 8:11) and "zeal" or "enthusiasm" (ζῆλος) of the Corinthians to participate in Paul's fund-raising effort for the believers in Jerusalem. But if the Macedonians traveling with Paul to Achaia after he leaves Macedonia find a only meager

---

activity (Hughes, *Paul's Second Epistle to the Corinthians*, 316), or from Macedonia, since he had been ministering in that area and lifted these churches up as model believers (Harris, *The Second Epistle to the Corinthians*, 603).

55. It is a matter of debate whether κύριος here refers to God the Father or to the Lord Jesus Christ. Most often the apostle uses κύριος as a term for Jesus Christ, though the later reference to δόξα Χριστοῦ in 8:23 might indicate that κύριος in 8:19, 21 refers to God the Father. In any case, we may never drive a wedge between the Father and the Son, for they are one triune God.

number of coins given to Paul as the Corinthians' contribution, the apostle admits that "we would be ashamed" (καταισχυνθῶμεν ἡμεῖς, 9:4), as would the Corinthians (ἵνα μὴ λέγω ὑμεῖς).

We noted above that the honor-shame culture of the Greco-Roman world played a role in the motivation of 2 Cor 8:1–5 (there Paul used the "honor" or praise side as a means to stimulate a bit of rivalry or competition between the Corinthians and the Macedonians). Here he works more on the "shame" side. Not only does he explictly use the verb καταισχύνω ("to be ashamed"), but he also hopes that neither he nor the Corinthians will have to hang their heads down low because Paul's boasting about them (τὸ καύχημα ἡμῶν τὸ ὑπὲρ ὑμῶν, 9:3) would be proven false. While Paul clearly did not like to boast about his own service to the Lord Jesus Christ (see 11:16–12:13), he did not hesitate to boast about the grace of God working in the hearts of those whom he had led to Christ (9:2–3; cf. also Phil 2:14–16).

Bassler agrees that Paul had "encouraged a rivalry between the regions in order to promote the collection in both."[56] She also recognizes that what Paul had said to the Macedonians about the Corinthians could easily backfire, especially if the Macedonians had been spurred on to participate in the collection by the example of the Achaians; but now if Titus, having returned from Achaia, has reported to Paul less than stellar cooperation in giving money from the Corinthians (cf. 7:13–15), the apostle fears humiliation for himself and his churches in Achaia. "Yet, as before, [Paul's] theological argument soon eclipsed his very human concern."[57] It is these theological arguments that deserve most of our attention.

In 9:1 Paul calls the collection a "service" (διακονία), a term that he uses elsewhere regarding the collection (Rom 15:31; 2 Cor 8:4; 9:12–13), along with the corresponding verb διακονέω ("to serve, administer," Rom 15:25; 2 Cor 8:19–20). Note that in Paul's discussion of the collection in Rom 15, therefore, as well as in 2 Cor 8 and 9, he both opens and closes his discussion with words from this word group. These words describe uniquely Christian acts of service to others. It became a term denoting loving action for brother or sister and neighbor, which in turn is derived from divine love; it also describes the outworking of koinōnia,

---

56. Bassler, *God and Mammon*, 106.
57. Ibid., 107.

fellowship."[58] Through using this word group, Paul is encouraging the believers in Corinth to a life of Christian service, one aspect of which is to share their resources with the impoverished Jewish Christians in Jerusalem.

Paul also calls the collection a "blessing" (εὐλογία; NIV "generous gift") twice in 9:5, a rich word from the OT that Paul developed into a uniquely Christian concept. In Gal 3:14, he stressed that the time had come for believers of all nations to receive "the blessing" that God had promised to Abraham in Gen 12:2–3—namely, the blessing of God's redemption in Christ (cf. Eph 1:3). By using this term here for the collection, Paul encourages the Corinthian church to think of their giving as a blessing—to "contribute ungrudgingly [rather than] grudgingly, so that through this gift God's blessing may be given tangible expression in the Jerusalem church."[59]

GENEROSITY FROM GOD AND PRAISE TO GOD (2 COR 9:6 – 15)

In v. 6, Paul continues the theme of blessing with the use of an agricultural metaphor—that of sowing and reaping. If a person sows sparingly (φειδομένως), that is what they will reap. Perhaps Paul already has in mind the thoughts he will express a few months later when he writes to the Romans from Corinth that God "did not spare [ἐφείσατο] his own Son" (Rom 8:32). If that is how God has treated us, and if we model our lives after God's blessed gift of his Son, surely we will want to offer our best. With that in mind, Paul gives the converse agrarian principle: those who sow "with blessings" (ἐπ' εὐλογίαις) will reap the same. As Betz suggests here, this Greek expression is perhaps best translated "bountifully" (NIV "generously").[60]

Paul is not offering the crass motivation that prosperity preachers today advocate by using greed as a motive: the more you give to God, the more he will give back to you; you cannot out give God. Paul has carefully used the word εὐλογία again, with all the spiritual connotations he has poured

---

58. Verlyn D. Verbrugge, *New International Dictionary of New Testament Theology: Abridged Edition* (Grand Rapids: Zondervan, 2000), 137.

59. Ibid., 218.

60. Betz, *2 Corinthians 8 and 9*, 103.

into that word thus far. Spiritual blessings are in store for us as we give to the needy.

This becomes clear in vv. 7–8. What God causes to abound (περισσεύω) to us is not material wealth but "all grace" (πᾶσαν χάριν), with the result that "we will continue to abound in every good work" (περισσεύητε εἰς πᾶν ἔργον ἀγαθόν). The joy in giving and in seeing one's money helping someone who has far less than we do becomes in itself an incentive to give even more. It is for that reason that Paul instructs the Corinthians to give not with pain (ἐκ λύπης) in their hearts or because someone is forcing them (ἐξ ἀνάγκης), but to do so voluntarily and cheerfully. No one enjoys giving if money is being extracted from them as a tax; blessings abound if it comes from the heart.

As noted in ch. 6, Paul does not even include an imperative in 9:7. Everything is based on the theology of giving voluntarily. "This approach means that if [the Corinthians] comply, they will do so out of obedience to their Lord who gave himself for them, not out of obedience to Paul."[61] Obedience to the Lord is the fruit of a life of gratitude and indicates spiritual maturity; moreover, the Corinthians will experience the love of God ("God loves a cheerful giver"). And since it seems apparent that the Corinthians had been resisting any authoritative command from the apostle, to get his point across without an imperative is a rhetorically powerful way to present a course of action that he hopes they will follow as believers in Jesus Christ.

In typical fashion, Paul then backs up his statement with a quotation from the OT, from Ps 112:9 (LXX 111:9): "He has scattered abroad his gifts to the poor, his righteousness endures forever" (NIV 1984). If the primary subject in this quotation is intended to be the Lord, Paul is suggesting to his audience that by their giving to the poor, they are, as it were, enabling God to do what he has promised.[62]

---

61. Garland, *2 Corinthians*, 406.

62. As Downs (*The Offering of the Gentiles*, 141–42) points out in an extended footnote, in the original psalm the subject of the singular verbs in this quotation is clearly the pious one who fears the Lord and delights to do his commands (Ps 112:1). But since God is the actor in 2 Cor 9:8 and again in verse 10, it would seem that Paul wants us to see God as subject of this quotation. Is Paul violating the OT here? Downs adopts the observation of Christopher D. Stanley (*Arguing with Scripture: The Rhetoric of Quotations in the Letters of Paul* [London: T&T Clark, 2004], 105–9) that "readers with different levels of familiarity with the biblical text would have interpreted this scriptural citation in different ways. Members of what Stanley calls the 'informed audience' might have recognized that the psalm

In v. 10 Paul clearly asserts that the one who supplies seed to the sower and bread to those who are hungry is God (cf. Isa 55:10–11). Moreover, just as God meets the needs of the poor through the gifts of his people, in a similar way God will see to it that those who give these gifts for the poor will themselves receive provisions. In addition, Paul once again stresses that they will grow spiritually (αὐξήσει τὰ γενήματα τῆς δικαιοσύνης ὑμῶν, "[God] will increase the fruits of your righteousness").[63] In the agrarian metaphor that Paul continues here, it was assumed in the Jewish mind that God is the one who makes things grow; this applies not only to a physical field, but also to hearts and lives of his people.

In 2 Cor 9:6–10, as Paul has been attempting to motivate the Corinthians to give for the poor saints in Jerusalem, he has emphasized its voluntary nature and its producing of spiritual blessings that will inevitably become a part of their lives as they participate in the collection. In the next few verses (9:11–14), he focuses on an additional result: the praise and thanksgiving to God that will be produced by their giving.[64] Although Paul does not use the unique language here of the patron/benefactor and client pattern of the Greco-Roman world, his audience would assume that praise and thanksgiving are due to anyone who gives a significant gift.[65] Note, however, what Paul says: if the Corinthians do come through with a sizable gift, they will not be the ones to receive heaps of praise and thanksgiving (εὐχαριστία); rather, it will go to God (v. 11).

Yet it is not as if there is nothing in it for the Corinthians; they will "be enriched [πλουτιζόμενοι] in every way" (v. 11).[66] Paul uses the verb

---

praises the righteous person who freely gives to the poor, whereas members of the 'competent' and 'minimal' audiences, who possessed less knowledge of the original literary context of this verse, would have understood God as the subject of the citation." Both are true theologically, that is, both God and the righteous person are involved in supplying gifts to the poor.

63. See Harris (*The Second Epistle to the Corinthians*, 75): "God will also increase ... the material and spiritual benefits that would accrue to them and to the poor in Jerusalem as a result of their generous benevolence."

64. We should note here that syntactically, verses 11–14 form a single sentence in the Greek text.

65. For more on this Greco-Roman cultural pattern of patron-benefactor, see the discussion in part 1 (ch. 3). A patron who provided for his clients did so to receive praise (see Downs, *The Offering of the Gentiles*, 142–43). While this would not be the prime factor that would motivate God to give to his people, the expectation of praise and thanksgiving would inevitably be there.

66. Thrall considers that the nominative participle πλουτιζόμενοι is loosely attached to the genitive ὑμῶν at end of the preceding verse (*2 Corinthians*, 2:585 n. 144). Technically, it is an anacoluthon.

πλουτίζω only two other times in his letters (1 Cor 1:5; 2 Cor 6:10), and in both cases he refers to spiritual blessings that come to us by God's grace. "Paul is not interested in the material understanding of the term *riches*. He gives it a deeper meaning by applying it to God, Christ, and the church.... To be rich is a spiritual gift unconnected with material possessions."[67] Paul must indeed think highly of the Corinthians since he has now used several arguments in order to motivate them to give toward the collection because of the spiritual riches that will accrue to them by God's grace.

Paul elaborates on this theme in vv. 12–14. Verse 12, introduced by ὅτι ("because"), gives the reason why the Corinthians will be enriched and why thanksgiving to God will occur. Their διακονία (see discussion of this word above at 9:1; the term is repeated in 9:13) will not only supply the saints in Jerusalem with what they need for their bodies, but it will also result in *many* thanksgivings offered to God.

> Indeed, God's gifts to Corinth will overflow back to God through the "many thanksgivings" that their generosity will generate. Grace here reveals its true nature, for it is the essence of grace to overflow any situation or vessel into which it has been poured (Rom. 5:15–21). It will overflow the Macedonian vessel into Corinth. It will overflow the Corinthian vessel as contributions for Jerusalem, and overflowing finally the Jerusalem vessel, it will return to God as undiminished thanksgiving and praise.[68]

Paul elaborates on this same thanksgiving theme again in v. 13, offering further perspectives on why so many thanksgivings will be offered to God: because of the Corinthians' "obedience" (ὑποταγή) and because of their "generosity" (ἁπλότης).[69] Note once again that the "obedience"

---

67. Verbrugge, *Abridged Edition*, 473. This applies also to the corresponding verb πλουτέω, which Paul uses five times. Only in 1 Tim 6:9 does it refer to physical riches, and Paul goes on in 1 Tim 6:18 to remind Timothy that those who are physically rich should be "rich in good deeds, and to be generous and willing to share" (see also comments on ch. 11).

68. Bassler, *God and Mammon*, 109.

69. As in v. 11, Paul has a participle (δοξάζοντες) that lacks an antecedent in the nominative (i.e., another anacoluthon). As Belleville (*2 Corinthians*, 243) points out, translations differ here. Some opt for the Corinthians as the ones praising God, others opt for those who receive the offering, and still others are vague (e.g., NIV 1984, "men will praise"). Belleville chooses the second option, arguing that "the subject must be supplied by the logic of the argument ... the logical subject is *eis autous* ('to them,' v. 13) — that is, the recipients of the offering." This is clearer in v. 14, where the genitive absolute αὐτῶν ... ἐπιποθούντων indicates the intense feelings of the prayers of the recipients.

referred to here is not to any command that Paul has given them (cf. 8:8); rather, it is obedience "to their confession of the gospel of Christ."[70] The Corinthians are merely responding with grace and gratitude to the grace they have received in Christ. It is for that reason that Paul refers in v. 14 to "the surpassing grace" (διὰ τὴν ὑπερβάλλουσαν χάριν) that God has wrought in the Corinthians. Moreover, Paul expresses confidence that the recipients of the collection, the poor Jewish Christians in Jerusalem, will offer intercessory prayers for the Gentile Christians in Paul's churches.[71]

Paul's final verse (9:15) is a doxology—thanksgiving to God for the marvelous gift he has given to us in sending his Son Jesus Christ to this earth and in offering us redemption through his blood. This verse offers the foundation for everything he has written in chs. 8 and 9. God's incredible gift to us calls for a response on our part, and in giving to the poor, we are demonstrating our gratitude to God.

CONCLUSION

In summarizing Paul's methods as used in 2 Cor 8 and 9 of raising a significant offering for "the poor among the saints in Jerusalem," Bassler says it best:

> The theological implications of the collection were so significant that Paul's words in II Corinthians have an insistent, even an urgent quality. Moreover, Paul used some problematical techniques. He pitted community against community and seemed to misrepresent the efforts of one to provoke the other to greater participation. He even seemed to make participation into a loyalty test for Corinth. At the same time the theological dimensions of the project provide constraints to these excesses. It

---

70. Garland (*2 Corinthians*, 414) rightly calls the genitive in τῆς ὁμολογίας ὑμῶν a subjective genitive, that is, "obedience created by your confession."

71. Garland (ibid.) and Thrall (*2 Corinthians*, 2:593) reflect on Rom 15:31 in this context, where Paul expresses a significant reservation about how this gift might be received in Jerusalem and asks the Christians in Rome to pray that for a favorable reception. Thrall even speculates that Paul heard rumors from Jewish visitors to Corinth that the animosity against Paul was increasing in Jerusalem rather than decreasing. But it is also fair to say that in writing to the Corinthians, Paul would not find this an opportune time to bring up his fears (if indeed he had them already by this time). Moreover, the apostle always tried to think positively about those whose lives had been shaped by God's grace in Christ—that Christians would act in a Christian manner and not let their petty biases and jealousies take over their lives.

is ultimately a matter of grace, and grace cannot be compelled. It is also a matter of fellowship and equality, not enrichment of one group at the expense of another. And Paul made it absolutely clear that this request for money into which he had poured so much time and energy was entirely and exclusively for the benefit of others.[72]

---

72. Bassler, *God and Mammon*, 112–13.

CHAPTER 8

THE AFTERMATH AND DELIVERY OF PAUL'S COLLECTION

THE LAST THREE CHAPTERS HAVE DEALT WITH THE MAJOR FUND-RAISING effort that Paul engaged in on his third missionary journey, which we now call the collection. Paul has only a few verses in Rom 15 about the success of the collection, and he refers there only to money that was raised in Macedonia and Achaia (15:25–27). That raises certain questions. For example, what about Galatia (1 Cor 16:1)? And what about Asia (Ephesus), from where Paul wrote 1 Corinthians and from where he sent Titus to Corinth to help motivate the Corinthians to resume their interest in the collection? Did he solicit money from his churches in Asia?

Moreover, Paul never writes anywhere about the delivery of the collection in Jerusalem and how it was received. This stands to reason, perhaps, since Paul's letters were occasional; they were not a diary of his life. But what does the unusual journey of Paul with a frequent change of plans as described in Acts 20:1–5 mean? What was "a plot against him by the Jews" (20:3)? And what about Paul's insistence that he go to Jerusalem in spite of several warnings that he would face significant danger there? Was this in any way connected with the collection and his deep feeling that he had to deliver it in person because he was the apostle to the Gentiles and this was his service (ἡ διακονία μου, Rom 15:31)? And why does Luke, a travel companion of Paul on this very trip (cf. Acts 20:7–16; 21:1–18), practically ignore the collection in Acts? Many see an allusion to the collection in Acts 24:17 in the phrase "alms for the poor"; is this so?

Questions, questions, questions! In this chapter, we need to probe such questions about the final stages of the collection, its aftermath, and its delivery in Jerusalem.

The Success of Paul's Fund-Raising

In ch. 5, where we talked about what the collection meant to Paul, we looked carefully at Rom 15:25–32. We examined mostly vv. 27–32, a passage that, so we argued, tells us more than any other passage why the collection was so important to Paul and what it meant to him as the apostle to the Gentiles. But Paul prefaces these comments with vv. 25–26, where Paul tells the Romans, in a few words, about the success of the collection. In v. 25 he simply reports that before he comes to visit them on his way to Spain, he is heading to Jerusalem "in order to serve the saints" (διακονῶν τοῖς ἁγίοις). As we have noted in ch. 5, some scholars consider "the saints" here as a technical term for the Jewish Christian community in Jerusalem. While we do not agree with that phrase as a technical term, there is no doubt that Paul has the church in Jerusalem in mind.

Moreover, the adverbial participle that Paul uses, διακονῶν, is rightly interpreted as an adverbial participle denoting purpose. While Paul went to Jerusalem after his first missionary journey because of the apostolic conference about the Gentiles and circumcision (Acts 15), and while he visited Jerusalem briefly after his second missionary journey and greeted the church in that city (18:22),[1] after his third journey he had a more specific goal: ἡ διακονία μου ("my service," Rom 15:31; see discussion of this expression in ch. 5).

Next, in Rom 15:26, Paul mentions the success of the collection in Macedonia and Achaia. The believers in these two areas "were pleased to make a certain contribution [κοινωνίαν τινά]" for the poverty-stricken Jerusalem believers. We do not know how much they gave, though in 2 Cor 8:1–5 (as noted in ch. 7), the Macedonian believers gave abundantly

---

1. While "Jerusalem" is not specifically mentioned in the text of Acts 18:22, the participle ἀναβάς (from ἀναβαίνω, which means "to go up") suggests going to Jerusalem (cf. NIV). Since Caesarea, where Paul's ship landed, was at sea level, and Jerusalem was in the central highlands, Paul had to go up. From there "he went down" (κατέβη), probably to Antioch, his sending church. Most scholars agree that these verbs allude to Jerusalem (see the discussion in Schnabel, *Acts*, 769).

(cf. the verb ἐπερίσσευσεν in 2 Cor 8:2; NIV translates "in rich generosity"). In any case, Paul was definitely pleased with what they gave (he uses the verb εὐδοκέω in vv. 25 and 26), and he puts both "Macedonia" and "Achaia" (where Corinth was located, as well as Cenchreae, Rom 16:1, and Athens, Acts 17:34) in the same category of churches with which he was pleased because of their response to the collection.

But what about the Galatians? In 1 Cor 16:1, Paul had written that he commanded the believers in that area also to participate in the collection. When did he communicate that? Downs reviews various theories as to when he may have written them a letter telling them about the collection and commanding that they participate.[2] But we see no reason why his instructions had to be in a letter. When Paul began his third missionary journey, the journey on which he intended to take up the collection, Paul set out from Antioch, traveled through Galatia and Phrygia, strengthening "all the disciples there," and finally ended up in Ephesus (Acts 18:23; 19:1). This means that he took essentially the same route as he did during his second missionary journey, when he stopped in Derbe, Lystra, and Iconium (all located in Galatia), visiting the churches he had organized on his first journey and had visited at the beginning of the second journey (15:41 – 16:6). It is entirely possible, and we think likely, that his instructions to the Galatians on the collection could have been oral rather than written.[3] Paul asked them (probably even commanded them) to make regular Sunday deposits in keeping with their income, just as he wrote sometime later to the Corinthians (1 Cor 16:1 – 2 and the verb διέταξα).

Yet Paul does not mention the Galatians in Rom 15:26. Did they or did they not participate? Scholars have taken different positions on this question. Downs confidently concludes that "the Galatians did not participate in the offering of the Gentiles."[4] He argues this from the silence in

---

2. See Downs, *The Offering of the Gentiles*, 40–41.

3. Note Martin Hengel and Anna Maria Schwemer (*Paul between Damascus and Antioch* [trans. John Bowden; London: SCM; Louisville: Westminster John Knox, 1997], 498 [n. 1554]): "Paul had presumably arranged this [collection] in Galatia on his journey through there to Ephesus." Note too Barrett (*The First Epistle to the Corinthians*, 386): "[These instructions] may have been given orally during the journey described in Acts xviii.23, or possibly in a special letter"; also James D. G. Dunn (*The Acts of the Apostles* [Valley Forge, PA: Trinity Press International, 1996], 248), who notes that we should understand this visit to Galatia and Phyrgia as background for the collection for the poor believers in Jerusalem.

4. Downs, *The Offering of the Gentiles*, 42.

both 2 Cor 8:1–5 and Rom 15:26 (though he does admit that "arguments from silence are always problematic").[5] We offer a different scenario. First, as we will discuss later in this chapter, as Paul heads to Jerusalem with the collection, according to Acts 20, he has an entourage of people with him from his churches, including Gaius from Derbe and Timothy from Lystra (Acts 20:4). Unfortunately, far too many scholars today feel that Acts offers little historical reliability because (so they argue) Luke is far too biased in his telling of the history of the church to be trustworthy. As we stated in the introduction, however, we disagree with that assessment. It is true that Luke has specific purposes he wants to accomplish in his two-volume work (cf. later in this chapter), and like any historian, he is selective about which stories to tell, but in what he does write, he writes with full historical accuracy.

If, as we believe, Acts 20:3 accurately describes those who accompanied Paul to Jerusalem, there were at least two representatives from Galatia. It is likely, in our estimation, that when Paul was about ready to leave from Corinth for Jerusalem in the spring of AD 56 or 57,[6] he sent Timothy to Galatia, perhaps to visit his mother and certainly to gather the collection;[7] Timothy then returned to either Corinth or Macedonia, along with Gaius from Derbe, with the contribution from these churches. In other words, the reason why Paul does not mention the response of the churches of Galatia in either 2 Cor 8 and 9 or Rom 15 is because at the time he wrote those letters, he simply did not know what their response was. But the fact that two respected representatives, Timothy and Gaius, were part of the entourage headed with Paul to Jerusalem strongly suggests that the churches in Galatia had made a significant contribution.

---

5. Ibid. See Downs's discussion on why he thinks Paul would have mentioned it to both the Corinthians and the Romans if the Galatians had participated. Ernst Käsemann (*Commentary on Romans* [Grand Rapids: Eerdmans, 1980], 381) argues that Paul wanted to conceal the collection effort in Gentile territory because it was a levy on the Gentiles by the Jerusalem pillars. Such a view, of course, denies 1 Cor 16:1.

6. If we follow the chronology of Richard Longenecker ("Acts," *EBC* rev ed. [Grand Rapids: Zondervan, 2007], 10:1021), which is attractive, Paul may have spent as much as a year before he returned to Corinth, during which time he evangelized Illyricum (Rom 15:19), and perhaps also Dalmatia (in 2 Tim 4:10, Titus is mentioned as traveling to Dalmatia, perhaps a return visit).

7. It is also possible that just as Paul spent the winter of AD 56–57 in Corinth, Timothy may have left from Macedonia (from where 2 Corinthians was written) to go to Galatia, spent the winter there, and finalized the collection during that time.

What about Ephesus in the province of Asia Minor, and perhaps other churches that Paul had organized (either directly or indirectly) in that province on his third missionary journey? Paul's first two letters to Corinth ("the earlier letter," 1 Cor 5:9, and 1 Corinthians), and most likely his letter of tears as well (2 Cor 2:2–4; 7:8–12), were written from Ephesus, where Paul preached for at least two and a half years (Acts 19:8–12). The collection was obviously well under way during this time. Did he also solicit money from the churches in Asia Minor for the impoverished believers in Jerusalem? Obviously here it is more difficult to claim, as we did for the churches in Galatia, that at the time Paul wrote Romans from Corinth, he did not know how the believers in this province had responded; he would not have kept his collection as a total secret while he was living in Ephesus. Yet Paul does not include "Asia" in his listing in Rom 15:26.

There is not much discussion about this issue in the literature. This issue is primarily a concern for those who write on the history of the collection. To begin, we must once again go to Acts 20:4, where Luke writes that among Paul's entourage heading to Jerusalem included "Tychicus and Trophimus from the province of Asia." If indeed these two people heading to Jerusalem with Paul were representatives of all the churches that participated in the collection, then churches in Asia Minor did participate.

Lüdemann takes issue with this. From the account Paul gives in 2 Cor 1, Lüdemann concludes that the apostle lost his authority in Ephesus and had to flee from the city.[8] But if we give credibility to the history recorded in the book of Acts, immediately after the uproar caused by Artemis over Paul's effect on the silversmiths' businesses, the apostle sent for the disciples from wherever he was, said good-bye to them, and left for Macedonia (Acts 20:1). The riot in the amphitheater is as good a candidate as any to explain what Paul reports in 2 Cor 1:8–11 and why he almost lost his life. In fact, this may tie in with Rom 16:3–4, where we read that Priscilla and Aquila at some point risked their lives for Paul. This couple had perhaps done much to prepare Ephesus to receive Paul on his third missionary journey (see Acts 18:18–21), and as we argued in ch. 2, presumably Paul stayed with them as a leatherworker, as he had in Corinth. So if the opposition to Paul in the business community of Ephesus was

---

8. Gerd Lüdemann, *Paul: Apostle to the Gentiles: Studies in Chronology* (trans. F. Stanley Jones; Philadelphia: Fortress, 1984), 86.

so vehement, Priscilla and Aquila were also in danger, and after making sure Paul was out of town safely, they left Ephesus to go back to Rome.[9] If this scenario is true, then the opposition Paul experienced in Asia was not from unbelieving Jews and certainly not from the church in Ephesus, but from unbelieving Gentiles who saw Paul's success in preaching the gospel as a threat.

Rick Strelan suggests that Paul had the greatest preaching success in Ephesus among the Jews in Ephesus.[10] If that is so, and if the collection was to be from Paul's Gentile churches, Strelan argues that Paul would not have sought to collect funds from the church of Ephesus. Downs, in fact, using the suggestion of Strelan, concludes that "considering all the available evidence, it does appear ... that the churches in Asia did not partake in the collection for the saints."[11]

However, at least two considerations argue against this. First, Acts 19:17–20 speaks about "the Jews *and Greeks* living in Ephesus" (italics added) being seized with fear after the incident of Sceva and his sons; they both came in significant numbers to faith in Christ. In fact, an enormous pile of scrolls about the practice of sorcery was burned. While we do know from ancient sources that there were Jews who practiced sorcery (witness, again, Sceva and his sons), many of these magicians were likely Gentiles. The church in Ephesus was a mixed community, like any of the other churches Paul established.

Second, we should note that Tychicus and Trophimus are not listed as from Ephesus, but from Asia (Acts 20:4; Tychicus is also mentioned in Eph 6:21; Col 4:7; Trophimus is mentioned again in Acts 21:29 as clearly being a Gentile). The book of Colossians, which Paul addressed to this church in Asia, along with an unknown letter to the church in Laodicea, clearly suggests that other churches in Asia were considered Paul's churches, even though he had never seen most the believers there (Col 2:1; cf. 4:15–16); there was likewise a Christian community in Hierapolis (4:13). From the

---

9. If, as we believe, Rom 16 is an integral part of the letter to the Romans, then a few months after Paul left Ephesus (and, presumably, Aquila and Priscilla left as well), we find them back in Rome (Rom 16:3–4). By this time it would have been safe to go to Rome, since Emperor Claudius, who had required them to leave Rome (Acts 18:2), was dead and Nero was the new emperor. Temporary laws often expired with the ascension of a new ruler.

10. Rick Strelan, *Paul, Artemis, and the Jews in Ephesus* (BZNW 80: Berlin: de Gruyter, 1996), 295.

11. Downs, *The Offering for the Gentiles*, 58.

content of the letter to the Colossians we know there was a significant Jewish element in this church (cf. 2:16–17; 4:11), but there are also strong hints of a Gentile element. Note the reference to τὰ στοιχεία τοῦ κόσμου in 2:20, which is more relevant to "hollow and deceptive [pagan] philosophy" than to the Jewish law. Moreover, 4:11–14 certifies that Epaphras and Demas were most likely Gentiles, and Paul, in writing that in Christ "there is no Gentile or Jew, circumcised or uncircumcised, barbarian, Scythian, slave or free" (3:11), must have listed these categories because there were some of each in the church at Colossae. We conclude, therefore, that like most of Paul's churches, there was a healthy mixture of Jews and Gentiles in the churches in Asia.

But this does not help us get any closer to explaining why Asia is not mentioned in Rom 15:26. To the best of our knowledge, two other factors have not been considered that may yield a more positive answer to whether the believers in Asia Minor participated in the collection. First, we know from ch. 2 above that Paul's policy was not to accept money and support from churches *while he was engaging in ministry there* (see 1 Cor 9; receiving support from Lydia in Philippi was the only clear exception). The situation in Corinth had clearly warned him how easily he could be charged with trickery if he collected money for any reason, and Paul avoided with every ounce of his energy even the slightest evidence of impropriety in this regard. Not even Paul's saying in Ephesus that the collection was for Jerusalem would be sufficient. Thus, if any money for his fund-raising project were to be gathered in Asia Minor, it would have to be totally outside of his hands. He would delegate this to trustworthy people (Tychicus and Trophimus?), and he would not even want to know how much it might be, until, perhaps, he was about ready to head to Jerusalem.

Second, as noted above, Paul had to leave Ephesus and Asia quickly. If perchance Paul had been getting brief updates on how much was being collected, his sudden removal from Asia meant that he had no idea what the final tally might be. In fact, how would he know if perhaps the money that had been gathered during the previous two years had been confiscated by the authorities after the riot? He would not know until he met up with Tychicus and Trophimus what the final amount might be, but that was long after the letter to the Romans had been written and sent off. As a result, just as we pleaded ignorance for how the collection had proceeded in Galatia when Paul wrote Romans, it is also permissible to plead ignorance for Asia Minor.

In sum, the only two provinces that Paul knew for sure as to their contribution to his collection when he wrote the letter to the Romans were Achaia and Macedonia, for he had personal knowledge of the results of the collection from those two areas.[12] But there is sufficient evidence to conclude that churches in both Galatia and Asia Minor had also participated.

THE JOURNEY TO JERUSALEM

In the spring of AD 56 or 57,[13] Paul was ready to go to Jerusalem with the collection. He intended to sail directly from Corinth to Syria as soon as the spring shipping season began (Acts 20:3). He perhaps wanted to reach Jerusalem by the time of Passover. But something changed; he heard rumors of a "plot against him by the Jews" (ἐπιβουλὴ αὐτῷ ὑπὸ τῶν Ἰουδαίων), so rather than going directly to the ship headed for Syria, he and his group of trusted friends headed north to Macedonia (by ship or on foot, we do not know), where Paul celebrated Passover (20:6). Some of these friends are mentioned by name in 20:4, and they appear to be representatives of the churches that had participated in the collection. Sopater was from Berea, and Aristarchus and Secundus from Thessalonica (churches in Macedonia). Gaius was from Derbe (in Galatia) and Timothy was from Lystra (also Galatia). Tychicus and Trophimus were from Asia. We can surmise that Luke linked up with Paul in Philippi.[14] The list given in Acts 20:4 may therefore not be complete.[15]

---

12. Note that according to the record in Acts, Paul was not intending to go back to Macedonia but to travel directly to Syria (Acts 20:2–3); thus he would have already asked to have delivered to him in Achaia what the Macedonians had given. Note too that among his entourage, Luke included "Sopater son of Pyrrhus from Berea, Aristarchus and Secundus from Thessalonica" (20:4) — three people from Macedonia.

13. Note that some scholars put this date as late as the spring of 58.

14. The last "we" section ended at Acts 16:18, at Philippi. Luke presumably stayed behind in Philippi, and Paul and Luke did not meet again until Paul traveled back there in Acts 20, or perhaps earlier in Paul's visit to Macedonia recorded in 2 Cor 2:12–13; 7:5–7.

15. Note too that there is no one from Achaia, one of the two areas that Paul says in Rom 15:26 gave generously for the collection. Richard Pervo suggests that "the list is evidently incomplete" (*Acts: A Commentary* [Hermeneia: Minneapolis: Fortress, 2009)], 509), citing Georgi (*Remembering the Poor*, 123). F. F. Bruce (*Acts*, 406), based on 2 Cor 8:16–24, argues that Titus plus two other trusted men served as representatives of Corinth.

What was this "plot against [Paul] by the Jews"? All scholars must acknowledge that any hypothesis about this plot cannot be verified. The standard theory for well over a century is that Paul's enemies found out which ship Paul would be traveling on and were plotting to kill him on board of the ship.[16] In any case, it was a plot "against [Paul]" (αὐτῷ) personally, not an attempt to steal the collection money Paul was perhaps rumored to be carrying. So rather than spend Passover in Jerusalem, Paul remained in Macedonia (20:6), though some of the rest of his entourage moved on to Troas.

Paul eventually joined up with the others in Troas. Since 20:6 begins a new "we" section in Acts, Luke and perhaps Titus (he is never mentioned in Acts) accompanied the apostle. From this point, the itinerary as recorded in Acts becomes somewhat convoluted, probably because Paul still did not trust the situation and kept trying to keep his enemies guessing as to what his plans were and where he might be.

When it was time to leave Troas, Paul decided to walk on foot to Assos while the rest took a ship. Why did Paul decide to walk? Once again, we simply do not know, and any suggestion is pure speculation.[17] Perhaps he wanted to have his team assess the situation before he would board a ship. In any case, Paul did board the ship at Assos. The ship they had selected was not scheduled for a stop at Ephesus. Schnabel gives a reasonable suggestion that Paul chose a ship with this itinerary because the apostle did not want to take a chance on becoming entangled with the situation that had been so dangerous in Ephesus (perhaps the riot caused by the silversmiths).[18] Thus, Paul disembarked at Miletus (a day's journey from Ephesus) and sent for the elders of the church to come to see him there (20:17). Much of the rest of Acts 20 is Paul's farewell address to the elders at Ephesus at Miletus (20:18–35).

In Paul's farewell address to the Ephesian elders, Acts 20:22–24 stands out for us here. Earlier we discussed Rom 15:31, where Paul expressed his

---

16. See Schnabel, *Acts*, 833. Cf. William M. Ramsay, *St. Paul the Traveller and Roman Citizen* (Grand Rapids: Baker, 1962 [orig. 1896]), 220.

17. Polhill gives several suggestions. "[Paul] may not have relished the difficult voyage around the Cape [Lectum], or he may have wished to spend the last possible moment at Troas, or perhaps the incident with Eutychus had delayed him" (*Acts*, 420).

18. Schnabel, *Acts*, 838. Certainly "saving time would not likely have been the primary factor in Paul's avoiding Ephesus" (Polhill, *Acts*, 421), since to send for the elders in Ephesus and have them come to Miletus would have taken as much as five days.

apprehension of what might happen to him when he arrived in Jerusalem. He expresses that same apprehension here. The Holy Spirit had warned Paul (διαμαρτύρεται) that prison and affliction were facing him if he went to Jerusalem (Acts 20:23). Nevertheless Paul feels "compelled in the Spirit/spirit" (δεδεμένος τῷ πνεύματι)[19] to go to Jerusalem in spite of that warning (20:22).

But what does Paul mean in this verse by τῷ πνεύματι ("in spirit"). Is it the Spirit of God that is compelling him to go to Jerusalem in spite of the dangers? Or is it his own spirit? It seems to us that with the word ἐγώ preceding the τῷ πνεύματι and with πορεύομαι following it (both first person singulars), it is more likely that Paul is speaking about his own inner spirit: "And now, behold, I personally, compelled in my spirit, I am traveling to Jerusalem" (cf. NRSV text note).[20] If, as we have argued, the collection was Paul's personal project in an attempt to heal the growing rift between Jewish Christianity and Gentile Christianity, there is no way that he would *not* go to Jerusalem, in spite of the dangers and in spite of warnings from the Holy Spirit (20:23). He certainly would not expect a group of Gentile believers to go to Jerusalem with the gift for saints there and he not be with them![21]

---

19. This verb, δέω, is often used for imprisonment (BDAG, 221–22, s.v. δέω, meaning 1b; cf. 9:2, 14; 12:6; 21:11). Paul uses this word as a figure of speech here (in the middle voice) to express an inward binding or compulsion he feels in his heart (Danker calls this use "a transcendent binding"). Note too the perfect tense, which suggests that this compulsion has been in his heart for some time (Schnabel, *Acts*, 841 n.48).

20. This would parallel Acts 19:21, which reads in the NIV that "Paul decided" ("decided in the/his spirit" ἔθετο ... ἐν τῷ πνεύματι) to go to Jerusalem. The NIV does have a footnote that reads, "decided in the Spirit." Obviously there is no way to determine with certainty which was Luke's intention.

21. There is another hint of the collection at the end of Paul's speech in Acts 20, and since Paul is speaking to the Ephesian elders, it suggests their participation in the project. Paul asserts that he had never been motivated by greed or covetousness; in fact, he had worked hard to support himself (20:33–34) so as not to take any money from those among whom he was preaching the gospel. In other words, if Paul had received money from people in Asia (Ephesus), it was for someone else, namely, the poor in Jerusalem. This is confirmed by Paul's expressing his concern for "those who are weak [τῶν ἀσθενούντων]," undoubtedly a generic word that includes the poor (BDAG, 142, s.v. ἀσθενέω, includes a meaning of this word as "to experience lack of material necessities, *be in need*"). He also reasserts the main personal benefit of giving that he had expressed in 2 Cor 8 and 9, namely, the personal blessing that comes from giving generously for the collection (cf. εὐλογία in Rom 15:29 and 2 Cor 9:5–6 with μακάριος in Acts 20:35, in a saying he attributed to Jesus [not recorded in the Gospels]). Pervo (*Acts*, 527) writes about this part of Paul's speech: "At issue is the never-mentioned but ever-present subject of the collection."

From Miletus Paul and his group continued on their journey to Syria and Jerusalem, landing at Tyre, where they stayed for seven days. Through the Spirit, the disciples at Tyre warned Paul not to continue on his journey to Jerusalem, and once again Paul refused to heed the warning (Acts 21:3b–6). Their next stop was Ptolemais and then the port of Caesarea Martima, where they stayed with Philip and his four unmarried daughters (21:7–9). This time it was the prophet Agabus who came from Judea; he would perhaps know better than anyone else what people in Jerusalem were saying about Paul. He took off Paul's belt, bound his own hands and feet,[22] and uttered a prophecy by the Holy Spirit: "As to the man who owns this belt, the Jews in Jerusalem will bind him in the same manner and will deliver him into the hands of the Gentiles" (20:11). These words were not just a pleading and an exhortation from a group of concerned believers; this is now a specific prophecy from a man with the known gift of prophecy. Paul himself had earlier acted on a prophecy from Agabus when he and Barnabas had brought a gift to Jerusalem for the poor during a time of famine (11:27–30; see discussion of this incident in ch. 4).[23]

The prophecy of Agabus led to more urging and pleading, with tears, that Paul give up his plans of going to Jerusalem. And once again, Paul rebuffed the pleas, though it was probably the most difficult one to resist. He asks, "Why are you making this commotion by weeping and breaking my heart?" (21:13). The project Paul had been working on for more than three years is so important to him that he is ready to die for it in Jerusalem, if need be. When the believers in Caesarea and Paul's traveling companions saw that Paul's resolve would not budge, they finally ceased their pleading and said, Τοῦ κυρίου τὸ θέλημα γινέσθω ("May the will of the Lord be done"). Whatever might happen was now in God's hands.

---

22. The verb form used here is δήσας, an aorist participle from δέω, the same verb that Paul used to describe his own compulsion to go to Jerusalem. Note the future tense of this same verb in the prophecy of Agabus (δήσουσιν, "they will bind"). See this discussion of this prophecy in Schnabel, *Acts*, 857.

23. It is important to note that the Holy Spirit is *not* instructing Paul to refrain from going to Jerusalem. All three messages that Paul received — Paul's own warning from the Holy Spirit in Acts 20:23, the message through the Spirit from the believers at Tyre in 21:4, and the one from the Holy Spirit through Agabus (21:11) — are simply prophetic of the dangers of what will happen if Paul does go to Jerusalem. Note what Longenecker ("Acts," 10:1033) writes: "It is probably best to understand the Greek preposition *dia* ("through") [in Acts 21:4] as meaning that it was the Spirit's message that was the occasion for the Christians' concern rather than that their trying to dissuade Paul was directly inspired by the Spirit."

It is important to note that there were a number of times when Paul took measures to escape persecution. He escaped danger by being let down over the wall of Damascus (Acts 9:23–25; 2 Cor 11:32–33). When he went to Jerusalem and tried to preach there, "the Hellenistic Jews tried to kill him"; he then agreed to leave Judea and head to Tarsus (Acts 9:29–30). Later, he quickly left Philippi, Thessalonica, and Berea when either Gentiles or certain trouble-making Jews tried to create a riot against him (Acts 16–17). A few years later he left Ephesus when he knew his life was in danger (2 Cor 1:8–11); presumably at this time Priscilla and Aquila risked their lives for him (Rom 16:3–4). He had taken several steps on this final journey to Jerusalem, as we have noted, to evade the threats rumored to be against him from the Jews (Acts 20:1–5).

But in this final stage of his trip to Jerusalem, his firm intention was to go there and personally deliver the money he had collected, in spite of numerous and specific threats, and so Paul would not yield. Nothing would stop him from handing over the collection to the church in Jerusalem in person, with a large number of Gentile believers at his side. He knew that his role as the apostle to the Gentiles, who became followers of Jesus without needing to be circumcised, had played a role in creating a rift between Jewish Christians and Gentile Christians, and he felt a deep sense of obligation to fulfill what God had laid on his heart as a project that would symbolize that the Gentile believers saw the saints in Jerusalem as brothers and sisters in Christ. The collection demonstrated that Paul's Gentile churches owed it to the Jewish Christians in the mother church of Jerusalem to share with them in material blessings (Rom 15:27).[24]

That, then, raises the question: How was the collection received in Jerusalem? Did it accomplish what Paul hoped and prayed with all his heart (and asked others to join in prayer, Rom 15:30–31) would be the result of the collection?

---

24. Downs takes the position that "in Luke's account, it is divine necessity, and not the collection, that compels Paul on his fateful trip to Jerusalem" (*The Offering of the Gentiles*, 65). This seems to pit Paul's own spirit against the Holy Spirit, as if it has to be one or the other. In NT theology, however, the Holy Spirit often shapes the human spirit, and the two work in tandem with each other. Yet as we have also seen, nowhere in the passages we have looked at does the Holy Spirit command Paul to cease his trip to Jerusalem. The Spirit allows Paul to make his own decision according to the will of the Lord as he felt it in his heart.

THE RECEPTION IN JERUSALEM

With Paul ready now to present the collection along with the Gentile representatives of his churches to the elders in Jerusalem, and with Luke, the author of Acts, being a longtime friend of Paul (and a Gentile himself), it may seem surprising and even anticlimactic that so little is said about the reception of the collection in Jerusalem. In fact, while there are hints about the collection in Acts, as we have been outlining in the previous section, there is no overt, uncontested comment about the collection anywhere in Acts. When Paul arrived in Jerusalem, here is what Luke records:

> When we arrived in Jerusalem, the brothers and sisters received us warmly. The next day Paul and the rest of us went to see James, and all the elders were present. Paul greeted them and reported in detail what God had done among the Gentiles through his ministry. When they heard this, they praised God. (Acts 21:17 – 20a NIV)

DID PAUL USE SOME OF THE COLLECTION FOR THE NAZIRITE VOW?

Then the elders continued by commenting on the rumors circulating about Paul and made a suggestion that Paul make a political move to squelch these rumors. The rumor was that Paul was teaching the Jews who lived among the Gentiles to forsake their Jewish traditions, including not circumcising their children (21:20b – 21). Nothing could be further from the truth; Paul's longstanding policy had been to honor Jewish ways when he was among Jews and to encourage them to do so as well, but when among Gentiles, he would live as one not under the law (1 Cor 9:19 – 23). So the leaders in Jerusalem suggested that Paul make a Nazirite vow and then join four other men in their purification ceremony — and pay the expenses for all five of them (Acts 21:22 – 24). That should convince the naysayers that Paul did, at least in Jewish territory, live in obedience to the law.

There is not a word about the collection. A number of scholars take this as evidence that either the church in Jerusalem rejected the funds, or at least they were lukewarm to the gift.[25] If that were the reaction, it might

---

25. Cf. James D. G. Dunn (*From the Beginning* [Christianity in the Making 2; Grand Rapids: Eerdmans, 2009], 972) who writes: "It is hard to shake off the suspicion that the collection was not welcomed and possibly *not* even received by the Jerusalem church."

be understandable why Luke would not choose to record that event. In his historical writing, Luke tends to choose to write about events that emphasize the unity and cohesiveness of early Christian community. While he records numerous conflicts with either Roman political authorities or the leaders of the various Jewish communities, his record of inner-church squabbles are few—limited to the controversy about widows in Acts 6, the issue about circumcision in Acts 15 (which was peacably resolved), and the conflict between Barnabas and Paul over John Mark (13:13; 15:36–40). Yet we know from Paul's letters that there were other difficult moments in the early church, such as Paul's confrontation with Peter in Galatia (Gal 2:11–14), the sharp words Paul addressed to the Galatian believers (1:6–9; 3:1–5; 5:2–12), the various frictions in Corinth as attested in both 1 and 2 Corinthians, and even the conflicts among Paul's coworkers in Philippi (Phil 1:15–18; 4:2–3).

It is for reasons such as these that, as noted in the introduction, some have rejected the historical realiability of Luke's writing about the early church. They claim that he presents an idealized picture of the church—history as he wished it were, not as it really was. Yet is Luke then unhistorical? Any historian has to pick and choose certain incidents from the vast array of historical happenings, and all writers of history have a slant they want to give to their story. We accept that from historians today, so there is no reason why we should not accept that from ancient historians. Moreover, there is a plausible reason why Luke may have decided not to write about the collection as one of the limited things he chose to talk about. He is entering into one of the longest and most important units of his book—"the significance of Paul's arrest and long imprisonment [which] completely overshadowed the collection" in Luke's mind.[26] In addition, if indeed the collection was not well-received in Jerusalem and Luke, looking back, knew about that when he wrote Acts, "he did not see the collection as having the significance which Paul attached to it in the period leading up to his final visit to Jerusalem."[27]

Furthermore, we have already noted an allusion to the collection undertaken in Asia in our comments on Acts 20:33–35. In the rest of Acts, it is

---

26. Schnabel, *Acts*, 871.
27. David Wenham, "Acts and the Pauline Corpus: II. Pauline Parallels," in *The Book of Acts in Its First-Century Setting*, vol. 1, *Ancient Literary Context* (ed. Bruce W. Winter and Andrew D. Clarke; Grand Rapids: Eerdmans / Carlisle: Paternoster, 1993), 254.

important to note that there are two more direct hints that allude to the collection. The first is right in this passage: Paul's agreement to undergo a Nazirite vow and to pay for the expenses of four others (21:24). Schnabel speculates on how much these expenses may have been, and he outlines three options — one of which was very expensive since it required several sacrifices, the other two less so.[28] But regardless of what amount of money would be needed, some outlay of cash would be requred to pay for five people — and let us remember that Paul had had no opportunity during his travel time to work in his leatherworking business. From where did he get the money to agree to this suggestion of the Jerusalem leaders?

It is possible and even likely that Paul may have used part of the collection for this purpose.[29] After all, if the main purpose of the collection was to help heal the growing breach between the Gentile Christian branch of the church and the Jewish Christian branch, then to use a portion of that money for a political move, under the assumption that it would help to accomplish that very purpose, I suspect that Paul would have readily agreed.[30] In fact, it is just as odd for Luke not to reflect on Paul's source of money here as it is to suggest that Luke either does not know anything about the collection or fails to mention it because of embarrassment over its reception. Perhaps both of these issues have the same answer: Paul did bring the collection to the Jerusalem church, and at least a portion of it was immediately put to good use to pay for a ceremony that, according to the leaders in Jerusalem, might help heal the growing rift in the church.

PAUL'S SPEECH IN ACTS 24:17

The second evidence of the collection in this part of Acts is Acts 24:17. This chapter records events after Paul's arrest and after his removal from

---

28. Pervo (*Acts*, 546) comments about paying for the expenses of others, that "this was a charitable benefaction associated with the wealthy." We have already placed Paul at best in the ES5 level or perhaps even ES6, well out of range for such expenses.

29. Note Robert W. Wall ("Acts" [NIBCNT; Nashville: Abingdom, 2002], 294): since Paul's agreement involved a significant financial cost, "might this be an allusion to Paul's collection, hitherto unmentioned in Acts?" While Wall ultimately rejects that interpretation, it seems plausible to us. Haenchen, by contrast, sees it as likely that some of the collection money might be used for this purpose, especially since "a redemption of Nazirites was considered particularly pious by every Jew" (*Acts*, 614).

30. Recall too that Paul readily accepted help for specific projects (such as writing letters) and for special projects that would help advance the kingdom (see ch. 3 for a discussion of this topic).

Jerusalem to being placed under guard in the royal palace in Caesarea (23:31 – 35). Five days later, the high priest, Ananias, went down to Caesarea with some of the Jewish elders and a lawyer named Tertullus, in order to charge Paul formally with being a troublemaker, creating riots all over the empire and destroying the sanctity of temples. Tertullus gets a chance to speak first and lays out the charges. Then Governor Felix offers Paul an opportunity to defend himself. Among the things that Paul says is that his main purpose for coming to Jerusalem after several years' absence was to "offer alms [ἐλεημοσύνας] for my people and to present offerings [προσφοράς]."

There is a virtual consensus among scholars that Acts 24:17 is at least a hint of the collection in this writing of Luke.[31] Downs, however, takes exception to this consensus and argues strenuously against it.[32] He links 24:17 with 24:11 since both verses have a first person aorist verb followed by a future participle of purpose. Verse 11 says that Paul went up to Jerusalem in order to worship; v. 17 says that Paul came to Jerusalem in order to bring alms for his people and offerings. Then v. 18 locates Paul in the temple. From this Downs concludes that all of the above occurred in the temple: worship, bringing alms, and offerings; the collection, however, would have been presented to James and the other church leaders elsewhere in Jerusalem, so that Paul's use of the word "alms" does not refer to the collection. Downs paraphrases v. 18 this way: "While I was in the temple offering alms and sacrifices, they found me completing the rite of purification, without a crowd or disturbance." Moreover, the phrase "for my people" would have to mean "for the Jewish nation" — certainly not "for my Christian brothers and sisters."

Furthermore, Downs traces the word ἐλεημοσύνη ("alms") in the book of Acts and concludes that it refers either to something that happened in

---

31. Downs (*The Offering of the Gentiles*, 62–63) acknowledges this: "the scholarly consensus has hardly changed since Clayton R. Bowen asked over eighty years ago, '[Does] Acts 24:17 refer to the collection at all?' With a few notable exceptions, Bowen's answer could appropriately describe the situation today: 'No commentator has, to the present writer's knowledge, hitherto doubted it'" (citing Clayton R. Bowen, "Paul's Collection and the Book of Acts," *JBL* 42 [1923]: 48–58). Downs cites at least eighteen prominent modern scholars who support a linkage between this verse and the collection. Two recent commentators who deny that link, however, are R. C. Tannehill, "Narrative Criticism," in *Dictionary of Biblical Interpretation* (Philadelphia: Trinity Press International, 1990), 300, and Beverly R. Gaventa, *The Acts of the Apostles* (ANTC; Nashville: Abingdon, 2003), 328.

32. The following section summarizes Downs, *The Offering of the Gentiles*, 66–68.

the temple (Acts 3:2, 3, 10) or was an act of personal piety (9:36; 10:2, 4, 31). Consequently it could not mean an act of bringing money from Gentile believers to the church in Jerusalem. But Downs has too narrow a definition of ἐλεημοσύνη in the NT and limits himself only to its uses in Acts.[33] Matthew uses the notion of giving ἐλεημοσύνη for what some people did publicly "in the synagogues and on the streets" (Matt 6:2–4), or (which Jesus considers preferable) for something that a person might do in private. Moreover, in Luke 12:33 (written by the same author as Acts), Jesus gives a generic command: "Sell your possessions and give alms [δότε ἐλεημοσύνην]"; there is nothing here about the temple or about personal piety (note that the imperative verbs are plural). Paul is not limited to the meaning that all almsgiving must have taken place in the temple by throwing money in one of the collection boxes for the poor or had to be done as a personal act of piety.

We acknowledge that the two future participles in 24:11 and 24:17 are participles of purpose. Paul did indeed go to Jerusalem in order to worship, and he did go to Jerusalem in order to bring alms. But it is too narrow a concept that these two purposes, via 24:18, had to take place in the temple. What surprises us even more is that whereas Downs's entire book comes to the conclusion that Paul viewed the collection as an act of worship and used many metaphors to describe it as an act of worship, when there is rhetorical evidence *in Acts* that Paul's bringing of funds to the church in Jerusalem is perhaps linked with worship, he severs that connection to the collection. Even more striking is the fact that the word that serves as a title to his book, *The Offering* [προσφορά] *of the Gentiles*, which comes from Rom 15:16, is precisely the word that Luke uses to describe one of the purposes why Paul came to Jerusalem, namely, to present προσφορά.[34]

Finally, Downs takes no account of the setting in which Paul talks about bringing "alms for my people" (in Acts 24:17–18). He is in a legal setting, in a trial before Felix. The lawyer for the prosecution, Tertullus, has just presented his best-case scenario, beginning with excessive flattery of the governor (not unusual in an ancient legal setting). Paul does not

---

33. See also our earlier discussion of the word ἐλεημοσύνη in ch. 4.

34. This word also occurs in 21:26 as Paul is engaging in the purification rites. The rest of the occurrences in the NT, apart from the one previously discussed in Rom 15:16, have allusions to the sacrifice of Christ (Eph 5:2; Heb 10:5, 8, 10, 14, 18).

stoop so low as to reciprocate with flattery, but he does intend to present the best case for his defense (and, we should note, he has no lawyer supplied for himself as the defendant). His goal is to present himself as a faithful, law-abiding Jew, who does all the legal things that Jews were permitted to do in the Roman empire: worship the God of their ancestors, believe the Law and the Prophets, seek to live a moral life, give alms for the poor, and present offerings in the temple. If there is any substance to the charge that he does in fact incite riots in other cities, well, that proof would have to come from Jews in Asia, and they are not present there (see 24:11–21).

Regarding the specific aspect of this listing about giving alms for the poor (i.e., the ἐλεημοσύνη), then, Paul would not have any problem if Felix perhaps thought that Paul was offering alms just like every other Jew did, in the collection boxes in the temple, while he in his own mind knew that the alms he was offering had been done in a more private setting earlier in the week, when he met with the elders and leaders of the church of Jerusalem. After all, the believers in Jerusalem were Jews—followers of the Way. While the setting for giving alms was different (though still within the semantic range of how alms could be given and received), the idea was the same—offering a substantial gift for "the poor among the saints in Jerusalem" (Rom 15:26).

CONCLUSION

Paul faced significant challenges after he had completed the collection. There were threats against his life, and Paul had to begin his trip to Jerusalem warily. The Jews in Asia knew that the key figure in this collection was Paul himself, for this was his fund-raising project. Moreover, Paul was warned a number of times how dangerous it would be for him to go to Jerusalem and that he could easily be killed. But he insisted on going; this is what God had called him to do. In our view, he did present the collection to the church leaders (James and the elders), and for nearly a week everything seemed to indicate that nothing bad would happen. On the seventh day, however, the Jews from Asia started a riot. Yet God continued to find ways to protect his apostle as he sat in Roman custody—through the tip-off from his nephew, through his protective custody in Caesarea, through using the advantages of his Roman citizenship, and even through a storm at sea, until he eventually reached Rome. Whether the collection had any lasting effect on the church in Jerusalem, we have no way to assess, but Paul certainly tried his best. He had presented an offering from the Gentiles to the church leaders in Jerusalem, demonstrating to them that Gentiles believers considered them as part of the one church—brothers and sisters in Christ.

PART 3

Other Issues concerning Finances in Paul

CHAPTER 9

THE THESSALONIAN FREELOADERS

ONE OF THE PRINCIPAL REASONS WHY PAUL WROTE THE THESSALONIAN correspondence was because a number of believers were freeloading off others in the church.[1] It seems that a group of people in the fellowship, for reasons that we cannot definitively ascertain,[2] refused to work and to take care of their own physical needs (2 Thess 3:8, 10 – 12). In these two letters, however, Paul writes that he valued work for all able-bodied persons to earn their own income. Consequently, he instructed the Thessalonians to deal with those who refused to work and to initiate church discipline in the hope of restoring these believers to a productive life. In this chapter we will examine four essential texts in 1 and 2 Thessalonians that discuss work and issues related to money, along with Paul's recommendation if no changes take place (1 Thess 2:9; 4:11 – 12; 5:14; 2 Thess 3:6 – 15). We will conclude with the considerations of the task of church discipline, into which this issue of Paul and money leads us.

---

1. This is certainly the case for 2 Thessalonians; it is less certain that these issues were front and center in Paul's mind as he wrote 1 Thessalonians.

2. Gary Shogren (*1 and 2 Thessalonians*, 331 – 35), outlines five different theories that scholars have proposed as to the historical situation behind what might be called "the Thessalonian freeloaders" (see n. 21 in ch. 2). On this issue, Gordon D. Fee (*The First and Second Letters to the Thessalonians* [NICNT; Grand Rapids: Eerdmans, 2009], 324 – 25) astutely notes: "Was it disdain for work itself, because they were people of God's kingdom and thus a cut above needing to work? Was it pressing the gospel of the kingdom a bit too far, *expecting/demanding* the rich to care for the poor? Was it related to their eschatological understanding? Was it an attempt on Paul's part to break up dependencies created by patron-client relationships? Or was it just plain laziness? We simply do not know and in fact getting an answer to this question would hardly affect our understanding of the text at all." [italics original]

THE BELIEVER'S WORK ETHIC (1 THESS 2:9)

Paul's first statement concerning work comes from the autobiographical section of 1 Thessalonians. Beginning in 2:1, Paul reflects on his experience when he and his missionary companions (Silas and Timothy) first arrived in Thessalonica. They had just been in Philippi, where Paul and Silas suffered severe physical abuse and imprisonment (cf. Acts 16:22–24). When they arrived in Thessalonica, they were still experiencing the physical and emotional trauma of having been imprisoned and severely beaten (2:2).[3]

In spite of the painful tribulations Paul endured, he expressed his love for the Thessalonians by supporting himself and laboring with his own hands (1 Thess 2:8–9; cf. Acts 18:3; 20:34) rather than burden[4] his converts by making financial demands of them.[5] His primary concern was that the gospel be "freely offered and freely received"[6] to avoid putting any hindrance in the way of potential or actual converts (cf. 1 Cor 9:12). As 1 Thess 2:3–8 indicates, Paul's motives were exemplary. He did not exercise his authority or seek personal glory. Instead, everything that he did was for God's glory *and* the good of the church.

Paul asks the Thessalonians to "remember the toil and hard labor" (μνημονεύετε τὸν κόπον ἡμῶν καὶ τὸν μόχθον)[7] that he carried out to support himself while undertaking his preaching of the gospel to them.[8]

---

3. The participles προπαθόντες ("suffered") and ὑβρισθέντες ("mistreated") are strong words that show the intensity of the animosity against Paul and his preaching of the gospel.

4. In 1 Thess 2:9 Paul's use of ἐπιβαρῆσαι ("to burden," in the phrase "not to be a burden") alludes to his own physical labors and clearly points to Paul's providing his own material support such as food and lodging. Shogren (*1 and 2 Thessalonians*, 106) notes: "The simple verb 'burden' (βαρέω) has a similar meaning in 1 Tim 5:16, where the church is burdened by a widow who should rely on other resources."

5. See our previous discussion in ch. 2, where we explored Paul's insistence on working with his own hands for his living expenses.

6. Ben Witherington III, *1 and 2 Thessalonians: A Socio-Rhetorical Commentary* (Grand Rapids: Eerdmans 2006), 81 n. 85.

7. Green (*The Letters to the Thessalonians*, 346) notes: "Paul writes the Thessalonian correspondence to remind his readers of what they already knew (see 1 Thess 1:5; 2:1, 2, 5, 9, 10, 11; 3:3, 4; 4:2; 5:2; 2 Thess 2:5, 6)." Paul typically uses οἴδατε ("you know"; cf. 1:5; 2:1, 5), but this time he uses μνημονεύετε ("you remember"), probably for the sake of stylistic variation. Paul uses the combination "our labor and toil" (τὸν κόπον ἡμῶν καὶ τὸν μόχθον) here and on two other occasions in relation to the support of his own living expenses while doing missionary work (2 Cor 11:27; 2 Thess 3:8).

8. While it is true that the Philippians sent financial aid to Paul more than once when he was in Thessalonica (Phil 4:15–16), such help was partial and did not alleviate his need to work continually and support himself. As we explored in ch. 2, while Paul refused to burden

Syntactically, 2:9 explains the statement in 2:7b–8, as the conjunction γάρ ("for") indicates.[9] The apostle's willingness to work hard for the gospel exhibits his maternal instincts for the Thessalonians ("just as a nursing mother cares for her own children").

Paul's heart drove him relentlessly and tirelessly. As the present participle ἐργαζόμενοι ("working") implies, he and his colleagues worked night and day, probably preaching the gospel at the same time.[10] The genitive case in νυκτός ("night") and ἡμέρας ("day") does not mean that they worked without sleeping but rather that they were able to work both at night and during the day.[11] The order of the words may indicate that they rose up to work before the sun and that their labors continued throughout the day.[12] Gene Green comments: "Labor contracts normally indicated the period of labor as 'from sunrise to sunset,' but these men went beyond the norm, rising before the dawn."[13] Hence, Paul had little choice but to use the workshop as a place for communicating the gospel since so much of his time was spent there.[14]

While not his primary motivation for mentioning his work patterns, Paul is laying a foundation for the appeal he will soon make to the Thessalonians to "work with [their own] hands ... and be dependent on

those among whom he was preaching the gospel to help support him for his general living expenses, once Paul had left, he was willing to receive money from churches that he had previously founded.

9. Wanamaker, *The Epistles to the Thessalonian*, 102; Green, *The Letters to the Thessalonians*, 129.

10. Wanamaker, *The Epistles to the Thessalonians*, 102. See also Wallace, *Greek Grammar Beyond the Basics*, 124. See also ch. 2, where we adopted the interpretation that one advantage of Paul's being a leatherworker was that he could witness to the people who came into the place where he was working.

11. Michael W. Holmes, *1 and 2 Thessalonians* (NIVAC; Grand Rapids: Zondervan, 1998), 65.

12. See esp. David J. Williams (*1 and 2 Thessalonians* [NIBCNT; Peabody, MA: Hendrickson, 1994], 42) who argues that the word order "reflects the fact that in the ancient world the working day started early, while it was still night (cf. Acts 20:31; 2 Thess. 3:8; also 1 Thess. 3:10)." See also Hock, *Social Context of Paul's Ministry*, 31–32; Green, *The Letters to the Thessalonians*, 129.

13. Green, *The Letters to the Thessalonians*, 130. See also Hock, *Social Context of Paul's Ministry*, 31–37; see also Hock, "Paul's Tentmaking and the Problem of His Social Class," *JBL* 97 (1978): 555; Abraham J. Malherbe, *Paul and the Thessalonians: The Philosophic Tradition of Pastoral Care* (Philadelphia: Fortress, 1987), 55–56.

14. Hock (*The Social Context of Paul's Ministry*, 37–42) has shown that Paul probably did not participate in street preaching and other forms of public mass appeal. Of necessity his mission work was with individuals and small groups. The workshop provided one of the recognized social contexts for this preaching. See also Earl J. Richard, *First and Second Thessalonians* (SP; Collegeville, MN: Liturgical, 1995), 102–3.

no one" (4:10b–12).[15] Moreover, Paul's conduct and work ethic among the Thessalonians further reinforces his own sincerity (2:1–12), which in turn will strengthen the Thessalonians' confidence in the gospel, which he preached.[16]

The Believer's Ambition (1 Thess 4:11 – 12)

In 1 Thess 4:11–12, Paul instructs the Thessalonians to be ambitious in their work because their work is a witness. He writes: "and to make it your ambition to lead a quiet life[17] and to attend to your own business and work with your hands,[18] just as we commanded you, so that you will walk[19] properly[20] toward outsiders[21] and not be in any need." In these verses there are three critical expectations that Paul has for the Thessalonians. First, he states, "make it your ambition to lead a quiet life" (4:11a). The apostle portrays a life that does its best to avoid unnecessary contention and seeks to be at peace with all people insofar as it is humanly possible (cf. Rom 12:18). The infinitive translated "make it your ambition" (φιλοτιμεῖσθαι) can also be rendered "aspire."[22] Gordon Fee explains that it could be translated, "strive hard to live quietly."[23] He also points out that the word "quiet" here does not carry the idea of "not speaking" or "being restful"[24]

---

15. See Abraham J. Malherbe, *The Letters to the Thessalonians* (AYBC; New Haven: Yale University Press, 2000), 161; Victor Paul Furnish, *1 & 2 Thessalonians* (AB; Nashville: Abingdon, 2007), 61.

16. Jon A. Weatherly, *1 & 2 Thessalonians* (CPNIVC; Joplin: College Press, 1996), 71.

17. The verb ἡσυχάζειν ("lead a quiet life") is used elsewhere in the NT only in Luke 14:4; 23:56; Acts 11:18; and 21:14. A related word, ἡσύχιος, is used to describe the wife with a "quiet spirit" in 1 Pet 3:4 (cf. also its use in 1 Tim 2:2).

18. Paul later gives a similar injunction to the Ephesians in the context of general ethical instructions (Eph 4:28).

19. The ESV, HCSB, and NKJV translate περιπατῆτε in its usual meaning, as "walk" (cf. 1 Thess 4:1). Those translations that render this term in a different way (e.g., NASB, NET, and NIV) prevent the English reader from seeing the *inclusio* between 4:1 and 12.

20. The adverb εὐσχημόνως ("properly") is used elsewhere in the NT only in Rom 13:13 and 1 Cor 14:40.

21. The term τοὺς ἔξω ("the outsiders") is only used by Paul in 1 Cor 5:12–13 and Col 4:5 (in addition to this passage).

22. BDAG, 1059, s.v. φιλοτιμέομαι: "have as one's ambition, consider it an honor, aspire." Its only other NT occurrences are in Rom 15:20 and 2 Cor 5:9.

23. Fee, *The First and Second Letters to the Thessalonians*, 162.

24. Contra Leon Morris (*The First and Second Epistles to the Thessalonians* [rev. ed.; NICNT; Grand Rapids: Eerdmans, 1991], 131) who thinks the idea is "to seek strenuously to be still."

but of not intruding into the lives of other people, especially brothers and sisters in the faith, and so becoming a burden to them. Paul is instructing his readers to live in such a way as not to create stress for others, but he is also warning them not to draw attention to themselves.[25] His point is that there is a time to share Christ, but more often than not, it is better to work diligently and when there is an opportunity, to listen and draw others out.

Second, Paul reminds the Thessalonians that he had already instructed them to work ("just as we commanded you," 1 Thess 4:11b). The expression "attend to" (πράσσειν) means "to do, accomplish, or act."[26] The phrase "your own business" means "your own affairs." We might say today "mind your own business." There is no place for a Christian to be a busybody.[27]

Third, Paul told the Thessalonians to work "with their hands" (4:11c). The upper classes of Rome and Greece despised manual labor. That is why they owned so many slaves. They hated to work with their hands. But Christianity brought in a new ethic based on personal responsibility and hard work. Jesus was a carpenter and Paul himself was a tentmaker/leatherworker.

It is important to understand that Paul is not being metaphorical here. He literally worked with his hands whenever he could so that he could support himself while he preached the gospel.[28] Even though he was highly educated, he did not mind hard work in the least and he did not find manual labor embarrassing.[29] So Paul urges the Thessalonians

---

25. Paul seems to clarify this command ("mind your own business") to do their own work in 1 Thess 5:14.

26. BDAG, 860, s.v. πράσσειν 1a.

27. The fact that the warning of unruly behavior occurs both in this context (4:11) and later (5:14), immediately after Paul's explicit teaching about Christ's final coming (4:13–5:11), suggests that some of the Thessalonians were not working because they believed Christ's return was near. See F. F. Bruce, *1 & 2 Thessalonians* (WBC; Nashville: Nelson, 1982), 91; I. Howard Marshall, *1 and 2 Thessalonians* (NCBC; Grand Rapids: Eerdmans / London: Marshall, Morgan & Scott, 1983), 117; G. K. Beale, *1–2 Thessalonians* (IVPNTC; Downers Grove, IL: InterVarsity Press, 2003), 125.

28. Jeffrey A. D. Weima ("1 & 2 Thessalonians," in *The Zondervan Illustrated Bible Backgrounds Commentary* [Grand Rapids: Zondervan, 2002], 408) writes: "It is commonly assumed that Paul won converts by preaching in the marketplaces ('street corner' evangelism). Nevertheless, there is good evidence his missionary work took place in the workshop and the private home. We can picture the apostle in Thessalonica laboring in a local workshop, perhaps one owned by Jason (Acts 17:5). During the long hours at his workbench, cutting and sewing leather to make tents, Paul would have had opportunities to share the gospel with fellow workers, customers, and other citizens who were interested in this tentmaker-philosopher newly arrived in the city."

29. See Still, "Did Paul Loathe Manual Labor?" 781–95.

to "work with your hands" so that they can provide for the needs of their own families and not give the gospel a reputation that it is intended for disorderly people.

The exhortation to "work with your hands" is particularly important in evaluating the way the Thessalonians were living compared with the early Jerusalem Christians. The way the believers in Jerusalem conducted themselves won the respect even of unbelievers and served as a means to help bring people to faith in Christ (Acts 2:46–47). By contrast, the behavior of some of the Thessalonians was bringing disrespect from their neighbors (and, as we will see, also from others in their believing community).

Paul does not give the Thessalonians bare expectations; he also provides reasons why they should live in this manner. First, the apostle tells them that they are supposed to live this way so that they might "walk [περιπατέω] properly before outsiders" (4:12a; cf. 4:1 where Paul uses περιπατέω). Second, Paul states, "so that you … [may] not be in any need" (4:12b). Paul uses the word "need" (χρεία) three times elsewhere in 1 Thessalonians to express the fact that he did not "need" to write or say anything further to the believers at Thessalonica (1:8; 4:9; 5:1). Here the thought is entirely different. In light of the command to work with their hands, the derived meaning no doubt involves financial matters. Bruce comments, "If all the able-bodied members worked with their hands, they would be able to support themselves and their dependents, and not fall into destitution and become a charge on the generosity of others."[30]

In Paul's mind, to be dependent on someone else in the congregation is unloving. That has been his point since 4:9, and he presses the conclusion upon them: it is a loving act to be self-sufficient in regard to their own work. But perhaps the apostle has an additional reason in giving this command. The Thessalonians are called to be dependent on the Lord to provide their daily bread, and if they get in a situation where they, of their own free will, are dependent on someone else, it could cause them to compromise some Christian convictions, which could adversely affect their walk before outsiders.

If the Thessalonians, however, live in a way that reflects brotherly love, it will be obvious to an on-looking world. They will not have to proclaim their faith loudly to outsiders, but the latter will see how the believers

---

30. Bruce, *1 & 2 Thessalonians*, 91.

are living. In the city of Thessalonica, everyone would have noticed the change of lives in these Christians. They did not participate in religious ceremonies and sexual immorality in the pagan temples. They did not cheat each other or strangers. They worked hard, they took care of each other, and they loved each other. As G. K. Beale notes:

> Indeed, the first mention of love in 1 Thessalonians is inextricably linked with labor: "we continually remember … your labor prompted by love" (1:3). Love for God and one another inspires the doing of good works, including doing literal work in the world to which God has called one.[31]

Paul believes that love expressed through good works can transform a culture. As the Thessalonians live out their faith at work, they will make their impact in the world.

THE BELIEVER'S RESPONSIBILITIES TO THE BODY (1 THESS 5:14)

Paul wraps up 1 Thessalonians with eleven verses that flesh out what it means to live soberly (5:6, 8).[32] He lays out four sobriety checkpoints: honor church leaders (5:12–13), shepherd church members (5:14–15), discover God's will (5:16–18), and worship with wisdom (5:19–22). The first of these checkpoints states the responsibilities of the church to its leaders; the remaining checkpoints consider the responsibilities of the church members to each other.[33] In 5:14 (our focal point here), Paul urges[34] church members to adopt a fourfold job description. He does not elaborate here why he chooses these four verbs, each followed by a specific adjective. But he may have been sensing something amiss in the congregation at Thessalonica.

---

31. Beale, *1–2 Thessalonians*, 125.

32. Morris (*The First and Second Epistles to the Thessalonians*, 166) explains, "while its tone is brotherly, it is big-brotherly."

33. Holmes (*1 and 2 Thessalonians*, 180 fn. 4) notes: "Some have argued that 5:14–15 are directed to the leaders referred to in 5:12–13, but this is unlikely. The entire community is addressed in 5:12–13 and 16–18 and the introduction of 5:14 is nearly identical to the one in 5:12 (note esp. the repetition of *adelphoi* 'brothers and sisters'). Had Paul intended a change in subject in 5:14 he would surely have signaled it more clearly."

34. Paul uses the verb παρακαλέω ("urge") a total of eight times in 1 Thessalonians (2:12; 3:2, 7; 4:1, 10, 18; 5:11, 14).

First, Paul urges the Thessalonians to "admonish the unruly" (5:14a). The adjective "unruly" (ἀτάκτους) is a military expression that means "those who break ranks, get out of line."[35] It refers to soldiers who are undisciplined and irresponsible. In the church there are unruly soldiers who are disrespectful and slanderous. When a brother or sister becomes unruly (as would happen if they failed to "lead a quiet life" [4:11]), Paul says the Thessalonians are to "admonish them" (see discussion below on 2 Thess 3:6–15, where the work ethic of some in the church is front and center). The verb translated "admonish" (νουθετεῖτε) is a strong word that means to "put into the mind" (cf. 5:12).[36] It implies a face-to-face confrontation, precisely the kind of situation most Christians want to avoid at all costs. It is painful, difficult work.

Second, Paul urges the Thessalonians to "encourage the fainthearted" (5:14b). The components of the adjective translated "fainthearted" (ὀλιγόψυχος) translate as "small-souled."[37] While nothing in the immediate context explains its meaning or its cause,[38] in the LXX ὀλιγόψυχος refers to discouragement due to trials. Paul, then, could be referring either to those who were shaken by the persecutions that the church had to endure (2:14; 3:1–5) or to those who were anxious about various aspects of Christ's return (4:13–5:11).[39] The church must "encourage" (παραμυθέομαι)[40] such people. This verb is a narrowly defined word meaning to comfort or cheer the heart (cf. 2:11), to instill courage, and to verbally affirm hurting people.

---

35. The adjective ἄτακτος ("unruly") is only used here in the NT. BDAG, 148, s.v. ἄτακτος, defines it: "of volitional state, pert. to being out of step and going one's own way, *disorderly, insubordinate*." The word "idle" (ESV, NRSV, NIV, NLT [lazy]) is not the best translation. The word does not mean "lazy," which is what we think of when we hear "idle." Beale (*1–2 Thessalonians*, 164) suggests that the word be translated as "disorderly" or "disruptive," and Fee (*The First and Second Letters to the Thessalonians*, 208–10) suggests the rendering "unruly." The translation "the idle" first appeared in the RSV in 1948 but apparently does not have a strong case. Fee (209) even says that it is "difficult to fathom" why this meaning took over NT translations "despite total lack of evidence for it" as well as the fact that "it does not in fact have a lexical leg to stand on." Instead, the word means "out of line." Note that in 2 Thess 3:6, 7, 11, other words in the word group describe those who are refusing to work and have become freeloaders on others in the church.

36. BDAG, 679, s.v. νουθετέω: "to counsel about avoidance or cessation of an improper course of conduct, *admonish, warn, instruct*."

37. The adjective ὀλιγόψυχος is only used here in the NT.

38. Holmes *1 and 2 Thessalonians*, 181.

39. Weima, "1 Thessalonians," 427; Beale, *1–2 Thessalonians*, 165.

40. Paul uses the verb παραμυθέομαι elsewhere only in 1 Thess 2:12; cf. John 11:19, 31.

Third, Paul urges the Thessalonians to "help the weak" (5:14c). He uses the verb ἀντέχω ("help") elsewhere only in Titus 1:9, where it refers to an elder's responsibility in "holding fast the faithful word." The adjective "weak" (ἀσθενῶν) can refer to physical, mental, emotional, and spiritual weakness.[41] Since the term follows up "fainthearted," it may refer to "those who lack in some physical manner in comparison to others, the sick, lame, blind or even economically destitute."[42] If so, it is not impossible that Paul may have partly in mind believers who, for one reason or another, are unable to earn their own living. Yet the apostle's main focus is probably not on physical health or some disability. Most of the commands in 5:14 apply to the spiritual realm. Thus, ἀσθενῶν may refer to a weakness in faith. Even though the church as a whole was characterized by a strong faith (1:3), Paul knew that not everyone in the congregation stood at the same level in their strength of faith.[43] The expression "help the weak" in this way is virtually synonymous with the phrase "encourage the fainthearted" (5:14b).

Finally, Paul urges the Thessalonians to "be patient with everyone" (5:14d). The verb μακροθυμέω typically indicates particularly the restraint of anger, in the NT especially enjoined on believers because God has offered forgiveness in place of wrath.[44] The readers must extend such patience to all because God has extended his patience to all. This instruction is, of course, applicable under all circumstances, but it may have had special relevance for Christians facing the pressures of persecution.

While we cannot say that Paul is writing this verse in order to set up the context for his later instructions at the end of his second letter (presumably at this point Paul does not anticipate needing to write another letter), nevertheless, the phrases studied here, which predominantly address the need for believers to be concerned about the spiritual well-being of their fellow believers, do help the interpreter to grasp a perspective of Paul that blossoms in a new direction in 2 Thess 3:6–15. We now turn to that unit.

---

41. BDAG, 142–43, s.v. ἀσθενής 1–2.

42. Beale, *1–2 Thessalonians*, 163.

43. David A. Black ("The Weak in Thessalonica: A Study in Pauline Lexicography," *JETS* 25 [1982]: 307–22) argues that the three phrases "warn those who are idle, encourage the timid, help the weak" are in the context of the three sections of the epistle. The "weak," therefore, refers to those who are having a difficult time understanding the death of loved ones and the apparent delay of the parousia.

44. Paul uses the verb μακροθυμέω elsewhere only in 1 Cor 13:4.

The Believer's Livelihood (2 Thess 3:6 – 15)

Paul wrote a follow-up letter to the Thessalonians just a couple of months after his first letter.[45] In it he clarified further certain issues regarding the second coming of Christ and once again was compelled to address the problem of disorderliness that existed in the church. Since some had not responded to his previous exhortations,[46] he had to take more extreme measures with those who were deliberately being disobedient to the apostolic tradition.[47]

Paul's words in 3:6 certainly reflect seriousness and apostolic authority. The verb παραγγέλλω ("to command") was often used to describe a general in the army who was giving orders to his troops. The adverb ἀτάκτως ("in an unruly manner," cf. 3:11; also 1 Thess 5:14) is another military word used to describe soldiers who were not maintaining rank.[48] Here, some of the Thessalonians had gone AWOL from their God-given responsibility to work. It was not that they were merely "idle" (e.g., ESV, NRSV, NLT; NIV adds "and disruptive"), but rather were distracted with other concerns. Hence, Paul authoritatively commands the church with the Savior's full title—"the Lord Jesus Christ" (cf. 3:12)—to "keep away" (στέλλεσθαι; cf. 3:14–15) from unruly believers who disregard the apostolic message ("tradition").[49]

---

45. Ernest Best, *The First and Second Epistles to the Thessalonians* (HNTC; Harper & Row: New York, 1972), 59. Contra Wanamaker (*The Epistles to the Thessalonians*, 28–44) who offers a reversed sequence of 1 and 2 Thessalonians, which has not proven convincing; hence, most commentators continue to favor the traditional sequence (see Fee, *The First and Second Letters to the Thessalonians*, 3 n. 1).

46. The disorderly Thessalonians refused to submit to the admonitions of the apostles (2 Thess 3:10) and (presumably) the leaders of the congregation (cf. 1 Thess 5:14; 2 Thess 3:4). Contra Wanamaker (*The Epistles to the Thessalonians*, 281–82) who suggests that the disorderly were not intentionally resisting authority or acting in disobedience, but merely acting irresponsibly.

47. Several textual variants exist for the last verb in 3:6, with the most likely options being παρελάβοσαν / παρέλαβον ("they received") or παρελάβετε ("you received"). While most English versions prefer παρελάβετε ("you received"), παρελάβοσαν ("they received") appears to best explain the other readings, enjoys external support, and is the more difficult reading (see also the NET translation and study notes). Hence, Paul is pointedly emphasizing that the offenders *themselves* have flagrantly disobeyed his tradition.

48. Morris, *The First and Second Epistles to the Thessalonians*, 100, 144. It is the adverbial form of the adjective ἀτάκτους used in 1 Thess 5:14.

49. M. J. J. Menken ("Paradise Regained or Still Lost? Eschatology and Disorderly Behaviour in 2 Thessalonians," *NTS* 38 [1992]: 275–80) plausibly proposes that the "tradition" is rooted in the OT, particularly in the divine institution of Gen 3:17–19, where hard work is presented as necessary for one's sustenance in a post-fall world.

In 2 Thess 3:7–9 Paul stresses, as he had done in 1 Thess 2, how he, Silas, and Timothy had modeled what it meant to work night and day to the point of pain ("labor and hardship"). Paul states: "We did not act in an undisciplined manner [ἠτακτήσαμεν][50] among you" (3:7b). During the daylight hours they taught, discipled, evangelized, and defended the faith, perhaps at their place of work. At night they made tents so as to provide for their own room and board. They worked hard, not because they weren't entitled to some support, but to give these Christians a "model" that they could "imitate."[51] As church planters, they did not want to be a burden to the Thessalonian believers (cf. 1 Thess 2:7–9).

Unfortunately, some Thessalonians were not imitating Paul's example. Instead, they were living disorderly lives and asking for assistance from others within the community. Hence, Paul did not mince words when he wrote: "If anyone is not willing to work, neither should that person eat" (3:10).[52] The key word is "willing" (θέλει). The apostle is referring to those who deliberately chose not to work, not those who were *willing* to work but could not find employment. In every age and culture, there are those who have a disability, who are too young or too old to be employed, or who cannot find a job. Such people are not under consideration here. Rather, Paul is concerned with able-bodied believers who are able to find work but who shirk it. Such people are ignoring the example Paul has set.[53] These believers should not receive from others the benefits that come from work.

The negative consequences of shirking work go beyond the burden placed on others. Those who dodge work often end up spending their time

---

50. This is the verbal form related to the adverb ἀτάκτως (3:6, 11).

51. Paul expresses his desire to be an "example" or "model" (τύπον, 3:9). Paul also uses twice (3:7, 9) the verb μιμέομαι, which may be his equivalent to the word "disciple" that Jesus used so often but Paul never does. So Paul was strategically providing a discipleship model for the Thessalonian Christians—a living, breathing example that they could look at to see how a devoted follower of Jesus lived. He says, in effect, "Imitate me as your model of conduct."

52. An early church document called the *Apostolic Constitutions* (ca. AD 375) used this verse as a ground for its instruction regarding the requirement to work for a living. It also provided instruction for ministers concerning how they should help those in need, as well as dealing with the "disorderly" who should not receive help from the church.

53. Victor Paul Furnish, *1 & 2 Thessalonians* (ANTC; Nashville: Abingdon, 2007), 176. Michael Eaton (*1, 2 Thessalonians* [PTB; Tonbridge: Sovereign World, 1997], 118) comments: "Paul has a lot of sympathy for people who are in need (Rom 15:26–29; 2 Cor 8–9; Gal 2:10) but he deals severely with Christians who love excitement but have no love for work."

on unhealthy pursuits. Paul's exhortation to the Thessalonian manual laborers "to aspire to lead a quiet life" and "to attend to [their] own business" (1 Thess 4:11) hints at what 2 Thess 3:11 states explicitly: "We hear that some among you are living in a disorderly manner, not doing their own work but being busybodies."[54] There is a play on words here since the participle περιεργαζομένους ("busybodies") is built on the root of ἐργαζομένους ("work"). Instead of working with their hands, they are working with their mouths. This is confirmed when we understand that περιεργαζομένους is better translated "meddlers"[55] and refers to meddling in other people's affairs.[56] "It is not that these people were inactive, but that they were active in an unproductive, irresponsible, and disruptive manner."[57]

Someone has compared meddlers to mules. When they are pulling, they cannot kick; when they are kicking, they cannot pull. A person who is working hard is generally not lashing out at those around him. In contrast, the individual who is inflicting pain on others is usually not pulling his or her load. Paul is saying: stop being an unnecessary burden on the rest of the community. Instead, mind your own business and work to provide for yourself and your family.

Now in 3:13 the apostle turns back to the majority of the church

---

54. A similar thought is expressed by Paul in 1 Tim 5:13, where Paul says of younger widows being supported by the church that "they are not only lazy, but also gossips and busybodies, talking about things they should not" (see comments in ch. 11 on the widows in 1 Tim 5). Proverbs 26:17 paints a vivid picture of what happens when we meddle: "Like one who takes a dog by the ears is he who passes by and meddles with strife not belonging to him."

55. BDAG, 800, s.v. περιεργάζομαι. Malherbe (*The Letters to the Thessalonians*, 453) notes that περιεργάζομαι was a "well-known term of opprobrium" and that "the emphatic position and sharpness of *periergazesthai* show the importance that this offensive behavior has for Paul."

56. Because περιεργάζομαι and related terms tend to be fairly general and occur in a wide range of contexts, it is impossible to determine from a purely lexical standpoint the precise nuance of περιεργάζομαι in the present passage. A scholar's reconstruction of the Thessalonian situation typically drives his or her understanding of the particular "meddling" in view: (1) whether "the Thessalonian freeloaders" were spreading false teaching (e.g., Beale, *1–2 Thessalonians*, 257), or (2) whether they were supporting the causes and the accolades of a patron (Green, *The Letters to the Thessalonians*, 351; see also Winter's lengthy arguments in *Seek the Welfare of the City*, 42–60, that some Thessalonians had apparently returned to a client-patron relationship after Paul left Thessalonians), or (3) whether they were speculating about and preaching doctrines of the unseen world (Shogren, *1 and 2 Thessalonians*, 327–28), or (4) whether they were merely keeping others from their work by useless chatter and meddling in other people's affairs (Marshall, *1 and 2 Thessalonians*, 224–25).

57. Holmes, *1 and 2 Thessalonians*, 273.

members who are acting responsibly.[58] Paul recognizes that it is easy to get discouraged when others in the community are doing things that are wrong. So he declares: "But as for you, brothers and sisters, do not grow weary of doing good." This exhortation could be a general reminder to continue doing good.[59] But in this context the expression seems to be dealing in some way with the problem of the unruly. Three possible nuances may be present. (1) Those who are working hard are not to lose their motivation[60] when they observe those who are hardly working.[61] (2) The faithful believers are not to let busybodies discourage them from withholding financial help from those with legitimate needs.[62] (3) The Thessalonians are to carry out disciplinary action against the disobedient members, if it is deemed necessary.

Verses 14–15 explain in detail how such disciplinary action is to be exercised. Paul urges the church to "take note" of those who are disobeying his mandates here (3:14a). This verb is plural and in the middle voice (σημειοῦσθε), which suggests, "note for oneself," with the implication that all the members of the congregation are to take responsibility for following these instructions.[63] This means that the whole church is to take this seriously by keeping an eye on the person who persists in going down a wrong path. They are to watch that person, so they can avoid him.

Paul also says, "Do not associate with him."[64] This means that the church is not to "get mixed up with" or "associate closely" (NET) with an unruly church member.[65] There is much debate on what this

---

58. The pronoun ὑμεῖς ("you") is in the emphatic position and stands in contrast to "such persons/people" and "their/they" in 3:12. Some scholars take the initial words of 3:13 ὑμεῖς δέ, ἀδελφοί, ("but you, brothers and sisters") as introducing a new section, but this is unlikely.

59. Galatians 6:9 is a nearly identical parallel, and it seems general in scope. However, the context of 2 Thess 3:6–12 seems to demand that Paul is speaking to the concerns at hand. See also Wanamaker, *The Epistles to the Thessalonians*, 288.

60. The verb translated "grow weary" (ἐγκακήσητε) means "to lose one's motivation in continuing a desirable pattern of conduct or activity, *lose enthusiasm, be discouraged*" (BDAG, 272, s.v. ἐγκακέω, 1).

61. Marshall, *1 and 2 Thessalonians*, 226, argues that Paul included here the continuing support of the busybodies because of the gracious nature of Christian love, though this did have a final limit expressed in 3:14. If this is Paul's point, however, little sense can be made of the injunction to keep away from these in 3:6 or "he shall not eat" in 3:10.

62. Shogren, *1 and 2 Thessalonians*, 329.

63. Church discipline will have little effect if not followed by the *whole* body.

64. The ESV goes so far as to render this verb: "have nothing to do with him."

65. In Hos 7:8 Israel "mixed" itself with surrounding nations by allowing their pagan religions to corrupt its religious and spiritual life. Hosea's concern is for the purity of the people of Israel.

disassociation looks like. Are such offenders "to be excluded from the community or somehow isolated within it"?[66] Many scholars suggest that the reference is to some form of *limited* disassociation, such as who should eat the Lord's Supper.[67] However, this view does not seem likely since Paul reminds them that he did not eat anyone's bread without paying for it (2 Thess 3:8); merely not eating bread is not the disassociation that is referred to here. Moreover, the verb in question (συναναμίγνυσθαι) is only used in two other places in the NT and clearly refers to a more complete exclusion or dis-fellowshipping of someone (1 Cor 5:9, 11). So, while we can appreciate certain circumstances where it may be appropriate to have a limited disassociation, as a general rule, we understand Paul to be referring here to full exclusion.

Admittedly, this notion is not widely accepted among commentators.[68] Nor is it politically correct in our day and age; many Christians expect the church to be solely a place of grace and compassion and rarely, if ever, deal with situations of overt sin. But our conclusion holds that the goal of church discipline is not punishment; rather, it is the restoration of the offender who has brought shame to God's reputation and character. Paul is relatively severe when dealing with these disorderly people in Thessalonica because he understands how damaging such behavior can be to the church as a whole.

In essence, disorderly believers are to be ostracized from intimate fellowship[69] with the community as a means of shaming them into repentance and change.[70] The verb "put to shame" (ἐντρέπω, 3:14c) has the meaning of "being turned in upon oneself."[71] The Roman world was an

---

66. Furnish, *1 & 2 Thessalonians*, 180.

67. See Best, *The First and Second Epistles to the Thessalonians*, 343–44; Bruce, *1 & 2 Thessalonians*, 211; Malherbe, *The Letters to the Thessalonians*, 460; Green, *The Letters to the Thessalonians*, 355. See esp. Witherington, *1 and 2 Thessalonians*, 254–57, "*Peroratio*—3.13-15 On Shunning and Shaming Without Excommunicating." Yet, Wanamaker (*The Epistles to the Thessalonians*, 290) rightly states: "there is no reason to think that admonishing someone excluded from the community could not take place outside the communal meeting."

68. Many scholars disagree with this conclusion and insist that the case in 1 Cor 5 is far more severe than 2 Thess 3 (Green, *The Letters to the Thessalonians*, 353). However, the text does not require this reading (see also Wanamaker, *The Epistles to the Thessalonians*, 288).

69. There is a difference between acquaintanceship, friendship, and fellowship; for fellowship (koinōnia) means "to have in common." For obedient saints to treat disobedient Christians with the same friendship they show to other dedicated saints is to give approval to their sins.

70. Holmes *1 and 2 Thessalonians*, 275.

71. BDAG, 341, s.v. ἐντρέπω, 1. Beale, *1–2 Thessalonians*, 262, suggests the translation: "he should be turned."

honor/shame culture.[72] Honor in Mediterranean societies came from the group to which one belonged, and the loss of honor resulted in shame. To be shunned by one's associates was a severe disgrace. The loss of public honor would bring shame, which in that society would thus serve as a strong motivation to such people to adjust their behavior within the norms of the community.[73]

In the case of Christians, separation from the church would throw the disorderly brother into a precarious social situation. He had already experienced rejection and dishonor from his contemporaries in the city (1 Thess 2:14), and now he would not be in fellowship with the new community to which he belonged and in which he found his new identity as a member of God's family. He would have lost his honor both in the society at large and within the new family. The resultant shame of exclusion would be a forceful influence to conform his conduct to the tradition/rule of the community (3:6, 10, 12).[74]

Unfortunately, there is much debate on how the seemingly clear command of 2 Thess 3:14 relates to what Paul writes in 3:15. G. K. Beale summarizes the dilemma well:

---

72. See Bruce J. Malina, *The New Testament World: Insights from Cultural Anthropology* (3rd ed.; Louisville: Westminster John Knox, 2001), 28–62.

73. One expression of honor bestowed on males was through the invitation to meals. Craig S. Keener (*The IVP Bible Background Commentary: New Testament* [2nd ed.; Downers Grove, IL: InterVarsity Press, 2014], 470) remarks: "Banishment was a common punishment in the Roman period. In Judaism, exclusion from the community was a spiritual equivalent of execution, applied in the NT period to capital crimes of the OT (capital sentences of Jewish courts could not be legally carried out without Roman permission)."

74. We can also point out, as we did in ch. 4, that in the Greco-Roman world, there was no social safety net for anyone to fall back on for basic life necessities for those who did not work. For various treatments on the subject of church discipline, see Verlyn D. Verbrugge, "The Idea of Excommunication: An Analysis of the Biblical Passages" (ThM thesis; Calvin Theological Seminary, 1979), 84–90; Jay Adams, *Handbook of Church Discipline* (Grand Rapids: Zondervan, 1986); Daniel E. Wray, *Biblical Church Discipline* (Carlisle: Banner of Truth, 2001); Mark Lauterbach, *The Transforming Community: The Practice of the Gospel in Church Discipline* (Fearn, UK: Christian Focus, 2003); Mark Dever, "Mark Seven: Biblical Church Discipline," in *9 Marks of a Healthy Church* (Wheaton, IL: Crossway, 2004), 167–93; John S. Hammett and Benjamin L. Merkle, eds., *Those Who Must Give an Account: A Study of Church Membership and Church Discipline* (Nashville: B&H Academic, 2012); Robert K. Cheong, *God Redeeming His Bride: A Handbook for Church Discipline* (Fearn, UK: Christian Focus, 2012); Jonathan Leeman, *Church Discipline: How the Church Protects the Name of Jesus* (Wheaton, IL: Crossway, 2012).

At first glance, this text does not appear to affirm excommunication, because Paul says that the person who continues in disobedience is still to be reckoned as a *brother* (3:15). On the other hand, the command *not* to *associate with him* in 3:14 seems to express something like excommunication. Therefore, it is difficult to determine how these verses line up with a traditional notion of excommunication. Any answer to the question must explain how the apparently disparate statements of 3:14 and 15 are to be reconciled.[75]

It seems that the solution to this tension is that *throughout* the disciplinary process, the disruptive person is not be regarded as an enemy, but admonished as a brother (3:15).[76]

Paul likely adds this proviso because of the tendency of believers, both ancient and modern, is to get angry with sinful believers. Yet the apostle dictates that the church gathered is to "admonish" or "warn" such believers.[77] However, even after community exclusion has occurred, lines of communication should be kept open for continued warnings. Thomas Schreiner suggests saying something to this effect: "We are all praying for you, that you would repent and come back [to the church]. We miss you so much!"[78] After all, the goal of church discipline is never punishment; rather, it is reformation and restoration to fellowship with Christ and the church.

Nonetheless, disobedient believers who refuse to work must be encouraged to repent of their meddling and unruly conduct. Again, Schreiner rightly states:

---

75. Beale, *1–2 Thessalonians*, 259.

76. Charles J. Bumgardner ("'As a Brother': 2 Thessalonians 3:6–15 and Ecclesiastical Separation," *DBSJ* 14 [2009]: 80–81 fn. 91) comments: "The grammar of 3:14–15 supports this conclusion as well. As noted above, μὴ συναναμίγνυσθαι is subordinate, not independent, and best seen as a purpose infinitive describing the aim of the 'taking note' (σημειοῦσθε). So Paul is not necessarily giving a progression of actions in 3:14–15, i.e., (1) take public note of the disorderly, (2) disassociate from the disorderly, (3) admonish the disorderly as a brother. Instead, it is better to understand Paul thus: (1) take public note of the disorderly so that (purpose infinitive) the congregation may disassociate from him, and (coordinate καί) (2) in relation to taking public note of the disorderly, do not treat him as an enemy, but admonish him as a brother."

77. Best, *The First and Second Epistles to the Thessalonians*, 343–44. On the verb νουθετεῖτε, see comments on 1 Thess 5:14.

78. Thomas R. Schreiner, "The Biblical Basis for Church Discipline," *Those Who Must Give an Account: A Study of Church Membership and Church Discipline* (eds. John S. Hammett and Benjamin L. Merkle; Nashville: B&H Academic, 2012), 178.

The church must not give the impression to the one being disciplined that "everything is fine," so that life with him proceeds just as it did before. On the contrary, any interaction with him must have as its motive and intention the repentance of the one who has strayed. If a believer eats with a person in sin and does not solemnly warn him to repent, the message that is conveyed to the person under discipline is that his sin "is not a big deal," for life goes on as normal. Under no circumstances, Paul warns, must life go on as normal.[79]

CONCLUSION

Paul has several issues to bring to the attention of the Thessalonians relative to money issues. He emphasized how his own pattern of working hard, night and day, for a living should remind the believers in that city how much he loved them and how sincerely he wished he could return to Thessalonica and give them further instruction in the faith. Moreover, he referred to those same work patterns to demonstrate to the able-bodied people in the church how important one's daily work was. And when the apostle heard that some among the Thessalonians had stopped working and were becoming freeloaders off others in the church, he wrote to admonish such believers to get back to work. He forcefully challenged the body to warn and encourage these people to follow in the apostolic example and not become a burden to the community. Those who persisted in rejecting this tradition would be liable to church discipline with the goal that they would be ashamed of their behavior and turn from their sin.

---

79. Ibid., 125.

CHAPTER 10

THE RICH AND THE POOR IN CORINTH

ONE CANNOT WRITE ON THE TOPIC OF PAUL AND MONEY WITHOUT DEAL-
ing with the complex issue of the rich and the poor and, in particular, what
attitudes these groups express toward each other through their wealth
(or lack of it). In the next chapter, we will examine some of Paul's more
general comments on the rich and the poor. But before we do so, we will
examine a specific situation in the church at Corinth where a significant
conflict developed between the different economic classes. This conflict
becomes apparent in how the members of the church celebrated the Lord's
Supper—or, more specifically, how they interacted with each other in a
common meal (often called an ἀγάπη feast) that apparently preceded the
actual event of the Eucharist.[1] We read about this in 1 Cor 11:17–34. We
now turn to examine those verses.[2]

THE CAUSE OF THE SOCIAL DIVISIONS IN CORINTH (1 COR 11:17 – 22)

It is evident from the force of Paul's rhetoric (11:17, 22)[3] and his repeated
warnings of judgment (11:29–32) that he is alarmed about divisions within

---

1. Such a practice fits the pattern of the Jewish Passover meal and seems likely in light of
Paul's reference to Passover motifs (1 Cor 5:6–8 and 10:16–17).

2. Many of the insights in this chapter are from Krell, *Temporal Judgment and the Church*,
185–215.

3. Harvey (*Listening to the Text*, 168) points out that 11:17–22 is framed by an *inclusio*
(ἐπαινῶ):

the Corinthian church (11:18 – 19), which are linked to the community's partaking of the Lord's Supper. Paul Barnett suggests that 11:17 – 34 are "amongst Paul's most severe words to any congregation."[4] This declaration is confirmed by divine discipline, which had resulted in weakness, sickness, and death (11:30).

There have been various proposals as to the cause of these Corinthian divisions. For years most scholars argued that the schisms stemmed primarily from theological disputes.[5] Now, however, it is more generally agreed that socioeconomic factors (see 1:26 – 31; 6:1 – 8; 8:1 – 11:1), rather than theological ones, are responsible for the Corinthians' fractured fellowship.[6] Presumably, some of the wealthier and socially superior members had been dishonoring the poor.[7] What is not so clear is what exactly transpired during the Lord's Supper (and the Love Feast that preceded

---

(11:17) τοῦτο δὲ παραγγέλλων οὐκ ἐπαινῶ ὅτι ...

(11:22) ἐπαινέσω ὑμᾶς; ἐν τούτῳ οὐκ ἐπαινῶ.

4. Barnett, *1 Corinthians*, 210.

5. See Robertson and Plummer, *A Critical and Exegetical Commentary on the First Epistle of St. Paul to the Corinthians*, 238.

6. See Gerd Theissen, *The Social Setting of Pauline Christianity: Essays on Corinth* (trans. John H. Schütz; Philadelphia: Fortress, 1982), 145 – 74; Wayne A. Meeks, *The First Urban Christians: The Social World of the Apostle Paul* (New Haven, CT: Yale University Press, 1984), 67 – 68; Stephen C. Barton, "Paul's Sense of Place: An Anthropological Approach to Community Formation in Corinth," *NTS* 32 (1986): 225 – 46; Ben Witherington III, *Conflict and Community in Corinth: A Socio-Rhetorical Commentary on 1 and 2 Corinthians* (Grand Rapids: Eerdmans, 1995), 241 – 52; Thiselton, *The First Epistle to the Corinthians*, 850 – 53; Garland, *1 Corinthians*, 533 – 37. A challenge to the socioeconomic view has been mounted by Meggitt (*Paul, Poverty, and Survival*, 4 – 99) who holds that the social and economic differences in antiquity were larger than has usually been assumed (see also comments in ch. 4). The lot of the Christians was poverty; all of them lived at or near the subsistence level and none of them belonged to a "middle class." Meggitt is too simplistic in his description of poverty. For detailed critiques, see Dale B. Martin, "Review Essay: Justin J. Meggitt, *Paul, Poverty and Survival*," *JSNT* 84 (2001): 51 – 64; and Gerd Theissen, "Social Conflicts in the Corinthian Community: Further Remarks on J. J. Meggitt, *Paul, Poverty and Survival*," *JSNT* 25 (2003): 371 – 91.

7. Lyle D. Vander Broek (*Breaking Barriers: The Possibilities of Christian Community in a Lonely World* [Grand Rapids: Brazos, 2002], 114 – 15) writes, "Historical evidence suggests that the city of Corinth itself was no stranger to class-consciousness. We know that when Corinth was refounded by the Romans in 44 B.C.E. (it had been destroyed in 146 B.C.E.), it was settled primarily by 'freedmen,' former slaves who had earned or had been given their freedom. Many of them became the new rich, the entrepreneurs and wealthy business people of this prosperous trade city.... Archeological discoveries and the literature of the period indicate that Corinth was as hierarchical as any other Greco-Roman city of the period, and was unusual only in that status was defined more by wealth than by family name."

it) that led to the humiliation of the poorer members who were present.[8] Thus, a reconstruction of the Lord's Supper and the events surrounding it will be considered as the text unfolds.[9]

RECONSTRUCTING THE SCENE AT THE LORD'S SUPPER

Paul begins this section with sobering words: "Now in giving this instruction, I do not praise you, because you come together not for the better but for the worse" (11:17). The conjunction δέ ("now") marks the introduction of a new topic. If a contrast is implied, the apostle is merely stating that in 11:2–16 he could praise the Corinthians, while in 11:17–34 he cannot.[10] In 11:2 Paul praises the Corinthians because they remember him in everything and maintained the traditions he passed on to them. But in 11:17 (cf. 11:22) he does not praise them, on account of their divisions (cf. 11:18). Instead, he declares that they "come together not for the better but for the worse" (11:17b).

Sadly, the gathering[11] of the Corinthian community is a blatant contradiction of the gospel. Hence, with more than a sprinkling of irony, he repeatedly describes the Corinthians as "coming together" while knowing full well that their eating is anything but "together" as a unified body. The very ritual that is intended to celebrate the gospel and symbolically act out their oneness in Christ has become an occasion for splitting the church on the basis of status.[12]

---

8. There is scholarly disagreement on nearly every issue in 11:17–34; therefore, it can be rather difficult to argue definitively.

9. Witherington (*Conflict and Community in Corinth*, 243–47) provides a helpful excursus that delineates association rules and teaching at meals.

10. William R. Baker, *1 Corinthians* (CBC; Wheaton, IL: Tyndale, 2009), 167.

11. The verb συνέρχομαι is used five times in 11:17–34 (11:17, 18, 20, 33, 34) and only used two other times by Paul (14:23, 26), where it is used of "coming together" for the purpose of corporate worship (see BDAG, 969, s.v συνέρχομαι 1). It is generally recognized that the Corinthian believers would have gathered in the homes of their three or four wealthiest members, whose homes could have accommodated approximately thirty people on a regular basis, whether daily or weekly (see Garland, *1 Corinthians*, 536; Baker, *1 Corinthians*, 166).

12. Paul acknowledges that different classes exist in the church and often names high status people: Gaius, who hosts Paul and has a house large enough for the entire Corinthian Church (1 Cor 1:14; cf. Rom 16:23); Erastus, a city treasurer (Rom 16:23), who may be the public official and benefactor named in an inscription found in Corinth; Crispus (1:14), a former synagogue ruler (Acts 18:8); Stephanas, the leader of a household (1 Cor 1:16), who was free to travel in the service of Paul (16:15); Phoebe of Cenchrea (Rom 16:1); and Aquila and Priscilla, leaders of a house church.

Paul continues his rebuke: "For, chiefly,[13] when you come together as a church, I hear that divisions exist among you; and I believe it" (11:18).[14] First and last on the apostle's mind are the σχίσματα[15] that are taking place in Corinth. Instead of treating one another with brotherly love and acting as the family of God,[16] those who have more than enough to eat and drink at the Lord's Supper are treating shamefully those who have insufficient quantities. He contrasts ὃς μὲν πεινᾷ ("one person is hungry") with ὃς δὲ μεθύει ("another person is drunk," 11:21), identifying a group within the church as τοὺς μὴ ἔχοντας ("those who do not have anything," 11:22), whose members are humiliated by the actions of their wealthy counterparts.[17] These divisions are not to be taken lightly. Jerome Neyrey argues that the σχίσματα in 11:18 threaten not only the wholeness but also the holiness of the body, just as in Lev 21:16–20 the wholeness of the animal determined its holiness. Lack of control at the Lord's Supper manifests a serious disregard of the social body's integrity and purity.[18]

---

13. Collins (*First Corinthians*, 421) points out that the phrase πρῶτον μὲν γάρ is emphatic since no "second" follows.

14. Bruce W. Winter (*After Paul Left Corinth* [Grand Rapids: Eerdmans, 2001], 159–63) argues convincingly that μέρος in 11:18 refers here to a "matter" (2 Cor 9:3) or "report" and should not be translated adverbially. Rather, Paul means that he is convinced of the report he has received from Chloe's people about their factions (1:10), which included reports of their divisions during the Lord's Supper. Thus, Winter suggests that the phrase μέρος τι πιστεύω be translated, "I believe a certain report."

15. There are two primary views on the nature of σχίσματα in 11:18: (1) Paul uses the exact term σχίσματα that he used in 1:10, which suggests he is connecting Chloe's report of σχίσματα (1:10–11) with what is taking place in 11:18 (see Thiselton, *The First Epistle to the Corinthians*, 850; Winter, *After Paul Left Corinth*, 162). This may be further confirmed by Paul's final use of σχίσμα (12:25), where he again expresses concern regarding preferential treatment within the church at Corinth. (2) Paul does not seem to be addressing the same groups in 1:10 as in 11:18. In 1:10 the issue is divisions generated by loyalty to rhetorically gifted leaders, by a desire for wisdom that occurs across class lines (see 1:26–31), and that may well pit one house church against another. In 11:22 the divisions pit poor against rich and probably happen within house churches, the basic unit for the celebration of the Lord's Supper (see Barnett, *1 Corinthians*, 211; Baker, *1 Corinthians*, 168). Either view is possible, but the latter seems preferable.

16. Roy E. Ciampa and Brian S. Rosner (*1 Corinthians* [Pillar; Grand Rapids: Eerdmans, 2010], 543) rightly note that "the community is to 'come together as a church' to represent the coming together of one body (10:17) of people who together participate in the body and blood of Christ (10:16)."

17. Barry D. Smith, *Paul's Seven Explanations of the Suffering of the Righteous* (New York: Peter Lang, 2002), 89.

18. Jerome H. Neyrey, *Paul: In Other Words* (Louisville: Westminster/John Knox, 1990), 123.

In 11:19 Paul goes on to state, "for there must also be factions among you," which is rather surprising in light of his earlier condemnation of factiousness in 1:10–17.[19] Does the apostle now tolerate Christ being divided? Certainly not! Contextually, he is concerned about the socio-economic divisions. The ἵνα clause states that factions are necessary to identify οἱ δόκιμοι. Most commentators and English versions translate οἱ δόκιμοι as "the approved." It is postulated that the apostle is discussing an eschatological necessity that distinguishes the saved (i.e., "approved") from the unsaved (i.e., "unapproved").[20] Yet, Paul's concern here is not to separate genuine believers from the false.[21] Rather, he is demonstrating that the socially elite among the Corinthian community are denying the message of the cross by failing to honor selflessly the less fortunate members of the church (cf. 11:23–26).[22] Paul seems to be using οἱ δόκιμοι with reference to those who have God's approval.[23] "The approved," then, are those who are "the tried and true Christian(s),"[24] who "pass the test" of behaving well in the midst of socioeconomic factions. These divisions are necessary, sad to say, to separate those faithful to God's Word from the rest.[25]

Verses 20–22 make possible a more detailed reconstruction of the situation at Corinth. Paul writes:

---

19. Fee (*The First Epistle to the Corinthians*, 538) calls 11:19 "one of the true puzzles in the letter." However, we would suggest that there is no mystery unless it's introduced.

20. Fee, *The First Epistle to the Corinthians*, 537–39; Baker, *1 Corinthians*, 168–69.

21. In Paul's other usages of δόκιμος (Rom 14:18; 16:10; 2 Cor 10:18; 13:7; cf. 2 Tim 2:15), he does not appear to be distinguishing between the saved and unsaved.

22. David W. J. Gill, "1 Corinthians" (ZIBBC; Grand Rapids: Zondervan, 2002), 160. Ciampa and Rosner (*1 Corinthians*, 544) allow for the possibility of irony. Garland (*1 Corinthians*, 539) suggests that Paul is using οἱ δόκιμοι sarcastically to denote the "dignitaries" who are causing factions in the church. These individuals are perceived as doing so for the purposes of distinguishing themselves as genuine or elite members of the group. Another possibility is that Paul concedes that social distinctions are a fact of life and will be reflected, in one way or another, at the meal. Nevertheless, that is no excuse for letting the poor go hungry. See BDAG, 256, s.v. δόκιμος 2: "pert. to being considered worthy of high regard, *respected, esteemed.*"

23. Michael Eaton, *1 Corinthians 10–16* (PTB; Tonbridge: Sovereign World, 2000), 34; Frank Thielman, "1 Corinthians," in *The ESV Study Bible* (Wheaton, IL: Crossway, 2008), 2207.

24. BDAG, 256, s.v. δόκιμος 1; see also Barnett, *1 Corinthians*, 211.

25. This view finds support in the apostle's use of δοκιμή where he tests the Corinthians to determine their attitude (2 Cor 2:9). Paul also uses δοκιμάζω to encourage the Corinthians to test themselves by a different measure (11:28). In this context, those who examine themselves, and are thus tested and approved by God, preserve their physical well-being (cf. 11:30).

Therefore [οὖν] when you come together at the same place, it is not to eat the *Lord's* Supper, for each devours his or her own supper during the meal, and one is hungry and another is drunk. Do you not have homes in which to eat and drink? Or do you despise the church of God and shame the 'have-nots'? What shall I say to you? Shall I praise you? In this [matter] I will not praise you.

The phrase συνέρχομαι ἐπὶ τὸ αὐτό, which is repeated in 14:23, is usually translated, "to come together at the same place"; thus, it is synonymous with, "to come together as a church" in 11:18. The entire phrase may be a double entendre. The prepositional phrase ἐπὶ τὸ αὐτό literally means "to the same place," but metaphorically, "together."[26] The dual meaning of the phrase seems to stress the irony of the Corinthians' factionalism—when they come together "in the same place," they are not "together."[27] This elucidates the language that follows.

VIOLATING THE PRINCIPLE OF UNITY

Paul's concern in 11:21 is for those individual members who are violating the principle of unity. Each one takes τὸ ἴδιον δεῖπνον ("one's own meal"). The adjective ἴδιον ("own") provides a sharp antithesis with κυριακόν ("Lord's"; 11:20). It is important to note that ἕκαστος ("each one") is fronted for focus in 11:21. In 1 Corinthians, ἕκαστος always stresses the individual as opposed to the community.[28] The apostle's point is that individual members of the Corinthian community are sinning against God and each other.[29] The sharing of food, a thing appropriate for the Corinthians when they come together, is not happening.[30] Rather than

---

26. BDAG, 363, s.v. ἐπί 1bβ.

27. Robertson and Plummer, *A Critical and Exegetical Commentary on the First Epistle of St. Paul to the Corinthians*, 240; Margaret M. Mitchell, *Paul and the Rhetoric of Reconciliation: An Exegetical Investigation of the Language and Composition of 1 Corinthians* (Louisville: Westminster John Knox, 1991), 153–54. It is not possible to know whether Paul consciously intended the ambiguity, but it is certainly present in what he wrote.

28. E.g., 1:12; 3:13; 7:2, 24; 12:7; 14:26. It is no coincidence that ἕκαστος appears twenty-two times in 1 Corinthians, more than any other NT letter.

29. Fee (*The First Epistle to the Corinthians*, 541) argues that ἕκαστος refers specifically to the rich who are abusing the Lord's Supper.

30. Bruce W. Winter, "The Lord's Supper at Corinth: An Alternative Reconstruction," *RTR* 37 (1978): 73–78; Brad B. Blue, "The House Church at Corinth and the Lord's Supper: Famine, Food Supply, and the Present Distress," *CTR* 5.2 (1991): 234–37; David W. J. Gill ("In Search of the Social Elite in the Corinthian Church," *TynBul* 44 [1993]: 323–37) points

serving to build up the church in love (cf. 8:1), which would be for the better, their meetings served to tear down and humiliate some members in the presence of others.

Furthermore, it appears that some of the Corinthians are eating too much and too greedily. The meaning of the verb προλαμβάνω (11:21) becomes crucial for determining the situational context.[31] Many underscore the temporal force of the prefix προ- to render it, "to take beforehand."[32] However, Winter argues persuasively that in this context the προ- prefix is not temporal, but intensive,[33] and that προλαμβάνω does not require the consumption of food *before* the arrival of others; it means, "to eat or drink, to devour."[34] Contextually, this view seems preferable. Paul is not pleased with the behavior of the Corinthians (11:17), so he uses a verb that can have a pejorative nuance to condemn their selfish and greedy behavior.

Winter also makes a compelling case that the aorist articular infinitive τῷ φαγεῖν (11:21) indicates that the sinful "devouring" took place *during* the meal itself;[35] "for each one of you devours your own meal during your time of eating." This is convincing and stands in contrast

out that it is likely that there was a famine in Corinth (1 Cor 7:26). This adversely affected the church, especially the "have-nots." This makes the insensitivity of the wealthy even worse as they would be gorging themselves in front of hungry brothers and sisters during a time of food shortage.

31. Christopher L. Carter (*The Great Sermon Tradition as a Fiscal Framework in 1 Corinthians: Towards a Pauline Theology of Material Possessions* [LNTS; London: T&T Clark, 2010], 173) calls 11:21–22 the *crux interpretum* for 11:17–34 because the verses "define the eucharistic malfunction to which Paul is responding throughout 11:17–34."

32. BDAG, 872, s.v. προλαμβάνω 1c; Robertson and Plummer, *A Critical and Exegetical Commentary on the First Epistle of St. Paul to the Corinthians*, 241; Collins, *First Corinthians*, 422–23; Alan F. Johnson, *1 Corinthians* (IVPNTC; Downers Grove, IL: InterVarsity Press, 2004), 204–5; Craig S. Keener, *1–2 Corinthians* (NcBC; Cambridge: Cambridge University Press, 2005), 98; Nigel M. Watson, *The First Epistle to the Corinthians* (EC; London: Epworth, 1992. , 2005), 116–17.

33. There are only two other NT uses of προλαμβάνω. In Gal 6:1 προλαμβάνω means "detect" or "overtake" (BDAG, 872, s.v. προλαμβάνω 2); in Mark 14:8, it conveys the sense of "to anticipate." The only LXX use of προλαμβάνω bears this meaning in Wis 17:16. Fee (*The First Epistle to the Corinthians*, 542) claims "there is no clear evidence of the verb προλαμβάνω being used this way [temporal priority] in the context of eating."

34. Winter, "The Lord's Supper at Corinth," 75–77. See also Fee, *The First Epistle to the Corinthians*, 542; Richard B. Hays, *First Corinthians* (IBC; Louisville: Westminster/John Knox, 1997), 197; Thiselton, *The First Epistle to the Corinthians*, 864; BAGD, s.v. προλαμβάνω 2a.

35. Winter, *After Paul Left Corinth*, 149–51. The temporal view does not seem to solve the dilemma of the text since it only affects the time of eating and not the manner. Therefore, some would remain hungry. Winter's reconstruction, however, does not suffer from this problem.

with the less specific anarthrous aorist infinitives in 11:20.[36] Thus, the wealthy members of the Corinthian church are guilty of gluttony and drunkenness *while* the poor go without. This reconstruction can also be supported from the customary practice at Greco-Roman banquets where wealthy patrons—those with homes large enough to host the communal meal—would have assigned the biggest and best portions of food to the more privileged (including themselves), while the household slaves would have normally been expected to serve the dinner guests and eat leftovers.[37]

SOCIAL GEOGRAPHY IN THE ROMAN HOUSEHOLD

Social geography may also have played a role in how the meals were conducted.[38] The host apparently invited socially elite church members to join him or her in the dining room (*triclinium*), creating a private supper. The rest were left outside in the larger entry courtyard (*atrium*) with the lesser quality fare.[39] Superior food and a dining position near to the host were visible symbols of favor in an honor-driven society like Roman Corinth.[40] Furthermore, the use of separate tables seating nine to twelve persons (though caused by space limitations) would have led to further complications of who would sit where—sometimes potentially a socially divisive decision.[41] The result of these practices was a portioning of the community between the "haves" and the "have-nots" (11:22).[42] No doubt

---

36. Thiselton, *The First Epistle to the Corinthians*, 863.

37. Ciampa and Rosner, *1 Corinthians*, 545.

38. See Witherington, *Conflict and Community in Corinth*, 247–52; Thiselton, *The First Epistle to the Corinthians*, 860–66; Garland, *1 Corinthians*, 535–44.

39. Jerome Murphy-O'Connor, *St. Paul's Corinth: Texts and Archaeology* (London; New York: T&T Clark, 1983), 153–61; Fee, *The First Epistle to the Corinthians*, 542; Jeffery S. Lamp, "The Corinthian Eucharistic Dinner Party: Exegesis of a Cultural Context (1 Cor 11:17–34)," *Affirmation* 4 (Fall 1991): 5; Thiselton, *The First Epistle to the Corinthians*, 860–64. Barnett (*1 Corinthians*, 213) by contrast, argues that this is speculation and states, "It is equally possible that all ate in Gaius's *atrium*."

40. Lamp, "The Corinthian Eucharistic Dinner Party," 1–15; Stephen M. Pogoloff, *Logos and Sophia: The Rhetorical Situation of 1 Corinthians* (SBLDS 134; Atlanta: Scholars Press, 1992), 237–71.

41. Robertson and Plummer, *A Critical and Exegetical Commentary on the First Epistle of St. Paul to the Corinthians*, 239. Cf. Luke 14:7–11; Jas 2:1–4.

42. Theissen, *The Social Setting of Pauline Christianity*, 151–53; Meeks, *The First Urban Christians*, 159; Susan Watts Henderson, "If Anyone Is Hungry: An Integrated Reading of 1 Cor 11:17–34," *NTS* 48 (2002): 203; John Inziku, *Overcoming Divisive Behaviour: An Attempt to Interpret 1 Cor 11, 17–34 from Another Perspective* (Frankfurt am Main: Peter Lang, 2005), 283.

this kind of discriminatory behavior against the poor and social nobodies would have seemed quite natural within the stratified world of Paul's readers.[43] Yet, Paul does not tolerate what is socially expected in Corinth. In 11:22 he closes out this subsection with four rhetorical questions (the second and third are joined by καί), creating a strong appeal. His words are punctuated with a righteous indignation. Paul will not tolerate a σχίσμα between the rich and the poor in the church.

Whatever the precise circumstances, a meal designed to express unity is being so abused as to highlight the disunity of the Corinthian congregation. The cliquish behavior of the community reflects significant social and economic divisions. Thus, members who bring nothing with them to the meal are being humiliated and going hungry.[44] What should be an inclusive community meal has become an occasion for simultaneously private meals.[45] This is an affront to Christ and his gospel. He lived a life of servanthood and died a sacrificial death (cf. 11:23–24). Paul wants no socioeconomic class-consciousness in his churches, and the Lord's Supper must reflect unity and concern for others.[46]

THE MOTIVATION TO AVOID THE SOCIAL DIVISIONS IN CORINTH (1 COR 11:23 – 26)

To address the divisions between the "haves" and the "have-nots," Paul recalls for the Corinthians the apostolic tradition[47] and the theology of the Lord's Supper (11:23–26).[48] His aim is to make clear the holiness of

---

43. David Horrell, "The Lord's Supper at Corinth and in the Church Today," *Theology* 98.783 (1995): 198; D. E. Smith and H. E. Taussig, *Many Tables: The Eucharist in the New Testament and Liturgy Today* (Philadelphia: Trinity Press International, 1990), 21–35. Oster (*1 Corinthians*, 266) remarks: "The potentially divisive character of Greek and Roman meals is well documented in ancient literary testimony from authors such as Plutarch, Juvenal, Pliny, Lucian."

44. Paul does not explicitly say what it is that the "have-nots" do not have. The nearest referent, however, is οἰκίας. Thus, οἰκία more likely refers to "household" (i.e., a patron's client group) than a house.

45. Victor Paul Furnish, *The Theology of the First Letter to the Corinthians* (NTT; Cambridge: Cambridge University Press, 1999), 79.

46. Ciampa and Rosner, *1 Corinthians*, 547.

47. The Corinthians are familiar with the Lord's Supper tradition (11:23a). See David Wenham, *Paul: Follower of Jesus or Founder of Christianity?* (Grand Rapids; Cambridge: Eerdmans, 1995), 144–47; Anders Eriksson, *Traditions as Rhetorical Proof: Pauline Argumentation in 1 Corinthians* (ConBNT 29; Stockholm: Almqvist & Wiksell, 1998), 180.

48. Verbrugge, "1 Corinthians," 359.

the meal in the face of the selfish practice of the elite who are destroying this holiness.[49] In doing so, he emphasizes that in the Lord's Supper the Corinthians commemorate Christ's self-giving on behalf of his people.[50] The wealthy Corinthians are hardly remembering Christ's example if they oppress the poor at the very time the Supper is celebrated.

The apostle reminds the community of the word of institution and expresses two realities. (1) The purpose of the institution of the Supper is to remember Jesus' body and his blood (11:23–25).[51] (2) The proclamation of the Supper is to show forth Christ's death until he comes (11:26). The result should be that the Corinthians will not overindulge themselves, despise and shame others, or allow brothers and sisters to go hungry. Unfortunately, their conduct at the Lord's Supper "proclaimed a culture of selfishness and status mongering."[52] Thus, Paul's accusation: "you are not really eating the Lord's Supper" (11:20b, NET).

THE JUDGMENT FOR THE SOCIAL DIVISIONS IN CORINTH (1 COR 11:27 – 34)

Those Corinthians who abuse the Lord's Supper are guilty of a most heinous sin. By dividing the church through rank and status, the community is bringing shame to the Lord and themselves. Paul expounds, "Therefore,[53] whoever eats the bread and drinks the cup of the Lord in a

---

49. Luise Schottroff and Brian McNeil, trans., "Holiness and Justice: Exegetical Comments on 1 Corinthians 11.17–34," *JSNT* 79 (Spring 2000): 57.

50. According to Peter Lamp ("The Eucharist: Identifying with Christ on the Cross," *Int* 48.1 [1994]: 45): "our love for others represents Christ's death to other human beings." Paul exhorts the Corinthians to imitate Christ's sacrificial humility by having an unselfish attitude and love for one another (1:18–2:2; 8:1, 11; 10:31–11:1; 13:1–14:1; 15:1–3; 16:14, 22).

51. The words of the tradition call the Corinthians twice to "remember" Christ's death (11:24, 25). Anthony C. Thiselton (*First Corinthians: A Shorter Exegetical & Pastoral Commentary* [Grand Rapids: Eerdmans, 2006], 185) remarks: This "denotes more than merely mental recollection, but less than any notion of 'repeating' the once-for-all death of Christ ... the remembrance is a dramatic *involvement* or *actualization* of placing ourselves *'there'* at the foot of the cross, just as to eat the Passover was not simply to think about it but to be *'there'* as one who *took part in* the remembered events. In this sense Christian believers proclaim the death of Christ as (a) an *event*; and (b) an event *'for me,' that* involves *me*" (his emphasis).

52. Hays, *First Corinthians*, 200.

53. The conjunction ὥστε (cf. 11:33; 10:12) indicates that the apostle now resumes his main discussion from 11:17–22 since the Lord's Supper is a proclamation of Christ's death, eating and drinking in an unfitting fashion is unconscionable.

way that is not fitting[54] [ἀναξίως] will be held accountable[55] for so treating the body and blood of the Lord" (11:27). In this context, to eat or drink the Lord's Supper ἀναξίως is to violate its purpose to proclaim Christ's death. The result is that the perpetrator becomes "liable [ἔνοχος][56] of sinning against" the death of the Lord.[57] The punishment, however, does not appear to be described. While some argue that the future tense of ἔνοχος ἔσται requires eschatological judgment,[58] such an interpretation does not fit the immediate context. Given the lack of clear temporal indicators that it is guilt assessed at the eschatological judgment (e.g., "on the day of the Lord"), most likely we have liability assessed at the moment of transgression (11:30). It is a charge incurred in real time after doing the wrong that fulfills the condition.[59]

THE NEED FOR SELF-EXAMINATION

In light of the dire threat of being liable of sinning against the body and blood of the Lord Paul warns, "But let a person examine [δοκιμαζέτω] himself or herself and in this manner eat the bread and drink from the cup" (11:28).[60] Presumably, self-examination serves to reveal whether an individual stands "accountable" for the behavior described in 11:21–22.[61]

---

54. BDAG, 69, s.v. ἀναξίως. See also Thiselton (*The First Epistle to the Corinthians*, 889) who notes: "Paul's primary point is that attitude and conduct should fit the message and solemnity of what is proclaimed." This is also in keeping with the corresponding adjectival form of ἀναξίως in 6:2, which according to Thiselton (889) "conveys the sense of incompetency or being not good enough for a task." The gloss "not fitting" is preferred over the prevalent "in an unworthy manner/way" or "unworthily."

55. Thiselton, *The First Epistle to the Corinthians*, 889; Hays, *First Corinthians*, 200–201; Collins, *First Corinthians*, 438 = "answerable for."

56. This is Paul's only use of ἔνοχος; however, it is used elsewhere in the NT primarily as a judicial word denoting guilt before the law (Matt 5:21–22; 26:66; Mark 3:29; 14:64; Heb 2:15; Jas 2:10).

57. BDAG, 336–39, s.v. ἔνοχος 2 bγ.

58. F. W. Grosheide, *Commentary on the First Epistle to the Corinthians* (NICNT; Grand Rapids: Eerdmans, 1953), 274; Simon J. Kistemaker, *Exposition of the First Epistles to the Corinthians* (NTC; Grand Rapids: Baker, 1993), 401.

59. Judith M. Gundry-Volf (*Paul and Perseverance: Staying In and Falling Away* [WUNT 2.37; Tübingen: Mohr-Siebeck, 1990], 101) rightly argues that the future tense here refers to temporal judgment subsequent to the action.

60. BDAG, 255, s.v. δοκιμάζω 1: "to make a critical examination of something, to determine genuineness, put to the test, examine." Cf. δόκιμος in 11:19.

61. Stephen Anthony Cummins, *Paul and the Crucified Christ in Antioch: Maccabean Martyrdom and Galatians 1 and 2* (SNTSMS 114; Cambridge: Cambridge University Press, 2001), 171; Carter, *The Great Sermon Tradition as a Fiscal Framework in 1 Corinthians*, 175.

Most likely the apostle is speaking directly to the "haves."[62] The present imperatives δοκιμαζέτω, ἐσθιέτω, and πινέτω are clearly iterative: whenever the Lord's Supper is observed, there is an ongoing responsibility to carefully examine one's attitude in relation to 11:21–22.[63] It is also worth noting that the adverb οὕτως implies that the eating and drinking is to be done only after the examining has been done and the person is not liable of partaking in an unfitting manner.[64] When this directive is followed, one can have confidence to participate in the Lord's Supper.

The theme of judgment intensifies in 11:29–34.[65] The forensic emphasis of the text is unmistakable and suggests that a judicial event is now taking place in the congregation, all because of how the rich are treating the poor.[66] Furthermore, Paul declares that God will continue to render a verdict of judgment unless the Corinthians repent of mistreating one another. He writes, "For the one who eats and drinks,[67] by failing to discern the body, eats and drinks judgment on himself or herself" (11:29). The reason (γάρ) that each Corinthian must examine himself or herself is to avoid eating and drinking judgment on oneself by failing to discern the body. In this case, διακρίνω could mean either "to differentiate by separating"[68] or "judge correctly."[69] In this context the latter, forensic sense may

---

62. Inziku, *Overcoming Divisive Behaviour*, 217–19.

63. Wallace, *Greek Grammar beyond the Basics*, 722.

64. In the context of the Lord's Supper, the Didache (14.2) says, "But every Lord's day gather yourselves together, and break bread, and give thanksgiving after having confessed your transgressions, that your sacrifice may be pure. But let no one who is at odds with his fellow come together with you, until they be reconciled, that your sacrifice may not be profaned."

65. Paul's use of paranomasia with words related to judgment is striking and gets lost in translation: κρίμα (11:29, 34); διακρίνων (11:29); διεκρίνομεν (11:31); ἐκρινόμεθα (11:31); κρινόμενοι (11:32); and κατακριθῶμεν (11:32). These words aid the ear and eye to pick up the dominant theme on the apostle's mind and heart.

66. Calvin Roetzel, *Judgment in the Community* (Leiden: Brill, 1972), 137.

67. There is a textual variant here. The UBS[4] and NA[27] omit τοῦ κυρίου, which was probably included by an early copyist to help explain τὸ σῶμα. The Robinson-Pierpont reading is: Ὁ γὰρ ἐσθίων καὶ πίνων ἀναξίως, κρίμα ἑαυτῷ ἐσθίει καὶ πίνει, μὴ διακρίνων τὸ σῶμα τοῦ κυρίου (words in italics omitted in UBS[4] and NA[27]). Bruce Manning Metzger (*A Textual Commentary on the Greek New Testament* [2nd ed.; New York: United Bible Societies, 1994], 562–63) argues for the "shorter reading" saying that "there appears to be no good reason to account for the omission if the words had been present originally."

68. BDAG, 231, s.v. διακρίνω 1. See also Leon Morris, *The First Epistle of Paul to the Corinthians* (TNTC; Grand Rapids: Eerdmans, 1958. 1985), 162.

69. Barrett (*The First Epistle to the Corinthians*, 274) points out that Paul's use of διακρίνων varies (see 4:7; 6:5; 14:29; Rom 4:20; 14:23), so that one cannot ascertain its meaning in 11:29 from Paul's previous uses.

probably be ruled out.[70] Thus, διακρίνω could refer to distinguishing the holy from the unholy or having the right estimate of Christ's body. But it can also mean "to recognize."[71]

"THE BODY": A DUAL FOCUS

The phrase τὸ σῶμα is disputed; however, it seems that this phrase refers both to the eucharistic elements and to the Corinthian church.[72] There is likely a double entendre here with the reference to the "Lord's body," referring literally to Jesus' physical body "which is for you" (cf. 11:24), and the church as the Lord's corporate body, which is being divided by the Corinthians' attitude (cf. 11:17–22).[73] If so, this represents an example of Paul fluidly moving between individual and corporate dimensions of τὸ σῶμα with the individual body in this case being Christ's (cf. 6:12–20). In other words, one who treats fellow believers poorly fails to discern that they are members of Christ's body.[74] One may also fail to discern the significance of Christ's death since by his death he created a people; and therefore, one who mistreats fellow believers at the Lord's Supper reveals that he or she has little understanding of why Christ died.[75] Consequently, just as the meal itself is both social and eschatological, so also the bread represents the social and eschatological significance of Christ's death.

The strength of this position is that it does not require the interpreter to choose between two valid positions. Instead, this view balances the two

---

70. Fee (*The First Epistle to the Corinthians*, 564) sees the meaning here as, "to discern, distinguish as distinct and different."

71. See BDAG, s.v. διακρίνω 3a. The participle may have conditional force ("if they fail to discern the body"), or this may be a causal clause ("because they do not discern the body"). See Wallace, *Greek Grammar Beyond the Basics*, 633.

72. Collins, *First Corinthians*, 439; Barnett, *1 Corinthians*, 220; Thomas R. Schreiner, *Paul, Apostle of God's Glory in Christ* (Leicester: Apollos; Downers Grove, IL: InterVarsity, 2001), 381; Verbrugge, "1 Corinthians," 361.

73. James D. G. Dunn, *The Theology of Paul the Apostle* (Grand Rapids/Cambridge: Eerdmans, 1998), 616–18; Mitchell (*Paul and the Rhetoric of Reconciliation*, 263–65) rightly denies any antithesis between "body" as congregation and as the eucharistic body of the Lord. On the contrary, because eating and drinking the symbols is a communal act of unity, both ideas are inextricably intertwined.

74. Inziku (*Overcoming Divisive Behaviour*, 235) observes: "The Corinthians had apparently no difficulties with the actual eucharistic action, but rather with divisive and greedy behavior by some at the common meal, spoiling it or, in the words of the text, making it (spiritually and morally) impossible to eat the Lord's food."

75. Schreiner, *Paul, Apostle of God's Glory in Christ*, 381.

themes that seem to color Paul's language and emphasis.[76] The ambiguity in the phrase μὴ διακρίνων τὸ σῶμα ("not discerning the body") may be deliberate, because one cannot separate the physical body of Christ and the spiritual body of Christ.[77] Moreover, the balance between the vertical and horizontal relationships of τὸ σῶμα also serves to remind the Corinthians that even though it is terrible to sin "against the body and blood of the Lord" (11:27), it is equally sinful to sin against fellow believers by making a distinction between the rich and the poor (11:29). Christ, after all, died for all. Paul admonishes those who flaunt their so-called "freedom" in Christ in a way that offends or scandalizes weaker Christians: "When you sin against your brothers and sisters in this way and wound their weak conscience, you sin against Christ" (8:12). A relationship with Christ demands loving those who make up his body.

APPLICATION TO THE SITUATION AT CORINTH

Paul now applies the general truths of 11:27–29 specifically to the situation at Corinth: "On account of this [διὰ τοῦτο, i.e., "not discerning the body," 11:29], many among you are weak and sick, and quite a few[78] are dead" (11:30). The apostle has probably heard of these repercussions from those who told him of their divisions (1:10–12), and he connects (διὰ τοῦτο) these events to their improper handling of the Lord's Supper and to God's judgment. The terms that follow refer to literal, physical suffering. Specifically, some of the Corinthians have received degrees of chastisement, possibly in proportion to the severity of their sins. Paul does not identify who or how many have become sick or have died. However, for his arguments to have force as a warning, one would assume that the Corinthians could readily identify those who are sick or have died as liable of despising and humiliating their brothers and sisters at the Lord's Supper.[79] Regardless, God's hand plays a role in the judgment of the Corinthian community.[80]

---

76. If this suggestion is correct, then 11:29 is a case of single meaning and multiple referents, allowing a seamless transition into Paul's use of σῶμα in ch. 12.

77. Horrell, "The Lord's Supper at Corinth," 199.

78. BDAG, 472, s.v. ἱκανός 4a.

79. Barton, "Paul's Sense of Place," 241; Garland, 1 Corinthians, 553.

80. Many scholars link God's judgment in 11:30 to the retribution theology of Deuteronomy. See Hays, First Corinthians, 205–6; Charles H. Talbert, Reading Corinthians: A Literary and Theological Commentary on 1 and 2 Corinthians (2nd ed.; New York: Crossroad, 2002), 99–100; Garland, 1 Corinthians, 553.

The means by which the Corinthians can avoid God's judgment is by judging themselves. Paul writes, "But if we were examining ourselves, we would not be judged" (11:31). The word δέ links 11:31 with some contrast implied to 11:30. The apostle's logic seems to be: judge yourselves so that the Lord will not have to judge you (11:31 – 32a).[81] His use of διακρίνω in 11:31 refers to self-judgment, whereby one becomes aware of selfish behavior toward less fortunate believers at the Eucharist or any other carelessness in observing the Lord's Supper.

The ultimate purpose behind God's temporal judgment is to correct the errant attitude and behavior of certain Corinthians. Paul explains, "But when we are judged by the Lord, we are being disciplined so that we may not be condemned with the world" (11:32). Here, he clearly states that God's judgment on believers is discipline, not condemnation. The apostle explicitly juxtaposes the two forms of judgment: παιδευόμεθα ["we are being disciplined"], ἵνα μὴ κατακριθῶμεν ["so that we may not be condemned"]. The contrasting objects of the two judgments reinforce their juxtaposition: present temporal judgment has fallen on certain members of the church,[82] whereas the world is destined for eternal condemnation.[83] The Corinthians could have avoided the present experience of judgment (11:31); nevertheless, it is disciplinary and will allow them to be spared God's ultimate judgment (11:32).[84] Moreover, παιδευόμεθα and κρινόμενοι act contemporaneously, which suggests that παιδεύω is

---

81. An explicit example of this principle is found in Ex 15:26 where Moses prophesied, "If you will diligently obey the LORD your God, and do what is right in his sight, and pay attention to his commandments, and give ear to his statutes, then I will not bring on you all the diseases that I brought on the Egyptians, for I, the LORD, am your healer."

82. Gundry-Volf, *Paul and Perseverance*, 100. See also Richard A. Horsley, *1 Corinthians* (ANTC; Nashville: Abingdon, 1998), 162–63; W. Baker, *1 Corinthians*, 173.

83. Contra James M. Hamilton Jr. ("The Lord's Supper in Paul: An Identity-Forming Proclamation of the Gospel," in *The Lord's Supper: Remembering and Proclaiming Christ Until He Comes* [ed. Thomas R. Schreiner and Matthew R. Crawford; Nashville: Broadman, 2010], 93) who argues that the sinful Corinthians are unbelievers. In support of his view, he claims Rev 2:20–23 as a parallel text.

84. C. F. D. Moule ("The Judgment Theme in the Sacraments," in *The Background of the NT and Its Eschatology: Studies in Honour of C. H. Dodd* [eds. W. D. Davies and D. Daube; Cambridge: Cambridge University Press, 1956], 477) states, "If these words [11:31 – 32] are to be pressed, they must mean that 'the world' is destined to be 'condemned'; but Christians, however culpable they may be, will only fall under remedial, educative judgment destined to rescue them from ultimate condemnation."

remedial chastening.[85] The apostle's goal is to motivate certain socially elite Corinthians to repent and stop dishonoring the poor within the community, but a failure to do so does not revoke their salvation.[86]

Paul's assurance of God's grace concludes the central unit of the exposition (11:23–32). The repetition of the phrase τοῦ κυρίου makes an important contribution to the semantic coherence of 11:23–32. τοῦ κυρίου ("of the Lord") appears thrice in each of the subunits of 11:23–26 and 11:27–32, twice in the opening sentences (11:23, 27), and once in the closing sentences (11:26, 32). It forms an *inclusio* marking the beginning and end of each subunit. The first subunit explains (γάρ, 11:23) what the Lord's Supper is, thereby clarifying why it is that what the Corinthians are doing is not eating the Lord's Supper (11:20). The second subunit gives the result and explains what obedience to Christ should look like when the church gathers to celebrate the Lord's Supper (11:28, 31).[87]

PAUL'S WRAP-UP

Paul concludes this passage by laying out specific instructions to evade God's judgment (11:33–34). The proper course of action from the Corinthians should be to honor and respect one another. Paul writes, "So then, my brothers and sisters, when you come together to eat, welcome one another" (11:33). The conjunction ὥστε (cf. 11:27) and the vocative ἀδελφοί ("brothers and sisters") indicates that the apostle is concluding his argument (11:17–32). The use of ἀδελφοί adds a touch of affection to a stern scolding and serves to mitigate the severity of his admonition. It also opens the hearts of his listeners to the counsel he is about to give. Finally, it implies that abusing the Lord's Supper does not eliminate one from God's family. συνερχόμενοι ("when you come together") links back to συνέρχεσθε and συνερχομένων (11:17, 18) and serves to bracket this unit. Paul then provides a direct answer to the issues raised in 11:21. Instead of some gorging themselves while others go hungry, the wealthy should eat,

---

85. This is further supported by Paul's only other use of παιδεύω in the Corinthian correspondence (2 Cor 6:9). He knows from fulfilling his apostolic commission that chastening [παιδεύω] is not a contradiction of God's love, but is rather to be understood on the basis of it.

86. E.g., Morris, *The First Epistle of Paul to the Corinthians*, 161; Craig L. Blomberg, *1 Corinthians* (NIVAC; Grand Rapids: Zondervan, 1994), 231; Collins, *First Corinthians*, 436.

87. Collins, *First Corinthians*, 437.

in Paul's mind, at home. In this way, the Corinthians are to reflect the unity of the body and avert God's judgment.

The phrase ἀλλήλους ἐκδέχεσθε is generally translated "wait for one another."[88] This rendering is in keeping with the common meaning of ἐκδέχομαι in the NT.[89] However, the obstacle to this rendering is that if the Corinthians merely "wait for one another," the problem at hand is not corrected.[90] The scandal in Corinth is that the rich are humiliating the poor by feasting in their presence. Hence, another possible translation for ἐκδέχομαι is "welcome" or "receive."[91] Three arguments seem to support this translation: (1) When ἐκδέχομαι is used of persons or in the context of a dinner, it means "to take or receive from another" or "to entertain."[92] (2) In the papyri, ἐκδέχομαι relates to hospitality with explicit references to the provision of food. (3) Paul generally uses ἀπεκδέχομαι when he means "wait," not ἐκδέχομαι (e.g., 1:7; Rom 8:19, 23, 25). Therefore, the imperative ἐκδέχεσθε demands that the affluent Corinthians "receive" or "welcome" the less fortunate to the full dinner and thus avoid humiliating them in the church gathering.[93] This use of

---

88. See major English versions (e.g., NET, NASB, ESV, HCSB, NRSV, NKJV, KJV). BDAG, 300, s.v. ἐκδέχομαι and L&N, 85.60, s.v. ἐκδέχομαι define 11:33 as "wait for one another." See also Morris, *The First Epistle of Paul to the Corinthians*, 162; Kistemaker, *Exposition of the First Epistles to the Corinthians*, 405; Collins, *First Corinthians*, 440; Barnett, *1 Corinthians*, 221; Thiselton, *The First Epistle to the Corinthians*, 898–99; Vander Broek, *Breaking Barriers*, 114; Johnson, *1 Corinthians*, 212; Watson, *The First Epistle to the Corinthians*, 124.

89. See John 5:4; Acts 17:16; 1 Cor 16:11; Heb 10:13; 11:10; Jas 5:7.

90. Winter, "The Lord's Supper at Corinth," 79; *After Paul Left Corinth*, 151–52; Blue, "The House Church at Corinth and the Lord's Supper," 231; Lamp, "The Eucharist: Identifying with Christ on the Cross," 42.

91. See Winter (*After Paul Left Corinth*, 151–52) for the following arguments.

92. MM, s.v. ἐκδέχομαι call this the "primary meaning"; similarly *EDNT*, s.v. ἐκδέχομαι 1:407. See 3 Macc 5:26; Josephus, *J.W.* 2.14.7 §297; 3.2.4 §32; *Ant.* 7.14.5 §351; 11.8.6 §340; 12.3.3 §138; 13.4.5. §104; 13.5.5. §148.

93. See Fee, *The First Epistle to the Corinthians*, 567–68; Blomberg, *1 Corinthians*, 232; Witherington, *Conflict and Community in Corinth*, 252; Hays, *First Corinthians*, 202–3; Horsley, *1 Corinthians*, 163; Eaton, *1 Corinthians 10–16*, 41. Thiselton (*The First Epistle to the Corinthians*, 898–99) and others still prefer the translation "wait" because they see the lexical argument for "receive" as weak, but none of these commentators seem to explain the glaring difficulty of the failure to "wait" to solve the eucharistic problem. It should be noted, however, that the eucharistic problem could be solved in the "wait" reading if the Eucharist takes place after the meal, in which case Paul solves the problem by eliminating the "Love Feast" aspect of the rite. See Conzelmann, *1 Corinthians*, 195.

ἐκδέχεσθε is closely analogous to προσλαμβάνεσθε ἀλλήλους ("Welcome one another") in Rom 15:7, the notable difference being that Paul is speaking more generally there, whereas in 1 Cor 11:33 he is focusing specifically on the Lord's Supper.[94]

The apostle concludes this text with these words: "If anyone is hungry, let him or her eat at home, so that you do not come together for your judgment" (11:34a).[95] "If anyone is hungry" refers not to the "have-nots," but to those who are wealthy,[96] who were gorging themselves on their delicacies in front of the poor. Paul's goal is that the Corinthians might truly proclaim Christ's death until he comes (11:26). To do so, in the midst of the materialism of Corinth, the rich need to show uncommon concern for the poor, just as the "strong" are to show concern for the weak (8:1 – 11:1). God has shown equal mercy toward each class in their salvation, and they must now reflect Christ's love and compassion in their relationship with each other.

The command to "eat at home" in 11:34 (ἐν οἴκῳ ἐσθιέτω) restates (as a command) 11:22a and connects to Paul's first warning that the Corinthians are worse off for having gathered together (11:17). If they are intent only on indulging their appetites, they should stay at home or at least eat enough at home to curb their bodily appetites. If the church's gathering is to be meaningful, it has to be an expression of real fellowship, which includes sharing.[97] Again, the apostle wishes to prevent the

---

94. See Inziku (*Overcoming Divisive Behaviour*, 322) who proposes an echo in Isa 58:6–7, 10 LXX where the prophet has Yahweh ask: "Is not this the fast that I choose? Is it not to share your bread [τὸν ἄρτον] with the hungry [πεινῶντι], and bring the homeless poor into your house [τὸν οἶκον]? If you give your food to the hungry [δῷς πεινῶντι τὸν ἄρτον] and satisfy the needs of the afflicted, then your light shall rise in the darkness and your gloom be the noonday."

95. Verses 17 and 34 form an *inclusio* with συνέρχησθε. Marion L. Soards (*1 Corinthians* [NIBCNT; Peabody, MA: Hendrickson, 1999], 249–50) writes: "Paul's words in 11:33–34 and 11:17–22 form an inclusio around his reflections on the Lord's Supper in the material found in 11:23–32. The nature of repetition is to create emphasis, both by repeating the information itself (11:17–22, 33–34) and by highlighting the material that is surrounded by the repetitive two parts (11:23–32). Thus, 11:33–34 both bring the final segment of Paul's discussion (11:27–34) to a conclusion and help focus and hold the entire reflection from 11:17–34 together."

96. See 16:19; Rom 16:5; Phlm 2; Col 4:15 for the elite in whose houses the early church met.

97. Garland, *1 Corinthians*, 555.

Corinthians from coming together for discipline, which goes back to κρίμα ("judgment") in 11:29.[98] The implication is that their gathering brings judgment on them rather than blessing.[99]

Paul concludes this section with the vague phrase: "As for the remaining matters, I will direct you when I come" (11:34b). He has discussed two critical issues in connection with worship: the wearing of veils by women (11:2–16) and the abuses taking place at the Lord's Supper (11:17–34). Apparently, there are other worship issues that need his input, but they are not so urgent that he has to write about them at this time. Rather, these instructions can wait a few months until he arrives in Corinth (cf. 16:5–7). One can only surmise what other issues these are.[100]

CONCLUSION

Instead of the Lord's Supper being a symbol of unity and spirituality, in accordance with what the meal was intended to represent—the gospel—the Corinthians made a sinful meal out of the celebration (11:17–22). In doing so, they painted a terribly depraved picture of the community partaking in a meal centering on the death of the Lord Jesus (11:23–26).

---

98. Mitchell (*Paul and the Rhetoric of Reconciliation*, 276) has suggested that in 11:34 "judgment" may be a double entendre—signifying both divine discipline and human-class-based stratification. Peter Oakes ("Urban Structure and Patronage: Christ Followers in Corinth," in *Understanding the Social World of the New Testament* [ed. Dietmar Neufeld and Roger DeMaris; London: Routledge 2009], 192) reconstructs the scene: "The group of Christ-followers from across the city comes to a single place. The host of this meal clearly has accommodation of some size. This makes it rather likely that he or she will be patron of a local network. If that is the case, then the behavior that Paul criticizes becomes quite easily explicable. Although patronage involved transfer of benefits—such as provision of a meal—between patron and clients, the relationship was founded on structural inequality. If a patron participated in a meal with clients we would expect the meal to reflect the structural inequality. Patrons stop being patrons if they do not generally eat more food, and more expensive food, than clients. This is sharpened by the fact that the patron's need to project his or her status goes beyond the people gathered at the meal." For more on the patron-client relationship and its inherent inequality, see ch. 3. Paul will not stand for such inequality in the church.

99. Inziku (*Overcoming Divisive Behaviour*, 324 n. 74): "Because of the use of μή plus the subjunctive, the ἵνα clause construction best serves as a warning or suggests caution."

100. Winter ("The Lord's Supper at Corinth," 80) suggests that these matters are difficult and "perhaps touch the very special structure of Corinthian society." Winter guesses that this instruction serves as an interim ethic. What the wealthy need to do for the poor, he will deal with later.

The purpose of the meal was: (1) to remember the suffering and death of Christ, and (2) to bring a unified, healthy body together as a testimony. Instead, the affluent members of the Corinthian church refused to share with those who were poor.

Consequently, they were participating in the Lord's Supper in an unfitting manner by demonstrating a complete lack of unity and concern for their brothers and sisters (11:29). The solution to the problem of discrimination against the poor Corinthians at the Lord's Supper is for rich Corinthians to share everything in the common meal and to save their own feasts for the privacy of their homes (11:33–34). The result of failing to exhibit the unity of the body in the observance of the Lord's Supper was divine judgment designed to restore oneness (11:30).

CHAPTER 11

A MESSAGE TO THE RICH IN THE WORLD

IN THE PREVIOUS CHAPTER WE EXAMINED THE SITUATION IN CORINTH, where distinctions were being made between the rich and the poor, which were especially evident when the Corinthian community gathered together for the Lord's Supper. Moreover, we know from ch. 4 that Paul had a special place in his heart for the poor, and this passion led, at least in part, to a special project on this third missionary journey to take up a collection for "the poor among the saints" in Jerusalem.

But did Paul have an independent message, apart from the collection, for Christians who had wealth? The answer to this question is a resounding yes. In various places in his letters, the apostle addresses those who are rich in the world—and in particular, those who have gained their riches by dishonesty and used their wealth to maintain power over other people. Since this is a book where we plan on examining all areas where Paul talks about money issues, we need to look at these passages. Many of them occur in the Pastoral Epistles, and interestingly, it is in these same letters that Paul often offers the antidote to clamoring after wealth.

WORDS TO RICH CHRISTIANS (1 TIM 6:9 – 10, 17 – 19)

One of the key, and perhaps most dramatic, passages in which Paul deals with the issue of wealth is the last chapter of 1 Timothy. We must remember the setting of this letter. Paul is writing to one of his protégés, Timothy, whom he has left in Ephesus to serve as pastor of the church there (1 Tim 1:3). The instructions Paul gives to Timothy do not outline how the young pastor should address problems in society at large; rather, these are instructions that he must teach and preach to the believers under his care.

We begin with 1 Tim 6:9–10:

> Those who want to get rich fall into temptation and a trap and into many foolish and harmful desires that plunge people into ruin and destruction. For the love of money is a root of all kinds of evil. Some people, eager for money, have wandered from the faith and pierced themselves with many griefs. (NIV)

Note the last sentence, "some people, eager for money, have wandered from the faith." The expression "the faith" is used a number of times in the Pastoral Epistles as a euphemism for the body of Christian truth (1 Tim 1:19; 4:1, 6; 6:10; 2 Tim 2:18; 4:7).[1] In other words, some people who are attached to earthly wealth and set their hope on it end up denying Christ as their Savior and the teachings of the Christian faith.[2] The problem is not money itself, but the love of it — the destructive, all-consuming desire for more, which Paul describes so graphically in this section. Love of money forms a "root[3] of all kinds of evil."[4]

After a parenthesis (6:11–16), Paul again returns to the topic of riches in 6:17–19.[5] Previously he was concerned about "those who want to get rich" (6:9). Now he addresses the issue of those who *are* rich (6:17–19, "the rich in the now age").[6] Paul does not denounce the possession of

---

1. See BDAG, 820, s.v. πίστις, meaning 3: "that which is believed, *body of faith/belief/teaching*" (all these verses are categorized here, though some of them, including 1 Tim 6:10, are also categorized under 2.d.α, "*faith, firm commitment*," as a synonym for being a Christian 819).

2. Note Paul's use of the word "some" (τινες). Thus, it is possible to have wealth and yet retain a commitment to the Christian faith, though such people face challenges that those without wealth do not.

3. Though the primary sense of ῥίζα is simply "root," as in the root of a plant, the meaning here is best seen in a more figurative sense. In secular Greek as well the word may be understood metaphorically as "origin" or "ancestry" (J. H. Moulton and G. Milligan, *The Vocabulary of the Greek Testament Illustrated from the Papyri and Other Non-Literary Sources* [Grand Rapids: Eerdmans, 1952], 564). Cf. also BDAG, 905, s.v., ῥίζα, meaning 1b, "of the beginning fr. which someth. grows" (905).

4. See the discussion of this verse in Blomberg, *Christians in an Age of Wealth*, 92.

5. Some scholars have argued that this discussion does not belong at this place in the epistle.

6. George W. Knight III (*The Pastoral Epistles* [NIGTC; Grand Rapids: Eerdmans, 1992], 272) suggests that the Greek word τοῖς πλουσίοις (meaning "the wealthy") refers to the

wealth as such. As we have seen in chs. 2 and 3, the contributions of wealthier believers were important to the early church and its missionaries. Paul endorsed the fact that other apostles were making their living from preaching the gospel, and he himself needed financial help in order to write letters and pay for travel fees on ships. Quite the contrary, he affirms that it is God "who richly gives us all we need for our enjoyment" (6:17).[7] Paul does not condemn wealth, but he does know the added temptations that the wealthy face. He is vitally concerned that Christians have the right attitude toward their wealth and make the proper use of it.[8]

Paul goes on to contrast right and wrong responses to the possession of wealth.[9] He urges Timothy "to instruct" (παράγγελλε)[10] such people "not to be conceited or to fix their hope on the uncertainty[11] of riches." The tense of the verb "to fix their hope on" is perfect, denoting a settled state of confidence in one's wealth, which is so easy for those who have wealth to experience. Instead, regardless of their financial status, these believers are to fix their hope on God, "who richly supplies us with all things for our enjoyment." "The reason everything may be enjoyed lies in the recognition that everything, including one's wealth, is a gift, the expression of God's gracious generosity."[12]

Rather than putting their hope in wealth, says Paul, the wealthy are to follow four admonitions that the apostle instructs Timothy to offer to the rich (6:17 – 18): (1) they are to "put their hope ... in God, the one who supplies us with everything"; (2) they are "to do good things" (ἀγαθοεργεῖν) with their money; (3) they are "to be rich in good deeds" (πλουτεῖν ἐν ἔργοις καλοῖς);[13] and (4) they are "to be generous [εὐμεταδότους] and

---

materially rich, particularly those who did not need to work for a living. In terms of the economic levels we discussed in ch. 4, this would probably be the ES4 level.

7. Linda Belleville, 1 Timothy (CBC; Carol Stream, IL: Tyndale, 2009), 121.

8. Lea and Griffin, 1, 2 Timothy, Titus, 174.

9. Fee (1 and 2 Timothy, Titus, 156) points out how similar 1 Tim 6:17 – 19 is to Eccl 5:18 – 20.

10. This is the military word for "command" (cf. 1 Tim 1:3; 4:11; 5:7; 6:13).

11. The Scriptures frequently speak of the uncertainty of wealth (Ps 39:6; Prov 23:4 – 5; 27:24; Eccl 5:13 – 14; Matt 6:19; Jas 5:1-2).

12. Fee, 1 and 2 Timothy, Titus, 157.

13. Although "to do good things" and "to be rich in good deeds" function as synonyms, the second phrase — "to be rich [πλουτεῖν] in good deeds" — provides a wordplay on the phrase "the rich" (τοῖς πλουσίοις) with which Paul began in 6:17. See Knight, The Pastoral Epistles, 273; Mounce, Pastoral Epistles, 367.

sharing with others [κοινωνικούς]."[14] One cannot help but think here about what we discovered in ch. 4, that Paul expected all believers, insofar as they were able, to show compassion for the poor and to help them with their present physical needs (as the early Jerusalem church showed in Acts 2–6).

Although Paul writes that God "richly supplies us with everything for our enjoyment" (v. 17), we should not understand the word "enjoyment" (ἀπόλαυσις) here to mean self-indulgence (cf. 5:6–10).[15] Rather, everything—in context, especially the wealth of those who are rich—is from God, and as Paul himself said on one occasion, quoting Jesus (in a saying not found in the Gospels), "there is a greater blessing that comes to us by giving than by receiving" (Acts 20:35). "By being generous, the rich are not losing their wealth. Rather, they are laying it away in heaven, and by doing so, they are establishing a firm foundation for eternity, for life that is truly life."[16]

In 6:19a Paul conflates banking and building metaphors. He commands God's people to pursue "storing up[17] for themselves" the treasure of a "good foundation" for the future. Being willing to part with their riches so that others may benefit is the sort of activity that builds that good foundation. In so doing, "they will be able to take hold for themselves [ἐπιλάβωνται] of that which is life indeed" (6:19b). Paul's only other use of the verb ἐπιλαμβάνομαι is in 6:12, where he exhorted Timothy to "take hold of the eternal life" to which God had called him. The verb means "to take hold of [something] in order to make it one's own."[18] The phrase "for themselves" emphasizes that while generous givers do know that they are helping others, they also are laying hold of eternal life in the here and now and storing up significant future benefits. As Lea and Griffin put it: "Christians who enter the life of love by unselfish behavior will enter gloriously into God's presence in the life to come."[19]

The thesis of 6:17–19, therefore, is that spiritual treasure provides a

---

14. Both of these adjectives are found only here in the NT.

15. See BDAG, 115, s.v. ἀπόλαυσις: "having the benefit of something, and so enjoying it."

16. Mounce, *Pastoral Epistles*, 368.

17. The participle ἀποθησαυρίζοντας ("storing up") is only used here in the NT. It is, however, reminiscent of θησαυρίζετε in Jesus' message in Matt 6:19–20.

18. BDAG, 374, s.v. ἐπιλαμβάνομαι, meaning 4. John Kitchen (*The Pastoral Epistles for Pastors* [The Woodlands, TX: Kress Christian Publications, 2009], 290) notes, "The middle voice (in which all nineteen of its NT usages appear) underscores the inward nature of this act."

19. Lea and Griffin, *1, 2 Timothy, Titus*, 174.

stable foundation against an uncertain future.[20] "The wealthy who are truly wise delay present personal gratification for future personal blessing."[21] The goal for every believer is to prepare in this present age for the coming age, and one of the best ways for the wealthy to do this is to share what they have with those who do not.

A related theme to the joy of giving is the theme of "contentment," which Paul had introduced in the earlier section (6:6). The term Paul uses here is αὐταρκεία. Although the Stoic and Cynic philosophers of Paul's day used this word to declare self-sufficiency a crowning virtue, Paul transformed the term for Christ's purposes. He uses αὐταρκεία to refer to a form of contentment that one can have, whether one has little or much. Paul had used the adjective related to this noun (αὐτάρκης) with respect to himself in Phil 4:11 – 12 ("as for me, I have learned in whatever circumstances I am, to be content [αὐτάρκης].")[22] In his own life, Paul knew this did not come automatically, for it is something he had to learn.

The reason for contentment given here in 1 Tim 6 is that "we have brought nothing into the world, so we cannot take anything out of it either" (6:7). The negative pronoun οὐδέν ("nothing") is absolute and categorical in its negation. Additionally, it is put in the front of the sentence to emphasize it. When we are born, we bring nothing, absolutely nothing, with us into the world. We must, therefore, be content with life's basic necessities (6:8). Otherwise, it is easy to succumb to the temptation of pursuing wealth, which (as already noted) can "sink people into destruction and disaster" (6:9) and cause them to live dissatisfied lives. In fact, if people become enamored with money and possessions, they can lose their desire to serve Christ and end up with no reward on the other side of the grave (6:10b).

---

20. Paul's words are much like those of Jesus (Luke 12:32–33; 18:22; cf. Matt 6:19–21; 19:23–24). Philip H. Towner (*1-2 Timothy & Titus* [IVPNTC; Downers Grove, IL: InterVarsity Press, 1994], 146) states: "Today's gains are tomorrow's losses. Even on the best of days, the value of this world's wealth is extremely limited; it pertains only to this present world."

21. Kitchen, *The Pastoral Epistles for Pastors*, 289.

22. Fee (*1 and 2 Timothy, Titus*, 143) states this mind-set is "not *self*-sufficiency but *Christ*-sufficiency."

False Teachers Seek Dishonest Gain (Titus 1:10 – 11; 2 Tim 3:1 – 2)

When the apostle Paul was in the midst of the controversy with his opponents in 2 Cor 10 – 12, his main goal was to defend his own integrity. This is why he wrote his so-called "fool's speech" (2 Cor 11:1 – 12:18), even though he desperately did not want to. Paul said little to attack his opponents directly in those chapters (his focus seems to have been not to push down his enemies but to regain his own confidence and respect of the Corinthians). In one verse (11:20) he uses a number of verbs to describe the deplorable actions of these opponents among the Corinthians, but none of them specifically has to do with financial matters, such as manifesting greed or trying to use gullible people for their own gain.

Paul writes differently, however, in the Pastoral Epistles. There is, as we might expect in the scholarly world, a variety of views as to precisely who Paul's opponents are in these letters and what actions they are doing. We do not need to settle this scholarly discussion here. What is clear from Paul's words in the Pastoral Epistles is the motivation of the false teachers. It is "greed"; their goal is to teach "for the sake of sordid gain" (αἰσχροῦ κέρδους χάριν, Titus 1:11). The noun κέρδος ("gain") describes whatever might be to one's profit or advantage. It is used only in two other places in the NT, both by Paul (Phil 1:21; 3:7). Those two references are clearly to nonmonetary gain; thus, Paul's intent in Titus 1:11 may not simply be financial, but could include social leverage, power, and clout as well.[23] Nevertheless, financial gain is a likely piece of the pie. Whatever form the gain may have taken, Paul is careful to point out that it is "sordid" (αἰσχρός), a word describing that which is shameful, base, or dishonest.[24]

In 1 Tim 6:5 Paul says a similar thing, that the false teachers think that "godliness is a pathway to gain [πορισμός]." Precisely how greed or desire for financial gain would be a part of the picture of these false teachers Paul does not spell out (presumably he doesn't have to, because Timothy knows the situation). They may be similar to the wandering philosophers whom we examined briefly in ch. 2 and from whom Paul consistently distanced

---

23. Kitchen, *The Pastoral Epistles for Pastors*, 503.

24. BDAG, 29, s.v. αἰσχρός. The word is used only by Paul in the NT and always of that which is either socially or spiritually shameful (1 Cor 11:6; 14:35; Eph 5:12).

himself.[25] It was indeed important to Paul that no one preaching the gospel of Jesus should think he was in that business just to make a quick, easy buck. That was at least one reason why Paul insisted on working for his own daily keep (see 1 Cor 9:15–18 and the discussion in ch. 2).

In 2 Tim 3:1–2a Paul comes out forthrightly and calls these false teachers "lovers of money" (φιλάργυροι), which is the adjective related to the word Paul had used in 1 Tim 6:10 as a danger for any believer: "love of money" (φιλαργυρία).[26] To this adjective Paul adds "lovers of themselves" (φίλαυτοι in 2 Tim 3:2). "Paul … has already taught that the love of money is a root of all kinds of evil (1 Tim 6:10); here he adds that behind the love of money is the love of self."[27]

Most students of the Pastoral Epistles consider that the varying characteristics of the false teachers described in these letters form an intersecting picture of a single group. If that conclusion is appropriate, it is little wonder, then, that the issue of love of money surfaces more than once — especially from an apostle/pastor who has sought to minister to his sheep with absolute integrity.

Paul tackles the sin of loving money with great sobriety. He urges Christians to disassociate themselves from people who are self-centered, materialistic, and hedonistic (2 Tim 3:5). The verb he uses — ἀποτρέπω ("to avoid") — occurs only here in the NT, but it restates a common theme in the Pastoral Epistles using synonymous verbs (e.g., "turn away from" in 1 Tim 6:20; "avoid" in 2 Tim 2:16; "don't have anything to do with" in 2 Tim 2:23). Kelly writes that ἀποτρέπω is a strong term indicating that "Timothy is to avoid them with horror."[28]

---

25. Admittedly, one feature of the teachings of these false teachers would not line up with the wandering Cynic and/or Sophistic philosophers, namely, their teaching of circumcision (Titus 1:10). Jews in the Greco-Roman world were seen as strange people in that they practiced circumcision on their children, refused to eat pork, and would not do work on the Sabbath.

26. The term φιλάργυρος occurs in the NT elsewhere only in Luke 16:14 in a description of the Pharisees.

27. Mounce, *Pastoral Epistles*, 545. He also states, "The threefold repetition of the requirement for overseers (1 Tim 3:3) and deacons (1 Tim 3:8; cf. elders in Titus 1:7) that they not be greedy for financial gain shows that this was one of the basic problems in the Ephesian church, which is explicitly stated in Titus 1:11 concerning the situation in Crete (cf. 1 Tim 6:5–10)."

28. J. N. D. Kelly, *A Commentary on the Pastoral Epistles* (HNTC; New York: Harper & Row, 1964), 195.

LEADERS WITH INTEGRITY AS THE ANSWER (1 TIM 3; CF. TITUS 1)

Paul is not only quick to describe the characteristics of false teaching in the Pastoral Epistles. He is also ready to describe the antidote. First and foremost, the answer is simple: ministry leaders who serve as examples to the flock of what integrity is all about. Such leaders are examples to the rest of the flock as to what Christian service consists of—including showing integrity with respect to money issues.

INSTRUCTIONS IN THE PASTORAL LETTERS

One of the key characteristics of an elder is to be hospitable (φιλόξενος in 1 Tim 3:2; Titus 1:8). The two components of this word mean "love for a stranger."[29] One might expect Paul to use the more familiar φιλαδελφία ("brotherly love"), which he often calls for the churches to exercise (Rom 12:10; 1 Thess 4:9; cf. also Heb 13:1; 1 Pet 1:22; 2 Pet 1:7 [2x]). Instead, he expects leaders to set an example for believers in opening up their homes to strangers.[30] That is, rather than having people cater to the needs of the leaders (the pattern advocated by the wandering philosophers), the church elders are to expend themselves for any strangers or newcomers to their worship gatherings.

Hospitality was a highly valued Greek and Jewish virtue. In NT times it was assumed that town residents would welcome guests traveling through their town. In the case of believers, hospitality was essential for the expansion of the gospel, as well as important for the image of the church among outsiders.[31] Hospitality was particularly important for the early church since Christians had little choice but to meet in homes. It is likely that those believers who had homes with sufficient room to accommodate a number of people were generally the ones selected to be elders in the NT churches.[32] This did not necessitate that the elders be affluent or have large homes, but they did have to be willing to minister to others in the church with what they had.

---

29. The word is used elsewhere in the NT only in 1 Pet 4:9.

30. Kitchen, *The Pastoral Epistles for Pastors*, 126.

31. Moss, *1, 2 Timothy & Titus*, 70.

32. E.g., Rom 16:5; 1 Cor 16:19; Col 4:15; Phlm 1–2; see Kevin Giles, *Patterns of Ministry among the First Christians* (San Francisco: HarperCollins, 1991), 41.

Second, in 1 Tim 3:3 Paul states that an elder must "not [be] loving money/not [be] greedy" (ἀφιλάργυρος).[33] This word is made up of the alpha privative for negation (ἀ-), "love" (φιλ-), and "silver" (ἄργυρος) — hence, "not loving silver/money."[34] Paul wants *no* greediness to be found in an elder. In Ephesus, however, it appears that a number of people were manifesting greed, as we have seen, including some believers. Regarding this issue, in Paul's farewell speech to the elders of Ephesus a number of years before this, he pointed to his own example in their midst of not coveting gold or silver; rather, he worked hard with his own hands to meet his own needs and those of his companions (Acts 20:33 – 35).

It is important to note that Paul does not say that leaders should be free from money but rather free from *the love* of money.[35] A church leader must have a detachment from wealth and its distractions. He should be an example of generosity and faithful dependence on God. His goals and decisions are not to be influenced by money.[36] He will habitually use his financial resources for God's glory and the advancement of his kingdom (cf. Matt 6:24).

Church leaders often have to battle the temptation to love money. If Satan can't trip up an elder in the areas of pride or sexual sin, he will lay a trap of covetousness. Fortunately, as we have noted above, the Lord has also provided a positive quality that can deliver us from covetousness: contentment (cf. Phil 4:11 – 12).

In addition to being "hospitable" and "not loving money," in Titus 1:7b Paul stipulates that an elder must not be "shamelessly greedy for money, avaricious, fond of dishonest gain" (αἰσχροκερδής).[37] The apostle is referring to "the desire to be rich beyond one's needs."[38] The quest for

---

33. BDAG, 157, s.v. ἀφιλάργυρος. This adjective appears elsewhere in the NT only in Heb 13:5.

34. Mounce (*Pastoral Epistles*, 177) notes that the same word without the alpha privative was used to describe the Pharisees of Jesus' day and the people of the last days as "lovers of money" (Luke 16:14; 2 Tim 3:2).

35. Philemon was a man who apparently had wealth but who did not love it (cf. Phlm 2, 6–7).

36. Knute Larson, *I & II Thessalonians, I & II Timothy, Titus, Philemon* (Holman New Testament Commentary 9; Nashville: Broadman & Holman, 2000), 184.

37. BDAG, 29, s.v. αἰσχροκερδής. L&N (25.26) states that αἰσχροκερδής has to do with an insatiable appetite for wealth. Peter also uses the related adverb αἰσχροκερδῶς in reference to a character trait that elders should not have (1 Pet 5:2). In Titus 1:11 the same two root words (αἰσχρός and κέρδος) are separated but used together to describe the opponents of the gospel on the island of Crete.

money becomes base whenever one makes personal gain rather than God's glory the prime object of life. Hence, perhaps, even more at the heart of Paul's prohibition is that the reckless pursuit of money points to misplaced priorities and questionable integrity.

Like elders, deacons must not be "shamelessly greedy for money [once again, αἰσχροκερδής]" (1 Tim 3:8). While the task of the deacon is somewhat uncertain in the first century, that ministry may have involved the handling of resources intended for the disadvantaged, thus giving opportunity for such sin.[39] Many scholars relate the origin of the deacon's role to the story in Acts 6, where the apostles established a group of seven Spirit-filled men to handle the distribution of benevolent needs of Hellenistic widows. In any case, a deacon must never use his position for personal financial gain. What Paul prohibited was the use of a spiritual office for material benefit, even if no dishonesty or illegality was present. The deacon must not be perceived as greedy.

PAUL'S PERSONAL INTEGRITY MANIFESTED IN 2 CORINTHIANS

The situation alluded to in the Pastoral Epistles is not the first time Paul expressed concern about integrity in financial matters for church leaders. He had earlier done so in connection with the collection, though we did not discuss it in ch. 6. In that chapter we spoke briefly about some of the issues that had developed in Corinth between the writing of Paul's first letter to the Corinthians and the letter we now call 2 Corinthians. Charges appear to have been made against Paul and his associates that they were exploiting (πλεονεκτέω) the Corinthians (2 Cor 12:17 – 18). In addition, in 12:16, we get the feeling that some in Corinth were charging Paul, or at least his associates, with "deceit" or "trickery" (δόλος), probably in connection with their solicitation of donations for the collection on behalf of the apostle.[40]

---

38. Mounce, *Pastoral Epistles*, 390. C. K. Barrett (*The Pastoral Epistles* [New Clarendon Bible; Oxford: Clarendon, 1963)], 129) phrases it this way: "It is the sordidness of making profit out of Christian service, rather than dishonest gain, that is here condemned." See also Fee (*1 and 2 Timothy, Titus*, 174) who approvingly quotes Barrett.

39. Kitchen, *The Pastoral Epistles for Pastors*, 140.

40. See Harris ("2 Corinthians," 537) who gives the conclusion of these opponents: "because Paul was unscrupulous (*panourgos* ... NIV 'crafty') by nature, he had exploited the

This charge seemed to weigh heavily on Paul's mind because in 2 Cor 8 and 9 (the unit in this letter in which he is trying to motivate the believers in Corinth to give generously for the collection), he includes a specific section asserting the integrity of those doing the collecting in Corinth. He writes that he is sending along with his letter Titus plus two other men who are known to the churches and are praised by them (8:18–19). The apostle goes so far as to say that one of them "had been chosen by the churches as a traveling companion [συνέκδημος]" to aid in the transportation of the collection.

In addition to comments about these three men, Paul describes in detail what he personally intends to accomplish through them (8:20). He is "trying to avoid" (στελλόμενοι)[41] at all costs a situation where someone might be able to "find fault with" or "criticize"[42] him and his company because of the way they are handling the money in the collection. As Betz comments:

> When Paul wrote 1 Thess 2:3–12, he was already obliged to draw a sharp distinction between himself and the religious charlatans who filled the Roman world. Such men had a reputation for raising funds for what were purported to be good causes, and then lining their own pockets. The apostle provided a similar defense of his intentions in 1 Cor 4:1–13.... But 2 Cor 8:20 looks back directly on the crisis that has just past [i.e., concerning the collection].[43]

In this way, Paul says, "we are taking careful thought ahead of time to do the right thing, not only in the eyes of the Lord but also in the eyes of other people" (2 Cor 8:21). In interpreting this verse, most commentators point out that Paul is citing the principle of Prov 3:4 (though he does not quote it exactly).

---

church's generosity and had gained surreptitiously through his agents what he had declined to accept personally. The collection for the poor in Jerusalem was simply a convenient way to get access to their money."

41. Ralph Martin translates this "we are taking this precaution" (*2 Corinthians*, 455).

42. BDAG, 663, s.v. μωμάομαι.

43. Betz, *2 Corinthians 8 and 9*, 76. This is not just a biblical virtue but one recognized even by pagan Roman writers; note Cicero, *Off.* 2.21.75: "the main thing in all public administration and public service is to avoid even the slightest suspicion of avarice" (noted by Martin, *2 Corinthians* [2nd ed.], 458).

This is the issue of integrity. There have always been people filled with covetousness and greed in this world, and human beings have an amazing capacity to find ways to take what does not belong to them in a sly and crafty manner, hoping to get away with it. This happened in the first century, and it continues to happen today.[44] Paul knew that a charge of financial mismanagement against his associates would bring dishonor to Christ; that is why he is pleased that the men chosen to assist him were known for their desire to bring honor to the Lord (2 Cor 8:19). This is equally a warning to us today to be completely open in our financial dealings within the church. As Paul reminds us here, there is no substitute for integrity.

Give Proper Attention to Widows in Need (1 Tim 5:3 – 16)

The directive to "honor" widows (1 Tim 5:3) introduces one of the lengthiest sections in Paul's letters (and in the NT as a whole) having to do with money (5:3 – 16). While Paul was addressing a unique cultural situation in the Roman Empire, what he wrote yields some relevant and helpful guidelines for Christians in every culture of the world.[45]

To understand this unit properly, however, we must first recognize that in Judea particularly, when Jews became Christians, they could easily be cut off from the welfare system in Israel (the laws in the OT that had to do with distributing to the needs of the poor and needy, including especially widows and orphans; cf. Jas 1:27). Furthermore, since there was no official governmental program in the Roman Empire to sustain such people with food (see comments in ch. 4), caring for truly needy Christians became the responsibility of local churches. As Christianity spread in the Roman world and grew in number, more people emerged with special needs. Inevitably, people began to take advantage of the generous spirit that existed among believers. Not only did older people tend to look to the church to meet their needs, but family members who had needy aging

---

44. For a powerful book on the issue of integrity in financial matters, with numerous examples of how people have sought to hide their theft from their church, see Rollie Dimos, *Integrity at Stake: Safeguarding Your Church from Financial Fraud* (Grand Rapids: Zondervan, forthcoming 2016).

45. See also Mounce, *Pastoral Epistles*, 299.

relatives also began to depend on the church rather than considering it their own responsibility to care for these needy relatives.[46]

Hence, in his first subsection (5:3–8), Paul states his main principle in clear language: "Honor widows who are widows indeed" (5:3). The imperative τίμα ("honor") is in the present tense, demanding repeated or continuous action. It means "to show high regard for, *honor, revere*."[47] In this context τιμάω includes the provision of an honorarium or monetary support.[48] This commitment is based on the fifth commandment, where the same verb is used: "Honor [τίμα] your father and your mother" (Exod 20:12, LXX).[49] "Honor" was understood to include providing financial support; note how Jesus made this clear by quoting this same command in his rebuke of the Pharisees and teachers of the law who were dodging their responsibility, through the use of the "Corban" exemption, to not take care of aging parents (cf. Mark 7:8–13).

Some issues must have developed in the early church over the care of widows that account for this section being included in 1 Timothy. It may even be that some church members were beginning to abuse the system, figuring that it was the duty of the church to care for widows. As a result, the financial resources of the church were being strained beyond the limit. In addition, some of the (younger) widows were becoming "busybodies" (περίεργοι, 5:13),[50] meddling in other people's business. In fact, perhaps because of an immoral lifestyle, Paul writes that some had apparently even turned away from the church to follow after Satan (5:15),[51] yet were still

---

46. Gene A. Getz, *A Biblical Theology of Materials Possessions* (Chicago: Moody, 1990), 315. For a thorough discussion of the Roman cultural and legal background to the issues faced by widows and how they were being handled in the first century, plus the relationship of these patterns especially to understanding Paul's instructions to the younger widows in 1 Tim 5:11–15, see Winter, *Roman Wives, Roman Widows*, 123–40.

47. BDAG, 1004, s.v. τιμάω, meaning 2.

48. Contra Fee (*1 and 2 Timothy, Titus*, 116) who understands τιμάω as merely respect or recognition.

49. See Winter, *Seek the Welfare of the City*, 69; see in this book pp. 40–46 for a thorough discussion of the Jewish and Greco-Roman social dynamics and expectations as they intersect with the situation of the widows in Ephesus that Paul discusses in 1 Tim 5:3–16. We should recall too that in the OT God expressed a special concern for the widow, the least, the little ones, the oppressed, and the powerless (Exod 22:22; Deut 10:18; 24:17; Job 29:13; Ps 68:5; Isa 1:17). This theme carries over into the NT, where the Christian community saw care for widows as a special responsibility (Luke 7:11–15; 18:2–8; 21:1–4; Acts 6:1; 9:39; Jas 1:27).

50. This word is related to περιεργαζομένους in 2 Thess 3:11; see comments on ch. 9.

51. See Winter, *Roman Wives, Roman Widows*, 132–35.

wanting the church to take care of them. Thus, Paul writes that children and other family members, not the church, should be the first[52] tier of people to provide for widows in their family (i.e., "children and grandchildren" who put their religion into practice, 5:4).[53] Such care is "pleasing in the sight of God" (cf. Jas 1:27).[54] By contrast, a widow who "lives for pleasure" should not receive support from the church (5:6).

In this section, Paul carefully describes the necessary characteristics of a woman who is truly a widow in need (ἡ ὄντως χήρα, "the genuine widow," 5:3, 5, 16). In other words, the church must use discernment in determining whose needs can be provided by the church. It even appears as if there was an official list (5:9) that Paul expected a church to keep as to who were the approved widows. Here, then, are the stipulations for who should be on that list.

(1) A genuine widow who has no living relatives who can care for her; her husband has died and she has no living children or grandchildren (5:4, 16).

(2) She is a godly woman who has been devoting herself regularly "night and day in supplications and prayers" (5:5). She is truly alone in this world, except for her relationship with God.

(3) Such a woman must be sixty years of age or older[55] and one who had been faithful to her one husband (ἑνὸς ἀνδρὸς γυνή, "a wife of one husband"). This may seem like an unusually strict characteristic, but since Paul goes on to say that younger widows should seek remarriage (5:14), this age factor suggests that a woman over sixty years old would in all likelihood never have any hope of getting remarried.

---

52. Paul bears this out by using the adverb πρῶτον ("first," 5:4) to emphasize the priority of this responsibility.

53. Bruce W. Winter ("Providentia for the Widows of 1 Timothy 5:3–16, " *TynBul* 39 [1988]: 83–99) points out that the Greco-Roman world demanded that a dowry accompany a woman into marriage so that it could provide her care whenever she became a widow. If the woman became a widow but had a son, this dowry came under the control of the son. Winter argues that the directives in 5:3–16 are intended to encourage individual family members to use the dowry they have in order to carry out the legal responsibility of support.

54. BDAG, 109, s.v. ἀπόδεκτος.

55. Is this a legalistic regulation, that a widow must be, without exception, at least sixty years old in order to receive this kind of help from the church? Not necessarily. The specific guideline, however, indicates that a widow should be up in years and not able to care for herself or provide for her needs.

(4) She must be known in the church for her good deeds and service to others, for her care in child rearing, and for her hospitality (5:10) — and not just in the past, but also in the present. In other words, the widows on the official list of the church had duties to perform within the Christian community (5:10b). They must be prudent in both conduct (5:11 – 12) and speech (5:13).[56]

In 5:7 Paul instructs Timothy to "command" (παραγγέλλω)[57] the widows to carry out the various exhortations given here.[58] Paul wants the widows to be "irreproachable" (ἀνεπίλημπτοι)[59] — a term he had used in 3:2 to introduce the qualifications of overseers.

Paul follows up this command with a warning in 5:8 that if[60] anyone does not provide[61] for his own family members, he has denied the faith and is worse than an unbeliever.[62] "Care for aging relatives is not an optional act of generosity: it is a fundamental part of Christian discipleship."[63]

---

56. Paul's concern throughout the book of 1 Timothy is that Christians live exemplary lives before the world (2:2; 3:1 – 7; 5:14; 6:1).

57. This is the same verb Paul uses in his instructions to Timothy for those who are rich in the world (1 Tim 6:17; see discussion earlier in this chapter). Note its use also in 1:3 and 4:11.

58. Fee, *1 and 2 Timothy, Titus*, 171.

59. BDAG, 77, s.v. ἀνεπίλημπτος.

60. Paul is most likely not speaking hypothetically here. The Greek is a condition of fact (εἰ + the indicative), which can sometimes even carry the meaning "since": "since they won't care for their relatives." See D. Edmond Hiebert, *First Timothy* (Chicago: Moody Press, 1957), 93 – 94; Fee, *1 and 2 Timothy, Titus*, 118; Belleville, *1 Timothy*, 94.

61. The verb προνοέω ("provide") means "to think ahead" or "to provide by seeing in advance." The only other NT usages occur in Rom 12:17 and 2 Cor 8:21. In this context, the word involves foreseeing and planning for the needs of one's family. Lock (*The Pastoral Epistles*, 59) suggests that by implication this term may include the duty of a Christian to provide for his wife in his will. Elsewhere Lock notes (125 – 26) that it later became Jewish law (imbedded in the Mishnah) that a husband must provide for his widow (cf. *m. Ketub.* 1.2).

62. Paul elsewhere says that even though pagans do not have the Scriptures, they do have "the work of the law written in their hearts" (Rom 2:15), e.g., they instinctively recognize the obligations of children to parents. Ray C. Stedman (*The Care and Feeding of Widows: Studies in First Timothy* ([1 Tim 5:1-16]: http://www.raystedman.org/new-testament/timothy/the-care-and-feeding-of-widows) writes, "The secular writings of the first century show that in the Roman, the Greek and the Jewish world, families were always expected to take care of their older parents. In fact, in Athens a statesman was not allowed to speak in public if he had any blot on his record in this regard; if he was not taking care of his older parents he was not allowed to perform as a politician or a statesman. It was widely accepted throughout the whole Roman world that it was a shocking and disgraceful thing not to meet the emotional needs of parents, and the financial needs, too, if necessary."

63. Dick France, *Timothy, Titus, and Hebrews* (Daily Bible Commentary; Peabody, MA: Hendrickson, 2001), 49.

In 5:11–16 Paul continues his discussion on widows, repeating some of the items he has just said.[64] We should note especially v. 16. If no family member was available to take care of elderly widows, then the church should consider supporting them.[65] But it is entirely possible that there might be some kind, believing woman in the church who would take a widow under her wing and care for her even if she were not a relative.[66] The church should honor the person doing that and not insist on taking over for the care of that widow (5:16).[67] In any case, one element Paul is clear about: the church has an obligation to care for widows who truly are alone, and it can only do so if it has the necessary resources.[68]

---

64. Some scholars, however, argue that it is better to understand "the list" in this section as a registry of widows capable of offering service. The stringent qualifications to get on "the list" are necessary for spiritual service. John Stott (*Guard the Truth* [Downers Grove, IL: InterVarsity Press, 1996], 129) writes: "Coming to 1 Tim. 5, we notice at once that the section on widows appears to be divided into two paragraphs, each of which is introduced by a different main verb. The widows in mind in verses 3–8 Timothy is to give proper recognition to, literally 'to honour, or rather support,' whereas those in mind in verses 9–16 he is to put on the list of widows, that is, 'register' or 'enroll' them. Commentators differ as to whether Paul is referring to the same group of widows in both paragraphs, or to two distinct groups. That different categories are in view is suggested not only by the different introductory verbs ('honour' and 'register'), but also by the different conditions for admission into the two groups. In the first case it is destitution and godliness, while in the second it is a combination of seniority, married faithfulness and a reputation for good works. I shall take it this way, understanding that the former group of widows is to receive financial support, and the latter opportunities for ministry, alongside the presbyters and deacons of ch. 3, although no hard and fast line is drawn between the groups, and they will probably have overlapped." However, as Towner (*1–2 Timothy & Titus* [IVPNTC], 116) points out, the evidence for the alleged office is quite late (third and fourth century), and the repetition of the same word for widow (χήρα, 5:3 [2x], 4, 5, 9, 11, 16 [2x]) and the similar opening and closing (5:3 and 16) hold the passage tightly together.

65. Mounce (*Pastoral Epistles*, 299) states, "Paul's primary concern in this passage is to help Timothy distinguish between widows the church should support and those whom it should not."

66. Note that if the person is not a relative, the one who takes care of her should be a woman, not a man. Even in the ancient world, one had to be careful about sexual issues.

67. There is a textual difficulty with 5:16. The shorter and better-attested reading is a bit problematic: "any woman who is a believer" (see NRSV note on this). The longer reading seems to fit better what one would expect here from Paul, "any man or woman who is a believer" (i.e., Paul is going back to the issue of family obligation here). Fee (*1 and 2 Timothy, Titus*, 124) has suggested that "the problem behind 5:4 and 8 was a specific case of a younger widow of means rejecting the care of a widowed mother and/or grandmother." While one need not see the "any woman who is a believer" as a widow, there may well have been a problem with women of means failing to care for widows within their households. If the shorter reading is adopted, the situation may be a kind woman of means who sees it as her mission to help widows, even if they are not blood relatives.

68. Mounce, *Pastoral Epistles*, 298.

OTHER PASSAGES OF MEETING NEEDS

There is one other text in the Pastoral Epistles that fits into the same category of verses we have been looking at — concern for the "needs" of other people. Paul writes in one of his closing instructions: "And our people must learn to devote themselves to good deeds directed to people's necessary needs [τὰς ἀναγκαίας χρείας], so that they may not be unfruitful" (Titus 3:14). A central goal of the Christian life and the role of the church is to meet the needs (χρείας) of people.

This word χρεία as a goal for the church (i.e., meeting the needs of people, esp. those of the household of faith) occurs elsewhere in Paul. In Eph 4:17 – 5:20, Paul contrasts the former manner of life of the followers of Jesus with what should be their lifestyle now. He covers a lot of different actions, such as sensuality, sexual immorality, greed, falsehood, lies, anger, unwholesome talk, drunkenness, and the like. Included in this listing is theft. It would appear that some of the members of the Ephesian Christian community had at one time made stealing a way of life for themselves; theft was certainly a lot easier than doing honest work for a living. Thus, Paul writes: "Anyone who has been stealing must steal no longer, but must work, doing something useful with their own hands" (Eph 4:28 NIV).

Definitely good advice! After all, one of the Ten Commandments is, "You shall not steal" (Exod 20:15, quoted by Paul in Rom 13:9). But Paul is not content to leave his instruction there. He goes on to speak about the purpose of work, namely, "that they may have something to share with the one who has a need [τῷ χρείαν ἔχοντι]" (Eph 4:28). It is not enough just to have an honest job; a central part of one's daily work is to be able to share with people who are truly needy.[69]

Finally, Paul also uses χρεία in his listing of instructions in Rom 12:9 – 21: "share with the needs of the saints" (ταῖς χρείαις τῶν ἁγίων κοινωνοῦντες, 12:13). What is interesting about this verse is that Paul had earlier identified the gift of generous giving, which only some people have (12:8). "Such people may give more, more sacrificially, and more freely or exercise more delight in the application of their gift than others do. But v. 13 addresses all believers: 'share with the Lord's people who are

---

69. It may be significant that the church Paul left under Timothy's care is the church in Ephesus (see 1 Tim 1:3), presumably the same church that is being addressed (at least in part, depending on one's textual-critical decision of Eph 1:1) in Eph 4:28.

in need.'"[70] Note that the verb "share" here is the verb κοινωνέω, which often includes the notion of financial sharing (Rom 15:27; Gal 6:6; Phil 4:15). This verb is also related to the word κοινωνία, used in Acts 2:42 to describe the sharing of food and other necessities that took place in the earliest Christian community as well as a word that was used for the collection, 2 Cor 8:4; 9:13. Believers are to share what they have with those who are in need.

CONCLUSION

When we began this chapter, we looked primarily at the message in the Pastoral Epistles that Paul directs to the rich—they are to be rich in good deeds and be willing to share. This is particularly applicable to the leaders (elders) of the church as part of their responsibility. One category of people is particularly singled out as those who generally have needs: older widows. The church must be specifically sensitive to them—especially if they have no family members who can give them assistance. Then, as we looked at a variety of other passages of Paul, we saw that this is the purpose of any working adult—not to build up one's own little kingdom on earth, but to share what one has with those who truly have needs.

---

70. Blomberg, *Christians in an Age of Wealth*, 117.

CHAPTER 12

ON TAXES, DEBT, AND TITHING

THERE ARE A FEW OTHER MATTERS PERTAINING TO MONEY IN THE LET-ters of Paul that we need to examine in order to complete our goal for this book. Paul has a couple verses on the paying of taxes in Rom 13:6–7. Then he goes on to talk about debt in 13:8. Moreover, we should examine one issue of the Christian and money that Paul does not talk about, namely, what he might think about tithing (that is, the idea of a set percentage, normally 10 percent, that all believers should return to the Lord, regardless of their economic situation). This chapter will look at these issues.

GOVERNMENT AND TAXES

We begin with Paul's statement on taxes. Romans 13:6–7 come at the end of Paul's discussion of the Christian and government (13:1–7). We cannot isolate the two verses about taxes from the broader discussion of Paul's view on government (which in Paul's day can only be the government that found its power center in Rome). Scholars who write on this passage run a whole gamut of interpretations about Paul's view of government and politics; it is not our goal here to summarize all of them and attempt to find which one best fits the evidence of these seven verses and other passages in Paul and Acts, for that would take us too far afield from the topic at hand.

PAUL'S VIEW OF GOVERNMENT

There are, however, several elements about the politics of the first century that appear beyond dispute. (1) The prevailing element in world government in Paul's day — and, indeed, that had been a part of the world at least since the international Neo-Babylonian Empire of the seventh and sixth centuries BC — is that "the powers [of world government] were exercised by a few by right of birth, or connection, or wealth, or ruthless self-advancement. For the rest, the great majority, there was no political power and no realistic hope of wielding it."[1] In other words, while people especially in the Western world are used to some form of democracy and self-determination of who their rulers will be, there was no such notion in the ancient world. One empire was displaced by another: Babylonian, Persian, Greek, Macedonian, Seleucid and Ptolemaic, and Roman. All of these had strong, powerful men in control, and when a weakness surfaced, a new empire poised ready to assume control. "It would not even have occurred to Paul and his readers that they could exercise political power in a Roman city, far less that they by their efforts might change its structures."[2]

(2) At the time Paul wrote the letter to the Romans, his experiences of the governing authorities of the Roman government, by and large, had not been negative. He had been able to use to his own advantage his Roman citizenship. From Gallio in Achaia Paul had received tacit endorsement for his right to continue preaching (Acts 18:12–18). He had friends among the officials of the province of Asia (19:31). In the imperial city of Philippi, where he had been unjustly beaten and imprisoned, the city magistrates appear to have apologized and personally escorted Paul and Silas from the prison (16:38–39).[3]

(3) Firmly entrenched in Jewish history was the awareness that the attitude of governing authorities could change quickly. Antiochus IV Epiphanes (one of the Seleucids) had attempted to wipe out Judaism through outlawing its uniquely Jewish practices, such as circumcision, the keeping of Sabbath, and the refusal to eat pork. In that situation, God

---

1. Dunn, *Roman 9–16*, 770.

2. Ibid.

3. Paul, of course, was fully aware that the Roman government could be unjust, as was apparent when Pilate sent Jesus to the cross (see Douglas J. Moo, *Romans* [NIVAC; Grand Rapids: Zondervan, 2000], 426).

had rescued his people through the Maccabees. More recently, there had been some sort of unrest in Rome in the Jewish community supposedly at the instigation of someone named Chrestus (Suetonius, *Claudius* 25.4, presumably meaning Christus), at which time Claudius expelled the Jews from Rome (cf. Acts 18:2).[4] For the most part, however, the religion of the Jews was a *religio licita*, a legal religion, in the Roman Empire, and Jews were able to practice their religion without hindrance.

(4) Nevertheless, even more firmly fixed in the minds of God's people was the principle that "political authority is from God."[5] When all is said and done, the Lord God is the one who determines the course of human history and the rise and fall of nation states. This is firmly taught in the book of Daniel: "The Most High is sovereign over all kingdoms of earth and gives them to anyone he wishes and sets over them the lowliest of people" (Dan 4:17). As a result, "YHWH would call pagan rulers ... to account [which] ... happened from time to time in history, and the book of Daniel sees the madness of Nebuchadnezzar and the fall of Belshazzar as examples."[6]

(5) The eschatological hope of God's people was that, at some point, God would break into history and restore the kingdom to David. As far as Paul was concerned, those days were now present, in that the Messiah Jesus, "a descendant of David" as well as "[God's] Son" (Rom 1:3), is now reigning at God's right hand (Rom 8:34; Col 3:1), and the days were imminent in which the prophecy of Isa 45:23 would be fulfilled, that before him "every knee would bow in heaven and on earth and under the earth, and that every tongue would confess Jesus Christ is Lord" (Phil 2:10–11).

It is in the light of these principles that N. T. Wright reads Rom 13:1–7. This passage, he asserts, "cannot therefore be pressed into service ... to make the point that Paul had no critique of empire in general or Roman in particular."[7] To substantiate this statement, Wright asserts three points about the connection between Rom 13:1–7 in its literary context in Romans. First, Paul stated just a few verses earlier (in 12:19) that "vengeance" (ἐκδίκησις) belongs to the Lord (quoting Deut 32:35).

---

4. Cf. Wright, *Paul*, 1283.
5. Dunn, *Romans 9–16*, 770.
6. Wright, *Paul*, 1298.
7. Ibid., 1303.

Now, however, he notes that God works that vengeance through structures of human authority (13:4); "whether or not the authorities are doing their job, it is vital for normal human life, and particularly normal Christian life, that they are there and carry that responsibility."[8] Romans 13 must not be divorced from the context of Rom 12.

Second, Wright emphasizes that "in a world where rulers have been accustomed to claim divine honours, [Paul's] statement that they hold their office as a vocation from the One God (13:1) constitutes a major demotion" for the present governing Roman authorities.[9] They are not the ones ultimately in power; God is the one who holds the true power, and "the powers that exist have been established by God" (13:1). This truth, of course, comes directly from Paul's Jewish heritage, as we have noted above, but it has been reshaped by the cross and resurrection of Jesus. "Unlike most Jews, [Paul] *believed that this holding-to-account had already happened, and that Israel's Messiah was already installed as the true ruler of the world.*"[10]

Finally, Paul's "exposition of how to live under alien rule is radically transformed, here as elsewhere, by his eschatology.... If what is coming to birth in the God-given new day is a world of love and justice, then it behooves followers of Jesus to live by, and in accordance with, that love and justice in the present, so as to be ready for the day when it comes."[11] Paul's eschatology, in other words, is the driving force behind his thoughts on the relation of the believer to the governing authorities. Romans 13:1–7 is not a piece of political thinking that Paul accidentally dropped into the book of Romans; rather, it is part and parcel of how those who belong to the kingdom of Christ should live in the midst of the kingdoms of the world.[12]

---

8. Ibid.

9. Ibid.

10. Ibid., 1283 (italics in original).

11. Ibid., 1303–4. Wright goes on to link this section, then, with Rom 14 and 15, where Paul emphasizes that all people will stand before the divine throne of judgment (14:4, 7–12) and that the risen Messiah will be the ruler of the nations (15:7–13).

12. A number of scholars have argued that Rom 13:1–7 seems to interrupt Paul's discussion of Christian love and it must have been inserted into this letter by a later redactor (see Moo, *Romans* [NIVAC], 421, for discussion). As one example, Moo cites W. Munro, *Authority in Paul and Peter: The Identification of a Pastoral Stratum in the Pauline Corpus and 1 Peter* (Cambridge: Cambridge University Press, 1983), 56–67. See also Dunn, *Romans 9–16*, 758.

THE CHRISTIAN'S RESPONSIBILITY TO GOVERNING AUTHORITIES

It is within this framework, then, that we must read Paul's instruction that believers are to be subject (ὑποτάσσω) to the secular (to use a modern term) governing authorities and even pay them taxes (φόρος) and revenue (τέλος, Rom 13:6–7). Until such time as the eschatological revelation of the lordship of Christ becomes universally apparent at the parousia and every knee bows to him, there must be order in society. "The One God wants human authorities to run his world, and ... the people of the One God should respect such authorities."[13] While ultimate allegiance always belongs to the true God rather than human authorities, God's people should be "prepared not only to obey those authorities under normal circumstances but also, when necessary, remind them of their proper vocation."[14]

To this extent, Paul is following the pattern of his Master, the Lord Jesus Christ. When Peter was once questioned whether Jesus paid the required temple tax, Jesus first claimed exemption in essence because he was the Son of God, but he nevertheless paid the temple tax for himself and Peter (albeit miraculously, Matt 17:24–27). Then later, when the Pharisees tried to trap Jesus with the question about whether it was "right to pay taxes to Caesar or not," Jesus (after looking at the image of Caesar on a coin) replied, "Give back to Caesar what belongs to Caesar and to God what belongs to him" (22:15–21). Paul was a loyal follower of Jesus; he advocated paying taxes to Caesar not out of a deep loyalty to the Roman government, but out of a recognition that until the kingdom of God came in its full power, human government was necessary and needed the required funds to operate. As much as people (especially God's covenant people) hated to pay taxes to support Rome, such taxes were obligatory for them.

CHRISTIANS AND DEBT

Immediately after Paul's discussion of government and taxes, he transitions into a section on Christians and moral behavior (Rom 13:8–10). His main message there is that "love is the fulfillment of the law" (v. 10). But he makes this transition in an interesting manner. He has just said

---

13. Wright, *Paul*, 1303; cf., 1298.
14. Ibid., 1303.

in 13:7: "Pay to everyone your debts [τὰς ὀφειλάς, i.e., what you owe them]"—taxes, revenue, fear/reverence, honor.

Then, picking up this theme in v. 8, he writes emphatically, "To no one, nothing, owe [μηδενὶ μηδὲν ὀφείλετε]—except to love one another." Obviously there is some linguistic connection between τὰς ὀφειλάς in v. 7 and ὀφείλετε in v. 8, but precisely what that connection indicates is not clear. This is mostly because there are two main definitions in the semantic range of the ὀφείλ- word group. It can mean "that which is owed in a financial sense," but it can also mean "obligation in a moral sense, duty."[15] So the question rises: What usage does Paul intend here? The word group in Rom 13:7 in at least a couple of the terms used ("taxes," "revenue") clearly denotes a financial sense, but Paul's message in 13:8b–10 speaks of a moral obligation to love one another. So, in the transition clause of 13:8a, how does Paul intend for us to read it? Does he have anything to say about whether it is appropriate for Christians to have financial debts?

There are two other places in the letters of Paul where the use of the ὀφείλ- word group does refer to financial matters. In Rom 4:4, where Paul is talking about God's free grace in crediting righteousness to us, he uses the contrasting image of a business owner who is obligated to pay his workers what he owes them (ὀφείλημα) because they have earned it. That is not how God operates; he does not credit us with righteousness as if he is paying a debt, but is offering it to us as a free gift. The second passage that has overtones of financial debt is Phlm 18–19. Paul says there that if Onesimus "owes" (ὀφείλει) Philemon anything, Paul will personally pay that debt—but then he reminds Philemon that he owes (προσοφείλεις) Paul his very self because Paul had been the one who pointed him to salvation in Christ. Once again here we have the ambiguity of an interplay between financial debt and moral obligation. But this much is clear: Paul knows that if Onesimus is in any way financially indebted to Philemon (perhaps by theft, perhaps by lost wages), those financial obligations need to be dealt with.[16]

---

15. See BDAG, 743, under three words: ὀφειλή, ὀφείλημα, and ὀφείλω. Note that ὀφείλω has a third definition in its semantic range: "to be constrained by circumstances," as in 2 Cor 12:11, "I ought [ἐγὼ ὤφειλον] to have been recommended by you."

16. Recall in Rom 15:27 the use of the ὀφείλ- word group insofar as the Gentiles are indebted to the Jews for the spiritual blessings they have received, and so they can "work off" that debt by making a contribution of the collection. But this usage clearly has nothing to do with financial borrowing; it is metaphorical.

But would Paul say it is ever appropriate for a believer in Jesus to borrow money and hence go into debt, or does Paul lay down a law, with his "to no one, nothing, owe" in Rom 13:8, that contracting debts (perhaps with interest) is simply wrong? Since his use of the ὀφείλ- word group in his letters is far too ambiguous, perhaps we can gain some perspective from the first-century patterns of borrowing money in the context of what is said about debt in the OT. In ch. 4 we explored briefly the laws in the OT about God's concern for the poor and how God made provision that their physical needs were to be met. What we did not discuss there in any detail were the laws in the OT concerning the lending of money. "Arguably the most distinctive laws [of the OT] by modern standards preventing ancient Israelites from earning more than they might have otherwise are those that forbid usury, that is, lending money at interest, to their fellow Israelites (Exod. 22:25–27; Lev. 25:35–37; Deut. 23:19–20)."[17]

There were occasions that could easily result in dire economic straits for an Israelite family (e.g., severe injury or illness of the male provider, natural disaster of some sort that wiped out crops, such as a locust plague), and the only way to obtain daily provisions, at least temporarily, was to ask a fellow Israelite for help. The ideal, of course, is that food would be given to the poor, but in order to restart one's herds or plant one's crops, the needy family would likely have to borrow (e.g., a pregnant animal or seed for grain crops). The laws of the OT did not prohibit such borrowing, but it did prohibit "Israelite moneylenders from ever charging interest on their loans to their kinsmen."[18] Moreover, the laws of the sabbatical year and the Year of Jubilee (Lev 25; Deut 15:1–11) were years for wiping out such loans. A lender was permitted to ask for something to be given as a pledge so that the loan would be promptly repaid, though "abusive liberties with pledges received [were] forbidden."[19] At the same time, God did permit that loans charging interest could be made to "foreigners," that is, non-Israelites, presumably whether they lived inside the land as aliens or lived elsewhere (Deut 23:20).[20]

---

17. Blomberg, *Christians in an Age of Wealth*, 70.

18. Ibid.

19. Bruce Chilton, "Debts," *ABD*, 2:114. The specific example given in Deut 24:12–13 was a "cloak," which doubled as a night covering; if a lender took such an item as a pledge, it had to be returned at nightfall to a fellow Israelite.

20. Mostly like such loans to foreigners would be "commercial loans ... which are the staple of international trade" (Blomberg, *Christians in an Age of Wealth*, 70).

Did the Israelites keep these laws against usury and predatory lending? There is plenty of evidence, both in the historical books (e.g., 2 Kgs 4:1–7; Neh 5:1–13) and in the messages of the prophets (e.g., Ezek 18:5–18; Amos 2:6; 4:1–2), that there were periods in which those who were wealthy engaged in "abusive lending"[21] and oppressed the poor. But it would take us too far afield to trace this history in detail through the OT. Suffice it to say that throughout history, both Israelite and non-Israelite, there has been a tendency on the part of the wealthy to boost their income at the expense of the poor.

Interestingly, however, Paul's message in Rom 13:8 is not to the lenders but to the borrowers: "to no one, nothing, owe." Naturally, had Paul been aware that within the early Christian communities he had organized predatory lending taking place, his summary of the fulfillment of the law to "love your neighbor as yourself" (Rom 13:9) would have elicited sharp words from him for those who initiated such loans (similar to the message he wrote in 1 Cor 6:1–8). But taking Rom 13:8a as it stands, we can ask the question: Is it wrong to borrow money, for whatever reason?

If that were Paul's intent, Paul would then be taking a position far more stringent than the OT law itself. While, as we have noted, there are strict regulations on loaning money or goods (e.g., food) to fellow Israelites, there is a clear assumption that it was appropriate for God's people to borrow, especially in times of unforeseen circumstances. Contemporary writers who claim that any and all debt is unbiblical are simply wrong. Moreover, if it was appropriate to borrow money in the agrarian society of Israel, it would certainly be appropriate to borrow money (and probably with interest) in the increasingly commercial culture of the Roman world, with all of its risks. The Roman world was filled with businesses that would have needed "start-up" money; it is not impossible that Paul himself may have needed to borrow money in order to start his leather-working business (though, of course, we have no evidence either way for that).

But Rom 13:8 has to mean something. If it does not mean that all borrowing is wrong, what does it mean? Doug Moo sets us on the right path when he writes that this verse "does not forbid a Christian from ever incurring a debt; it rather demands that Christians repay any debts they

---

21. Chilton, "Debts," 2:114.

do incur promptly and in accordance with the terms of the contract."[22]
Or, as Moo expands this concept in his NIVAC commentary:

> [Paul] is not prohibiting us from borrowing money but demanding we
> pay back what we owe. If I have entered into an agreement with a bank
> to pay them $800 per month for thirty years to buy a house, I need to
> discharge my obligation by paying that money on time. So what the text
> calls us to do is to be careful, prudent financial planners, not taking on
> any more debt than we are sure we can handle.[23]

That Paul himself practiced what he taught here seems clear from
the book of Philemon, as alluded to earlier. Paul writes in Phlm 18: "If
he [Onesimus] has done you wrong or owes [ὀφείλει] you anything, put
[ἐλλόγα] this on my account." Then, in the next verse, as if make it official, Paul signs his name to what today might be called a "promissory
note": "I, Paul, write this with my own hand: 'I will make compensation
[ἀποτίσω] for it.'" That Paul sees this as a legally binding commercial
transaction seems clear from the use of the verb ἐλλογέω and ἀποτίνω.[24]

It is impossible to know for sure what Paul has in mind that may
have brought about this obligation or debt. Those scholars who argue
that Onesimus was a runaway slave suggest that he has stolen money from
his master, Philemon. But the ὀφείλει can also refer to "the loss of service incurred when Onesimus was away from Philemon."[25] In fact, some
scholars argue that the conditional clause with the promise to repay in
Phlm 18–19 is simply a rhetorical strategy of anticipating an objection
that might come from Philemon. It seems to us, however, that the most
natural way to view these verses is that Paul does indeed acknowledge that
Philemon has incurred some financial loss in the absence of Onesimus,
and Paul wants to make sure that such a debt is repaid.[26] If the situation

---

22. Moo, *Romans* (NICNT), 812.

23. Moo, *Romans* (NIVAC), 436. For many practical comments on the issue of debt and
the Christian, see Randy Alcorn, *Money, Possessions, and Eternity* (rev. and updated; Wheaton,
IL: Tyndale, 1989; 2003), 305–26.

24. Both of these verbs have strong commercial and legal overtones; see BDAG, 319,
s.v. ἐλλογέω (which calls this verb a "commercial t.t. [technical term]"); BDAG, 124, s.v.
ἀποτίνω, which calls this verb a "legal t.t." for paying damages.

25. See Pao, *Colossians and Philemon*, 407. See his entire discussion, 407–10.

26. Note too our discussion of Philemon and Onesimus in ch. 3, where we looked at this
small letter from the standpoint of the patron–client relationship.

is such that the runaway Onesimus has been serving Paul instead of Philemon, Paul may even have felt an obligation to pay Philemon for those lost wages from which he benefited. In any case, such an interpretation would correspond well with our view of Rom 13:8 that while Paul recognizes debts are inevitable in the lives of many people, they should be repaid as quickly as possible.

WHAT ABOUT TITHING?

As we suggested at the beginning of this chapter, there is no place in Paul's letters where he talks about tithing. Tithing, as is well known, formed a significant portion of the OT law (e.g., Lev 27:30–33; Num 18:8–32; Deut 14:22–29). Are there any clues as to why there is no mention of this issue in the writings of Paul or in the book of Acts? Is it simply that there was no occasion in the life of Paul's churches that might have elicited some comments on this issue in a letter? Or is there enough written in the letters of Paul that we can deduce something about how he felt about tithing?

To answer these questions, we need to return to the issue of the collection, specifically, to the guidelines that Paul did give in 1 Cor 16:1–2 when he "commanded" the Corinthians to participate in his fund-raising project for the impoverished believers in Jerusalem. Paul's first instruction is that giving should be regular—in fact, weekly ("on the first day of every week"). Paul does not explain why it should be regular, but presumably if Paul is hoping for a significant gift for the saints in Jerusalem from the saints in Corinth, it is better to put aside a small amount each week than to try to come up with a significant lump sum within just a short time.[27]

Second, the selected amount is to be stored up at home (παρ' ἑαυτῷ θησαυρίζων, "storing it up by oneself"). The NT era, of course, was not an age in which there were central banks in which money could be deposited for safekeeping, and without formal church buildings, the only other option would be to allow one trusted individual to serve as the guardian of the money being set aside. This could easily become a setup for temptation or, if word got around that a certain person living in Corinth had a significant amount of money stored somewhere in his house, for possible theft. It made the most sense for each family to have its own small deposit location.

---

27. Garland (1 Corinthians, 753) writes: "setting a portion aside each week makes it easier to give a larger amount."

The most important instruction — and the one that has the most interpretive difficulty — is "with respect to whatever he is being prospered" (ὅ τι ἐὰν εὐοδῶται). The verb used here (εὐοδόω) occurs only four times in the NT: here, in Rom 1:10, and twice in 3 John 2. Using the two Greek words that make up this single word, BDAG notes the word would mean (in the passive, as it is used in the NT): "to be led along a good road."[28] But the lexicon goes on to point out that this serves as a metaphor for to "have things turn out well, prosper, succeed." In 3 John 2 it is a stock phrase, also used in the papyri, in which the writer offers the addressee well-wishes for success. In Rom 1:10, Paul hopes that things will work out so that he will succeed in coming to Rome. In 1 Cor 16:2, it would therefore seem, Paul is suggesting that the guideline to use for how much to give for the collection is in accordance with how each one has been prospered.[29]

In other words, Paul places a significant emphasis on the freedom of individual giving. He will do so again in 2 Cor 9:7: "Each of you should give what you have decided in your heart to give, not reluctantly or under compulsion, for God loves a cheerful giver" (NIV). Cheerful giving is voluntary giving — giving because one wants to give. This theme is also in keeping with the word "generosity" (ἁπλότης) that occurs in 2 Cor 8:2; 9:11, 13. By its very nature, generosity is something that comes from the inside, not from outer compulsion (that certainly was the case for the Macedonians, whose spirit of generosity was so strong that they begged Paul to receive more of their income for his collection).

The point of all this is that if there were any place in Paul where he would have mandated a certain amount for Christians to give, it would have been in 1 Cor 16:1–2. He was in an "ordering" mood,[30] and he was

---

28. BDAG, 410, s.v. εὐοδόω.

29. As Garland (*1 Corinthians*, 754) and Thiselton (*The First Epistle to the Corinthians*, 1323) both point out, the specific form of this verb (without an accent in the original) could be present passive subjunctive, a perfect passive indicative, or perfect middle subjunctive. The indicative is all but ruled out with the presence of ἐάν, and the perfect middle subjunctive is an exceptionally rare form. That leaves the most likely candidate to be a present passive subjunctive, which fits well with the context — "with respect to whatever he may be prospered." This is most likely a "divine passive," for God is the one who gets the credit for whatever success we have in life.

30. Recall the use of the imperative in 1 Cor 16:1 and the verb διατάσσω, "to order," as discussed in ch. 6.

attempting to raise money for a divine cause that was dear to his heart—for the poor believers in Jerusalem. Put otherwise, if there was ever a time in Paul's life in which he could easily have demanded at least a "tithe," it would be in this situation. But Paul clearly leaves all giving up to the conscience of the individual: "with respect to whatever he may be prospered." Paul refuses to do so much as to suggest a minimum amount—or any amount whatsoever. "It might be less than a tithe; it might be far more than a tithe."[31]

Why does Paul manifest such a resistance to a set tithe? There appear to us to be at least two reasons. First, this fits in with Paul's entire view of the role of the law in the life of the believer. Much has been written on Paul's view of the law, and we do not need to repeat it here. Suffice it to say that for Paul, the nitty-gritty, minute details of the law of Moses have no role in the life of a believer, who is filled with the Spirit. As Paul says in Gal 5:1: "For freedom Christ has liberated us; stand firm, therefore, and do not again become burdened with a yoke of slavery." Or Rom 10:4: "For Christ is the end of the law so there may be righteousness for everyone who believes." Or, again, to use the text quoted earlier in the present chapter, Paul's summary of the fulfillment of the law is to "love your neighbor as yourself" (Rom 13:9); this replaces a legalistic emphasis on the splicing and dicing of the Ten Commandments into a legalistic nightmare.

Second, nowhere in the words of Jesus is there an emphasis on some form of tithing that would remain in effect after his death and resurrection.[32] Paul was indeed following in the tradition of Jesus in his view of the law, who charged some of the Jewish leaders with letting go of the commands of God in order to hold on to "human traditions" (Mark 7:8; cf. the entire passage, 7:1–23). Moreover, when Jesus noticed the wealthy putting into the temple treasury what was probably their tithe, he saw a poor widow put in two copper coins but made no attempt to stop her. Rather, he said: "Truly I tell to you, this poor widow has put more into

---

31. Garland, *1 Corinthians*, 754.

32. Blomberg (*Christians in an Age of Wealth*, 128–29) shows that Jesus did endorse the Mosaic law as in force in his day especially for the Pharisees, including the laws of tithing (Matt 23:23; Luke 11:42). In Jesus' fulfillment of the Law and the Prophets, however (Matt 5:17), he emphasizes that "no Old Testament law should be obeyed exactly as it was in pre-Christians times until one examines to see if Jesus' life and death have in any way changed things with respect to that category of commandments."

the treasury than all the others. They all gave out of their wealth; but she, out of her poverty, put in everything—all she had to live on" (12:43–44 NIV). Jesus himself, therefore, emphasized not a set amount that God's people should give, such as a tithe, but voluntary giving from the heart. Blomberg's summary for the apostolic age is pertinent here:

> When one turns to Acts through Revelation ... one looks in vain for a reference anywhere to the tithe for believers. In fact, the only reference to a tithe at all emerges in Hebrews, as the author recounts the story of Abram giving a tenth of his increase to Melchizedek (Heb. 7:1–10). While the point of Hebrews 7 is that Jesus is a high priest of the order of Melchizedek, one who is superior to the Levitical priesthood, the writer makes no deduction at all about the significance of this point for tithing ... one cannot infer logically [from this passage] a regular, systematic tithe.[33]

As Blomberg goes on to stress, however, there is ample evidence for Christ-followers to follow principles of good stewardship: giving to the needy, supporting Christian teachers and leaders in full-time ministry, supporting those engaged in the outreach of the gospel throughout the world, and the like. But there is no fixed percentage. "Indeed, a more detailed scrutiny of 1 Cor 16:1–4 and 2 Cor 8–9 suggests that if all Christians gave one identical fixed percentage of their income, they would actually violate Paul's mandates. Some would be giving sacrificially, some generously, some ordinarily, and others stingily!"[34]

CONCLUSION

The conclusion to this chapter can be brief. Amidst all the comments Paul has made on financial issues, he (like Jesus) occasionally talked about taxes. Believers are to live as law-abiding citizens of the state in which God has placed them. The government provides necessary services that a single-family unit cannot afford. Through its army the government protects the nation from outside invaders and its citizens from those bent on crime and violence within its borders. Such things, along with other needed services,

---

33. Ibid., 129–30.
34. Ibid., 130.

cost money, and so taxes are necessary. Even though believers are members of a spiritual kingdom, they do live in an earthly kingdom and must cooperate with their neighbors near and far to help create a livable space.

Christians must also pay their debts; to do otherwise means to participate in cheating someone else of what is due them. Already in the Ten Commandments Yahweh said, "You shall not steal" (Exod 20:15), a text that Paul himself quotes in Rom 13:9 (note also his warning against stealing in Eph 4:28).

Finally, while this is perhaps not in keeping with our overall theme of a book where we seek to understand everything the apostle Paul says about money, we did discuss briefly one thing that Paul did *not* say about money. While his instructions regarding participation in the collection and his instructions elsewhere on helping those who are genuinely in need are clear, Paul (a former Pharisee who would certainly have promoted tithing) never advocates a set percentage that everyone should give. That is, he has no mandate in his letters about tithing. If anything, those who are wealthy in the world should give far more than one-tenth; the apostle never ceases to advocate generosity for those who are rich in the world (see chs. 4 and 7).

CHAPTER 13

A THEOLOGICAL AND PRACTICAL CONCLUSION

THIS BOOK, FOR THE MOST PART, HAS BEEN AN ACADEMIC EXERCISE OF carefully exegeting the Greek NT and studying with the broader world of NT scholarship in order to understand how the apostle Paul interacted with the world of money and finance. Only the most primitive of societies (e.g., a barter society) can avoid interacting with other people through buying and selling, having some sort of job, helping others (especially the poor) with goods and services, paying taxes, and the like. It would be presumptuous for us to claim that we have written the final word on how Paul managed these aspects of life in the Greco-Roman world, though no one to our knowledge has been as comprehensive as we have tried to be. We have attempted to fix our conclusions on textual exegesis and our knowledge of the Greco-Roman world, but undoubtedly there will be more discoveries and different conclusions. What we wish to do in this final chapter is to outline some of our conclusions and to ask where to go from here. In addition, we hope to spell out some of the "So what?" issues. What does our analysis mean for us as we try to live a Christian life in a world vastly different from the world in which Paul lived?

EXEGETICAL AND THEOLOGICAL PERSPECTIVES

We begin with a few perspectives that we have sought to demonstrate about Paul as he lived in the first century.

1. Paul appears to have grown up in what we might call a middle class

Jewish home. But after he became a Christian on the Damascus Road, his personal status in the Roman Empire seems to have been downgraded to what might be called at best a lower middle class lifestyle (or perhaps even lower—from ES4/ES5 level to an ES5/ES6 level, to use the categories of Bruce Longenecker). It is impossible to determine whether this was deliberate on Paul's part, or involuntary. After all, Paul grew up a zealous Jew and apparently received support from his family to become a Pharisee (a family tradition). Was Paul disinherited when he became a Christian? Or did he take his share of his inheritance and plunge it all into his missionary activity, so that his downgrading happened when the money ran out, and he accepted this as his lot in life?

2. In any case, what becomes plain is that Paul was often strapped for cash for his daily living expenses. There were times when he had relatively little to eat or drink and no place where he could comfortably sleep. Nevertheless, he refused (for the most part; recall Lydia) to accept lodging and food from the people whom he was evangelizing; this was part of his personal boasting (1 Cor 9:15–18). Yet he argues vigorously that it was his personal choice to work as an artisan in leather to raise his own support, for he clearly indicates that the other apostles (including Peter) and the Lord's brothers had every right to expect food, drink, and lodging from those among whom they were working. Only Paul and Barnabas insisted on earning their own living expenses.[1]

3. However, surprisingly, Paul had no problem asking for money if it was not for his own *personal* needs. He would ask for money for travel expenses (cf. the verb προπέμπω), even from the Corinthians. On a number of occasions he asked for money for those who were struggling financially with being able to pay for basic life necessities (particularly the believers in the church in Jerusalem). And when a spontaneous gift from Macedonia (perhaps from Lydia?) came while he was working and ministering in Corinth, he does not appear to have plunged that money into better living conditions for himself but simply used it for food (and he temporarily stopped working for Aquila and Priscilla) so he could do full-time evangelism until the money ran out (Acts 18:5). Moreover, we

---

1. Note, of course, that we did not include a section on why Barnabas took this same position. It would be an interesting study to try to understand whether Paul convinced Barnabas to live this way, or whether Barnabas had already come to accept that same lifestyle prior to meeting Paul. Or is it even possible that Barnabas convinced Paul?

argued Paul also needed to solicit significant funds so he could write letters to his churches.

4. So why did Paul make life so hard for himself? Here again, we will probably never know. One element seems certain: he did not insist on this difficult lifestyle in order to set an example to other believers for a proper work ethic. It is true that he used his work ethic as an example to instruct believers in both Thessalonica and Corinth, but by that time his years of working for his own living expenses had been well established. In other words, his lifestyle was a convenient ad hoc argument that helped make his case to the Thessalonians to get to work, but we cannot push that argument back to the time when he himself started living in that manner.

So, is there any clue as to why Paul was so hard on himself? The answer is mixed. In 1 Cor 9:25 he suggests it was in order to get an incorruptible crown, but if we interpret that crown to be eternal, we will end up with a Pauline theology that champions works righteousness.[2] That would be false. We suggested that an answer may lie deep within Paul's soul—that he may have struggled his entire life with guilt over his year or two of persecuting Christians. Much more work needs to be done on "the psychology of Paul," although admittedly scholars have hesitated trying to get a handle on Paul's inner psyche, because there is no way to reach a conclusion that is scientific enough to meet modern research standards.

5. No one can truly understand the NT world without knowing the system of patronage in the Roman Empire. Patronage was an integral part of the Greco-Roman financial world. It was one way for a person to get money for daily living expenses. But Paul would have none of this lifestyle. A client was essentially a servant to a patron, and the patron called the shots. Paul knew that if he sought a wealthy patron to sponsor him as a missionary-evangelist, he would likely at some point have to compromise his message in order to keep his patron happy. His personal freedom to preach the gospel as the Lord revealed it to him was vital to his ministry.

But the disadvantages of the patronage system did seem to cease being a concern when a person became a believer, for believers formed a new community, a koinōnia in which everyone was part of a new family. Perhaps this is why Paul eventually was willing to give in to Lydia's persuasiveness,

---

2. See the exegesis of this text in Krell (*Temporal Judgment and the Church*, 141–54) who cogently argues that we should read 1 Cor 9:24–27 to indicate that the crown is an eternal reward, not eternal salvation.

for just as Paul owed her for supplying food and lodging, Lydia owed Paul her new life as a member of God's kingdom. They were now brothers and sisters in Christ. The same argument seems to be made in the case of Philemon, where Paul feels free to make demands of Philemon regarding Onesimus and even himself.

6. The apostle Paul was a huge promoter of concern for the poor and wasted no words in criticizing those who were promoting godliness as a way of great gain and those who were greedy. Moreover, in 1 Cor 11:17–34 he took to task the wealthy in Corinth who were using their socio-economic status to shame the poor and the servant class. To treat servants unkindly and shamefully was par for the course in the Greco-Roman world, but the church had different values.

Furthermore, on at least two occasions Paul spearheaded an offering for the poor among the saints in Jerusalem. Believers in Jerusalem perennially had difficulty making ends meet, especially during times of food shortage (which, according to records, happened frequently during the first century). With respect to the collection Paul organized during his third missionary journey, Paul's primary goal was to collect a significant monetary gift that would show the Jewish Christians in Jerusalem that the Gentile Christians in Galatia, Asia Minor, Macedonia, and Achaia considered them brothers and sisters in Christ; this gift, he hoped, would help heal the growing rift between these two segments of first-century Christianity (see Rom 15:26–27).

7. We have taken aim at the present-day consensus that in Gal 2:10, the "pillars of the church" placed some sort of mandate on Paul to take up this collection. Since by most calculations this letter was one of Paul's earlier letters (reflecting a time shortly after Paul's first missionary journey), it makes no sense to say that for seven to eight years, Paul did not act on that request (or mandate) to bring money to Jerusalem, especially since he appears to have gone to the holy city empty-handed after the second missionary journey. The only hints in Acts and Paul's letters that the apostle was bearing a gift for the Christians in Jerusalem appear at the end of the third missionary journey. If anything, Gal 2:10 reflects his first collection for Jerusalem, which was mostly limited to Antioch.

8. One of the surprising results of the collection was the insight we receive about Paul's skills as a church leader. There is no doubt that when Paul wrote to the Corinthians in 1 Cor 16:1–2, he did not feel it was

necessary to try to motivate them to give; he simply commanded them to do so and gave a few instructions about the process. But by the time we get to 2 Cor 8 and 9, Paul writes thirty-nine verses on the collection, giving all sorts of reasons why the Corinthians should donate, and he includes only one mild imperative. More study needs to be done to account for this switch in tactics and what it says about Paul as a church leader.

9. One of the puzzling elements of the NT, if we have read it correctly up to this point, is Luke's almost total silence about what appears to be one of Paul's most important projects, namely, trying to use the collection to heal the growing Jewish-Gentile rift in the church. There is no uncontestable record of the reaction of the Jerusalem church to the significant gift from the Gentiles that Paul and his entourage brought at the conclusion of the apostle's third missionary journey. There are a couple of hints (Paul's possible use of some of the funds to help four other people and himself complete a Nazirite vow, and the reference to "alms" in Acts 24:17), but we must remember two items: Luke was a regular travel companion of Paul, and Luke had probably been involved in the collection during much of the third missionary journey. So why is there no resounding affirmation of the delivery of the gift and a record of its reception? Further study needs to be done here, both on Luke's authenticity as a historian and on the aftermath of the collection in Jerusalem.

10. Church leaders absolutely must lead with integrity.[3] It is surprising how often Paul talks in the Pastoral Letters and elsewhere on the issues of integrity, not being greedy, and not loving money, especially for church leaders. After all that Jesus had said about the rich and after so many similar warnings by Paul, one would think that Christians would have gotten the message that "the love of money is a root of all kinds of evil" (1 Tim 6:10 NIV). But the allure of wealth is as strong today as it was in Bible times.

11. We looked briefly at the teaching in the NT on the kingdom and the interaction between the government and the church. This comes particularly in the matter of taxes and whether believers in Jesus as the Messiah should have to pay them. Paul is forthright about this issue: "Give

---

3. See Andreas J. Köstenberger, *Excellence: The Character of God and the Pursuit of Scholarly Virtue* (Wheaton, IL: Crossway, 2011). See especially the chapters entitled "Integrity" and "Fidelity" (159–76). Other helpful resources include Howard Hendricks, *A Life of Integrity* (Sisters, OR: Multnomah, 1997); Joe E. Trull and James E. Carter, *Ministerial Ethics: Moral Formation for Church Leaders* (2nd ed.; Grand Rapids: Baker Academic, 2004).

to everyone what you owe them: If you owe taxes, pay taxes; if revenue, then revenue" (Rom 13:7 NIV). The relationship of the church to the kingdom of this world has many ramifications, only part of which involves finances, so this section was not fully developed.[4] Suffice it to say, "Jesus is Lord, Caesar is not."[5]

12. Finally, we felt it was important to raise the significant issue of tithing, since so many preachers believe that tithing is a mandate for NT believers.[6] However, as to the letters of Paul, there is not so much as a hint of a command to tithe. But if we read the letters of Paul and the book of Acts carefully, it is fair to say that the principle of being as free and generous with our resources as God was in giving his Son Jesus as a sacrifice for our sins would require much more than a mere 10 percent of our income.[7] Especially in an affluent society such as we live in, we have the potential to do so much good with our money, and we need to root out every smidgen of greed from our lives.[8] In the OT world, giving never had to come from the heart. In the NT world, that is the key.

A Practical Look at Paul and Money

We have sought to be academically robust in our analysis in this book. Yet it has been difficult, at times, not to shift the reader over into exhortation and admonition, for while both authors of this book are academicians, we are also pastors. For years we have preached God's Word faithfully every Sunday, not just explaining the meaning of the text to its original audience but also seeking to apply it to the lives of our parishioners. It would not be right to finish this book without reflecting, ever so briefly, on the application of Paul's thinking about money to our own personal lives and

---

4. See Wayne Grudem, *Politics—According to the Bible: A Comprehensive Resource for Understanding Modern Political Issues in Light of Scripture* (Grand Rapids: Zondervan, 2010), 285–308.

5. This is the title of an excellent collection of essays edited by Scot McKnight and Joseph B. Modica, published in 2013 by InterVarsity Press.

6. E.g., R. T. Kendall, *Tithing: A Call to Serious Biblical Giving* (Grand Rapids: Zondervan, 1983).

7. See Randy Alcorn, *Money, Possessions, and Eternity*, 173–222; Ken Hemphill, *Making Change: A Transformational Guide to Christian Money Management* (Nashville: Broadman & Holman, 2006); Sam Storms, *A Sincere and Pure Devotion to Christ Volume II* (Wheaton, IL: Crossway, 2010), 33–84.

8. See Brian S. Rosner, *Greed as Idolatry: The Origin and Meaning of a Pauline Metaphor* (Grand Rapids: Eerdmans, 2007).

the lives of those who sit in the pew. Thus, we will end this book with a few practical applications from the principles discussed throughout the book. We offer these applications in no particular order.

1. We live in a world in which money is at the center of much that we do.[9] Huge transfers of money take place instantaneously today. This rapid transfer of money was not true, of course, in the Greco-Roman world, but that world was one of history's first commercial societies — that is, a society that had a standard monetary system throughout the then-known world and in which financial interactions among its people were not based on a barter economy. Paul's collection for Jerusalem, for example, could hardly have taken place were this common monetary system not a part of the fabric of the Greco-Roman world. Just as we today cannot engage in our day-to-day lives without money, so also with the world in which Paul lived. Many people in the first century AD did not live directly off the land; Paul himself was a leatherworker, and he made products that people wanted to purchase. What is needed in all such transactions is integrity — products that are not part of shoddy workmanship, and coins that are genuine and maintain a worldwide standard. Paul has much to say about integrity in all financial dealings.

2. When church leaders and church workers are chosen or appointed, Paul insists that they must not be greedy or dishonest in financial dealings.[10] One of the key characteristics of a false teacher in Paul's day was a person who sought dishonest gain. The same is true today. There is nothing that brings more shame on a church than a pastor or church treasurer or other church worker who finds ways to fill up his or her own pockets from money that has been donated to the church. Whenever embezzlements or thefts of church funds become public, it brings shame to the cause of Christ. Church leaders need to do everything possible to choose leaders known for their integrity and to have checks and balances in place so that if there is a lack of integrity, it is caught early.[11]

---

9. R. Kent Hughes (*2 Corinthians: Power in Weakness* [Preaching the Word; Wheaton, IL: Crossway, 2006], 158) remarks: "Some say that the average American spends 50 percent of his or her time thinking about money — how to get it, how to spend it. Whether the statistic is accurate or not, it is generally true. And it is also true that our handling of money defines our affections, the things we truly treasure, how tightly we are bound to the world, and so on."

10. See Alexander Strauch, *Biblical Eldership* (Colorado Springs, CO: Lewis & Roth, 2003); Thabiti Anyabwile, *Finding Faithful Elders and Deacons* (Wheaton, IL: Crossway, 2012).

3. Not only should church workers manifest integrity; everyone should put in an honest day's work. Paul states this in so many words in Eph 4:28, and he also implies this with the situation of the Thessalonians busybodies. Paul instructs able-bodied believers to get busy and earn their own living rather than sponge freely off church people. Such a message is important today as well, for there are so many ways for anyone to cheat his or her employer out of an honest day's work or to get something for nothing.[12] While the apostle recognized that there were people who had genuine needs (such as certain widows),[13] there were others who were eager to abuse the system.

4. In connection with the previous paragraph, we even learned something about church discipline. Paul ordered other church members to refuse to associate with anyone who was ready to abuse the church's charity if that person was able to work. The goal of such discipline, however, is not punishment, but to steer that person into living the full-orbed Christian life. Effective church discipline is sadly lacking today.[14]

5. From the beginning of his ministry to the end, the apostle Paul believed that those involved in full-time ministry had every right to expect to be paid for their work. "The worker deserves his wages" (1 Tim 5:18). Just because Paul personally did not avail himself of this right to receive financial support did not mean he expected others to imitate him in this respect. This applies not only to the other apostle-missionaries (1 Cor

---

11. Aubrey Malphurs and Steve Stroope, *Money Matters in Church: A Practical Guide for Leaders* (Grand Rapids: Baker, 2007); John Temple, *Make Your Church's Money Work: Achieving Financial Integrity in Your Congregation* (Leominster, UK: Day One Publications, 2008).

12. See the following helpful resources on work: Doug Sherman and William Hendricks, *Your Work Matters to God* (Colorado Springs, CO: NavPress, 1987); Kenneth Boa and Gail Burnett, *Wisdom at Work* (Colorado Springs, CO: NavPress, 2000); David W. Gill, *Doing Right: Practicing Ethical Principles* (Downers Grove, IL: InterVarsity Press, 2004); William Carr Peel and Walt Larimore, *Workplace Grace: Becoming a Spiritual Influence at Work* (Grand Rapids: Zondervan, 2010); Tom Nelson, *Work Matters* (Wheaton, IL: Crossway, 2011); Ben Witherington III, *Work: A Kingdom Perspective on Labor* (Grand Rapids: Eerdmans, 2011); Gene Edward Veith Jr., *God at Work: Your Christian Vocation in All of Life* (Wheaton, IL: Crossway, 2011).

13. See Wesley M. Teterud, *Caring for Widows: You and Your Church Can Make a Difference* (Grand Rapids: Baker, 1993).

14. See Hammett and Merkle, *Those Who Must Give an Account: A Study of Church Membership and Church Discipline*; Leeman, *Church Discipline: How the Church Protects the Name of Jesus*; Cheong, *God Redeeming His Bride: A Handbook for Church Discipline*.

9:3 – 14), but also to elders involved in leading the affairs of the church
(1 Tim 5:17 – 18).

6. Every Christian should give a portion of his or her income to the
church. The apostle Paul never mandates a fixed percentage of our income,
such as a tithe (10 percent), but each one should give to the church regularly in proportion to what they earn. Those who have more should give
more. In the NT era this practice was inevitable, since without independent church buildings, those who were better-off opened up their homes
for the early Christians to meet there regularly for worship.

7. Those who are rich in the world have a duty to be generous with
their money by sharing with people in need. That applies to most of us
in the Western world, who have far more than most people in Majority
World countries ever dream of having. There are many worthy nonprofit
organizations out there which are doing great work in the name of Christ
to help boost the standard of living of people in poorer countries. It is
important, of course, that we give to organizations that make wise use of
their funds.[15] Unfortunately, a number of organizations spend the majority
of the money they collect on administrative costs (including fund-raising
campaigns), with the result that only a small percentage goes to the cause
for which the fund-raising was done. Every church and every Christian
organization should be familiar with the standards of the Evangelical
Council for Financial Accountability (www.ecfa.org) and abide by them
to the best of their ability.

8. Every church should use a portion of its income to establish a benevolent fund to help the needy.[16] The needy in the local church take priority
over the needy in the community and throughout the world (see esp. Gal
6:10). Giving money to the needy, of course, does require investigation and
great care, for once again, there are people everywhere who are willing to
take advantage of the generosity of others.[17] The church should especially
be eager to help others in situations of natural disasters, for at such times
there is little question of the urgency of immediate needs of those who have
suffered the loss of their homes and do not have easy access to life-saving

---

15. See Alcorn, *Money, Possessions, and Eternity,* 243 – 78.

16. See Steve Corbett and Brian Fikkert, *When Helping Hurts: How to Alleviate Poverty
without Hurting the Poor ... and Yourself* (Chicago: Moody Press, 2009).

17. Ibid., 223 – 42.

food and water.[18] Emergency medical supplies are also critical in times of natural disaster, and we should be eager to help supply those needs.

9. The attitude that Christians manifest toward one another can often be affected by economic issues.[19] As we saw in the celebration of the Lord's Supper in Corinth, those who were wealthier had a snobbish attitude toward those of the servant class and showed it in the way they gorged themselves on the best food and wine and left little or nothing for the poor. Such an attitude destroys a sense of community in the body of Christ. We must always remember that Christ died for all of us equally, and we have a responsibility to respect all believers equally—the rich as well as the poor. The apostle would not be pleased with churches in which those who donate more threaten to withhold their money in order to wield more influence in the church and to "get their way."

10. While we did not draw specific attention to the following practical issue, Paul's attempt to monitor his churches' activities and to personally raise money from all his churches for the collection suggests that the apostle was a "hands-on" administrator, where he tried to micromanage his growing list of churches from a distance. He found it increasingly difficult and frustrating to use this style of management, especially as other people, who had different ideas on how the believers should live, settled into the areas where Paul had organized churches (cf. the resistance in Galatia and the opponents who had settled in Corinth) and began to develop relationships with the believers there. This shows that giving leadership to a church requires a physical presence; you cannot manage a church effectively without nurturing personal relationships on site.[20] It is significant to see how Paul eventually changed his style of leadership. He left personal representatives Titus in Crete and Timothy in Ephesus, and he wrote letters to *them* as to how to solve some of the issues he heard about that were troubling the churches he started.[21]

---

18. Interestingly, there is even evidence of philanthropic aid that crossed city-state borders in the Greco-Roman world. See Verbrugge, *Paul's Style of Church Leadership*, 176–83.

19. James makes the same point in Jas 2:1–13.

20. For helpful church administration works, see Bruce P. Powers, ed., *Church Administration Handbook* (3rd rev. ed.; Nashville: B&H Academic, 2008); Robert H. Welch, *Church Administration: Creating Efficiency for Effective Ministry* (Nashville: B&H Academic, 2011).

21. See Thomas K. Ascol, *Dear Timothy: Letters on Pastoral Ministry* (Cape Coral, FL: Founders Press, 2004). This book contains twenty letters written from experienced, active pastors (e.g., Mark Dever, Ray Ortlund Jr, Ligon Duncan) to a young, inexperienced pastor.

11. Taxes are a necessary part of life, and each believer should be willing to pay their fair share.[22] Trying to sidestep this teaching of the Word of God can take a variety of forms. There are those who find creative ways to hide a certain amount of income so that they do not have to pay taxes on it (i.e., they cheat on income tax). Far too many people today advocate that the central role of government is to reduce taxes while keeping the services we expect from the government at a high level. To make up the shortfall, they are okay with the government borrowing large amounts of money that will never be paid back, at least, not in the short term, and thus they push the increasing debt to future generations. The apostle Paul would not have us live with outstanding and increasing debts.

12. As to personal debt, it seems clear from the little Paul says about this topic that no one should ever contract a debt that they know they can never pay back.[23] Bankruptcy is never a way to handle our debts. We can be fortunate in our society to have the avenue for squeezing out of debt, but the only way to handle an unpaid debt in the ancient world was through slavery. We feel confident that if the choice we faced in our legal system was between slavery or being careful how much we borrowed in the first place, there would be far less bankruptcy. Moreover, we should not simply let the government be our safety net. The church needs to be far more involved in ministering to those who are truly needy because of illness, accident, or some other natural catastrophe.[24]

Some of the most difficult parts of our lives in our homes, our churches, our community, and our world have to do with financial issues. May God give us the grace to make decisions that correspond with the principles of God's Word.

---

22. Harold O. J. Brown, "Civil Authority and the Bible," pp. 109–25 in *The Christian and American Law: Christianity's Impact on America's Founding Documents and Future Direction* (ed. H. Wayne House; Grand Rapids: Kregel, 1998); D. A. Carson, *Christ & Culture Revisited* (Grand Rapids: Eerdmans, 2012); John S. Feinberg and Paul D. Feinberg, *Ethics for a Brave New World* (2nd ed.; Wheaton, IL: Crossway, 1993, 2010), 697–736.

23. See "A Biblical Perspective on Borrowing and Debt" in Gene A. Getz, *A Biblical Theology of Material Possessions* (Chicago, IL: Moody Press, 1990), 263–79.

24. See Steve F. Echols and Allen England, *Catastrophic Crisis: Ministry Leadership in the Midst of Trial and Tragedy* (Nashville: B&H Academic, 2011). See also Michael R. Milco, "Fumbling with Figures," pp. 111–25 in *Ethical Dilemmas in Church Leadership: Case Studies in Biblical Decision Making* (Grand Rapids: Kregel, 1997).

Select Bibliography

Ascough, Richard S. *Lydia: Paul's Cosmopolitan Hostess*. Collegeville, MN: Liturgical, 2009.

Baker, William R. *2 Corinthians*. CPNIVC. Joplin: College Press, 1999.

———. *1 Corinthians*. CBC. Wheaton, IL: Tyndale, 2009.

Barnett, Paul. *Romans*. Fearn, UK: Christian Focus, 2003.

———. *1 Corinthians*. Fearn, UK: Christian Focus, 2000.

———. *The Second Epistle to the Corinthians*. NICNT. Grand Rapids: Eerdmans, 1997.

Barrett, C. K. *A Commentary on the First Epistle to the Corinthians*. HNTC. New York: Harper & Row, 1968.

Barton, Stephen C. "Paul as Missionary and Pastor." In *The Cambridge Companion to Paul*. Edited by James D. G. Dunn; Cambridge: University of Cambridge Press, 2003.

———. "Paul's Sense of Place: An Anthropological Approach to Community Formation in Corinth." *NTS* 32 (1986): 225–46.

Bassler, Jouette M. *God and Mammon: Asking for Money in the New Testament*. Nashville: Abingdon, 1991.

Beck, James R. *The Psychology of Paul: A Fresh Look at His Life and Teaching*. Grand Rapids: Kregel, 2002.

Belleville, Linda L. *1 Timothy*. CBC. Carol Stream, IL: Tyndale, 2009.

———. *2 Corinthians*. IVPNTC. Downers Grove: InterVarsity Press, 1996.

Best, Ernest. *The First and Second Epistles to the Thessalonians*. HNTC. Harper & Row: New York, 1972.

Betz, Hans Dieter. *2 Corinthians 8 and 9: A Commentary on Two Administrative Letters of the Apostle Paul*. Hermeneia. Philadelphia: Fortress, 1985.

Blomberg, Craig. *Christians in an Age of Wealth: A Biblical Theology of Stewardship*. BTFL. Grand Rapids: Zondervan, 2013.

———. *1 Corinthians*. NIVAC. Grand Rapids: Zondervan, 1994.

Blue, Brad B. "The House Church at Corinth and the Lord's Supper: Famine, Food Supply, and the Present Distress." *CTR* 5.2 (1991): 221–39.

Bock, Darrell L. *Luke: 9:51–24:53*. BECNT. Grand Rapids: Baker Academic, 1996.

Briones, David E. *Paul's Financial Policy: A Socio-Theological Approach*. LNTS 494. Bloomsbury: T&T Clark, 2013.

Bruce, F. F. *1 & 2 Thessalonians*. WBC. Nashville: Nelson, 1982.

———. *The Book of Acts*. NICNT. Grand Rapids: Eerdmans, 1954.

Campbell, Constantine R. *Basics of Verbal Aspect in Biblical Greek*. Grand Rapids: Zondervan, 2008.

Carson, D. A. *The Gospel according to John*. Pillar. Grand Rapids: Eerdmans, 1991.

Carter, Christopher L. *The Great Sermon Tradition as a Fiscal Framework in 1 Corinthians: Towards a Pauline Theology of Material Possessions*. LNTS. London: T&T Clark, 2010.

Chang, Steven S. H. "Fund-Raising in Corinth: A Socio-Economic Study of the Corinthian Church, the Collection and 2 Corinthians." PhD diss. University of Aberdeen, 2000.

Ciampa, Roy E. and Brian S. Rosner. *1 Corinthians*. Pillar. Grand Rapids: Eerdmans, 2010.

Cohick, Lynn H. *Philippians*. SGBC. Grand Rapids: Zondervan, 2013.

Collins, Raymond F. *1 & 2 Timothy and Titus*. NTL. Louisville: Westminster John Knox, 2002.

———. *First Corinthians*. SP. Collegeville, MN: Liturgical, 1999.

Conzelmann, Hans. *1 Corinthians*. Translated by J. W. Leitch. Hermeneia. Philadelphia: Fortress, 1975.

Dickson, John P. *Mission Commitment in Ancient Judaism and in the Pauline Communities*. WUNT 2/159. Tübingen: Mohr Siebeck, 2003.

Downs, David J. *The Offering of the Gentiles: Paul's Collection for Jerusalem in Its Chronological, Cultural, and Cultic Contexts*. WUNT 2/248. Tübingen: Mohr Siebeck, 2008.

Dunn, James D. G. *The Acts of the Apostles*. Valley Forge, PA: Trinity Press International, 1996.

———. *Romans 9–16*. WBC 38. Nelson: Nashville, 1988.

Eaton, Michael. *1 Corinthians 10–16*. PTB. Tonbridge: Sovereign World, 2000.

Fee, Gordon D. *1 and 2 Timothy, Titus*. NIBC. Peabody, MA: Hendrickson, 1988.

———. *The First Epistle to the Corinthians*. NICNT. Grand Rapids: Eerdmans, 1987.

Furnish, Victor Paul. *1 & 2 Thessalonians*. ANTC. Nashville: Abingdon, 2007.

Garland, David E. *1 Corinthians*. BECNT. Grand Rapids: Baker, 2003.

———. *2 Corinthians*. NAC. Nashville: Broadman & Holman, 1999.

Garrison, Roman. *Redemptive Almsgiving in Early Christianity*. JSNTSup 77. Sheffield: JSOT Press, 1993.

Gasque, W. Ward. *Sir William M. Ramsay: Archaeologist and New Testament Scholar: A Survey of His Contribution to the Study of the New Testament*. Grand Rapids: Baker, 1966.

Green, Gene L. *The Letters to the Thessalonians*. Pillar. Grand Rapids: Eerdmans, 2002.

Gundry-Volf, Judith M. *Paul and Perseverance: Staying In and Falling Away*. WUNT 2/37. Tübingen: Mohr-Siebeck, 1990.

Haenchen, Ernest. *The Acts of the Apostles: A Commentary*. Translated by R. McL. Wilson. Philadelphia: Westminster, 1971.

Harris, Murray J. *The Second Epistle to the Corinthians*. NIGTC. Grand Rapids: Eerdmans, 2005.

Harvey, John D. *Listening to the Text: Oral Patterns in Paul's Letters*. Grand Rapids: Baker, 1998.

Hays, Richard B. *First Corinthians*. IBC. Louisville: Westminster/John Knox, 1997.

Hendricksen, William. *Exposition of the Pastoral Epistles*. NTC. Grand Rapids: Baker, 1968.

Hengel, Martin. *The Pre-Christian Paul*. Translated by John Bowden. London: SCM, 1991.

Hiebert, D. Edmond. *Second Timothy*. Chicago: Moody, 1958.

Hock, Ronald. *The Social Context of Paul's Ministry: Tentmaking and Apostleship*. Philadelphia: Fortress, 1980.

Holl, Karl. "Der Kirchenbegreiff des Paulus in seinem Verhältnis zu dem der Urgemeinde," 1921 article reprinted in *Gesammelte Aufsätze zuer Kirchengeschichte*, 2:44–67. Tübingen: Mohr [Siebeck], 1928.

Holmberg, Bengt. *Paul and Power: The Structure of Authority in the Primitive Church as Reflected in the Pauline Epistles*. Philadelphia: Fortress, 1978.

Holmes, Michael W. *1 and 2 Thessalonians*. NIVAC. Grand Rapids: Zondervan, 1998.

Horrell, David. "The Lord's Supper at Corinth and in the Church Today." *Theology* 98.783 (1995): 196–202.

Horsley, Richard A. *1 Corinthians*. ANTC. Nashville: Abingdon, 1998.

Inziku, John. *Overcoming Divisive Behaviour: An Attempt to Interpret 1 Cor 11, 17–34 from Another Perspective*. Frankfurt am Main: Peter Lang, 2005.

Johnson, Alan F. *1 Corinthians*. IVPNTC. Downers Grove, IL: InterVarsity Press, 2004.

Keener, Craig S. *1–2 Corinthians*. NcBC. Cambridge: Cambridge University Press, 2005.

Kistemaker, Simon J. *Exposition of the First Epistles to the Corinthians*. NTC. Grand Rapids: Baker, 1993.

Kitchen, John. *The Pastoral Epistles for Pastors*. The Woodlands, TX: Kress Christian, 2009.

Knight III, George W. *The Pastoral Epistles*. NIGTC. Grand Rapids: Eerdmans, 1992.

Krell, Keith R. *Temporal Judgment and the Church: Paul's Remedial Agenda in 1 Corinthians*. Garland, TX: Biblical Studies Press, 2011.

Kruse, Colin G. *2 Corinthians*. TNTC. Downers Grove, IL: InterVarsity Press, 1987.

Lamp, Jeffery S. "The Corinthian Eucharistic Dinner Party: Exegesis of a Cultural Context (1 Cor 11:17–34)." *Affirmation* 4 (Fall 1991): 1–15.

Lamp, Peter. "The Eucharist: Identifying with Christ on the Cross." *Int* 48.1 (1994): 36–49.

Lea, Thomas D., and H. Payne Griffin Jr. *1, 2 Timothy, Titus*. NAC. Nashville: Broadman & Holman, 1992.

Levine, Lee I. *The Ancient Synagogue: The First Thousand Years*. 2nd ed. New Haven, CT: Yale University Press, 2005.

Lock, William. *A Critical and Exegetical Commentary on the Pastoral Epistles*. ICC. Edinburgh: T&T Clark, 1924.

Longenecker, Bruce W. *Remember the Poor: Paul, Poverty, and the Greco-Roman World*. Grand Rapids: Eerdmans, 2010.

Longenecker, Bruce W., and Todd D. Still, *Thinking through Paul*. Grand Rapids: Zondervan, 2014.

MacGillivray, Erlend D. "Re-evaluating Patronage and Reciprocity in Antiquity and New Testament Studies." *JGRChJ* 6 (2009): 37–81.

Malherbe, Abraham J. *The Letters to the Thessalonians*. AYBC. New Haven: Yale University Press, 2000.

———. *Paul and the Thessalonians: The Philosophic Tradition of Pastoral Care*. Philadelphia: Fortress, 1987.

Marshall, I. Howard. *1 and 2 Thessalonians*. NBC. Grand Rapids: Eerdmans; London: Marshall, Morgan & Scott, 1983.

Martin, Ralph P. *2 Corinthians*. WBC. 2nd ed. Grand Rapids: Zondervan, 2014.

Matera, Frank J. *II Corinthians*. NTL. Louisville: Westminster John Knox, 2003.

Meeks, Wayne A. *The First Urban Christians: The Social World of the Apostle Paul*. New Haven, CT: Yale University Press, 1984.

Meggitt, Justin. *Paul, Poverty and Survival*. Edinburgh: T&T Clark, 1998.

Mitchell, Margaret M. *Paul and the Rhetoric of Reconciliation: An Exegetical Investigation of the Language and Composition of 1 Corinthians*. Louisville: Westminster John Knox, 1991.

Moo, Douglas J. *The Epistles to Colossians and to Philemon*. Pillar. Grand Rapids: Eerdmans, 2008.

———. *Romans*. NIVAC. Grand Rapids: Zondervan, 2000.

Morris, Leon. *The First and Second Epistles to the Thessalonians*. Rev. ed. NICNT. Grand Rapids: Eerdmans, 1991.

———. *The First Epistle of Paul to the Corinthians*. TNTC. Grand Rapids: Eerdmans, [1958] 1985.

Moss, Michael. *1, 2 Timothy & Titus*. CPNIVC. Joplin: College Press, 1994.

Mounce, William D. *Pastoral Epistles*. WBC. Nashville: Nelson, 2000.

Munck, Johannes. *Paul and the Salvation of Mankind*. Translated by Frank Clarke. London: SCM, 1959.

Ng, Esther Yue L. "Phoebe as *Prostatis*." *TJ* 25 (2004): 3–13.

Nickle, Keith. *The Collection: A Study of Paul's Strategy*. Naperville, IL: Allenson, 1966.

Osiek, Carolyn. "The Politics of Patronage and the Politics of Kinship." *BTB* 39 (2009): 143–52.

Oster, R. E. *1 Corinthians*. CPNIVC. Joplin: College Press, 1995.

Pao, David W. *Colossians and Philemon*. ZECNT. Grand Rapids: Zondervan, 2012.

Payne, Philip. *Man and Woman: One in Christ*. Grand Rapids: Zondervan, 2009.

Pervo, Richard. *Acts: A Commentary*. Hermeneia. Minneapolis: Fortress, 2009.

Peterman, G. W. *Paul's Gift from Philippi: Conventions of Gift-Exchange and Christian Giving*. Cambridge: Cambridge University Press, 1997.

Peterson, David G. *The Acts of the Apostles*. Pillar. Grand Rapids: Eerdmans, 2009.

Polhill, John B. *Acts*. NAC. Nashville: Broadman, 1992.

Richard, Earl J. *First and Second Thessalonians*. SP. Collegeville, MN: Liturgical, 1995.

Richards, E. Randolph. *Paul and First-Century Letter-Writing: Secretaries, Composition, and Collection*. Downers Grove, IL: InterVarsity Press, 2004.

Robertson, Archibald, and Alfred Plummer. *A Critical and Exegetical Commentary on the First Epistle of St. Paul to the Corinthians*. 2nd ed. ICC. Edinburgh: T&T Clark, 1914.

Safrai, S. "Education and the Study of the Torah." Pages 945–70 in vol. 2 of *The Jewish People in the First Century*. Edited by S. Safrai and M. Stern. Leiden: Brill, 1988.

Saller, Richard P. *Personal Patronage under the Early Empire*. Cambridge: University of Cambridge, 1982.

Savage, T. B. *Power through Weakness: Paul's Understanding of Christian Ministry in 2 Corinthians*. SNTSMS 86; Cambridge: Cambridge University Press, 1996.

Schnabel, Eckhard. *Acts*. ZECNT. Grand Rapids: Zondervan, 2012.

Schreiner, Thomas R. "The Biblical Basis for Church Discipline." Pages 105–30 in *Those Who Must Give an Account: A Study of Church Membership and Church Discipline*. Edited by John S. Hammett and Benjamin L. Merkle. Nashville: Broadman & Holman Academic, 2012.

———. *Galatians*. ZECNT. Grand Rapids: Zondervan, 2010.

———. *Paul, Apostle of God's Glory in Christ*. Leicester: Apollos; Downers Grove, IL: InterVarsity Press, 2001.

Shogren, Gary S. *1 and 2 Thessalonians*. ZECNT. Grand Rapids: Zondervan, 2012.

Soards, Marion L. *1 Corinthians*. NIBCNT. Peabody, MA: Hendrickson, 1999.

Still, Todd. "Did Paul Loathe Manual Labor? Revisiting the World of Ronald F. Hock on the Apostle's Tentmaking and Social Class." *JBL* 125 (2006): 781–95.

Sumney, Jerry L. *Colossians: A Commentary*. NTL. Louisville: Westminster John Knox, 2008.

Theissen, Gerd. *The Social Setting of Pauline Christianity: Essays on Corinth*. Translated by John H. Schütz. Philadelphia: Fortress, 1982.

Thiselton, Anthony. *The First Epistle to the Corinthians*. NIGTC. Grand Rapids: Eerdmans, 2000.

Towner, Phillip H. *The Letters to Timothy and Titus*. NICNT. Grand Rapids: Eerdmans, 2006.

———. *1–2 Timothy & Titus*. IVPNTC; Downers Grove, IL: InterVarsity Press, 1994.

Thrall, Margaret E. *2 Corinthians*. ICC. 2 vols. Edinburgh: T&T Clark, 2000.

Vander Broek, Lyle D. *Breaking Barriers: The Possibilities of Christian Community in a Lonely World*. Grand Rapids: Brazos, 2002.

Verbrugge, Verlyn D. "1 Corinthians." Pages 239–414 in *Revised Expositors Bible Commentary*. Edited by Tremper Longman III and David E. Garland. Grand Rapids: Zondervan, 2008.

———. *Paul's Style of Church Leadership Illustrated by His Instructions to the Corinthians on the Collection*. San Francisco: Mellen Research University Press, 1992.

Wallace, Daniel B. *Greek Grammar Beyond the Basics: An Exegetical Syntax of the New Testament*. Grand Rapids: Zondervan, 1996.

Wanamaker, Charles A. *The Epistles to the Thessalonians*. NIGTC. Grand Rapids: Eerdmans, 1990.

Watson, Deborah E. "Paul's Collection in the Light of Motivations and Mechanisms for Aid to the Poor in the First-Century World." PhD diss. Durham University, 2006.

Watson, Nigel M. *The First Epistle to the Corinthians*. EC. London: Epworth, [1992], 2005.

Weatherly, Jon A. *1 & 2 Thessalonians*. CPNIVC. Joplin: College Press, 1996.

Weima, Jeffrey A. D. "1 & 2 Thessalonians." Pages 404–43 in *The Zondervan Illustrated Bible Backgrounds Commentary*. Edited by Clinton E. Arnold. Grand Rapids: Zondervan, 2002.

Williams, David J. *1 and 2 Thessalonians*. NIBCNT. Peabody, MA: Hendrickson, 1994.

Winter, Bruce W. *Roman Wives, Roman Widows: The Appearance of New Women and the Pauline Communities*. Grand Rapids: Eerdmans, 2003.

———. *Seek the Welfare of the City: Christians as Benefactors and Citizens*. Grand Rapids: Eerdmans, 1994.

———. "The Lord's Supper at Corinth: An Alternative Reconstruction." *RTR* 37 (1978): 73–78.

Witherington III, Ben. *Jesus and Money: A Guide for Times of Financial Crisis*. Grand Rapids: Baker, 2010.

———. *1 and 2 Thessalonians: A Socio-Rhetorical Commentary*. Grand Rapids: Eerdmans, 2006.

———. *The Acts of the Apostles: A Socio-Rhetorical Commentary*. Grand Rapids/Cambridge: Eerdmans; Carlisle: Paternoster, 1998.

———. *Conflict and Community in Corinth: A Socio-Rhetorical Commentary on 1 and 2 Corinthians*. Grand Rapids: Eerdmans, 1995.

Wright, N. T. *Paul and the Faithfulness of God*. Minneapolis: Fortress, 2013.

Scripture Index

SUBJECT INDEX

Author Index